Regulation and Repression

Studies in Society

Titles include:

The Migrant Presence Martin
Race, Class and Rebellion in the South Pacific Mamak and Ali
Children and Families in Australia Burns and Goodnow
Johnsonville Pearson
Australian Community Studies and Beyond Wild
Open Cut Williams
The Ethnic Dimension Martin/Encel
The Aging Experience Russell
Australian Cinema Tulloch
Strikes in Australia Waters
Class Consciousness in Australia Chamberlain
Heathcote Wild
Practice and Belief Black/Glasner
Law, Capitalism and Democracy O'Malley
Eclipse of Equality Pearson and Thorns
The Family in the Modern World Burns, Jools and Bottomley
Medical Dominance Willis
Women, Social Welfare and the State Baldock/Cass
Ideology of Motherhood Wearing
Indians in a White Australia de Lepervanche
Confronting School and Work Dwyer, Wilson and Woock
Ethnicity, Class and Gender in Australia Bottomley/de Lepervanche
The Faith of Australians Mol
Social Theory and the Australian City Kilmartin/Thorns/Burke
The First Wave Lewins/Ly
Surveys in Social Research de Vaus
Australian Ways Manderson
Custody and Control Asher
Where it Hurts Russell and Schofield
Caring for Australia's Children Brennan and O'Donnell
Shaping Futures Wilson and Wyn
Health Care Issues Bates and Linder Pelz

Studies in Society

Regulation and Repression

The Study of Social Control

Anne R. Edwards

ALLEN & UNWIN
SYDNEY WELLINGTON LONDON BOSTON

First published in 1988
Allen & Unwin Australia Pty Ltd
An Unwin Hyman company
8 Napier Street, North Sydney, NSW 2059 Australia

Allen & Unwin New Zealand Limited
60 Cambridge Terrace, Wellington, New Zealand

Unwin Hyman Limited
15–17 Broadwick Street, London W1V 1FP England

Allen & Unwin Inc.
8 Winchester Place, Winchester, Mass 01890 USA

National Library of Australia
Cataloguing-in-Publication entry:
Edwards, Anne R. (Anne Rosalie), 1941-
Regulation and repression: The study of
Social control.

Bibliograpy.
Includes index.
ISBN 0 04 332136 4.

1. Social control. I. Title. Series:
Studies in society (Sydney, N.S.W.).

303.3'3
Library of Congress Catalog Card Number: 88-81539
Set in 10/11pt English Times, Linotron 202 by
Setrite Typesetters Ltd, Hong Kong.
Printed by Dah Hua Printers, Hong Kong.

Contents

1 The concept of social control

This is a book about social control. Social control is both a concept that sociologists use and something that happens in the social world of which people are aware. Whenever we use such terms as persuade, restrain, discipline, coerce, penalise, reward, direct, manage or regulate to describe aspects of the activities of individuals, groups, organisations or society, we are talking about the exercise of social control over people's bodies, minds and behaviour. The most obvious instances of control are when it is direct and overt, when it comes from identifiable authority figures and is aimed at particular individuals or groups. Social settings in which control operates in this way include families and schools, where children are subject to rules set by adults, and workplaces, where employees are required to perform tasks laid down by employers. Society as a whole is governed by means of a complex system of legal statutes and law enforcement mechanisms which regulate behaviour in a wide range of areas.

Social processes may also have an important control element where this is neither intended nor recognised by the parties, where no coercion is involved, and/or where no particular agents or target groups can be readily identified – professionals like doctors and social workers, for instance, in the course of handling the problems with which they are presented may come to exercise a more general influence over their clients' lives. In either case, the effect of control, when successful, is the shaping of people's attitudes, beliefs and actions, in some cases reinforcing existing patterns and in others changing them.

Since social control is both a sociological concept and a social phenomenon, we need to give attention both to the changing definitions, meanings and usages of the notion and to the social practices, institutions and processes where control is being exercised. Our understanding of social control is advanced by a critical history of theoretical ideas about control and by analysis of the forms, functions and development of social control apparatuses in the modern world. This book attempts both. We will start with some discussion of the concept itself.

Control, with or without the 'social', is not only a term with a specialist technical meaning but it has a wide general usage. Though it is indeed a key term in sociological discourse, it is also part of our everyday language. In our culture, the word has a diverse range of applications and a variety of things are seen as requiring control, for instance: one's temper; people in the position of subordinates such as workers or wives and children; special problem groups such as drug addicts, the unemployed or those with disabilities; behaviour in public places; use of natural resources; and major institutions, including the unions, government bureaucracies, and the economy. Frequently, the emphasis is placed on the object(s) of the control rather than on the means of control, and the reasons for its exercise are assumed to be self-evident.

Control often appears in the company of related concepts such as discipline, authority, law and order and morality; together they convey a particular image of how a society should be organised and managed. The implication is that at every level individuals need to be restrained and regulated, and that social control is absolutely essential for the maintenance of social order. However, this is very much a perspective of those responsible for ensuring adequate social control (politicians, officials, community leaders, etc.) and those who benefit from it (the majority of 'solid citizens', with positions and interests that need protecting). Those who are its targets are likely to take a rather different view, seeing control as selectively and unequally imposed repression and rejecting the ideological representation of control as a set of regulations and rules applied uniformly and universally across the society for the benefit of all its members. Versions of these alternative lay conceptions of social control, one giving it a positive and the other a negative evaluation, are also to be found in sociology, as we shall see.

From the classical social theorists (Marx, Durkheim and Weber) on, the problems of social order and social control have been a primary concern. Although 'social control' has not figured universally or continuously as a key term in sociological writing, all major theorists, using this or related concepts like regulation, domination, integration, or coercion, seek to answer the fundamental question of how societies achieve and maintain order.

Many of the definitions of social control that have been given are little more than tautologies, since they treat social control and the maintenance of social order as more or less synonymous, leaving open the crucial issues of what it is that control does to maintain society and what the maintenance of society means anyway. Hollingshead, for instance, in a classic early article states: 'the essence of social control is to be sought in the organisation of people' (1941:220). Coser and Rosenberg, in the introduction to a section on 'social control' in their famous book of readings on sociological theory, make the following assertion: 'Social control refers to those mechanisms by which society exercises its dominion over component individuals and enforces conformity to its norms' (1966:87). Janowitz, in a survey of the variety of writings on sociological theory and social control, says a common conception of social control, particularly in the earlier work, is that it refers to 'the capacity of a society to regulate itself according to desired principles and values' (1975:82). As Lemert, an early American contributor to the subject who did not fall into this trap, and whose work contributed to a whole new approach in the 1960s, pointed out, there are major problems with general formulations of this kind. In particular:

> . . . the most glaring deficiency in extant works on social control has been the common failure to distinguish between the regularities in behavior and the techniques employed to induce these regularities. (1942:396)

We must start then with a recognition of the necessity to draw a distinction between 'normal' conforming behaviour patterns (the bases of social 'organisation' or social 'order') and the mechanisms by which these are produced and sustained.

The 'problem of social order', or the question of how social order is achieved and maintained, logically precedes the question of what is social control. Watkins (1975) starts his book *Social Control* by making this point. Questions about sociological writers' conceptions of social control cannot therefore be answered without looking carefully at the particular perspective or viewpoint on the social world from which they operate. Since there are as many different approaches to the problem of social order in sociology as there are models of society, there are also a number of different conceptions of what social control is and what it does.

We will now look briefly at some of the theories about social order and social control that have influenced sociologists working in this field over the past fifty or so years. The main theoretical approaches to the study of social control will be examined in detail in subsequent chapters. The purpose of a preliminary discussion here is to identify the principal perspectives and to trace the recent development of the concept within sociology.[1]

Davis, the author of one of the best overall reviews of sociological conceptions of deviance and social control, starts with a comparison between classical European social theory and traditional American approaches. As she puts it:

> European founding fathers of sociology used social problems as a vehicle for uncovering, chronicling, and explaining the social workings of modern society. Anomie, for Durkheim, and alienation,

> for Marx, were metaphors for a radical attack on the conventional order. In their approaches, social stratification was the central mechanism of social control, contributing to unequal distribution of political and economic resources. Deviance, interpreted as social conflict, was conceived of as a normal social process that was built into ongoing social arrangements and perpetuated by powerful groups and collectivities. (1975:3)

American sociology (specifically the early 'social pathology' and 'social disorganisation' schools and modern structural-functionalism), by contrast, moved away from these kinds of concerns and from 'critical analysis of modern institutions' (Davis, 1975:3), and it was not until the 1960s that the issues of inequality, power and conflict reemerged as important issues.

For a major part of the present century, the sociology of crime, deviance and social control took an almost entirely uncritical view of the major structures of modern society. Though in some respects these various perspectives differ significantly,[2] certain common underlying assumptions about social order and social control can be discerned. They all share the basic notion that social control is an essential and entirely desirable function on which the survival of society as a whole depends. Social control involves the utilisation of various mechanisms and techniques to discourage, restrict, prevent, divert or otherwise alter the behaviour of those who constitute an actual or potential threat or problem for the majority. Social control from this perspective means certain specific activities and processes which are the responsibility of special categories of persons and of special institutions. The obvious examples of control agents in contemporary society are the police, magistrates, psychiatrists, teachers, social workers and doctors; and the principal control institutions are the mental health system, and the legal-judicial system. The actions of control agents are seen as having been provoked by some instance of disturbing, disruptive, dangerous or, to use the sociological term, 'deviant' behaviour and their responses as justifiably directed towards its management and containment. A particular temporal and causal sequence is presupposed: anti-social act occurs, concern is expressed and some sort of social reaction follows. Deviance produces the need for social control. 'Control' thus implies a negative response to something undesirable that has already happened, a response aimed at the 'unmaking' of the deviance (Cohen, 1966:38).

Deviance, social control and the moral order of society are thus defined in terms of their mutual interdependence. The moral code of a society determines what is considered deviant, social control is whatever society deems appropriate for dealing with deviance, and it is both justified by and a necessary element of the moral order. From the perspective of structural-functionalism, Parsons provides a clear example of this: deviance, he says, is the 'tendency ... to behave in contravention of one or more institutionalized normative patterns' and social control consists of 'processes...to counteract deviance' (1951:250). As does Black: 'Social control is the normative aspect of social life, or the definition of deviant behavior and the response to it' and deviant behaviour is conduct that is 'subject to social control' (1976:1–2, 9).

This general conception of deviance and social control rests on the assumption that the prevailing norms in any given society are the appropriate standards for the sociologists to apply in determining what constitutes deviance. In this the sociologist takes the same view as do the dominant groups in the society, namely that conformity is good and deviance is bad, that norms must be defended and enforced, that effective methods of deviance detection and containment are all important, and that the stability of the social order should be the primary concern. One of the critics of this view, Matza (1969), points to three key features of this general approach, which he characterises as taking a 'correctionalist' stance: its reliance on an overly simple and allegedly objective division into 'good' and 'bad', 'conventional' and 'deviant', or 'normal' and 'pathological' categories of individuals and actions, both defined from a society's point of view; its more or less unquestioning acceptance of the necessity of social control in general and in its particular social forms; and its commitment to providing academic knowledge that would assist in preventing deviance and in making social control more successful. This view prevailed until relatively recently in sociology, though in the case of Durkheim and some modern American functionalists, the equations of deviance = bad, social control = good were somewhat qualified. These writers acknowledged that the activation of control mechanisms (and hence the existence of deviance) might have some beneficial social aspects: in particular, it provides an opportunity for the general population to be reminded of the moral boundaries of the society and to affirm support for general community values.[3]

Matza contrasts the correctionalist with an anti-correctionalist or 'appreciative' stance, which emphasises human diversity, societal complexity, and social conflict and division. Consequently, from this perspective, the moral order of society is characterised by pluralism or relativism rather than consensus. Defining moral and social norms, deciding on which standards are relevant to particular acts and matching evaluations with actual behaviour pose problems for society and its members as well as for social scientists. The existence of competing groups and moralities causes uncertainty, ambiguity, confusion and conflict. In the 'real' world, judgements about 'good' and 'bad' aspects of human behaviour and social life are problematic. Unwelcome events may bring beneficial consequences, and valued institutions and customs may be indirectly responsible for undesirable occurrences.

The new perspective on deviance and social control that emerged in the 1960s, commonly described as labelling theory and interactionism, started from this relativist position. As Rubington and Weinberg, the editors of a major text exploring the interactionist perspective on deviance, put it: from this standpoint, it is necessary to treat deviance as 'subjectively problematic rather than as objectively given' (1968:4). What constitutes deviance becomes an empirical matter and how deviance is defined varies from group to group and society to society. Deviance is the label attached by a more powerful group or section of the population to weaker individuals and groups whose behaviour is viewed as undesirable or offensive in some way. Of central interest are the mechanisms and processes within groups and organisations as well as at the level of society as a whole by which standards and norms are established and enforced. Who gets labelled 'deviant', how and why, and what are the consequences of labelling and application of sanctions for the deviant and for society? In short, the main emphasis has shifted from deviance and what causes it to social control—what forms it takes, how it operates, in whose interests, and with what effects.

What this entails is a reinterpretation of the relationship between deviance and social control. Social and societal responses to anti-social behaviour are now seen as constituting part of the social 'production' or 'manufacture' of deviance. As Becker expresses it in a famous passage in his book *Outsiders*:

> . . .social groups create deviance by making the rules whose infraction constitutes deviance, and by applying those rules to particular people and labeling them as outsiders. From this point of view, deviance is not a quality of the act a person commits, but rather a consequence of the application by others of rules and sanctions to the 'offender'. The deviant is one to whom that label has been successfully applied; deviant behavior is behavior that people so label. (1963:9)

He and others point out that attention needs to be given to the differential processes of perception, definition, evaluation and reaction. These can result in potential or putative cases of deviant behaviour being ignored, tolerated or accommodated as often as they are singled out for special control treatment on the grounds that they pose a problem for social order.

This 'new' conception, that developed from the work of Lemert (1951), Becker (1963) and others, offered a redefinition of deviance and social control and a reconceptualisation of how sociology should deal with these phenomena. Deviance, it was argued, can refer to a much broader and more diverse range of behaviours than simply those that involve infringements of the criminal law and other such major societally enforced codes of conduct. Social control can encompass a wider variety of modes and models than those previously recognised, chiefly the legal-judicial system and psychiatry: at the level of formal, official, institutional social control, welfare, education and medicine generally all are to be treated sociologically as major control systems.

But social control, for those adopting this perspective, is not only an activity carried out in formal, public settings, such as courts of law, or as part of the official duties of professionals and personnel working for major societal organisations, such as government agencies—it occurs also as part of the informal, everyday interactions of individuals and groups where society as a whole is neither directly affected by the deviant behaviour nor actively involved in the social control process.

Social control, furthermore, is not confined to reactive measures. The concept is extended so that it covers not only methods of detecting violations of norms and rules and the range of penalties and treatments for known offenders, but also mechanisms and techniques aimed at deterrence and diversion. In other words, some forms of social control seek to anticipate where deviance is likely to arise, and intervene before it occurs. Persuasion, exhortation and the utilisation of various material and social inducements are positive means of encouraging the observance of rules and hence preventing rule-breaking. People may want to behave conventionally as a result of internalising the beliefs, values and norms on which such behaviour rests and/or because it is consistent with what is expected of them in roles they play or groups they identify with. Any social mechanisms that contribute to social conformity may thus be considered to have a social control function. Socialisation itself may be regarded as a form of social control,[4] though one which ensures conformity with prevailing moral codes and cultural practices directly, as distinct from other methods that achieve compliance by making the consequences of engaging in deviance sufficiently painful or disadvantageous.

Sociologists with this broad conception of social control reinforced Durkheim's original observation that moral norms can at the same time be both attractive and restrictive, they can enable as well as compel—individuals are 'trained' and 'constrained' by their presence (Hollingshead, 1941:220). Social control in some of its forms may be welcomed and sought after, perceived as helpful and constructive guidance or assistance, rather than something to be automatically disliked and avoided. To be effective, social control need not always be or be seen to be unpleasant. The obviously hardline punitive and repressive control institutions (police, courts, the law, government departments, 'the state') are not the only ones engaged in the business of regulating society. This task is the responsibility also of socialisation agencies, such as the family, the school, religion and the media, which rely on the 'softer' techniques of education and persuasion. Since social control in these forms is never totally successful, however, all societies and groups have to develop institutionalised modes of accommodation and regulation with respect to deviance. These can include licensing certain types of questionable conduct for certain people in certain places (brothels for prostitution), tolerance of the beliefs and practices of socially segregated minorites (ethnic or religious communities) and, sometimes, the recognition that the 'deviant' culture of an outsider group may possibly offer an alternative towards which the rest of society might well consider moving.

Most social change starts out as a form of deviance. Durkheim, who originally advanced the view that a certain level of deviance is a positive element ensuring the 'health' of a society, put it this way: what may be regarded as an undesirable expression of 'individual originality' at one time may at another provide the basis for a 'new morality and faith' (1938:71). Although labelling and interactionist writers share Durkheim's view that what society perceives as deviance may later be welcomed as positive social change, unlike Durkheim and the functionalists they do not subscribe to a consensus model of society. For them, since society comprises a plurality of groups with often competing interests and moral values, the designation of behaviour as conformity, deviance or desirable social change depends on which group's perspective one takes and whether that group is powerful enough to impose its evaluation on others, power being the critical variable.

Thus, the alternative accounts of deviance, control and the nature of social order given by functionalists and by labelling/interactionist theorists reflect more fundamental differences between what have been described respectively as the 'normative' and the 'interpretive' paradigms,[5] over which there was considerable debate in sociology in the late 1960s and early 1970s.

During the 1970s another perspective emerged, variously described as 'radical', 'critical' or 'marxist', which mounted an attack not only on functionalist consensus theories but also on the interactionist and labelling approaches. Though in fact these critiques began to appear in the late 1960s (Gouldner, 1968; Horowitz and Liebowitz, 1968), the main works came later: in England, the book by Taylor, Walton and Young entitled *The New Criminology: For a Social Theory of Deviance* was published in 1973, and in America there were a number of significant articles around the same time (Liazos, 1974; Schervish, 1973; Spitzer, 1975a; Thio, 1972). These writers adopted a particular type of structural model of society, one characterised by an emphasis on class, conflict and political economy. Their main point of dispute with interactionism was over the latter's subjectivist and pluralist conception of power and social structure. Their perspective emphasised the repressive use of force and the coercive aspects of social control, in particular the criminal law and the justice system, which they linked to class domination. They rejected altogether sociological definitions (whether functionalist or interactionist) of deviance and talked instead about forms of social and political conflict, protest and revolution, and their relationship to the class struggle and the capitalist system.

Over broadly the same period, feminism started to make a contribution to the subject of deviance and social control, and to develop some understanding of the gender-differentiated nature of these phenomena

(Klein, 1973; Millman, 1975; Smart 1976). Feminists combined a new woman-centred orientation to the analysis of the social world (accompanied by a different set of philosophical and value assumptions from those found in conventional sociology) with some of the current ideas about deviance and social control, constructing a perspective which was different from the other approaches but had elements in common with both marxism and labelling/interactionist theory.

In the following two chapters, these four perspectives will be examined in some detail and comparisons and evaluations made of them. These four were chosen because, unlike their predecessors, all have contributed significantly to current understandings of deviance and social control. All recognise the subtle and complex social and sociological nature of deviance and social control and the critical role social control plays in the 'creation' or 'production' of deviance. All see social forces as not only responsible for the amount and types of rule-breaking that occur in society, but as key determinants of the standards of behaviour that people are expected to observe and of the measures adopted to deal with those who fail to do so.

Not all perspectives nor all those writing in this field regard social control as a useful concept. Some argue it has come to be associated too closely with functionalism and hence it carries particular and (for non-functionalists) undesirable theoretical and ideological connotations. A number of mainly marxist critics claim that the way in which it has been employed in (so called 'revisionist'[6]) historical analysis has led to the confusion of intention and effect and to the misrepresentation of the nature of power and the state.[7] It is worth noting, however, that despite serious reservations being expressed about social control as a concept, no preferred alternative has yet emerged within marxist or other critical discourses and over recent years it is once again attracting a significant amount of academic sociological interest. In the 1980s several books have appeared that treat social control as a central topic and indicate this by including the term in their title (Black, 1984; Cohen, 1985; Cohen and Scull, 1985; Gibbs, 1981, 1982).[8] Its long history seems to suggest that, whatever its limitations, it is a concept sociology finds hard to manage without. Though some see the problem as being one of 'a concept in search of a theory' (Donajgrodzki, 1977:14), it may rather be that too many different theories have laid claims to it and that what is needed is clarification of its various meanings and applications and greater care and precision in its usage.

One of the primary objectives of this book is to provide a systematic theoretical analysis of the concept of social control. All the four major current perspectives in sociology, briefly discussed in this introductory chapter, have much to say about social control and social regulation and their contribution to social order. We will therefore start by comparing the ways in which control as a concept is defined and used in functionalism, labelling and interactionist theory, marxism and feminism, and make brief reference to Foucault. It is worth commenting at this point that it is still highly unusual for feminism to be treated within academic sociology as one of the major contemporary perspectives and hopefully the present case will demonstrate how important it is that feminist theory be given a proper place in the discipline.

Although there may be danger in organising a theoretical discussion around such a broad notion, and one which it is often hard to distinguish from the idea of social order or society itself, the generality of the concept is also a major asset. It allows for a wide variety of apparently disparate processes and practices to be treated as part of the same phenomenon and for common factors and patterns in relation to the management of deviant behaviour to be identified. By acting as a sensitising concept[9] it provides an overall framework for the analysis of the various mechanisms and processes by which society, dominant groups, the ruling class, the normative system, patriarchy or capitalism (whatever conception of the collectivity one prefers) at the macro level, and groups and individuals at the micro level, seek to protect their values and interests against what they perceive as threats. It is then possible both to compare alternative theoretical accounts of the bases of social control in general and to explore differences and similarities between the various control institutions and mechanisms that exist in every society.

Similarities in the characteristic modes of organisation and functioning of social control as between different social contexts and types of institution can only emerge when a broadly defined control perspective is adopted. Without this broad, general, conceptual framework, the study of social control breaks up, as it traditionally has, into separate subject areas such as the sociologies of law, medicine and welfare within each of which the relevant control apparatuses are treated as distinct and discrete social phenomena.

A second major objective of the book is to further our understanding of particular control institutions and ideologies, specifically the three which in modern western societies have assumed responsibility for the main problem categories of the population: the legal-judicial system, the medical-psychiatric system and the welfare system, which respectively have jurisdiction over the problems of crime, illness and dependency. We devote some attention to the historical development of these three systems in Britain, the United States and Australia, and to alternative explanations for their changing forms and functions, before moving on to a detailed consideration of each one in turn. As the book progresses, we move therefore from the abstract and general to the substantive and historically specific. Chapters 2 and 3 are entirely theoretical, concerned with the presentation and evaluation of the four perspectives, with a primary focus on what they have to say about deviance and social control. Chapter 4 combines some discussion of the key dimensions of social control (derived from material presented in the preceding chapters) with an overview of the main trends in how social control has been exercised at the institutional and societal level over the past two hundred or so years. This chapter bridges the gap between theories of social control and empirical examples of social control systems. In the remaining three chapters of the book then, we apply the theoretical discussion and the conceptual frameworks developed in the earlier chapters to the analysis of the legal, medical and welfare systems, the dominant systems for the control of deviance in western capitalist patriarchal society, with particular reference to Australia.

2 Sociological perspectives and social control

Over the past twenty or so years, there has been a considerable volume of sociological literature devoted to the subject of crime, deviance and social control, in the form both of presentations of new theories and empirical research, and of secondary analysis and assessment of such work by supporters and critics of the various approaches. This became for a while in the 1970s one of the most popular and productive substantive areas within sociology, particularly in England (Cohen, 1981) and provided an arena for the discussion of key theoretical, methodological and ideological issues in the discipline. In time, the decline of interactionism, the ascendancy of marxism and the contribution from feminism resulted in a move away from the deviance area as previously defined by the members of the labelling/interactionist school (covering a variety of institutions and mechanisms of social control, including psychiatry and social work as well as the legal/judicial system). Instead there was a preoccupation with crime, law, justice and later the state in relation to social control; there was an overt rejection of 'deviance' and 'the deviance perspective' as bourgeois, ahistorical and apolitical (Manders, 1975). Feminists and some marxists subsequently turned their attention to other types and areas of social control—in particular the welfare state, with its effects on families and dependency (Corrigan ed., 1980; McIntosh, 1978) and ideological forces such as education and the media (Hall, 1974; Hall et al., 1978). It is interesting and perhaps surprising that some of these had been given a place in Parsons' categorisation of social control institutions (on the basis of their functioning as agencies of socialisation, ensuring the effective transmission and internalisation of prevailing normative expectations and values[1]), yet they had in the main been ignored by the labelling and interactionist theorists.

There have been many classifications and comparisons of approaches to deviance and social control. Most deal primarily with different approaches to the explanation of criminal and deviant behaviour or 'social problems' and consist mainly of a description in chronological sequence of the various types of causal theories. But there are also some 'deviance' perspectives (and some commentaries, for instance, Pfohl, 1985) where social control is specifically acknowledged as a significant conceptual issue: and this is true of all four sociological perspectives with which we are concerned in this book. Theories of deviant behaviour are not in themselves relevant here.[2] We are interested in approaches to social control, in particular in typologies that attempt to compare the basic theoretical and conceptual characteristics of perspectives on social control and in the process to expose major philosophical and epistemological differences between them. The choice of functionalism, labelling/interactionism, and marxism as three of the major perspectives on social control to be considered here conforms with general sociological practice. Differences between these perspectives turn out to be a reflection of their various fundamental presuppositions about human nature and social reality and of differences between the three major sociological traditions that can be traced back ultimately to the work of the classic theorists, Durkheim, Weber and Marx.

In the earlier part of this century, American sociology had on the whole given relatively low priority to what was at that time described as the field of 'social problems', 'social disorganisation' or 'social pathology'. This is partly explicable by the fact that during this period most sociologists apparently accepted without question the prevailing social and scientific belief that undesirable and problematic human behaviour (or 'social deviance') could be traced back to the presence of abnormalities or deficiencies in the biological and/or psychological make-up of individuals. Exceptions were the approach of the Chicago School which linked crime and other urban problems to the patterns of city development and conditions in inner slum areas, and the culture conflict theories of Sellin and others which had particular relevance at a time of high rates of European immigration into North America (Davis, 1975: Chapters 3 and 6).

The most illuminating classifications of theories of social control are those that rest on distinctions between sociologically meaningful theoretical and analytical dimensions; good examples would be the division between consensus and conflict models of society (Douglas, 1970; Gibbs, 1977; Horton, 1966), between macro and micro levels of analysis (Orcutt, 1983), between objectivist and subjectivist perceptions of social reality (Rubington and Weinberg, 1968), between normative and interpretive or relativist conceptions of social action (Hawkins and Tiedeman, 1975; Orcutt, 1983), between a correctionalist and a naturalist methodological stance (Matza, 1969) or between active and passive models of human nature (Beyleveld and Wiles, 1979). On such fundamental dimensions as these the various theorists subscribing to the four perspectives can be assigned a position. Perspectives do not necessarily differ on every feature and sometimes, unexpectedly, similarities may be found, as for example the acknowledgement already noted by both Parsons and modern marxists of socialisation and the normative system or dominant ideology as significant bases of social control. Nor can we assume internal consistency or homogeneity of ideas among the various exponents of each approach, in many cases there are significant variations in conceptualisation and emphasis within perspectives.

The presentation of the four perspectives will be in chronological order, starting with Parsons' social system approach which builds on some of Durkheim's ideas. This is generally recognised as being the first major perspective to treat both deviance and social control as serious sociological subjects.[3] It became the paradigm of establishment sociology in America. Our other three perspectives all distance themselves from, and claim superiority to it. However, chronology is not to be regarded necessarily as a measure of conceptual sophistication or progression of ideas. Changes in theoretical and ideological concerns over time reflect the changing social and intellectual environment as Davis (1975), for instance, shows.

With the exception of structural functionalism (which is represented by the work of one individual and deals with a particular set of his writings[4]), in the account given here, there is recognition from the outset of the existence of alternative orientations, foci and levels of analysis within each perspective. A distinction can usefully be made between the different versions of these perspectives to be found in the writings of their various exponents along the basic sociological dimension of individualism/structuralism or agency/structure (Giddens, 1979:Chapter 2), which in turn encapsulates other related dualisms (micro-macro, voluntarism-determinism). This should help us present the principal ideas of the various schools of thought in a way that is truer to the diversity that they contain and avoid endless and pointless terminological disputes over whether, for instance the labelling/interactionist perspective is 'really' social psychological or sociological, voluntarist or determinist, processual or structural (Davis, 1975; Liska, 1981; Taylor, Walton and Young, 1973). Similar difficulties which arise when one attempts to treat marxism and feminism as unitary perspectives can also hopefully be overcome.

Most surveys give the greatest detailed coverage to functionalism and anomie theory, labelling and interactionist theory, and to marxism and 'radical' or 'critical' criminology, and to the longstanding debate over the relative merits of these latter two schools of thought—the exponents of neither of these two approaches being willing to concede that there is any longer much of value in using the normative or functionalist paradigm in sociology. None of the major commentaries has yet included feminism as a distinct theoretical perspective worthy of consideration alongside the established male-dominated models and theories. An important contribution of this book, then, lies in its treatment of feminism as a major sociological perspective, and one with a significant contribution to make to our understanding of social control.

Marxism and feminism have some characteristics in common: both can loosely be described as conflict approaches and both disagree theoretically and ideologically with many of the assumptions of mainstream academic sociology. Marxism's main contribution to the sociology of deviance and social control is seen to lie in its critique of previous conceptions of the bases of social order and of power in particular. Feminist theory similarly challenges at a fundamental level conventional sociological concepts of power and social structure, but it also rejects 'straight' marxism, arguing for gender, the sex-gender system, and male domination or patriarchy to be incorporated in our models of society as well as or, in the view of some radical feminists, instead of class and the mode of production. Both types of 'radical' social theory direct their critiques equally at what they regard as the bourgeois nature of consensus functionalism and at humanism, idealism and pluralism which they believe are unavoidably and undesirably associated with interactionism.

Feminist theory contains the conceptual tools necessary for analysing and explaining gender as a fundamental principle of social organisation and a dimension of social inequality (along with class and race-ethnicity) and for incorporating the gender order or patriarchy into our understanding of the structures of power and domination characteristic of modern capitalist societies. Many feminist writers in the area of deviance and social control have been concerned to expose both gender discrimination in the criminal justice system, and bias and neglect in the treatment of women by academic criminology (early examples are Heidensohn, 1968; Klein, 1973). However, the potential of feminism goes far beyond a critique of sexism in attitudes and practices, important though this is. It offers a woman-centred framework for interpreting women's experience of and relationship to social control and for exploring the reasons for systematic differences along sex-gender lines in the nature and operation of social control mechanisms and institutions.

The presentation and comparison of the four perspectives will be based on a consideration of the way certain social concepts are defined and used by their exponents. These key concepts include perceptions of human nature and of social order, definitions of deviance and social control, conceptions of power, political order, and the sources, nature and functions of social control, and methodological, value and policy issues. With the exception of feminism, much of the material covered has already been subjected to extensive academic discussion, debate and critique. What is relevant for present purposes is the question of what each perspective has to say about social control and the examination and evaluation of the relative strengths and weaknesses of the different modes of conceptualising and analysing the nature and role of social control in society.

The Parsonian social system model and structural-functionalism[5]

> . . . the stable equilibrium of the interactive process is the fundamental point of reference for the analysis of social control just as it is for the theory of deviance. But our attention will be focused on one aspect of the interactive process, the forestalling of . . . deviant tendencies, and the process by which, once under way, these processes can be counteracted and the system brought back, in the relevant respects, to the old equilibrium state . . . .
> The prevention and forestalling aspects of social control consist in a sense of processes which teach the actor not to embark on processes of deviance. They consist in his learning how not to rather than how to in the positive sense of socialization. The re-equilibrating aspects on the other hand are a special case . . . in that they involve the unlearning of the alienative elements in the motivational structure. (Parsons, 1951:298)

The first and most important feature of Parsons' work is that he regards both deviance and social control as having social causes and consequences, as being socially interdependent, as being universally present in all human societies and therefore as qualifying as subjects for the serious attention of sociological theory. He clearly and explicitly identifies social control as a 'normal' social phenomenon, an indispensable part of the interactional processes that go to make up 'the social system'. Social control practices and techniques are not something exceptional or special, but an often unnoticed and not necessarily conscious component of everyday social interaction. Social control is a basic property of societies rather than something imposed on some sections of the population by others; it serves the interests not of particular individuals but the whole community. It is in this context that his comments about socialisation and social control having parallel functions are to be understood.

Parsons' account of the mechanisms of social control is in the form of a description of general social processes directed at deviance reduction: social control for him covers a variety of techniques and agencies (of which force is of relatively minor importance) and occurs at different levels and in different sectors of 'the social system'.[6] Social control is defined by its functions rather than by particular methods, institutions or structures. Parsons distinguishes between socialisation and (reactive) social control on the basis that, in the former case, the concern is with bringing people into conformity or normality, while in the latter, the need is to 'bring them back into accord when they have deviated' (1962:66). Then, using this general framework, he compares the professions of teaching, medicine and law, all of which he sees as being involved in social control, but each of which fulfils in different ways its control functions.

Parsons is usually also credited with being the first sociologist to offer a systematic treatment of medicine as both a major social control system (Stacey, 1978:282) and as the main alternative to law and criminal justice in the modern world. He describes both illness and crime as institutionalised deviant roles with a number of common though some different characteristics: one important difference he identifies is that the sick role confers a 'relative' or conditional legitimacy (and this may weaken its deterrent capacity), while criminality is regarded as illegitimate. This has the consequence that the occupant of the sick role has a greater exposure to 'reintegrative forces' as compared with the criminal who experiences predominantly negative effects associated with 'extrusion from the social group' (1951:312–3). However, as de Espinosa (1980) argues, law and the legal system are treated unsatisfactorily in Parsons' writings, which is surprising in view of the extent to which Parsons makes use of Durkheim's work (and considering also the attention paid to the legal order by Weber and many marxists). De Espinosa shows how Parsons, in giving theoretical priority to moral norms over others and to the internalisation—and hence acceptance—of the moral authority of norms, leaves himself with problems in dealing with legal norms, resting as they do in part on coercive power rather than normative consensus.

With respect to his conception of social order and social control Parsons is best categorised as a 'macro' and a 'normative' theorist (Orcutt, 1983). He worked with a theoretically constructed model of the self-regulating and self-maintaining 'social system'. For him the problem of social order was solved by postulating the existence of an underlying normative order or shared set of moral and social norms and values, which is ontologically prior to and independent of the social relationships within a given society. This ensures that the expectations attached to the roles and institutions which go to make up the structure of each society are consistent, compatible and uniform. The socialisation process provides the means whereby the norms and expectations of any given society become part of the personality of its individual members and hence determine their attitudes, motives and behaviour in the roles they are given. Important conditions, therefore, that are essential for the existence of a social system are a high degree of societal consensus and adequate socialisation. Individuals become social as they internalise the core values and norms of their society and, so long as this is done effectively and what they internalise is indeed a representation of the overall cultural system, society can function as a harmonious whole. The integration of the various parts of 'the social system' rests ultimately then on value consensus.

Though in practice societies fail to achieve the degrees of consensus and integration required for the perfect functioning of 'the social system' as conceived in the theoretical model, there are various mechanisms by which order or equilibrium can be maintained or restored. Parsons' model involves the idea of 'natural' social mechanisms or processes through which certain basic internal needs of the system are met: in his language these are described as the 'functional imperatives' or 'prerequisites' of integration and latency (this latter covering pattern-maintenance and tension-management)[7].

Parsons recognises that 'real' societies generate pressures and tensions which can result in deviance. In particular he points to problems with respect to socialisation and various forms of normative and role conflict as societally-produced sources of deviance. Social control is necessary to contain and counteract such tendencies and to reestablish order. Imperfections in society cause deviance and thus make social control mechanisms a necessary and indispensable part of the equipment of any viable social system.[8]

Following Durkheim, Parsons and some other modern writers—such as Coser (1962) and Erikson (1966)—point to some positive aspects for 'the social system' of the presence of deviant tendencies and the necessity for counter-measures of containment and control. Social control can result in the reaffirmation of important values, the clarification of norms and expectations, the expression of group solidarity, and attempts to remedy structural defects (the sources of tension, disequilibrium and deviance). Far from deviance and the problems it poses for society being seen sociologically as totally negative in both nature and consequences, they are treated as useful and even necessary for the health of society, as being 'functional'. Besides the generally recognised problems associated with the notion of 'function', there is, as Roshier (1977) argues, some conceptual confusion here over whether it is the deviance or the social control response that is of social benefit. For Parsons, it is clearly the activation of social control processes and the various ways in which the social system readjusts and is thereby strengthened (and the boundary-maintaining tension-management functions being fulfilled) that he is primarily thinking of. Unlike Durkheim, Parsons can see no value in deviance as an expression of healthy human diversity or as part of a continuing process of social change. For him, deviance is unavoidable but undesirable; it simply indicates the presence of defects or malfunctions in key social structures or institutions and the fact that human societies in the 'real' world are only imperfect versions of his model of the fully integrated and balanced social system.

Parsons' conceptualisation and analysis of social control attracts the same kinds of criticism as are levelled at his general theory (Pfohl, 1985:195–7). Both the social system model and the functionalist mode of analysis are regarded as highly problematic. Deviance and social control are portrayed as taking place in a 'social world that is unproblematically meaningful, based on moral consensus, homogeneous, stable, closed, and deterministic' (Douglas, 1970:371). Though this may be an over-simplification of Parsons' position, the elements of moral consensus, stability, closure and determinism are generally agreed to be a fair description of the key characteristics of his model of society. Piven summarises the case as follows:

> What Parsons calls the 'sociological theorem' is the proposition that society is a palpable reality, and that the essence of that reality is a shared normative orientation. Human beings are social beings, and the social part of that being can be recognized by the internalization of the normative consensus that is group life. The Hobbesian problem of order is solved, in other words, by definitional fiat. Conflict is relegated to the peripheries of the social, and the repressive role of the state is incidental and exceptional. It is not conflict that is rooted in nature, but consensus and conformity. And since understandings of conformity are inevitably also understandings of nonconformity, it follows that behaviors that deviate from the normative consensus are unnatural and abnormal, a symptom of a breakdown or a fissure of some sort in the consensual essence represented by society. The Hobbesian problem of enforcing social order among essentially power-seeking women and men is thereby converted to a problem of realizing the natural consensus that is society. (1981:490)

Though Parsons includes force as a method of social control, his discussion is chiefly about social and particularly normative techniques and mechanisms of social regulation. He concentrates mainly on the exercise of social control by agents enjoying full societal authority and their actions carry official legitimacy.

Society is conceived of as a well coordinated and integrated set of institutions, practices and processes centred around a core value-system, all of which work without conscious human intention or direction (Gibbs, 1977:411–12) in the collective interests of all to ensure the continuing operation and maintenance of the social whole: a highly abstract and reified depiction of society and social processes. Insofar as individuals are considered, it is as the players of pre-scripted roles in social institutions and organisations whose behaviour is the product of their culture and socialisation, there being no room for human will or agency, for the pursuit of interests or the exercise of power in this account.

> While Parsons' voluntarism places great importance on man's effort to realize certain ends, it is paradoxically true that those ends are no longer seen as derived from him; though they reside *in* him, they derive *from* social systems. Man is hollowed-out, empty, being filled with substance only by society. Man thus is seen as an entirely *social* being, and the possibility of conflict between man and society is thereby reduced. Man now has and is nothing of his own that need be counterposed to society. (Gouldner, 1971:206, original emphases)

The result is that normative expectations and actual behaviour are equated and only nonconformity is seen to need explanation. What Lemert said in 1942 about earlier American sociologists' analysis of the relationship between social control, social norms and conformity seems to apply equally to Parsons:

> . . . the most glaring deficiency in extant works on social control has been the common failure to distinguish between the regularities in behaviour and the techniques employed to induce these regularities. This is to be seen in monotonous references to folkways, mores, beliefs, laws and institutions as *means* of social control. (Lemert, 1942:396)

Structural-functionalist or 'normative' theories of deviance, like those of conformity, treat individuals as the puppets of societal forces (whether these take the form of a consensual normative order or its opposite—anomie) and are therefore heavily determinist. In Wrong's famous statement, Parsons' perspective rests on 'an over socialized conception of man' and an 'over integrated notion of society' (1961:184).

There are implicit moral judgements about deviance and social control in all this.[9] It is assumed to be in the interests both of society in general and of individual deviants that social control processes be extensive, readily available, regularly employed and effective, though Parsons and other functionalists do acknowledge that some types of deviant behaviour are problem-solving or otherwise beneficial for the individuals concerned, given the kinds of structurally induced difficulties and frustrations people in their social situations may be forced to encounter.[10]

In addition to the criticisms made of Parsons' conception of 'the social system'—specifically, his determinism, holism, idealism and reliance on a consensus model of social order—the notion and use of the term 'function' have also been called into question. Major institutions are seen as being linked to each other and to the whole society through the functions they perform. Two of the four 'needs' or 'functional prerequisites' of a 'social system' (latency and integration) refer in part to the control of deviance. Functional logic is offered as a method of understanding what social institutions and processes do in and for society. Although the concept 'function' may help us analyse the effects of a particular pattern of behaviour or institutional practice on other institutions and areas of society—and its value is certainly enhanced by such conceptual refinements as the distinctions between 'manifest' and 'latent' functions and between bad functions or 'dysfunctions' and good functions (Merton 1957:Chapter 1)—functional analysis cannot explain why or how particular institutions or practices have come to perform given functions nor why they take the form they do. It can only provide a language in which to describe and interpret the effects or consequences of social processes (Giddens, 1976).

In the case of the mechanisms of social control, therefore, we can only describe the forms they take in a specific situation or society, how they operate, what their relationships are with other parts of the social system. We can compare different types of social control within or across societies and, being careful not to confuse social control methods with what they are supposed to achieve, assess whether they are more or less successful in reducing tendencies towards deviance of various specified kinds. We can draw no inferences about the reasons for or desirability of their existence from the analysis of their nature and function. Social control may indeed be a universal component of all human groups and societies and be related in significant and complex ways to other aspects of the social order, but that is basically all that structural functionalism allows us to say about social control. For answers to questions about sources or causes of particular modes of social control, who is subject to social control, on whose behalf it is exercised and with what purposes and interests, and how social control mechanisms are linked to the political structure and other centres of power, we need to move away from structuralism-functionalism and consensus models of society and look at the work that has been carried out by those who prefer other sociological perspectives.

Interactionism and labelling theory[11]

> A sociological theory of deviance must focus specifically upon the interactions which not only define behaviors as deviant but also organise and activate the application of sanctions by individuals, groups, or agencies. . . . Socially significant differentiation of deviants from the non-deviant population is increasingly contingent upon circumstances of situation, place, social and personal biography, and the bureaucratically organised activities of agencies of control. (Kitsuse, 1962:256)

> In addition to recognizing that deviance is created by the responses of people to particular kinds of behavior, by the labeling of that behavior as deviant, we must also keep in mind that the rules created and maintained by such labeling are not universally agreed to. Instead, they are the object of conflict and disagreement, part of the political process of society. (Becker, 1963:18)

Since the 1960s there has been a considerable volume of published material contributing to the development and application of the labelling or social reaction approach to deviance and social control and to critiques and defences of this type of perspective. There are now available several excellent and up-to-date analyses of the current state and status of the labelling/interactionist perspective (in particular Downes and Rock eds., 1979; Hawkins and Tiedeman, 1975; Krohn and Akers, 1978; Liska, 1983; and Suchar, 1978). We will take for granted here that some of the conceptual problems and confusions have been satisfactorily resolved or at least clarified. Schur (1971:13–36), for instance, clears up a number of initial criticisms and misunderstandings. The main features of this perspective will be outlined, concentrating here on the more sophisticated formulations, and its major strengths and weaknesses assessed.

What the diverse contributors to this loose-knit category of theory and research (covering both 'labelling theory', and 'the interactionist approach') have in common is their rejection of the previously well-entrenched paradigms within sociology of empiricism and structural-functionalism and their advocacy of an alternative approach to the field, one which shifts the emphasis from a preoccupation with the nature and causes of criminal and deviant behaviour to issues related to social reaction and social control. There are some continuities between the Parsonian conception and the 'new' approach, in particular the idea of social control as a process of interaction between deviant and other members of society, an emphasis on norms and values, an interest in the workings of different social control mechanisms and in the diversity of types of deviance. Overall, however, most of the theorising and research carried out from the labelling/interactionist perspective is significantly different from the kind of work produced by Parsons and those from the functionalist school.

From the labelling/interactionist perspective, social control is involved in a fundamental sense in the social construction or creation of deviance: without rules there would be no deviance. (According to Quinney, 1974:8, as early as 1933, a similar view was expressed by two criminologists, Michael and Adler, who wrote: 'If crime is merely an instance of conduct that is proscribed by the criminal code it follows that the criminal law is the formal cause of crime. That does not mean that the law produces the behavior which it prohibits. . .only that the criminal law gives behavior its quality of criminality.') Compared with previous approaches, including functionalism, the 'new' deviance theorists have a much broader conception of the nature and scope of social control and therefore extend the field of study for sociologists interested in the phenomenon. It is now seen to include the processes of rule-making and norm-defining, in other words the setting of standards of what is socially appropriate and acceptable behaviour, as well as the processes involved in fixing the label 'deviant' to particular individuals and subjecting them to various types of sanctioning.

The 'new' deviance theorists are also concerned to highlight another aspect of the interdependence of deviance and social control with their attention to 'secondary deviation' (Lemert, 1951) and the 'deviant career' (Becker, 1963). A basic contention is that the labelling and social reaction that the deviant individual receives may be responsible for the continuation, 'stabilisation' (Scheff, 1966), or 'amplification' (Ditton, 1979) of precisely those behaviour patterns that they were supposed to stop, may in a sense be the causes of further deviance. For these reasons, when we are considering the labelling/interactionist approach it is not so easy to separate theories of deviance from theories of social control in the way one can with most of the other approaches.

'Labelling theory' is a misleading term, since it is now generally accepted that it is 'neither a theory, with all the achievements and obligations that go with the title, nor focused so exclusively on the act of labeling as some have thought. It is rather a way of looking at a general area of human activity, a perspective' (Becker, 1974:44). As such, it should be evaluated in terms of its capacity to pose questions and raise issues and to deal theoretically with aspects of the phenomena of deviance and social control not adequately handled by other perspectives. It cannot simply be reduced to a set of empirical propositions about the effects of social reaction on deviants which can then be refuted, though this is often what critics of the labelling school such as Gove (1975) misrepresent it as being. Its specific focus is 'the nature, emergence, application and consequences of deviancy labels' (Plummer, 1979:88; Pfohl, 1985:284–5) but these are conceptualised as complex and diverse sets of interaction processes.

Its theoretical orientation has been variously described as 'subjectivist', 'interpretive', 'relativist' and 'interactionist'. As Schur pointed out early on, it makes use of theoretical ideas drawn from a range of different perspectives, including functionalism, the most influential of which are symbolic interactionism, phenomenology and ethnomethodology (1971:Chapter 6), ultimately traceable to Max Weber; none of the original so-called 'labelling theorists' defined themselves as such (Petrunik, 1980:222–3). Those interactionists (for example Schur himself) who seek to retain a more macro dimension in their analysis alongside the more micro-sociological orientation characteristic of 'pure' interactionism may also draw on either functionalism or structuralism (Turk and Grimes, 1981:260). Plummer, who gives an account of this perspective very similar to that being offered here[12] admits this leads to 'theoretical contradictions' and incompatibilities (1979:90) and reflects 'the unresolved tensions of generations of social theorists': namely 'how to weld analyses of the structural with those of the situational; how to reconcile phenomenalism with essentialism, absolutism with relativism, idealism with materialism, formalism with *verstehen*; and how to abstract and generalise without reification' (1979:91).[13]

It is for this reason that it makes better sense to recognise the existence of at least two divergent sets of theoretical ideas and interests among the writers generally considered to be operating from this perspective. These can be differentiated according to their positions with respect to the micro/macro and voluntarist/determinist dimensions of social theory. Of the books dealing with this perspective, the best (such as Liska, 1983; Suchar, 1978) devote separate chapters to the work of the labelling theorists and that of those with a more phenomenological and ethnomethodological orientation, and this even includes some of its critics (for example, Taylor, Walton and Young, 1973).

They tend to favour a division along the following lines. On the one hand, they group together those writers who concentrate their attention on labelling and social reaction, in particular on how these operate at the official societal level, and on the effects of these on those individuals whose deviance has been formally recognised and sanctioned (effects which may be rather different from, even quite the opposite of, what is intended). On the other hand there are sociologists who regard the definition of acts and actors as deviant as highly problematic, theoretically and empirically, as subjectively determined, as relative to norms and contexts, and as a process, not a single event or decision; these sociologists are therefore more interested in identifying the competing sets of meanings and judgements and the processes of negotiation that characterise situations where imputations of deviance are made and then examining the stereotyping, stigmatisation and sanctioning that follow the designation of an individual as deviant and the social and psychological responses of the deviant to these processes. (Phenomenologists and ethnomethodologists go even further and claim that deviance does not exist independently of the perceptions, actions and contexts responsible for its production—though we need to remember this is not a uniform group.)

In all these writings social control is portrayed as an ambiguous, somewhat unpredictable, if not arbitrary, and multi-dimensional phenomenon. It covers self-control in the form of an internalised moral code, a variety of interpersonal and group techniques of accommodation and restraint, and the diversity of strategies for containment and control employed by large-scale regulatory organisations and institutions acting in a formal capacity as the agents of society as a whole.

Although there are significant variations in orientation and emphasis, there are also a number of themes and ideas common to most contributors to the labelling/interactionist approach—we will now consider some of these before returning to the differences. The most obvious common denominator is the unquestioning priority given to social control or social reaction as an important area of study in its own right and as a powerful factor in the social production and reproduction of deviant behaviour—(though even here as Suchar, 1978:174 points out, there are differences of focus to be found among the leading exponents of this approach, and he names Kitsuse, Becker, Goffman, Erikson, Garfinkel and Scheff). The major emphasis on labelling and social reaction in some cases is expressed in the form of the simple generalisation that the stigmatisation of deviant individuals causes their continued deviance, but most theorists prefer more sophisticated formulations. Their analyses of the relationships between both deviance and social control reflect the complexity and diversity of these phenomena. They recognise the need to specify particular types of social control (formal labelling being only one), the conditions under which they occur and the different motives and circumstances of various categories of deviants, in order to account satisfactorily for the diversity of deviant outcomes. The 'deviance' or 'social reaction' theorists also share an interest in the analysis of social control as an independent variable (i.e. in terms of its effects), an observation made by Black who is himself more interested in it as a dependent variable (1984: Chapter 1).

Those who argued for a 'new' deviance approach started from a set of assumptions about the nature of the social world and of sociology that differs from those that shaped the thinking of previous theorists of deviance and social control. For these later writers social reality is a construction, it is created by human action and consciousness. Human beings are diverse and complex creatures who interpret and reflect on what they see and experience and are capable of exercising will and choice. The part that subjective internal factors play in human behaviour is seen as less directly linked to external social forces (and hence less sociologically predictable) than would be the case in Parsons' model, for instance. Society therefore is also seen differently. Integration, cohesion and consensus are not taken as given, or regarded as the defining properties of 'the social system', but as historically variable aspects of social order. Society is characterised by pluralism, by the existence of groups with diverse and often competing ideas and interests who form more or less organised and permanent coalitions. Negotiation, competition and conflict, and the political process, replace consensus and the normative system as the main features of society.

Social control is now no longer a 'natural' social process mechanically activated by disturbances to the equilibrium of the system, but a deliberately chosen response by those enjoying a superior power position in a given situation to others who, for whatever reason, exhibit behaviour or personal characteristics considered incompatible with the standards set by those with the power to decide such matters. Hence, deviance is not an intrinsic quality of certain acts and cannot be objectively described as any particular type of behaviour; rather it is situational and contingent (Davis, 1975:173) and must be defined relative to people, situations, values and interests. From this perspective, official statistics purporting to record the extent of various types of deviant behaviour have to be reinterpreted. They too are a social construction, in this case a product of the priorities and practices of the general public and of processing agencies rather than a more or less accurate reflection of the incidence and distribution of the behaviour they are designed to measure (Kitsuse and Cicourel, 1963).

Social control is not simply a specific set of social reactions to deviance, but a concept that covers a range of subjective processes such as perception, categorisation and ascription of motives as well as various types of more concrete social action. Consequently, the important phases in the process of social control which are identified by the writers include detection, interpretation and evaluation of behaviour, identification and stereotyping of individuals, their designation or labelling as deviant, various modes of accommodation and reaction to such individuals, including stigmatisation, and the imposition of penalties and sanctions (Hawkins and Tiedeman, 1975; Schur, 1971). There is also the possibility of processes of 'delabelling' and 'relabelling' occurring (Trice and Roman, 1970).

This change of emphasis has led to particular types of empirical studies. On the one hand, there is socio-historical research on the 'creation of deviance' in the form of analyses of the processes of definition and redefinition of particular 'social problems' and categories of 'social deviance' which Becker (1963), for instance, suggests can be interpreted as 'moral enterprises' or 'crusades'. Well-known examples of this kind of work include the American drug laws (Becker, 1963; Dickson, 1968; Lindesmith, 1965), alcoholism (Gusfield, 1963), juvenile delinquency (Platt, 1969), 'mental illness' (Foucault, 1967; Scull, 1979) and 'new' medical conditions like hyperactivity (Box, 1980 and Conrad, 1975). On the other hand, there are analyses of social control agents and agencies involved in the processing of deviant individuals from an organisational point of view. These studies attempt to account for the patterns that emerge in the treatment of deviants by control agencies and organisations, by looking at their organisational characteristics (such as goals, ideologies, resources, structures of power and authority, and including external pressures and constraints) and aspects of the broader societal context in which they operate, such as, in the modern world, increasing state control and the processes of professionalisation, bureaucratisation and medicalisation (Hawkins and Tiedeman, 1974). Some (for example, Ermann and Lundman, 1978) extend the analysis of deviance and social control as an interactive process by developing a model to cover cases of the social control of organisations by other organisations. Researchers have also drawn attention to the significant role played by the media in contemporary society in shaping notions of deviance, transmitting knowledge about deviance, selectively reporting and interpreting deviant behaviour in a form that reflects and promotes sectional interests, reinforcing dominant norms and values, and generally participating in a variety of ways in the social control process (Cohen and Young eds., 1973; Hall, 1974; Young, 1974).

Social control is portrayed in these accounts as a complex set of actions and reactions, affected in different ways and at different stages by a variety of contingency factors and with a number of possible outcomes. All the 'deviance' perspective authors present the actual labelling of individuals as deviant as a (some say the) critical element in the process. Some stress the necessity for considering also the prior processes involved in determining what the rules, norms and standards of behaviour will be and what types of behaviour will be defined as deviant by a group or society. Dinitz et al., for instance, describe the different categorisations of deviance that are currently used in western societies; in our culture, they say, five negatively defined types of deviant are recognised—the 'freak', the 'sinful', the 'criminal', the 'sick' and the 'alienated' (1969:13).

All labelling/interactionist writers share the view that the role and status of an officially defined social deviant is a highly negative one, involving to varying degrees discrimination, deprivation, isolation and devaluation. It is also one that becomes a 'pivotal' or 'master' status, dominating the lives of those on whom it has been conferred. It can thus be expected to have a profound effect on the attitudes, self-identity, group attachments and social circumstances of those concerned. They advance the proposition that, instead of deterring individuals from deviance, the treatment they receive may be a powerful force pushing them in the direction of further and maybe more serious deviance. This is the 'narrow' version of the so-called labelling thesis (Plummer, 1979:117–8) which offers only one, though an important, prediction as to what the consequences of labelling can be for deviance.

Accompanying this kind of analysis of deviance and social control is a recognition of the value implications of this type of approach: the reasons for and consequences of social control cannot be unquestioningly accepted as either necessary or socially beneficial. Indeed for many labelling/interactionist theorists exactly the opposite judgement should be made. Since the labelled deviant is by definition someone lacking the power to defend his/her own values and interests, he/she should be regarded by the mainly liberal-minded 'new' deviance theorists as an object of sympathy and concern and, if any blame is to be allocated, it should be directed at the social control system, not at its victims. Deviants' experience and points of view are to be treated as valid in their own right. 'Taking the side' of the underdog and interpreting the processes that constitute social control from the point of view of those at the receiving end becomes an essential part of our understanding of the way deviance is socially produced and maintained.[14] The importance of research into the processes of making deviants or 'deviantising' (Schur, 1980:5) from the position of those involved in the process (not only the deviants themselves) means that the kinds of methods favoured in labelling and interactionist work are those found in more 'interpretive' or 'action-oriented' sociology generally, and in particular participant observation and in-depth interviewing.

The fact that every society treats certain forms of human diversity as deviance and that this in turn involves moral and social 'differentness' and unacceptability, an individualisation of the problem or condition, and a depoliticisation of the relevant social issues, provides us with an important subject for investigation and explanation (Horowitz and Liebowitz, 1968). Examining the factors influencing the selection of certain forms of behaviour and categories of individuals as deviant and the application of various kinds of control, can lead us to question the whole process and more particularly certain sorts of social and cultural legitimations for the use of social control. One of the major criticisms of this perspective, as we shall see later, is that it lacks an adequate theory of structure, power and ideology and cannot therefore properly address such questions either theoretically or morally (Liazos, 1972; Manders, 1975; Thio, 1973). Consequently, despite the intentions of its proponents to 'demystify' deviance and social control, what are considered to constitute proper topics continues to be determined more by society than by the sociologist. As one critic puts it:

> . . . whether they accept the judgements of the powerful or give a sympathetic ear to the complaints of the oppressed, deviancy theorists allow their field of study to be circumscribed by the givenness of social definitions. (Pearce, 1976:45)

The major differences between the different categories of writers who come under the heading of labelling/interactionist theorists can be linked to the way they perceive the relationship between labelling, social reaction and deviant behaviour and the importance they attach to that relationship in their work. At a fundamental level, one basis for differentiation is the question as to whether social control transforms or creates deviance; the relative importance attached to the central labelling thesis and the form in which this is posed is another.

In the view of many of its critics (those, for example, in Gove ed., 1975), all theorists taking this approach accept the proposition: rule-breaking→labelling→persistence or amplification of deviance. It is certainly true that much theoretical and empirical attention has been devoted to the exploration of relationships involved in this proposition, but to reduce a whole body of theory to a single such generalisation is to set up and then knock down a 'sociological strawman' (Petrunik, 1980). In most formulations, various factors or contingencies are all expected to have an influence on the deviant outcome. These include: the motivations for the initial rule-breaking; reference groups, and the resources, perceptions and responses of the labelled deviant to the processes of social control he/she experiences; social distance and relative power between the parties; visibility, publicity and privacy of the rule-breaking and the labelling; and degrees of formality and organisation of social control responses. The individual deviant's capacity to exercise agency to a greater or less extent is included in the analysis and social reaction is treated as a more complex and less predictable factor.

Despite the potential of this broad conceptualisation of deviance and social control, those theorists who tend to focus on the more serious forms of deviance often begin at the point where the rule-breaking is officially recognised and thereby perpetuate the traditional sociological preoccupation with such standard deviant categories as 'nuts, sluts and preverts' (Liazos, 1972). They, therefore, inevitably concentrate more on formal control mechanisms and agencies (principally the medical and criminal justice systems in modern society). Consequently, they may also present an image of social control as an impersonal, ruthless and all-powerful force and of social control systems as monoliths accountable to no-one but themselves. The result is that social control appears to be a one-way, irreversible, deterministic process and its nature and exercise is presented in a highly reified way (Davis, 1975:181; Schur, 1980:25).

This kind of 'labelling theory' contains a distinctive view of human nature as the passive puppet essentially shaped by external social forces (Schervish, 1973), of social control as exercised by middle-level officials in 'care-taking institutions' (Gouldner, 1968:107), and of society as a relatively loose-knit collection of groups and organisations engaged in the task of regulating behaviour and administering the rules of society. It is these characteristics which have attracted most of the well-known criticisms. The labelling thesis, and especially the 'narrow' version of this thesis, is said to lack any sense of human beings as exerting will or agency, of making choices in situations, and of resisting the effects of stigmatisation and sanctioning, and hence any sense of the 'production' of deviance as a process involving contest and struggle. Though it totally misrepresents the work of such theorists to accuse them of confining their analysis simply to the micro-sociological level, they do fall short of providing an adequate overall picture of the main structural features of modern society and of the state and capitalism in particular (Hall and Scraton, 1981; Piven, 1981; Plummer, 1979).

Interactionism by contrast is generally perceived as having a more wide-ranging set of interests, the nature and consequences of official and societal labelling being only one of its concerns. It is seen as offering a framework for the analysis of the interactive processes of deviance creation and social control at a number of different levels, ranging across the intrapersonal, interpersonal, situational, organisational and societal. There is some question about the extent to which its full capacity has so far been realised, particularly with respect to the structural level of analysis. (Both Becker, 1974:6 and the critics Taylor, Walton and Young, 1973:167 agree that this is a problem of 'under-application' or neglect rather than an inherent limitation in the perspective.) It treats the processes of norm-defining and rule-making as of equal importance in the production of deviance with those of labelling and reaction. Interactionists pay attention to the informal processes of interaction and negotiation over meanings and labels that occur in groups, as well as processes of social control of a more formal and official nature. They give greater weight to the investigation of the variability and influence of subjective motives, perceptions and interpretations and of competing and contested definitions and evaluations in both informal and formal settings. They therefore present a picture of the social construction of deviance and of social control as being far more ambiguous and interdeterminate phenomena than is the impression conveyed by the more narrow labelling approach.

Though the perspective has considerable theoretical potential, the fact that many interactionists have in practice concentrated on 'the immediate participants in localised dramas of deviance' (Becker, 1974:60) has resulted in their work being heavily criticised by more structurally-oriented theorists. The perspective then becomes vulnerable to the accusation that it offers only a micro or social psychological account of deviance and social control and runs the risk of lapsing into total idealism and relativism (Davis, 1975; Liska, 1981; Orcutt, 1983; Taylor, Walton and Young, 1973). Paradoxically, others attack the perspective from the opposite standpoint: they contend that some authors move uneasily between true phenomenology and interactionism and end up doing justice to neither (Fine, 1977; Rains, 1975; Warren and Johnson, 1972). These sorts of weaknesses lead some of its critics to see this approach and particularly 'labelling theory', though useful in its time, as on the way out: 'Labelling theory is perhaps best seen as a transitional stage in the move from traditional criminology to the new criminologies' (Wiles, 1976:18).

Those who still support this perspective but who take seriously the kinds of criticisms which have been levelled at it, particularly by marxists, over the past ten years are now advocating a move towards a greater recognition of the importance of historical specificity, the role of the modern state, conflict and political struggle, and of ideology. Hence they see the need for the incorporation of elements from conflict, class and political economy models into what is still regarded as basically an interactionist (rather than a structuralist) framework (Conrad and Schneider, 1980a; Grimes and Turk, 1978; Hils, 1981; Pfohl, 1985; Piven, 1981; Schur, 1980; Suchar, 1978). This blend of perspectives they believe has the potential for handling both agency and structure and permits the retention of a broad definition of the field of study, not restricted only to crime and the law, as tends to be the case with marxist approaches.

To gain a better understanding of precisely those dimensions of social structure and power that the labelling/interactionist school is accused of disregarding, we turn now to a consideration of modern marxism and critical criminology.

3 Radical social perspectives and social control

To call any theory or perspective 'radical' is to invite controversy. My purpose here is simply to draw a distinction between mainstream sociological traditions and other categories of social theory, which though sociological in content and implication originated elsewhere, usually in association with social movements and political action, and which, more particularly, at their initial conception reflected an explicit and fundamental rejection of both the prevailing social order and established bodies of theoretical and scientific knowledge.

'Radical' is thus used in its literal sense of going to the root of something. However, it must be acknowledged that the judgement as to whether an idea is 'radical', even in this limited sense, is highly subjective and open to challenge. In *Radical Sociology* (edited by Colfax and Roach, 1971), Colfax in a provocative paper makes clear how different values about the nature and purpose of knowledge influence judgements about what constitutes 'radical' thought. He distinguishes two dimensions of 'radical scholarship'—ontological and epistemological or in other words moral/political and intellectual/methodological—and argues that few works can qualify as radical in this dual sense.

Claims can be and have been made that the two perspectives which form the major part of the content of this chapter qualify as 'radical' on both these dimensions. First, for marxists and feminists, society (seen either as capitalist or patriarchal) and accepted bodies of social theory (which are bourgeois and/or sexist) are to be regarded as fundamentally flawed and in need of critical intellectual reappraisal, thorough transformation and reconstruction. Second, both categories of thinkers ground their analysis and proposals for change on moral absolutes, on basic values about human nature, freedom and liberation, which in their view cannot be realised under existing modes of social organisation. To avoid confusion, one should also add that, though particular theories within both marxist criminology and feminism have been given or have claimed for themselves the designation 'radical', 'radical' in such cases has a different meaning and this is not the reason for their inclusion here in the category of radical social theory.

At the end of this chapter, brief mention will be made of the work of Foucault. This French theorist, now dead, who has become such an influential figure in the social control field, is particularly hard to categorise, and although he has defined himself as neither sociologist nor marxist in the accepted sense, he should—in my view—be included here.

Marxist perspectives[1]

> If every State tends to create and maintain a certain type of civilisation and of citizen (and hence of collective life and of individual relations), and to eliminate certain customs and to disseminate others, then the Law will be its instrument for this purpose (together with the school system, and other institutions and activities)...the State must be conceived of as an 'educator', in as much as it tends precisely to create a new type of level of civilisation...The State...is an instrument of 'rationalisation'...It operates according to a plan, urges, incites, solicits, and 'punishes'...The Law is the repressive and negative aspect of the entire positive, civilising activity undertaken by the State. (Gramsci, 1971:246–7)

> Contrary to conceptions that treat it as a Thing or a Subject, the State is itself divided. Class contradictions are the very stuff of the State: they are present in its material framework and pattern its organization; while the State's policy is the result of their functioning within the State...
>
> We must therefore discard once and for all the view of the State as a completely united mechanism, founded on a homogeneous and hierarchical distribution of the centres of power moving from top to bottom of a uniform ladder or pyramid. According to this conception, the homogeneity and uniformity of the exercise of power is ensured by juridical regulation within the State: by a constitutional and administrative law that demarcates the fields of competence and activity of the various apparatuses. This is a radically false image, however. (Poulantzas, 1978:132, 133)

In the same way as labelling and interactionist theorists formulated their approach to deviance and social control as a deliberate attempt to correct the perceived defects and misrepresentations in accounts given by functionalists such as Parsons, so marxists and advocates of the new 'critical' criminology approach[2] presented their alternative view specifically to counter what they regarded as limitations in the work of both functionalists and interactionists. Functionalism was criticised particularly for the idea that the basis of social order is an overriding and pervasive normative or cultural consensus, for the assumption that all parts of society necessarily work together harmoniously for the benefit of all, and for the emphasis placed, when making comparisons between societies and over time, on structural and functional continuities at the expense of historical variability, contradiction and chance. They saw value in some of the features of the 'deviance' approach: namely, its anti-correctionalist stance;[3] its negative view of social control; its emphasis on power as a key factor in determining the definition of what constitutes deviance and in the identification, labelling and treatment of deviant individuals; its preference for a pluralist or conflict model of society over a consensus one; its questioning of the moral and social status of prevailing norms and standards and of those carrying out the business of social control; and its attempt (albeit not entirely successful) to deal with 'structure' adequately without sacrificing 'agency'.

> It is important not to throw out all the insights of labelling in the rush to class analysis and to acknowledge its role in the regeneration and re-orientation of psychological [meaning presumably social-psychological] theorising about crime and deviance. (Muncie and Fitzgerald, 1981:427)

The main task, however, was seen by the critics of the sociology of deviance perspective to be the formulation of a new 'radical' approach, benefiting from the insights gained from previous theory and research, but starting from a very different set of philosophical assumptions about the nature of the social world and leading to different kinds of social theory and political practice (Taylor, Walton and Young, 1975: 23–8). The aspects of labelling and interactionist approaches which attracted most opposition included the following: the ontological priority accorded by interactionists to subjectively defined meanings and situations over (in particular) material factors; their preference for analysis of social phenomena at the level of interaction between individuals and groups and their neglect of the structural dimensions of social reality; related to this, and to their view of society and power as pluralistic, their inability to confront the possibility of power structures, ruling classes, dominant institutions and ideologies, systemic sources of discrimination and inequality, and a whole social order resting on subjection and oppression; and their sociological and moral relativism and consequent inability to tackle issues of social policy, political action and social change.

An alternative position on most of these issues is present if not fully articulated in the critical literature that appeared in the early 1970s in England and America. The most famous example was the book by Taylor, Walton and Young (1973), *The New Criminology: For a Social Theory of Deviance*, whose somewhat ambiguous title reveals a main tenet of the new school of thought, namely that the principal form of deviance is crime and the primary mode of social control is the law and criminalisation. Accompanying this is the impression the authors give that the removal of class inequalities and the capitalist system would eliminate crime (and/or deviance) and the necessity for social (i.e. legal) controls (Cohen, 1979b:42–5). This somewhat restrictive view was subsequently modified as the work of certain western marxists (such as Gramsci and Althusser) became more widely known and was broadened to include all the agencies of the modern state, various ideological modes, and the economy as factors to be considered in the theoretical analysis of social control. In fact, on their own admission, Taylor, Walton and Young (1973:269) only outline the direction the new 'radical' approach should take, identifying marxism as the guiding light, and specifying some of the theoretical traps to avoid and problems to solve, mentioning particularly voluntarism/determinism, subjectivism/objectivism and correctionalism.

As time passed a number of different versions of the 'radical' perspective emerged, all claiming Marxian origins. Some remained closer to interactionism and labelling theory (and to one of its original intellectual inspirations, the work of Max Weber), while others, particularly those inclined towards structuralism such as the Althusserian school, adopted such a broad conception of the state as the regulator of society that they had more in common with Parsons' systems approach and structural functionalism.[4]

Several authors of books on sociological theories of deviance and social control include chapters on what they call 'conflict' theories. As the pioneering work from a 'critical criminology' perspective (the book by Taylor, Walton and Young) shows, this term covers a wide range of different approaches to crime and deviance. However, though marxist theories can certainly be described as 'conflict' theories, the latter term seemed to lose currency as marxism took over during the 1970s as the dominant 'radical' perspective in this field as in many areas of sociology. For that reason, after a brief discussion of non-marxist 'conflict' theory, we will concentrate here on marxism, and specifically on modern western marxism.

Though labelling and interactionist writers had shown that the definition of deviance and the exercise of social control are political as well as social processes, they have been much criticised for their treatment of power, which it has been claimed is pluralist and a-structural.[5] The labelling/interactionist perspective and the modern alternatives to that approach (both 'conflict' theory and marxism) all share the view that societies are based on social difference and division, and that therefore power relations, conflict and contest are a central feature of every social order. 'Labelling theory ties into conflict theory to the extent that the struggle for power constitutes the contingencies for action and reaction' (Grimes and Turk, 1978:55).

The major source of difference between pluralist and other conflict theories and among different types of conflict theory lies in the degree to which power is defined in structural terms and in the way 'structure' is interpreted. While non-marxist conflict theories recognise a number of sources of power (and hence conflict) they, like the pluralists, concentrate their attention on the political arena and on political groups and institutions. Whether the political units are relatively free-floating interest groups (as in pluralist models) or major social organisations and coalitions (as in elite theories), they are seen as essentially operating on their own behalf—hence questions as to the differential distribution of power and resources, the social origins of interest groups and organisations, and the broader societal contexts within which these operate are ignored (Alford, 1975; Head, 1983:Chapter 2). The political system, it is assumed, is concerned with finding compromise through negotiation and exchange or with maintaining the dominance of existing groups of leaders or elites; in both cases the main focus is on the processes involved in the reaching of political decisions by government.

By contrast, marxists look behind these phenomena in order to uncover what they believe are more fundamental structures and processes, the forces and relations of production. In classic marxism, the basic division in society is into two groups (classes) with unequal access to power and other resources, determined by their differing relationships to the means of production. This gives rise to a social structure characterised by conflict and struggle, in which the dominant class has to employ various means of coercion, regulation and repression in order to maintain its control over the productive system and the subordinate class; one important mechanism of control being the legal system. The predominant trend among 'radical' sociologists in the 1970s seemed at first to be 'the disinheritance of the wider "sociology of deviance" rubric, in favour of a concentration on "crime, law and the state"' (Cohen, 1981:241), though as we shall see this was only one aspect of modern marxism's approach to social control.

For most marxists, the processes of regulating and maintaining the (capitalist) social order are both more diverse and more impersonal or systemic than the notions of class oppression and material determinism associated with some forms of classic marxism. Marxist structuralists, such as Althusser and Poulantzas, confer relatively equal theoretical status as determinants of the modern capitalist system on three 'levels' or 'moments'—the economic, the political and the ideological—regarding these three as the key structures of society (and giving each some degree of 'relative autonomy'). They then concentrate their attention on the major roles they perceive the modern state and ideologies as playing in the production and reproduction of the social conditions and relations of capitalism.

Modern marxist theories of the state emphasise the less obvious, non-coercive mechanisms of social regulation and control, particularly such ideological apparatuses as the family, education, representative democracy, and 'welfarism' (which they regard as part of 'the state'), and the subtle ways in which these provide 'legitimation' and support both for the state itself and for capitalism. They suggest that the institutions responsible for carrying out state functions, being highly professionalised and bureaucratised, appear to be 'neutral' and detached from any particular political or economic interests or groups. So, what Parsons perceived to be the 'true' benign nature and function of social institutions and structures, modern marxists would interpret as an ideological mystification, their 'real' purpose or effect (and some marxists are as guilty of teleological reasoning and reification as functionalists) being the protection and perpetuation of an exploitative and oppressive system.

For marxists, the 'problem of social order' (and its solution) is produced by particular historical conditions and social practices; it is not the result of conscious intentions and actions by individuals or groups nor of an essential tension between individual human beings and society. The conditions and practices in question are those responsible for creating and maintaining social inequality and exploitation, and hence the necessity for an imposed order of domination and repression so as to safeguard the system and its beneficiaries, the ruling class or property-owners, from risk of attack by the disadvantaged and oppressed majority of the population. We will look briefly at the overall perspective developed by Marx and Engels and then at the additions, modifications and extensions made by modern western marxists, which are of particular relevance here.

For Marx and Engels, the original sources of inequality and exploitation were the division of labour and the institution of private property, and their basic form is economic. At a given level of technological development these made possible the production of a surplus and its appropriation by those in the dominant position in society. Since the key structure in society is the mode of production, the dominant group (or class) is the one that owns the means of production. With the capitalist mode of production (involving factory production, the money economy, and a 'free' market in goods and services, including labour), the capacity to generate a surplus (in the form of profit) greatly increased and with it the accumulation of wealth, the exploitation of workers and the polarisation of the two classes. Since the nature and main sphere of operation of the primary institutions of society—the system of production and distribution of goods and services—and the most important and powerful social group—the ruling class—are essentially defined in economic terms, the other structures and institutions in society are seen as dependent on, conditioned (some say determined) by and supportive of the material base and the interests of the dominant class.

Underlying the internal divisions and conflicts which are a feature of all class societies and are a constant source of tension and instability are structural contradictions which work themselves out in history. History, in Marx's view, involves an overall process of social change and development both within each epoch and as societies move from one major social form or epoch into another. As conflict (overt or repressed) characterises the social relations between the classes, so contradiction (or the dialectic) is the fundamental constituent of social order at least up to now. All societies, therefore, require institutions and mechanisms to manage workers in the factory and in the city, and to regulate class relations in such a way that the interests, position and wealth of ruling class members are protected without causing too much general resentment among workers. At the same time they need to ensure that the necessary conditions for the maintenance of capitalism as an economic, political and social system be preserved, and the optimum environment created within which capitalism's (alleged) infinite potential for expansion and development can be realised.

For Marx, the maintenance of capitalism meant a politico-legal institutional structure that would guarantee the necessary conditions for capitalist expansion, namely the unrestricted operation of market forces, free enterprise, capital accumulation, the profit motive, commodification and technological innovation. In this was included where necessary the enforcement of criminal laws and special regulatory procedures (such as the poor law system) whose principal targets were the propertyless, workers, and various sections of the non-productive population, and ideological support for such essential capitalist institutions and values as private property, freedom of contract, competition, individual responsibility and economic self-sufficiency.

For Marx, therefore, key features of social control under capitalism are (a) the relatively unlimited exercise of power by capitalists over labour in the workplace and in some industrial towns outside it as well; (b) laws which uphold employers' rights and powers and those of property-holders generally; (c) a legal-judicial system which, by the selective enforcement of laws against certain sections of the population and application of repressive and punitive sanctions, attempts to contain and restrain unruly elements of the oppressed classes; (d) a political system which, with the aid of liberal ideology, (mis)represents itself as providing an opportunity for the equal participation of all citizens or at least those who are 'responsible' i.e. property-owning males) in the decision-making processes of government and as operating as neutral arbiter between groups; this political system was seen as occupying a defined and limited territory, the 'public' sphere, quite separate from 'civil society' and in particular the 'private' sphere of industry, business and commerce; it was a political system that, at least in his time, intervened directly in the economy with reluctance, usually to protect ruling class and national interests;[6] (e) a social organisation of production for surplus which itself constitutes a 'despotic' system of social control (Melossi, 1980) whereby capital rules over work, the worker and the labour process;[7] and (f) various supportive 'secondary' institutions, such as ideology and the bourgeois family.[8] The state, a universal feature of capitalist society and one which comes to assume such a central place in modern marxist thought, is regarded as a subsidiary institution or structure, responsible for providing an overall legal and social framework for productive activities and processes and for capitalism as a whole socio-economic system.

Modern western marxism has developed and expanded Marx's own theoretical analysis in a number of important ways which have consequences for our understanding of social control under capitalism; essentially they involve ideas about the form and function of the modern capitalist state. Of particular significance are the changed nature and greater centrality of the role of the state in advanced western capitalist countries; the expanded scope and enlarged range of mechanisms associated with the operation of the modern state; increased emphasis on the non-coercive, ideological mechanisms and functions of the state (though some recent events suggest a swing back to more repressive methods, a trend we will discuss in Chapter 4) and on the various ideological apparatuses and instruments of social control. From the point of view of the sociology of deviance and social control, particularly interesting is the shift in recent marxist writing from a predominant concern with crime and the law to equal consideration of other 'problem populations' (Spitzer, 1975a) and of other state-based regulatory institutions and mechanisms. Accompanying these are different conceptualisations of the relationships between the state (its 'ideological' and 'repressive' apparatuses), class, and the capitalist system; all share a basic notion of the state as 'relatively autonomous'. This results in differences in the positions adopted on the agency-structure and determinism issues in particular, and in the extent to which internal contradictions and opportunities for resistance and change within the state and capitalism as a whole are recognised by theorists.

The modern capitalist state for marxists is 'the principal institutional locus of political power in capitalist societies' (Jessop, 1978:10) and it comprises a number of social institutions—'executive, legislative, administrative, military and police, judiciary and subcentral government' (Gough, 1975:64). It operates in a number of arenas, economic, political and socio-cultural or ideological (Therborn, 1982), through a range of agencies both public and private (including welfare and community services, education, the media, as well as government and the legal/judicial system). It employs a number of strategies such as 'legitimation, regulation, modification and the creation of institutions and practices' (Littlejohn, 1978:9) or such, mechanisms as 'facilitation, support and direction' (Winkler, 1977:44). Marxists deny the state has ever played a strictly laissez-faire role or that such interventions as were made were the natural outcome of the heightened humanitarian consciousness that accompanied developing industrialism. They maintain that, contrary to bourgeois theory and ideology, the state has always contributed to capitalist development by supplementing, protecting and assisting private enterprise and market forces (and thereby shaping directly and indirectly the lives of all sectors of society), though its functions and activities have become vastly more extensive, diverse and critical as capitalism has grown.

Jessop starts his useful survey of 'recent theories of the capitalist state' with a summary of six different conceptions of the relationship between the state and society to be found in the classic texts of Marx and Engels, four of which are of interest here. Briefly these are as follows: 'the state and state power as epiphenomena' of the economic and class systems; the state as 'regulator' of class struggle, responsible, through repression and concession, for achieving social cohesion; the state as a set of institutions and structures defined by its administrative and regulative functions; and the state as a system of political domination with structural and institutional links to capital and the class struggle (1977:354–6).

Jessop and many modern marxists draw distinctions between marxist approaches to understanding the nature and functioning of the state in instrumentalist terms and those which take a more structural(ist) view, and between economic reductionist, class relational and structuralist accounts. It is in the form of a choice between instrumentalism and structuralism that the famous debate in modern marxism between Miliband and Poulantzas is cast (Blackburn ed. 1972; Miliband, 1973; Poulantzas, 1976).

Instrumentalist conceptions of the state present it as the servant of the ruling class and explain this either in voluntarist terms (the members of the ruling class manipulate political processes for their own ends) or in an economic determinist fashion (the state does whatever is necessary to meet the needs and demands of the capitalist mode of production). This split between 'class-theoretical' and 'capital-theoretical' forms of marxist thought[9] (or, as Jessop 1982:25–6, also puts it, between an emphasis on control and one on the reproduction of capital) is reflected even within structuralist approaches.

The tendency to favour a structuralist model is associated with modern marxism's concern to develop a better appreciation of the ideological functions of the state and to move beyond the more narrowly defined (economic and materialist) conceptions of what 'the production and reproduction of the conditions of capitalism' means. The capitalist state came to be seen as not only exercising a 'monitoring' or 'housekeeping function' (Solo, 1975:100), but at least by the twentieth century, as being heavily involved in developing and monitoring social and ideological mechanisms aimed at securing compliance and reinforcing legitimacy through persuasion and artificially created consensus ('hegemony'). The state is also seen to be concerned with remedying, through publicly supplied services and benefits, the worst excesses, injustices and deprivations of the capitalist mode of production (thereby averting dissatisfaction with and opposition to the system).

By appearing to be separate from the economy and thereby 'neutral', the state masks by various means (both material and ideological) the exploitation and oppression inherent in capitalism and the part played by the state itself in ensuring the conditions necessary for capitalist production and accumulation, and in supporting and maintaining the system as a whole.

Gramsci (1971), Althusser (1971) and Poulantzas (1973) draw an important distinction between two major social control approaches or strategies—the 'repressive' and the 'ideological'—both of which are present in the institutions and operations of the modern state.

> . . . by the 'State' should be understood not only the apparatus of government, but also the 'private' apparatus of 'hegemony' or civil society . . . one might say State = political society + civil society, in other words hegemony protected by the armour of coercion. (Gramsci, 1971:263)

Repression involves the utilisation of physical violence, force and coercion, specifically by such agencies as the military, the police and the penal system, and under capitalism the state has a legally defined and protected monopoly on their use. The repressive function is exercised through a relatively integrated set of mechanisms under the direction of government in the interests of capital and/or the ruling class. Ideological apparatuses and techniques are intended to obtain voluntary compliance and consent through indoctrination and persuasion. They comprise a more diverse and 'independent' range of agencies and, though ultimately under the broad jurisdiction of the state, ideological functions may be performed by organisations in the 'private' sector of society (Althusser, 1971:135–41; Poulantzas, in Blackburn, 1972:251).

Historically, 'the maturation of non-coercive hegemony in the west has been accompanied by a decisive trend for the social processes involved . . . to become incorporated in the state' (Shaw, 1974:440). The modern state is characterised by its 'interventionism' and 'welfarism', which have meant a vastly increased administrative apparatus and an expanded range of institutions and functions. It is seen to have moved beyond the 'regulator and protector' role of the liberal state (Held, 1983:14) which involved meeting the basic infrastructural requirements of early capitalism, ensuring the continued supply of the factors of production and, to a limited extent neutralising and compensating for the negative aspects of competitive capitalism. In modern capitalism the state does far more.

> Aside from the field of social policy, it regulates business and commerce, intervenes in the labour market and industrial relations, conducts relations with other states, provides infrastructure services such as transport and communications, directly produces goods and services for sale, and since the Second World War has assumed responsibility for overall economic management. (Gough, 1979:49)

The modern state is set several major broadly defined functions or tasks. Clark and Dear give a useful summary of these: to secure the conditions of production and reproduction of the system, and to create and maintain social consensus and social integration; they add what they call an 'executive function', or the monitoring and regulating of its own activities and its relations with other non-state agencies. Though an apparatus can serve more than one function, they group apparatuses (or sub-apparatuses as they term them) according to their main function. 'Apparatus' refers to 'the set of institutions and organisations through which state power is exercised' (1984:45). Under consensus they list political, legal and repressive apparatuses; under production, public production, public provisions and treasury; under integration, health, welfare and education, information, communications and media; and under executive, administration and regulatory agencies (1984:50–54).

Alternative formulations of the expanded functions of the modern state are provided by Habermas who describes four major categories of government activity: constituting and maintaining the mode of production; market-complementing adaptations; market-replacing actions; and compensating for dysfunctional consequences of the accumulation of capital (1975:53–4).

The modern state 'regulates' and 'manages' all sectors of society and 'intervenes' in significant and major ways even in the direction of the economy and in production itself. The state now exercises a controlling hand in every aspect of life in society. This control takes a variety of forms, in addition to the basic one of force or coercion, ranging over the directly political (legislation and government policy), the administrative (government departments, statutory bodies and instrumentalities), the economic (taxes, subsidies, trade and pricing policies, as well as direct economic responsibility for state employees and state supplied goods and services), and the socio-cultural (policies and practices in the family, community and welfare areas affecting the circumstances, opportunities and ideological beliefs and values of individuals and groups in society). Common to all state institutional forms and modes of operation in modern capitalism are rationalisation, bureaucratisation and professionalisation, and the application of scientific knowledge and technology.[10]

Since the nineteenth century, the state has steadily assumed responsibility for many aspects of the functioning of society and for many sections of the population and their problems, and moved beyond a narrow reliance on repressive, punitive and moralistic methods of control to the development of an extensive range of what are broadly defined as 'welfare' provisions. In so doing it has cast off a largely negative image and, by demonstrating the 'good' side of capitalism, it has strengthened the perceived value and legitimacy of such a system. Many emphasise the ideological underpinning of capitalism achieved through a complex system of rewards and deprivations, described by Young (1975:83) as 'the soft machine of control'. However, as all marxists (and others)[11] point out with respect to the 'welfare' aspects of the state:

> ...the services of the welfare state are not major accomplishments, as some commentators would have it, but, rather, are meagre compensations for the price of industrial development....the welfare state in its historical development has been following the path of 'compensation' and 'offset' rather than the path of improvement and the widening of life chances...(Offe, 1972:483)

Gough sees the 'welfare state' as an important part of the modern capitalist state; it is that part which is concerned with extracting revenue through taxes and distributing it through goods and services. Its institutional areas cover education and training, health care, housing, transport, the environment, social security, family and single parent support, and the old age and unemployment provisions. The social policy aspects of welfare state activity do not only concern the provision and allocation of money and services, either on a non-paying or subsidised basis, but also, either as part of the deal for recipients of benefits or in other ways, the exercise of social control, mainly through...

> taxation policies and a whole range of social legislation from the Factory Acts to modern consumer protection, from building by-laws to the statutory compulsion on children to receive education. (Gough 1979:4)

The welfare state 'simultaneously embodies tendencies to enhance social welfare, to develop the powers of individuals, to exert social control over the blind play of market forces; and tendencies to repress and control people, to adapt them to the requirements of the capitalist economy' (Gough, 1979:12). A good example of what this involves is the explanation put forward by Piven and Cloward (1972) in their famous American study entitled 'Regulating the Poor' for changes in the levels of and conditions for receiving relief over various periods. Their thesis is that the expansion of state relief policies at certain times is not a simple response to increased economic need, but rather occurs when there are also threats of civil disorder and benefits are still kept at a level which preserves the differential between worker and non-worker. Contraction and restriction of relief programmes similarly reflect social not economic conditions, and are imposed as soon as the relief programme is perceived to be exercising a disincentive effect on the work ethic.[12]

However, the welfare state, as most modern marxists see it, is theoretically even more complex. Gough goes on to say: 'Each tendency will generate counter-tendencies in the opposite direction; indeed, this is precisely why we refer to it as a contradictory process through time' (1979:12). He rejects the view that 'the state, and thus the welfare state, can only act in the interests of capital and the capitalist class' (1979:13–14) and emphasises the conflicts, contradictions and crises that inevitably beset capitalism and the capitalist state, and create further problems of control for the state and the system.

For marxists, the effect of an increasingly complex inter-penetration of state, society and the economy, which makes it harder to separate the state from the rest of society, or isolate its specific mechanisms and functions, along with the occurrence of serious crises during the 1970s in western societies (crises affecting the economic, political and social-ideological bases of social order), has presented the state and specifically governments with threats to their existence and to that of capitalist society. The 'management of crises' in the view of writers such as Habermas and Offe (Held and Krieger, 1983; Held, 1984) has become a major and pressing task for the modern state and crises in 'legitimation', 'integration' and 'mass loyalty' pose as serious a challenge as the economic crises of inflation, recession and unemployment. All crises confront capitalist society and principally the state with a problem of social control (Clegg, Dow and Boreham, 1983; Gough, 1979; Habermas, 1973, 1981; Offe, 1975; O'Connor, 1981). Further, financial and other pressures on the state have resulted in cuts to welfare and other state expenditures which in turn threaten the value of the ideology of 'welfarism' as well as its material benefits as a significant source of social support for the system. Habermas (1981) and Offe (1984:171–3, 292–5) stress problems arising in the arenas of cultural reproduction, socialisation and integration and the threats posed by 'new social movements' (which direct their energies towards peace, ecology and women's issues rather than the traditional capital-labour struggle) to the conventional political processes, centralised bureaucratic structures and institutionalised administrative methods for handling conflict.

Marxists totally reject the 'logic of industrialism' account of the development of the welfare state, with its implicit technological determinism, that is favoured by functionalists (such as Smelser, 1964; Wilensky and Lebeaux, 1965). They prefer an explanation in terms of the nature and problems of the capitalist mode of production. Marxists divide over the issue of whether the institutions, activities and functions of the modern state are best understood as the result of the structural conditions, processes and inter-relationships characteristic of modern capitalism or as shaped by the social and economic conflicts and struggles between classes and organised groups, and particularly between capital and labour: in other words whether they are best analysed at the structural or at the class relational level.

Structuralism, and Althusser and Poulantzas in particular, have been heavily attacked by other marxists for 'abstractionism', 'superdeterminism' and 'theoreticism'. They, it has been alleged, merge or conflate 'the political' and 'the ideological' in their accounts and blur the distinction between 'the state' and 'civil society', which leaves no room for the possibility that the state's control strategies could fail or for the capacity of groups and organised interests other than those representing capitalism to influence the institutions of government and the state. The alternative view, which recognises the importance of class divisions and class conflict as a fundamental feature of capitalism, suggests that this affects the state in two ways: firstly, the struggles between the classes representing capital and labour (and between different class fractions) which arise in the economic or productive sector (and maybe those between other groups) are fought out also in the political arena, in a political system based on democratic principles[13] which offers some opportunities for labour to modify and moderate aspects of capitalism; and, secondly, the state itself contains internal conflict and division and in some respects operates as a relatively independent source and context of struggle (Corrigan, 1980:Introduction; London Edinburgh Weekend Return Group, 1980). The latter approach seems to be more likely also to generate research into the historical development and current operation of specific areas of state policy and activity (see for example Corrigan ed., 1980; Kennedy ed., 1982), empirical research having played little part in the almost entirely theoretically-determined work of the structuralists.

The marxist theories of the state of the kind that have just been described and the work of particular named authors have been extensively used by writers interested in the broad range of institutions and policies that comprise the 'welfare state' and in 'welfarism' as a philosophy or ideology; this includes also those working in the areas of health care, medicine and education.

However, law and the legal, judicial and penal systems (the 'repressive' side of the state) have been relatively neglected in the literature on the 'welfare state'. Much of the marxist material on law and crime draws also on the Weberian tradition and on Foucault and often appears separately from the mainstream work on the state. However, the theoretical frameworks and key concepts and concerns are broadly similar: for instance, the relationships between capitalism and the state, and between law, economy, ideology and the state; and the role of agency, of class interests and class conflict in the formation and administration of the law (Brown, 1978; Hall and Scraton, 1981; Sugarman ed., 1983; Young, 1981).

In summary, then, modern marxism has made an important contribution to our understanding of social control. It has applied critical theory and a materialist perspective to the analysis of the social processes of regulation, management and control, with a particular focus on capitalist society. With the aid of various concepts derived originally from the work of Marx, a comprehensive picture can be built up of the central role played at all levels of society by the modern state. Modern marxists examine the state's recourse to both coercive and persuasive methods, its utilisation of a vast array of institutional apparatuses and mechanisms, and the influence it exerts over so many aspects of human and social existence: on material circumstance, mental and moral attitudes and beliefs, working lives, family and personal relationships, political action, belief systems, culture, and so on. What capitalism and the state seek to regulate and control, from the point of view of marxists, is far more than crime and the limited range of phenomena defined as 'social deviance' by functionalists and labelling/interactionist theorists.

In the work of some marxists, such as the structuralists, this account becomes so abstract, theoretical and generalised that the state in a sense takes over completely and becomes society. Such an overly deterministic approach to the problems of social order (and social control in its broadest sense) has much in common with the consensus social systems model of Parsons discussed earlier in the chapter (DiTomaso, 1982). It suffers from some of the same theoretical weaknesses: the processes whereby social order is to be achieved are assumed to be successful, means are equated with ends or effects, and a high degree of social conformity to dominant morality and ideology is taken for granted; there is a reliance on functionalist and teleological forms of explanation; and the intricacies of the inter-relationships between the structural components of societies are given theoretical and even ontological priority over the minds, bodies and actions of real live human beings.

Recently, marxists have tended to favour theoretical perspectives which give more of a place to human agency and the dynamics of social relations and to the importance of the exercise of power and control by organisations and groups as well as by institutions and structures. This results in a focus on contestation, conflict and resistance (though such writers tend to define these only in terms of class and to ignore other bases of social division such as gender and ethnicity) which balances the structuralists' emphasis on domination, cultural hegemony as they understand this term, and over-determination by the capitalist mode of production.

Talking of the state as if 'it' were a single entity or subject (or even a 'structural ensemble') becomes, from an anti-structuralist perspective (such as that found in Poulantzas' later work), a misleading oversimplification. Instead the notion of 'the state' should be treated with great caution. 'It' should be conceptualised and treated as a collection or association of institutions, mechanisms, relationships and practices, being as likely to contain within its 'forms, apparatuses and functions' (if we continue to use such terms) division, conflict and contradiction as it is to operate as an integrated, cohesive and united force in defence of capitalism and the capitalist class.

What all conceptions of the state have in common is the recognition that the institutions of the state play an important part in the regulation and management of society. Though the specific concept 'social control' may not figure prominently in marxist discourse, the use of terms such as regulation, repression, surveillance, discipline, domination and control are commonplace. There seems little justification or support for Stedman Jones' (1977) rejection of the concept of social control altogether, on the grounds that it is defined in ideological terms and is therefore reductionist and contaminated by its bourgeois sociological connotations.[14]

This view is challenged by another historian, Donajgrodzki, who includes the term 'social control' in the title of his book on nineteenth century Britain. He admits that it became a central organising concept within a particular American sociological tradition, which led eventually to its identification in some circles with a consensus model of society as developed by Parsons and others. However, for him, it is 'trans-ideological' (1977:10). He sees social control as a valuable conceptual tool in the study of relationships between the powerful and the powerless in society (1977:14) particularly when used in conjunction with class analysis, and when part of an explanatory framework he contends it need imply neither structural or ideological determinism nor conscious manipulation or conspiracy theory. Basically he likes the opportunity the concept gave the authors in the book he edited to treat as a theoretical unity a wide range of social institutions and practices, not only the more obvious ones associated with the work-place and the penal system, but also including 'religion...family life...leisure and recreation, education, charity and philanthropy, social work and poor relief' (1977:9). The concept is also discussed in a similar way and a similar conclusion reached by Windschuttle (1982), one of the contributors to a comparable collection of essays on Australian history, which also focuses on welfare (public and private) and the increasing role of the state since the nineteenth century as an instrument of class control. Marxist writers in the crime field also claim that, when redefined and relocated in a class or materialist framework, the status of 'social control' as a useful and ideologically acceptable concept in the marxist vocabulary is reaffirmed. (For example, Michaelowski and Bohlander (1976), Spitzer (1975a) and Sugarman (1983) take this view.)

As a 'critical' theory marxism on balance has much to offer the study of social control, apart from possible reservations about the more abstract and determinist versions of structuralism, the restriction of the notion of human agency to a class context, and the interpretation of the social control nature and functions of the modern state being almost exclusively in terms of various features of the capitalist mode of production. Though it is the formal, official, societal modes and levels of social control that marxists to date have defined as the appropriate primary objects of their attention, there seems in principle no reason why the processes involved could not also be examined at the micro level from a marxist perspective (especially if informed by interactionism) (Melossi, 1985).

Finally, the heavy if not exclusive emphasis on class and capitalism as the basic components of society needs to be moderated by revising, extending or transforming existing theoretical perspectives (whether marxist or not) in order to give proper recognition to the dimensions of gender and patriarchy to which feminist theory has drawn our attention, as we shall see in the next section of the chapter.

Feminist perspectives[15]

> Clearly in a class-divided society both women and men are subject to material, repressive and ideological forms of social control, although they are usually affected differently, women being subjected to control principally within the private domain where they are in fact economically and legally subordinate to men. In addition, however, there are dimensions of social control which women alone experience; these are in relation to the following: (a) the reproductive cycle; (b) a double standard of morality; (c) a subordinate social and legal status (vis-a-vis men) in the family; (d) the separation of 'home' and 'work' and the ideology of the woman's place. (Smart and Smart, 1978:3)

> . . . the use of force and its threat, even though highly masked, is of sufficient importance in our own western industrialised society to be recognised as a major component in the social control of women by men. . . force and its threat is the basis for the extraction of all benefits that men make from women; that is, economic, sexual and prestige gains. As with subservience based on social class, ethnic group or third world country, that of sex, too, rests ultimately on force and its threat. (Hanmer, 1978:219)

Over the same period that saw the establishment in Britain and America of the labelling/interactionist and the critical/marxist perspectives, feminism also developed as both a socio-political movement and a body of knowledge and social theory. At its most basic, feminism means a moral, social and intellectual commitment to women, their rights, needs, interests and points of view, and to the elimination of the conditions responsible for their subordination and oppression. Feminism makes use of all means available, including the acquisition of new knowledge, critiques and reconstruction of existing 'male-oriented' (Oakley, 1974) or 'malestream' (O'Brien, 1981) academic thought and cultural traditions as well as personal example and collective action. The feminist perspective, therefore, is distinguished by its twin objectives: uncovering the sources of sex and gender inequality; and working to change the position of women.

Initially attempts were made by those sensitive to feminist issues to modify and extend the two major theoretical models in sociology, structural-functionalism and marxism, in order to answer the demand that 'the woman question' be taken seriously. Functionalism's contribution consisted of the application of role[16] and socialisation theory to the analysis of the modern nuclear family as based on the reciprocity or complementarity of instrumental (masculine) and expressive (feminine) dimensions. This was to cover sex roles and relationships and the location of women primarily in the 'private' or domestic sector of the social system. Countering the neglect of women by traditional sociology meant little more than paying more attention to sex roles and the position of women in the family.

Gender, like the social system generally, rested for functionalists on a complex structure of norms, values, roles and institutions, all depending ultimately on cultural consensus. Thus what sex roles define as appropriate behaviour for women (and men) is theoretically justified in terms of their consistency with prevailing norms and values and hence their necessary contribution to the maintenance of the social system. This disguises the fact that 'the female role' (in its traditional or modern form) is part of a sexual division of labour and gender order that gives dominance in the hierarchy to men and keeps women as women in subordinate positions (Edwards, 1983; Eichler, 1980:Chapter 2; Eisenstein, 1984:Chapter 1; Moulton and Rainone, 1984).

This theoretical framework fitted in well with a 'liberal' or 'equal opportunities' approach to the question of women's rights. 'Liberation' was seen as largely a question of removing constraints and obstacles to women's freedom, and specifically changing women's roles through re-education and socialisation and making adjustments to the allocation of child-care and domestic responsibilities in the family, thus permitting more women to participate in the male occupational world. Both sociology, in the form of 'role theory' and structural-functionalism, and 'liberal' feminism subsequently came under attack for their uncritical acceptance of the overall social system and their unquestioning reliance on a particular cultural representation of sex and gender in their model of society. In this model not only is gender taken as given (and as partly biologically determined) but what most feminists perceive as gender inequality is explained away as the result of socially necessary and even desirable sex-role differences (Elshtain, 1981:228–55). Though this kind of approach has lost favour with feminists, it remains a significant force both in sociology and in 'reformist' sections of the women's movement and political parties in western societies.

At first marxism also attempted to explain the subordination of women without making any fundamental alteration to either its basic model of the social order, or its key concepts—the mode of production, the class structure, productive labour and surplus value. In sharp contrast with the normative or cultural determinism of functionalist role theory, marxism placed responsibility for the subordination of women (as for the exploitation of the working class) on material conditions and in particular, following Engels, on the concepts of private property, the division of labour and the distinction between production and reproduction. These were applied to the analysis of women's position in relation to marriage and the family on the one hand and, on the other, to their place in the work force and the economic system (Delmar, 1976; Burton, 1981). The oppression of women was attributed to the power associated with class position and the control of surplus wealth, and to the institutions of private property, monogamy and later the state.

The separation in capitalism of the spheres of production and consumption and the confinement of women to the private domestic world of the home and family mean that the key features of the marxist conceptual framework—productive labour, class, capital, and the market—have only indirect relevance to the situation of women as women. The whole 'domestic labour debate' which occupied British marxist feminists for much of the 1970s was an attempt, ultimately abandoned, to stretch marxist categories sufficiently to explain women's work in the family and its significance for capitalism (Molyneux, 1979). The basis of sex differences and the sexual division of labour is taken by Engels and others as natural (i.e. biological) and as given, and hence not subjected to the kind of critical materialist analysis applied to all other major aspects of human and particularly capitalist society (Barrett, 1980:19–29; Jaggar, 1984:27–31; March, 1982:105). In addition to the tendencies in these forms of marxism to economic determinism and functionalism, feminists criticised early marxist analyses of women for their inability to explain the gendered nature of the division of labour and why it is men who operate in the productive sector of the capitalist system and women who service its reproductive needs.

> Marx's theory of the development of capitalism is a theory of the development of 'empty places'...Just as capital creates these places indifferent to the individuals who fill them, the categories of marxist analysis...do not explain why particular people fill particular places. They give no clue about why *women* are subordinate to *men* inside and outside the family and why it is not the other way around. *Marxist categories, like capital itself, are sex-blind*. The categories of marxism cannot tell us who will fill the empty places. Marxist analysis of the woman question has suffered from this basic problem. (Hartmann, 1979:7–8, original emphases)

Ultimately this type of marxist approach subordinates 'the woman question' to some other question—typically gender is subsumed by class (Gould, 1980:38, note 1; MacKinnon, 1982:524–6)—and relies on a biological reductionist, not a socio-historical, account of male-female differences.

As the 1970s progressed, rather than simply 'adding women in' or inserting 'the woman question' into existing academic theories and bodies of knowledge (Kuhn and Wolpe, 1978:2) more seemed to be required. Modern feminists began to argue for different approaches to the study of women and the social world and for a transformation, rather than merely a 'revision of knowledge'. What has come to be described as the 'radical' feminist position (and one that has also been taken seriously by later marxist and socialist feminists) started from the assumptions that the primary basis for social division is that between men and women and that hence the most fundamental principle of social organisation is sex/gender.[17] They then postulated, following Millett (1972), the notion of 'patriarchy', the name they gave to male dominance, a universal feature of all human societies. They claimed the oppression of women was 'normal' and inevitable in such a social order, given that the major institutions, values and practices of patriarchal societies reflect and maintain the dominance of men as a category over women as a category.

At the same time, the most activist branches of the women's movement were mobilising around certain specific current issues that particularly dramatically illustrated male dominance and the abuse of male power at the expense of women: these issues included rape, prostitution, restricted access to abortion and contraception, and wife battering. These campaigns, along with the attention drawn to educational and occupational inequalities of opportunity by other feminists, exposed the presence of systematic discrimination against and victimisation of women. Feminism put much of its energy in the 1970s into 'giving women a voice' and into devising collective strategies and services for women that would be controlled by women themselves. This woman-centred approach was applied both in the political and community context (leading to the establishment of special facilities for women, such as rape crisis centres, refuges and health centres) and in the academic sphere.

> If we conceive of feminism as more than a frivolous label, if we conceive of it as an ethic, a methodology, a complex way of thinking about, more responsibly acting upon, the condition of human life. . . Feminism means that we renounce our obedience to the fathers and recognise that the world they have described is not the whole world. Masculine ideologies are the creation of masculine subjectivity; they are neither objective, nor value-free, nor exclusively 'human'. Feminism implies that we recognise fully the inadequacy for us, the distortion, of male-created ideologies, and that we proceed to think, and act, out of that recognition. (Rich, 1979:213, 207)

The traditional disciplines of marxism and social science were seen to be guilty not only of neglecting women but of bias and misrepresentation. As the editors of *The Prism of Sex* put it:

> The prism of sex has all too often become a prison that has locked male scholars into a one-sided mode of thinking, and has locked women out of the pursuit of knowledge altogether. (Sherman and Beck, 1979:7–8)

In America and Britain during the 1970s women academics were beginning to explore the problems posed for women, for feminists and for the various disciplines by the fundamentally male-biased nature of most subjects. Bernard (1973) and Oakley (1974) examined the principal forms of male sexism in sociology: first and most obviously, the absence of women and considerations of sex and gender from most accounts of the social world; and secondly, a much more subtle and serious form of bias, sociological concepts, categories, assumptions and perspectives are themselves male-centred or male-oriented—thus, they reflect a view of social reality taken from the male standpoint, though unacknowledged as such. Even when women are included, they are likely to be stereotyped and misrepresented in accordance with dominant male cultural preconceptions. As Bernard said, sociology is not only a 'science of male society' but also a 'male science of society' (1973:781, 784). Women are not only invisible, they are unaudible (Spender, 1980:54). Women's experience and perspective is systematically concealed and distorted in a variety of ways (March, 1982; Millman and Moss Kanter, 1975:vii-xvii; Oakley, 1974:Chapter 1).

The identification of male bias in sociology and other social sciences formed (along with class and race biases) part of a broad radical critique of the liberal case for the value neutrality of modern western science. On this issue marxism and feminism were in agreement. Both claimed that knowledge is socially produced, that perspectives reflect particular interests and experiences, that 'truth' and 'objectivity' are never attainable and are often only relative, and that control over the realm of ideas and knowledge is tied to access to power in other spheres of society (Smith, 1974, 1979).

Over the past fifteen years or so, our understanding of sexism and androcentrism in the spheres of science, knowledge and academe, as in the rest of the social world, has become more sophisticated. Correspondingly there has been a reconceptualisation of what taking a woman-centred perspective means. Initially, when the problem was seen as one of women being excluded, in writing and research, the solution seemed obvious and straightforward: put them back in, fill in the gaps and redress the balance.

> But it is not enough to supplement an established sociology by addressing ourselves to what has been left out, overlooked, or by making sociological issues of the relevances of the world of women. That merely extends the authority of the existing sociological procedures and makes of a women's sociology an addendum. (Smith, 1974:7)

Feminists moved beyond simply the inclusion of women (what Stanley and Wise, 1983: 31 call the '"women and..."syndrome') and began to work on the analysis of gender as a theoretical construct and on the idea of gender division as a fundamental structural component of human society. All the major areas of human activity and social organisation required re-appraisal. They began to talk more in terms of a whole new perspective or frame of reference, a different approach to knowledge, with different language, philosophy, concepts and modes of analysis, through which women's experience and consciousness could be expressed and their social reality represented and understood.

In different ways both 'radical' feminisms and marxist/socialist feminisms over the past decade or so have attempted to develop a feminist perspective, feminist language and feminist modes of analysis which would take account of the more fundamental critiques of malestream theory in general and sociology in particular. 'Radical' feminisms have some affinity in their basic philosophical approach with subjectivist, phenomenological-existential or sociology of knowledge theoretical traditions in sociology, placing emphasis on experience, consciousness and the ontological status of the individual, and in some versions the importance of the embodied nature of human, and especially female, beings (Bartky, 1977; Daly, 1978; Stanley and Wise, 1983). This has led to some criticism of this type of feminist theory being 'idealist'.

Marxist and socialist feminisms on the other hand start from a materialist position, in which primacy is given to the economic and productive system. Use is also made of modern marxist theoretical developments, in which, as we saw earlier, greater significance is attributed both to the political system and the state and to ideological factors and processes than was the case in the classic Marxian model.

As feminist theory became a more substantial and more significant force through the 1970s and 1980s, it became also more diverse and complex, moving beyond classic marxism, functionalism, role theory and early adaptations of sociology of knowledge and subjectivist sociological orientations, to draw on more recent theoretical developments such as structuralism, psychoanalysis, critical theory and feminist social anthropology. (It also attracted the intellectual attention of some male theorists, Connell 1983, 1985 being a prime example.) It is just as difficult to present a coherent account of the variety of theoretical ideas and orientations in feminism as it is in marxism. Though some clusters of intellectual and political positions and interests can be identified, considerable variations occur within such groupings.[18]

Since it is totally impractical to summarise the basic ideas of each of the key modern feminist thinkers, we need to identify some fundamental conceptual and philosophical dimensions of feminism as social theory and then locate particular theories and theorists in relation to these dimensions. Such a strategy is at least consistent with the approach adopted in previous sections of this chapter where both the labelling/interactionist perspective and marxism presented something of the same problem. Though analytical distinctions between subjectivism and structuralism, voluntarism and determinism, and materialism and idealism have some relevance also to feminist theories, we need to be wary of these and other dualistic forms of western malestream thought.

We will look briefly at two issues with which all social theories have to deal and at the specific forms of these that confront feminists. These are: on the one hand, how human nature is perceived and specifically how male-female differences are interpreted and explained;[19] on the other, how society is conceptualised and what elements are regarded as the most fundamental or significant, and specifically how the relationships between class and gender, capitalism and patriarchy, and men and institutions are handled. Then we will move on to the topic of particular relevance for this book, how different feminist theories have analysed the sources and types of social control to which women specifically are subjected.

There is a variety of conceptions of human nature and of sex and gender differences to be found among the writings of modern feminists. In a recent attempt to provide an overall categorisation of feminism, McFadden (1984) uses this fundamental question as the basis for her differentiation between marxist and socialist feminisms, and radical feminisms. She identifies two dimensions or continua of views which she calls 'minimalist' and 'maximalist', meaning respectively a de–emphasis on sex differences in favour of integration of human beings compared with a stress on dissimilarity and disparity and the importance of differences. There exists a diversity of positions ranging between the conservative and the radical pole of each continuum.

Those forms of feminist theory usually described as 'radical' feminism, start from the assumption of sex and gender differences, divisions and inequalities as universal features of human society and as the starting point for feminist analysis. The importance placed on sex/gender as the fundamental determinant of individual identity and social structure is characteristic of all feminists in this category. Since the early 1970s the material and ideological structures of male dominance have come to be understood as considerably more sociologically complex and not, at least in the eyes of most 'radical' feminists, simply the external social manifestations of male biological superiority. However, a minority has always retained the belief that, in O'Brien's (1981:44) words, 'mute, brute biology', in the form of men's aggressive use of their physical and sexual powers and of women's reproductive function and relative physical weakness, is the ultimate basis of male supremacy. This is found particularly among feminists with a special interest in those forms of male physical and sexual abuse of women that involve violence and physical force such as rape, of whom Brownmiller (1976) is perhaps the most famous example. Some (such as Daly, 1978) have also asserted the intrinsic superiority of women as human beings over men, advocating various forms of separatism as at least a temporary strategy for modern feminists seeking to evade, resist or modify the effects of what continues to be an overwhelmingly patriarchal world.[20]

Some commentators have described what they perceive as a shift in feminism from an almost exclusive preoccupation with the nature and sources of *gender* distinctions between men and women, and correspondingly a focus on the 'politics' aspect of the theory of 'sexual politics' (Millett, 1972) to, by the later 1970s, a much more serious interest in *sex* and '*the sexual*' (English, Hollibaugh and Rubin, 1982:42). Aided by insights from psychoanalytic theory, feminists were able to develop their understanding of the processes of production and reproduction of not only the social identity of gendered subjects but of sexuality itself, and more particularly of female sexuality. Some links had earlier been made between female oppression and male sexuality (Griffin, 1971 and Brownmiller, 1976). Among the first of the second-wave feminist theorists, such as Mitchell (1971), there had been some recognition of the importance of cultural notions of femininity and sexual repression in the control of women. The more recent radical feminists, however, treat the social construction of female sexuality as a central concern (Shulman, 1980). By 1982, MacKinnon could write:

> Sexuality is to feminism what work is for marxism: that which is most one's own, yet most taken away. . . As work is to marxism, sexuality to feminism is socially constructed yet constructing, universal as activity yet historically specific, jointly comprised of matter and mind. As the organized expropriation of the work of some for the benefit of others defines a class—workers—the organized expropriation of the sexuality of some for the use of others defines the sex, woman. Heterosexuality is its structure, gender and family its congealed forms, sex roles its qualities generalized to social persona, reproduction a consequence and control its issue. (1982:515–6)

MacKinnon then argues that for women, gender reduces to sexuality.

> Sex as gender and sex as sexuality are thus defined in terms of each other, but it is sexuality that determines gender, not the other way around. . . Sexuality, then is a form of power. Gender, as socially constructed, embodies it, not the reverse. Women and men are divided by gender, made into the sexes as we know them, by the social requirements of heterosexuality, which institutionalizes male sexual dominance and female sexual submission. If this is true, sexuality is the lynchpin of gender inequality. (1982:531, 533)

Though early marxist feminists placed primary responsibility for the oppression of women (and of the working class) on socio-economic institutions—principally the division of labour, private ownership of the means of production, market forces, and the needs of capital—following Marx and Engels, they also took the view that a fundamental basis of the differences between males and females in all human societies is ultimately women's (biological) reproductive function. This leaves women dependent on men for their protection and subsistence and makes them valuable assets as sources of fertility and for their sexual and domestic services. As Kelly has pointed out:

> Sex oppression was taken to be 'private', as having to do only with sexuality and procreation, while causes were all in the 'public' domain of capitalism's productive relations. (Kelly, 1979:218)

Male dominance and female subordination are seen as the result not simply of biology or human will (men's aggression or self-interest) but of socio-historical factors. The same institutions and processes which are held responsible for class exploitation and oppression are blamed also for the subordinate position of women. This situation is only to be remedied by the abolition of private property and the socialisation of both production and reproduction. Feminism is thus subsumed under marxism (Campioni and Gross, 1983).

Later marxist feminists, and some prefer the term socialist feminist to denote a change within this perspective (Eisenstein, 1979; Jaggar, 1983; Oakley, 1981:Chapter 16), using a more complex sociological model of the political economy of capitalism, have explored the dimensions of class and sex/gender (and race/ethnicity in some cases) with respect to oppression and in a number of structural contexts—paid work and the economy, marriage and the family, and the state. They treat these latter two spheres as concerned with social reproduction or reproduction of the social conditions on which the system rests (Edholm, Harris and Young, 1977; MacIntosh, 1977) and emphasise the ideological and political as well as the more narrowly material or economic mechanisms involved in production, reproduction and consumption (for example, Barrett, 1980). Whether or not they accept the term patriarchy (Barrett for one does not), they recognise that structures of male dominance or the 'sex-gender system' (Rubin, 1975) contribute to the creation and maintenance of social divisions and inequalities and that sex/gender relations based on male power and female subordination permeate all levels and spheres of society. They reject some feminists' characterisations of male dominance as primarily a cultural, ideological or 'psychic structure' (Hartmann, 1979:1), and are also unhappy with what they consider to be the a-historical and static conceptions of male domination or patriarchy as a universal and undifferentiated phenomenon found in the work of some 'radical' feminists (particularly early modern feminists like Millett (1972) and Mitchell (1971)).

The critical (and unsolved) theoretical problem is how, without lapsing back into economic reductionism or biological essentialism, to express the nature of the relationship between the two major systems of capitalism and patriarchy (and cope analytically with the notion of contradictions within and between these systems) and therefore how conceptually and politically to connect class with gender and socialism with feminism.[21] Although these marxist feminists acknowledge that significant and deep-rooted gender divisions underlie the structures of all human societies, they regard these divisions as socially produced and historically variable in character. Whatever their conception of human nature, it is one that emphasises common human rather than sex-differentiated qualities, and socio-historical constructs such as class and modes of production over the more essentialist notion of sex differences.

Nonetheless, despite some differences, many feminists now share certain common ideas. They believe that the traditional analytical dichotomies of western philosophy, such as reason/emotion, culture/nature, private/public, mind/body, which are implicit metaphors of the differences between men and women, are not only intellectually suspect but also sexist and oppressive to women (Brown and Jordanova, 1981; Lloyd, 1984; Pateman and Gross eds., 1986). They agree that sex/gender, along with class and race/ethnicity, is socially constructed and that all three dimensions are fundamental to human identity and social organisation; and that male dominance is manifested in all spheres of social existence and is maintained by means of both material and social/ideological institutions and practices.[22]

Without denying the general importance of the economy and the state to the maintenance of patriarchal social order, many feminists have concentrated their attention on those areas of society of most direct relevance to the lives of women. Eisenstein (1979:33) describes five spheres of female activity—reproduction, child-rearing, maintenance of the home, sexuality and consumption—and then compares the different class situations of women across these five areas. Ortner (1972) shows how in many societies femininity is identified with 'nature' and masculinity with 'culture'; or as O'Brien puts it, with civilisation men are given the opportunity to cultivate a 'second nature' which is 'man-made' through which they rise above their first, more physical nature, while women remain determined by their pregiven bological makeup (1981:118). Of particular significance also is the sexual division of labour (Eisenstein, 1979; Young, 1981) and the fact that paid and unpaid 'labour' are differentially rewarded. Access to power, status and other socially valued resources is tied to participation and performance in the public world[23] and this is the province of men: in Millett's classic generalisation:

> . . . the military, industry, technology, universities, science, political office, and finance—in short, every avenue of power within the society, including the coercive force of the police, is entirely in male hands. (1972:25)

Mitchell (1971) identifies four social structures responsible for the oppression of women: those concerned with production, reproduction, sexuality and the socialisation of children. Ehrlich (1981:120–7) and Rich (1980:638–40) point out that men are in a position to draw on a wide range of techniques of control, from the extreme of 'physical brutality' to 'control of consciousness' (1980:640). These include ideological manipulation, psychological persuasion, emotional pressure, material advantage, patriarchal authority, legal and moral codes of conduct, legitimate use of physical and social coercion, as well as violence. Often these different mechanisms operate in conjunction. As Klein says in an important paper entitled 'Violence Against Women':

> Of the facets of sexism, it is difficult to know where to draw the line separating what is from what is not violence, particularly once one recognizes the interconnections among economic exploitation, political domination, and psychological oppression. (1981:65)

When dealing with modern capitalist partriarchies, feminist theorists lay stress particularly on the labour market, the sexual division of labour, the various ideologies supporting restrictive and dependent gender roles for women (especially heterosexism, romantic love, monogamy, and motherhood), and the state. Recent 'radical' feminist theorists, such as Barry (1979), Dworkin (1981) and Rich (1980) stress particularly the ideological and psychological levels of women's 'colonisation' or 'enslavement' and not only the directly sexual. Dworkin (1981:13–24), for example, identified seven forms of male power and these include 'a metaphysical assertion of self', and the powers of naming and owning (as well as superior physical and financial resources). She sees male control (and especially sexual control) of women as an essential component of all social institutions—law, marriage, health care, economy, religion, etc.—and not only those where sexual exploitation of women is explicit and recognized as in prostitution, rape, pornography or wife battering. Others turn their attention to the state in its various capacities as regulator of all aspects of social existence.[24]

Feminists have also pointed to the importance of cross-cultural comparisons of the forms and mechanisms of male power and the control of women. But they warn of the need to avoid over-generalisation and of the danger of universalising particular historical characteristics of patriarchy or structures of male dominance (Collier and Rosaldo, 1981; Edholm, Harris and Young, 1977; Rogers, 1978; MacCormack and Strathern eds. 1980; and Rosaldo, 1980). One theory that has been proposed (by Young and Harris, 1978) suggests a shift from control in the form of unmediated violence in 'simpler' societies to ideological and economic control as societies 'develop'. By contrast (and unlike many of the earlier second-wave feminists[25]), later modern feminists are on the whole more inclined to emphasise the continued role physical and sexual violence plays in maintaining male dominance and the continued vulnerability of women to abuse and exploitation by men in modern western societies. Hanmer (1978) who comments favourably on the Young and Harris thesis advances as her main argument in a major theoretical paper on 'Violence and the Social Control of Women' that:

> . . . force and its threat is never a residual or secondary mode of influence rather it is the structural underpinning of hierarchical relations; the ultimate sanction buttressing other forms of control. (1978:229)

There is also a group of mainly American feminists who are currently attempting to develop a better theoretical understanding of the nature and sources of various types of male physical and sexual coercion and exploitation of women (rape, wife-battering, incest, sexual harassment and pornography) and of the interconnections between these phenomena. They focus on institutional and ideological factors (such as aggressive modes of masculinity and male sexuality, the dependency and objectification of women, and sexist biases in the law, the professions and the criminal justice system) which permit, encourage and legitimate male violence in our so-called 'civilised' and 'rational' modern societies (Barry, 1979; Hirsch, 1981; Klein, 1981; MacKinnon, 1983; Rich, 1980; and Tong, 1984).[26]

Finally there are a few writers who have looked specifically at the institutions and organisations of social control (with their mainly male agents) that form part of the male-dominated structures of the modern state and of capitalist patriarchy. We are thinking here of the radical and feminist sociological literature treating the law, the judicial system, the 'welfare state', medicine and psychiatry, social work and the so-called 'helping' professions as instruments of social control, whose activities reflect and reinforce social divisions and inequalities, particularly those of class, race/ethnicity and sex/gender. In the process they have succeeded also in exposing the sexist biases of much academic theory and research in this field. There is now a substantial volume of books and articles criticising malestream writers, particularly in the areas of criminology and the sociology of deviance, for their failure to take women and sex/gender seriously in their accounts of the nature and incidence of various forms of deviant and criminal behaviour and of the operation of social control systems and processes.[27]

In the context of this chapter, it is noteworthy that in the latest textbook on criminological and deviance theory by Pfohl feminism is given a passing reference (1985:339) as a contemporary social movement, along with black rights and other such causes, all of which have had a radicalising influence on sociological models of power and social structure. However, other authors of similar works that have been cited here not only fail to mention feminism's theoretical contribution to the area, but also its socio-political impact.[28] With one exception, it is only in books by female authors directly on the topic of women and crime that feminist criminology is given its proper place (Heidensohn, 1985; Leonard, 1982). The exception is the recent book entitled *Labeling Women Deviant: Gender, Stigma and Social Control*, whose male author has already written extensively in the areas of crime and deviance from a labelling/interactionist perspective. Schur, drawing on mainly feminist material, explores the way the major categories of gender norms contribute to the systematic 'inferiorisation' or 'devaluation' of women by men generally in society and more particularly in the patterns of response from official control agents and the community to women as 'victims' of male criminal maltreatment, abuse and violence. Though he provides a thoughtful and well-documented account of these processes, his analysis is limited theoretically by the framework within which he places it: his conception of the 'gender system' responsible for distinctive patterns of labelling and social control of women is one which focuses only on its normative components, and in particular those norms governing appearance, maternity and sexuality for women (Schur, 1984:Chapter 3).

Feminist critiques in this field have exposed the way established academic disciplines like sociology and criminology have relied in their descriptions and explanations of female criminality, 'mental illness' and deviance generally not on careful empirical investigation but on prevailing (and sexist) stereotypes of women as irrational, immature, suggestible and basically governed by their biological and sexual nature. Feminist accounts of the treatment received by girls and women at the hands of the mental health, welfare and penal/judicial systems also demonstrate the extent of the 'sexualisation' of female deviance and the devaluation of women by professionals and social control agencies.[29]

The control of women, however, is exercised to a significant extent through informal mechanisms. It is more likely than is the case with men that particular individuals known to a woman—a male relative, family, close friends or community members—will take responsibility for her regulation and disciplining rather than officials in society. This, as feminists have pointed out, means that even in modern capitalist societies, the state and the legal system may not intervene, even where 'private' methods of controlling women involve violence, sexual abuse and the deprivation of basic individual rights, otherwise guaranteed to all citizens. In respect to sexual harassment, domestic violence and rape, as well as other more 'normal' aspects of marital and family life, the state is not neutral or impartial (Hanmer, 1978:226–9; MacKinnon, 1983; Smart, 1982, 1984). Nor strictly can one say in such cases that the state is not involved in the regulation of the lives of the members of society: by not taking the side of the weaker, it is indirectly and implicitly supporting the interests of the dominant (male) party.

In modern western societies, 'women's liberation' has challenged the institutionalised sexism and discrimination involved both in the state's preference for non-intervention in private domestic relationships, and in the considerable paternalistic enthusiasm with which it intervenes in cases of prostitution and adolescent female delinquency, for example. The existence of fundamental contradictions in the state's regulation of women and management of gender relations seems to be a major feature of capitalist patriarchies (see, for instance, Edwards, 1981, 1984; Harrison and Mort, 1980; and Smart, 1982). There is also evidence that in this form of society, males and females are seen as requiring referral to different types of state agency or apparatus. Overall there is a tendency for the criminal justice system to concern itself with men, the welfare system and health services with women (Bryson and Edwards, forthcoming; Hartz-Karp, 1981; Smart, 1976:Chapter 6).

As in society generally, social control systems and their staff have traditionally operated on the basis of gender stereotypes when dealing with women. Whether the woman is seeking medical or psychiatric care, welfare benefits, or legal or professional assistance and protection from male violence, her problems are likely to be trivialised, individualised and attributed to her own inadequacies. The role of other (male) people or of socio-economic circumstances is likely to be played down (the 'blaming the victim' phenomenon). Research on the topics of rape, domestic violence and incest has demonstrated a systematic bias by social control agencies and officials and by academics working in these areas to ignore, excuse or even justify male behaviour even in those instances where a criminal offence is involved. There is a reliance instead on explanations based on women's presumed emotionality, passivity and vulnerability, but which, somewhat paradoxically, give weight to the alleged female capacity for incitement, sexual provocation and 'victim-precipitation'.[30] Subsequent chapters will explore in some detail the question of sexism and gender discrimination in the legal/judicial system and in other major social control systems.

Powerful and persuasive though feminist theory may be both as critique and as an alternative perspective on society and on knowledge, a major weakness that many commentators have noted concerns the problem of over-generalising about women's position not only across different cultures and historical periods but even within one society. There is the danger of conveying the impression that patriarchy is a monolithic structure which has a uniform impact on all women. Economic and material circumstances, religion, ethnicity and age are important social variables which are to be found in all societies. They exercise considerable influence on the lives and situations of every individual and mediate the effects of structures and processes on the members of society. Differences of class and race/ethnicity in particular result in socially patterned variations in the experiences, opportunities, resources and social conditioning of women (and men). Hence the necessity for the social theorist to find a satisfactory way of conceptualising the relationships between sex/gender and class and between patriarchy and capitalism, as analytically separable entities. The work of Eisenstein (1979) and Hartsock (1979, 1985), both major American feminist materialist theorists, reflects this concern.

A second problem lies in the concentration on exposing and condemning the nature and extent of discrimination and injustice experienced by many women. For feminist theory, as for marxism, all institutions and practices in gender- and class-divided societies are regulatory, coercive and repressive, acting as mechanisms for maintaining the dominance of particular groups and structures. But both marxists and feminists have warned of the dangers and distortions which some forms of radical analysis of injustice and inequality can produce. While it is important for feminists (and others) to challenge the dominant ideological assumptions about how our society works and in whose interests, by exposing classism, racism and sexism, those who are working for change must be chary of giving the impression that 'the oppressed' are totally powerless, downtrodden and pathetic, at the mercy of those with the power or authority to decide their fate. The more convincing the analysis of the structures responsible for exploitation and oppression, the more likely is the conclusion that the forces in question are overwhelming.

The other side of the picture is that protest, struggle and resistance by oppressed and less powerful groups is as much a part of human history as is the victimisation and oppression of the weak by the strong (Cloward and Piven, 1979). The structures of domination and oppression always contain weaknesses and contradictions that can be used against those in power; a crucial task for radical theories like feminism is to identify and exploit such flaws.

> The point is to make sense out of this rather than to catalog centuries of horrors. The world is not one of undifferentiated patriarchy where women are fair game for whatever brutalities men may choose to inflict for their own power of amusement. This would insult both women, who are not simply the helpless victims of history, and men, most of whom do not necessarily approve of or voluntarily engage in abuse of women. Not all men have the individual power to place women at their command—in fact, hardly any do—and most women actively fight back in myriad ways against their own victimization. The point of analysis should be to make this struggle as effective as possible. (Klein, 1981: 66–7)

Before turning to a detailed consideration of the principal forms of social control in western societies and of changes in the preferred modes and models of control since the nineteenth century, there is one further theoretical contribution to the study of social control that should be mentioned, and that is the work of Foucault. Though Foucault, like labelling/interactionist theory, marxism and feminism, regards power as central to any analysis of social control, his treatment of these phenomena is distinctly different. Foucault distances himself from classical and modern marxism, from French structuralism (he has been termed a post-structuralist), from psychoanalysis and from conventional sociology;[31] and the last book published before his death, *The History of Sexuality* (1978), though exploring a subject of central interest to feminism, does not treat the category 'woman', gender, male sexuality or sexism as problematic in the way a feminist perspective would.[32].

Foucault's major contribution is to the 'revisionist history' of deviance control systems and ideologies (Cohen, 1985:8; Cohen and Scull, 1985:

3) and the processes and emergence of a whole new 'technology of subjection' he calls the 'disciplinary society'.

> There are two images, then, of discipline. At one extreme, the discipline-blockade, the enclosed institution, established on the edges of society, turned inwards towards negative functions, arresting evil, breaking communications, suspending time. At the other extreme, with panopticism, is the discipline-mechanism: a functional mechanism that must improve the exercise of power by making it lighter, more rapid, more effective, a design of subtle coercion for a society to come. The movement from one project to the other, from a schema of exceptional discipline to one of a generalised surveillance rests on a historical transformation: the gradual extension of the mechanisms of discipline throughout the seventeenth and eighteenth centuries, their spread throughout the whole social body, the formation of what might be called in general the disciplinary society. (1977: 209)

Starting with the construction of the modern concept of 'madness' and a whole new 'moral' approach to treatment (1967), Foucault then moved on from psychiatry to modern medicine (1976), to prisons and a whole range of institutions based on the same principles (1977), and to the consideration of the development of a whole new set of institutions, techniques and ideologies (or 'discourses') for the management of human beings. This new 'discipline' operated through control of minds, wills and behaviour, rather than over bodies; it was based on rationality, depersonalisation, objectification, individualisation, surveillance and training, and its aim was 'normalisation' not permanent exclusion or repression.

> Instead of bending all its subjects into a single uniform mass, it [the new disciplinary power] separates, analyses, differentiates, carries its procedures of decomposition to the point of necessary and sufficient units. . . . it is the specific technique of a power that regards individuals as both objects and as instruments of its exercise . . . it is a modest, suspicious power, which functions as a calculated, but permanent economy. These are humble modalities, minor procedures, as compared with the majestic rituals of sovereignty or the great apparatuses of the state. (1977:170)

With capitalism, knowledge and technology are applied to the processes of social regulation and control just as they are to the processes of production. What is distinctive about this process is the importance of the connection between knowledge and power and the dispersal or diffusion of power.

Foucault, like interactionists and some marxists, seeks to avoid essentialist modes of thought and analysis. This leads him to reject both the idea of human agency and reified notions of rationality, the economy, the state, social structure, and society (Wickham, 1983). He also aims to avoid the usual causal methods of explanation. His 'discourse theory' denies that thought is about preexisting objects, rather it constitutes them. So that, with the change to new 'disciplinary' modes of social control, the people subjected to these ideologies and techniques were not only treated differently, they were defined differently as human beings, as being possessed of mind and reason, but also as machines to be made as efficient and useful as possible. Power is seen as positive and productive, not only negative and repressive and, most importantly (and this view is shared by Poulantzas (1978)[33] and feminists) not as a thing to be used, taken, possessed, but as a relation, as something exercised through particular techniques and strategies in particular situations. Power is everywhere, it is diverse and widely dispersed through a heterogeneous range of situations and relations, it is a basic element or force and is not reducible to anything else. The analysis of power must start for Foucault at the lowest, or smallest, most micro level and work upwards and he denies the existence of any structural economic or political determinants of power. This view brings Foucault closer to interactionists than to marxists, given the latter's reliance on such concepts as the capitalist state, the market, and the ruling class.[34]

To date, Foucault's work stands in a category of its own. Alongside the work produced by writers who fit more readily into one or other of the four major perspectives considered here, Foucault must be recognised as having made a major but separate contribution to our understanding of social control and the 'problem of social order'.

4 The study of social control

In the two previous chapters we looked at various theoretical conceptualisations of social control and the place this concept occupies and what meanings are given to the notion in different perspectives. In this chapter we move from social theory to social reality. Informed by theory, our purpose is to investigate and attempt to understand the nature of social control as a social phenomenon, or rather as a complex, diverse and changing set of institutions, ideas and practices. We will find the different theoretical approaches assist us in different ways and, depending on the aspect or form of social control we are considering, to different extents.

Labelling/interactionist theory, marxism, feminism and Foucault each offer a general framework, some key concepts, theoretical insights, and empirical analysis and make the study of social control an interesting and important subject of sociological theory and research (functionalism having significantly less to contribute). As a very broad generalisation, as the preceding two chapters have demonstrated, the members of the labelling/interactionist school and Foucault have provided us with detailed and perceptive accounts of the major forms of social control in the modern western world, how they operate, their underlying philosophies and their effects on deviants and on society, and, aided by those in what has come to be called the 'revisionist' school, they have attempted to put all this in some sort of historical perspective. Marxism and feminism go beyond this kind of description and analysis, sophisticated and illuminating though it may be, and advance various structural explanations for the forms and functions of social control in capitalist patriarchies, and for the emergence and development of particular control systems, ideologies and agencies.

In this chapter we are interested in social control in the more restricted and specific sense of societal mechanisms and systems for dealing with social deviance and social problems. We will therefore be examining the various mechanisms, techniques and forms of social control, the modes, models and systems of control characteristic of western industrial society, and how and why these have changed since the late eighteenth century and are still changing: what Cohen has described as 'master patterns and strategies' (1985:13) and 'shifts and movements' (1985:3) in these over time.[1]

We will be concerned more with the basic sociological aspects of 'the social control systems' found in modern capitalist patriarchies than with a detailed characterisation of the historical development and current nature of social control apparatuses in Australia. This material will be left for the later chapters. This chapter is intended to form a bridge between, on the one hand, broad theoretical perspectives on social control and 'the problem of social order', and, on the other, sociological analysis of institutions, agencies and techniques responsible for the regulation of social relations in particular societies, such as Australia.

We will begin this chapter with a general description of some of the major conceptual elements and distinctions that emerge from the literature on social control. We will then move to a comparison of the main features of the three major 'formal' systems for the social control of deviant, dependent and other problem categories of the population in modern western societies—welfare, medicine and psychiatry, and law, criminal justice and corrections. We will end with an examination of the changing modes of social control over the past two centuries, seen against the background of changes in capitalism, in western democracy, in the state, and in patriarchy.

Conceptual aspects of social control

Social control includes all social measures which involve the management, containment, punishment, repression, direction or redirection of individuals and groups who are perceived to constitute a threat or a problem for society.

Social control can use a variety of means—physical, psychological, economic, moral, ideological, political—and can adopt positive or negative forms. It is a component of all social relations and a part of the everyday activities of the social institutions and organisations (such as schools, factories, hospitals and families) that make up the main fabric of society. It may also be the business of specially designated agencies and occupational groups (such as the police, magistrates, psychiatrists, and social workers), sometimes operating in particular types of premises and physical settings (typically prisons, mental hospitals, and day-centres and residential homes for delinquents, the intellectually handicapped, the emotionally distressed, drug addicts, and other such categories).

Thus pretty well all sociological theory and research on social control starts from the position that social control is a response to undesirable forms of behaviour and types of individual, though there is some acknowledgement that deviations from the norm can exceed expectations as well as fall short of them.[2] However this concentration on negatively-defined deviance does not mean that the responses to it necessarily always take the form of punishments: 'inducements' may be offered in the shape of rewards and opportunities (contingent on a returning to the fold). A. K. Cohen (1965) and Ditton (1979) both explore the various ways in which negative and positive responses can produce deviance amplification or reduction. In a recent Australian article, Freiberg (1986) surveys the wide range of ways in which the modern welfare state, as well as negatively sanctioning behaviour, also uses legal and regulatory machinery to allocate rewards and benefits as part of the exercise of control over its citizens.

Although there is some agreement that social control is basically about attempts to contain deviance, differences emerge between the various perspectives in their conceptual treatment of social control.

Some perspectives, as we have seen, are mainly concerned with social control at the societal level by major institutions and superordinate groups. A considerable body of marxist and feminist literature has been devoted to the analysis of capitalism and patriarchy as social systems that produce and are reproduced through a broad range of social control apparatuses, structures and mechanisms. Some writers, both historians and sociologists, and Foucault is a prime example here, concentrate their attention on particular institutions and social programmes (for instance, therapeutic forms of treatment, welfare policies, the prison system).

Historical analyses of the reasons for the emergence of particular forms and institutions of control have come under recent criticism: 'reformist' accounts for their uncritical treatment of the stated motives and objectives of those concerned with a particular system or policy; structural-functionalists for overestimating the degree of consensus and the collective power of shared values and norms; and marxists for over-simple instrumentalist or functionalist explanations. 'The social control theory of the 1920s...placed so much stress on the consensual that it neglected the coercive; the social control literature of the 1970s exaggerated the coercive at the expense of the consensual' (Ignatieff, 1985:99). What is needed is more of a balance between consensus and coercion, and between powerful structures (especially the state) and human agency and struggle.

Others engaged in work on social control have been content with more limited aims: they have sought to provide detailed and often highly critical accounts of the components and modes of operation of a given control agency or mechanism. Social control for these authors is usually assumed to be a social entity or system in its own right (with its own history and logic) and the analysis is seen as adequate even when lacking investigation of the interconnection between particular control institutions and ideologies and broader societal factors and processes. Others again, particularly labelling and interactionist writers, may define their task as the general exploration of the dynamics of the deviance-control relationship, but in practice there has been a tendency for the interpersonal and micro dimensions of labelling and social control to receive preferential attention over the more macro and structural aspects.

As a broad generalisation, functionalists, marxists and some feminists perceive social control primarily in terms of functions or effects on the maintenance of the social system (whether they define this as a question of ensuring conformity to the integrated set of shared norms and values on which society is based, or of defending and reinforcing entrenched power positions and interests).[3] The key dimension to social control for these theorists is that of its effects or results for society as whole—but in many cases no conceptual distinction is drawn between intended, presumed and actual effects or outcomes; in other words, social control is assumed to be always and fully effective and successful. All this is often further confused by being placed within an abstract structuralist and/or functionalist interpretive framework.

Some radical and marxist authors talk loosely of the 'functions' of social control and of control 'apparatuses' (particularly state apparatuses). Social control as a whole and particular control systems are described as instruments of coercion, regulation or repression and this is presumed to explain why they exist.[4] Apart from being tautologous, this kind of formulation permits such writers to avoid specifying whether they are referring to forms of social control, methods of social control, objectives or results. A good example of this is Higgins who, in a paper intended to clarify the literature on social policy and social control, poses the basic 'composite' question—'who is being controlled, by whom, how and for what purpose?' (1980:15)—but in her discussion fails to keep these aspects separate.

An overall impression tends to be conveyed by work of this kind that social control is relatively undifferentiated, all-powerful, the tool or servant of macro societal forces, and that it is theoretically best defined and understood in relation to its presumed role in helping to maintain a particular regime or social order. A substantial proportion of this kind of work (both marxist and feminist) is at a purely theoretical level. Even where some empirical material is introduced, any postulated associations between intentions and effects with regard to particular policies are more likely to be in the nature of temporal correlations rather than providing evidence for a causal explanation.

Labelling theorists and interactionists by contrast are interested in social control *per se:* that means (in a quotation used earlier) the 'nature, emergence, application and consequences' of labels (Plummer,

1979:860). For them the issue of the broader societal significance of the exercise of social control is not so central, but rather the detailed analysis of the variety of control mechanisms and processes and their modes of operation.

From these sociologists we derive a technical vocabulary and elaborate analytical and classificatory concepts to help us cope with the diversity and complexity of social control phenomena. Within this broadly defined school, there are several orientations and emphases. Some, and the work done by writers in this category includes and overlaps with that of 'reformist' and 'revisionist' historians in this field and with that of Foucault, have set themselves the task of investigating the processes of emergence and establishment of particular systems and ideologies of control. Well-known examples are Platt's (1969, 1974) study of the 'child–savers'; Foucault's (1967) account of the emergence of the modern conception of 'madness' and of new modes of control to deal with it; and Rothman's (1971) and Ignatieff's (1978, 1985) analyses of changes in approaches to punishment and correction and in the prison system from the late nineteenth century. More recently, some marxists have brought their more structural perspective to bear on the questions of how and why social control systems develop in particular ways. An example is the analysis of the process of 'rationalisation of crime control in capitalist society' that has been developed by Spitzer (1979) and Spitzer and Scull (1977a).

Since on the whole the labelling/interactionist perspective has been responsible for most of the detailed conceptual analysis of dimensions of social control, we will concentrate in this section of the chapter on the work produced within this tradition.

The basic vocabulary used to identify elements and aspects of social control includes the following terms: norm, reaction, label, stereotype, sanction, instrument, technique, mechanism, institution, agency, ideology. Gibbs (1977:410) has identified five basic aspects of the exercise of control:

What is subject to social control?
Who can exercise social control?
Who is subject to social control?
What are the goals or consequences of attempts at social control?
By what means can social control be exercised?

Gibbs is more of a critic than a supporter of labelling theory (see Gibbs, 1966), but in various articles (for example, Clark and Gibbs 1965) he has attempted to define and refine theoretically some of the key concepts in that approach, such as 'norms', 'sanctions' and 'reactions'.

Others have sought to identify some of the social variables which influence the level, type and likelihood of a social control response, some of which relate to the nature of norms and norm-violations and others to characteristics of agencies and mechanisms concerned with the enforcement of norms. In his pioneering work in the field, Lemert dealt with both categories of factors: he suggested that a certain degree of visibility[5] (of deviant behaviour) and a certain tolerance quotient (in the community) were necessary before any social or more particularly societal response was likely (1951:54, 57). He mentioned a number of factors which influence the 'formal societal reaction', such as power differentials between controller and controlled, authority, resources of control agencies, and personal idiosyncrasies of their personnel (1951:56).[6] Scheff (1966), in his classic theory of the social construction of mental illness, suggests seven major contingency factors affect reactions to the type of problem behaviour that may attract the label of 'mental illness'; these are—the amount, degree and visibility of the rule-breaking, the power and social distance of rule-breaker relative to control agents; tolerance levels and the availability of non-deviant cultural role alternatives in the community where the rule-breaking occurs.

Labelling theorists are interested not only in the factors responsible for rule-breaking behaviour being labelled or typed as deviant, but also in the results of various kinds of labels and reactions for the deviant and for society. Indeed, the so-called 'labelling thesis' (or in Lemert's words, theory of 'secondary deviation') is precisely about the nature and consequences of the stigmatisation and sanctioning of deviant behaviour; specifically, and contrary to the official objectives of social control measures, one particular effect is posited as the most likely outcome, that of ensuring the commission of further deviant acts and deepening the involvement and attachment of individuals, once labelled, to their deviant activities and associations. This is not the place to discuss in detail the theoretical arguments and empirical evidence for and against this thesis.[7] What is significant here is that such formulations as well as the earlier 'reformist' accounts of control systems (which described them only in terms of their avowed or idealised objectives) pay insufficient attention to the distinction between intentions, practices and outcomes. Lemert himself early on (1951:68–9) warned that the publicised 'functions' of social control often differ from the real, and that control agencies regularly fail in their task.

Several of the contributors to the recent volume edited by Cohen and Scull (1985) discuss the problems that arise when analyses of social control institutions merge motives with actions, and confuse intentions, methods and effects (Ignatieff, Ingleby, Mayer). Cohen in another book compares five different types of explanation for the emergence and operation of particular control systems in the social control literature and concludes that none of them gives a satisfactory account of all these dimensions (1985:Chapter 3).

Nearly all writers in this area rely on one or more of a range of dualistic or dichotomous variables. Social control agencies and measures are described as either formal or informal, official or unofficial, public or private, societal or social,[8] these qualities frequently being seen as mutually exclusive. Some interpose a third intermediate category (for instance semi-official, which Simmons 1969:120–2 uses to refer to middle-range control personnel such as teachers, landlords and barmen).

Grimes and Turk posit a continuum between 'small-scale, informal', personal relationship settings and 'large-scale, formal', impersonal settings (1978:41). Newman (1976:26–7) suggests such factors as legitimate authority and status, tradition, bureaucratisation, and power to sanction influence where on the continuum particular agents or agencies should be placed. He then uses these criteria to differentiate between types of control institution and types of deviance, the institutions ranging from the military and the law (with a high level of formality) through health, education, work and religion (with medium levels) to family and village (with low levels).

In general the terms formal/informal, official/unofficial and public/private tend to be used interchangeably and often without definition. 'Formal', 'official' and 'public' typically refer to those institutions and agencies whose major responsibility is the identification and management of problem cases of various kinds (dependency, disease, disturbance, deviance and crime); 'informal' and 'unofficial' are reserved for social control processes within primary groups or between individuals.

Public/private has several meanings. In one common usage of these terms, 'public' is used to denote those spheres of society and types of organisation which come under legal or governmental jurisdiction, regulation or supervision: one traditional practice is to equate 'public' with the state. Hence organisations, arenas and forms of activity, and categories of norms and rules, are 'public' if they are under direct governmental administration or direction. 'Private' then means so-called 'civil society'[9] and includes all other institutions and areas of social life, and specifically the economic sector. An alternative conception (and many feminists take this view) is to identify as 'public' not just government or the political sphere, but any set of practices or type of institution or body that is officially (that is either legally or by established tradition) authorised to operate in a particular way; 'private' then becomes equivalent to personal, 'informal' or 'domestic', and refers to the domain of primary, non-institutionalised, relationships and groups. When used to designate methods and techniques of control, the contrast is between those prescribed or at least sanctioned by legislation and government mandate, and interpersonal (often psychological and emotional) mechanisms of persuasion, chastisement and correction. One of the major problems in much of this literature is the imprecise meaning and use of these concepts. They may refer to categories of control agents and agencies, or to types of control methods and techniques, or to levels of control response, or reaction, or to a mixture of all three dimensions of social control.

Some of the feminist theorists who use this terminology to explore gender differences with respect to forms and contexts of social control have also been criticised for their lack of conceptual rigour and failure to distinguish between these separate dimensions of control (by for example, Hagan et al., 1979; Millman, 1975:253; Smart and Smart, 1978). Others, however, are well aware of the theoretical issues and attempt to discriminate between the different aspects or dimensions of social life and hence of social control to which these pairs of related concepts refer. The public/private dichotomy has attracted the most attention from feminists. As was indicated earlier, these feminists have called into question the assumed ontological primacy of the 'formal', 'official' and 'public' areas and aspects of social existence (including social control). They argue for wider recognition of the underlying social connections between the organisational features, normative standards, and social practices in the private domain and the 'official' institutional and ideological mechanisms and structures of the wider society.

MacKinnon (1982, 1983), for instance, reexamines the meaning of 'the political' and the relationship between 'the personal' and 'the political' from a feminist standpoint. She contends that sexuality (conventionally regarded as a supremely 'private' matter) is 'the primary social sphere of male power' (1982: 529); in her view, as every aspect of female experience, including the most intimate and personal, is subject to male control at the individual and at the collective or societal level (through the mechanisms of the state), women can have no 'private' identity or existence (1983:640–5, 655–8).

The dichotomous categorisation of dimensions of social control (public/private, formal/informal, exclusive/inclusive[10]) is at least a misleading over-simplification, if not a distortion, of the nature of social control. In reality, different elements and dimensions of social control may be present together. For instance, at the same time as a court is carrying out its 'official', 'formal' duty (to determine the guilt or innocence of the accused), its officers may indulge more or less openly in 'informal' modes of demonstrating disapproval (by inflicting insults, discomfort or injury on those in their custody). Nor should we assume that 'official' types of social reaction have a greater impact than 'unofficial' on the future behaviour of deviants who are subject to both.[11]

Contests[12] between controllers and those they seek to control take place on a number of different levels, and the outcome may not be a straightforward victory for one side or the other (Schur, 1980). Sociologists of deviance and social control must avoid portraying the target of labelling and social reaction as, to borrow Gouldner's highly expressive (though sexist) phrase, a 'man-on-his-back' (1968:107).[13] An interesting phenomenon here is the emergence in western societies of collective and organised protest and liberation movements—from women, the aged, ethnic minorities, gays and lesbians, to welfare claimants, mental patients, ex-prisoners, chronic disease sufferers, and other disability groups. Their main objective is to challenge the structural arrangements of society and the prevailing ideologies, social expectations and moral codes which they see as resulting in their own marginalisation and devaluation.[14]

All this shows that we need to exercise care and discrimination when using the basic terms in the social control vocabulary in order to avoid confusing or conflating what are very different elements and dimensions of social control.

Consistent with the position being advanced here, and a useful way of summarising this section of the chapter, is Mayer's proposed conceptual schema for the analysis of the creation and operation of control programmes and policies.

> One could look at the desires or intent of those who set up a control effort, and one could also analyse the operation of the control process itself. That there might be differences between these two requires making distinctions between them. A full analysis would also attempt to measure effectiveness: how many persons subjected to a particular controlling process behaved or expressed attitudes in conjunction with the ends or goals of the controlling effort? One must also consider regular behavioural changes resulting without regard to ends or goals, that is, unintended consequences. Each of these three might differ from each other. The amount of power that originating reformers desired to exert might have differed significantly from the power that the eventual controlling process actually did exert; and the effectiveness of the controlling process might actually have been inversely related to the amount of power exerted. (Mayer, 1985:26)

Modes, models and systems of social control

When we wish to examine the nature and exercise of social control, whether at the interpersonal, organisational or societal level, a limited range of types of approach (or models), sets of institutional arrangements (or systems) and patterns of interrelated perceptions and practices (or modes) can be identified. Each model and system of social control has a range of problems or forms of deviance for which it is responsible. Each has a conceptualisation of the nature and causes of the phenomena with which it has to deal and a set of strategies and policies for handling individual cases when they arise.

The most common sociological characterisation of the major categories of deviance across human societies is the three-fold division into sin, crime, and illness, to which correspond three kinds of social control orientation and organised pattern of response—the religious, the legal/judicial/penal, and the medical (Fox, 1977:11; Freidson, 1970: 247–50; Spector, 1981; Twaddle, 1973:755–6). Black (1976, 1984), who has made a major theoretical contribution to the study of social control, offers a different but compatible typology; his four 'styles' of social control are penal, compensatory, therapeutic and conciliatory and he contrasts them on a number of dimensions, including allocation of responsibility, focus of attention, type of institutional mechanism employed, and whether it relies on coercion or persuasion (see also Horwitz, 1984:213–5).

The major division in modern society is between crime, handled by legal/judicial methods (which may take the form of penal, compensatory or conciliatory measures) and illness which is managed by the medical system (working with a therapeutic orientation). Whereas crime has been universally and unequivocally classified as deviance, illness and 'the sick role' was first recognised by Parsons (1951), as also being 'deviant' in the sociological sense. Aubert and Messinger, in a classic article, describe the different philosophies associated with the socially defined roles of 'the criminal and the sick'. In the former case, an individual enters this role because he/she has performed a 'motivated act', while in the latter all that is necessary is for the individual to 'undergo an apparent change for the worse' (1958:139). This is also seen as the key element distinguishing Stoll's two 'images' of deviance and social control, termed the 'sickness' and the 'wickedness' models: sickness invokes a determinist explanation of human behaviour and wickedness a voluntarist one. When sick, one is entitled to sympathy, treatment and care; when criminal, one receives castigation and restriction (1968: 121). 'Sin' can imply either or both: original sin is part of the general human condition, but individual sins are regarded as volitional acts (Stoll, 1968:120, note 8).

Thus, the most fundamental distinction between sources or causes of deviance is between voluntary and involuntary actions, between choice and accident or determinism, and all cultures operate on the basis of one or the other or both of these constructions of human nature and behaviour. Which of the two sets of assumptions is in operation will be reflected in the moral and social orientation taken by control agents and the sort of treatment recommended. However, although distinguishing between two fundamentally different conceptualisations of deviance and approaches to social control in this way is analytically important and useful, it is only a first stage in the study of the control systems and ideologies found in the empirical world. How wickedness and crime or sickness and disease are defined, perceived and treated in particular contexts and under different cultural and social conditions is highly variable and provides the subject-matter for the sociology of deviance and social control. In the 'real' world, the distinctions between categories are blurred and the areas of jurisdiction of different systems may overlap; for instance, violence may be subject to the control of both criminal justice and medicine/psychiatry. Even the defining characteristics of voluntarism and determinism may appear in some form in the model to which logically or formally they do not belong. As an example, Freidson (1970a:238–9) points to cases of illness or injury where, due to the individual's negligence or risk-taking, the unconditional status of 'sick' is denied.

Crime as a concept is recognised across all or most societies, but the specification of particular acts as crimes is highly variable from culture to culture, though there does seem to be a common core of almost universally proscribed anti-social acts covering violence, sexual 'deviance' and offences against property.[15] Crime is defined in relation to particular types of social norms, specifically those embodied in the law, and hence the processes that determine which social norms are enshrined in law are responsible for what is categorised as criminal deviance in any given society. The characteristics of criminal law as 'an instrument of formal social control' are described by Quinney as follows: it relates to a set of 'explicit rules of conduct created by political authority'; it contains 'provisions for punishment'; designated officials have the task of making, interpreting and enforcing the rules; and there is 'uniform administration of the codes for all persons in a given territory' (1965: 133).

The concepts of disease and illness are also dependent on certain sorts of social norms, in this case norms relating to the body, its appearance and its functioning, to physical and psychological states of well-being, and to pain, discomfort and dis-ease, such norms coming from cultural and folk knowledge as well as from science and modern western medicine. The term disease is used to refer to a biological, physical state which is more or less observable and relatively objectively recognisable from the presence of certain signs and symptoms. Health, illness and 'the sick role' by contrast are social constructs (Twaddle, 1973).

In the process of uncovering complexities and even contradictions in the social definitions and conceptualisations of crime, illness and deviance, one is reminded that these are human creations, not independent objective entities. As the labelling and interactionist sociologists have argued, deviance is not a quality inherent in the person or the act. Where consensual definitions of deviance exist within or even in some cases between societies, this means only that the norms and values against which these phenomena are measured and found wanting are very widely held. Whereas, however, interactionists simply interpret this to mean that all deviance, including the categories of crime and illness, is socially relative and that sociologists should take as their subject-matter whatever society defines and treats as deviant, the more 'radical' theorists (critical criminologists, marxists and feminists) go further.

They point to the connections between the distribution of wealth, power and status, the class structure, the sex/gender system and other key features of society, and the prevailing norms and values which determine societal definitions of and reactions to deviance. Put at its simplest, the deviance (and particularly this is true of criminal deviance) that comes to official, public and hence sociological attention is the deviance of the powerless.[16]

Systematic patterns and biases occur in the selection of what constitutes 'deviance' out of the whole range of behaviours that are harmful, dishonest, threatening, or anti-social in some way. The designation 'crime' and the criminal law as a control mechanism is applied to certain categories of individuals and acts and not others. Though, as Young (1975) warns, marxists should not therefore conclude that the criminal law in capitalist societies offers no protection or benefit to the working classes, nor assume that working-class support for the law is simply false-consciousness. Moreover, the criminal law is mainly used to regulate the activities of individuals as individuals and not those of governments, statutory bodies, influential groups and organisations, or powerful sections of the population.[17]

It is not, therefore, satisfactory to settle for a definition of crime as simply whatever the criminal law prohibits or of illness as whatever medical science sees as disease or non-health. Indeed one of the major contributions by sociology to these areas has been to demonstrate how social factors and processes influence definitions, perceptions and practices in both law and medicine. But social control models and systems do much more than simply define and categorise types of behaviour and types of individual. We need also to consider how rules are administered, how knowledge and procedures are used and how these institutions or systems actually operate. Both law and medicine involve complex sets of ideas and norms, bodies of knowledge, working principles and procedures, techniques and methods that have developed, and are modified, over time. It is important to understand the whole range of mechanisms and processes by which deviance, and in particular crime and illness, are socially produced and reproduced, and how power-related social variables such as sex/gender, class, age, and race/ethnicity affect the nature and exercise of social control.

As we have seen, there are some major differences in the way control is perceived and exercised in these two systems. The law is seen as an involuntary, regulatory type of control, relying on coercion, constraint and penalisation, while medicine, it seems, combines the application of objective, scientific knowledge with a caring, compassionate attitude so as to bring benefit to all. Nonetheless, they both operate as control agencies, by propagating ideological notions about human nature, morality and the maintenance of social order, by identifying and labelling in some way individuals who fall into certain categories, and by exercising power and control over them with the objective of deviance management, treatment and prevention (Schur, 1980:146–53).

Our argument is that, although medicine (unlike the criminal law and the judicial system) is not perceived by society or by its own practitioners primarily or explicitly in control terms, it can be seen as both a model (or ideology) and a system of social control. The theory and practice of medicine has moral and social as well as technical and scientific aspects; the physician is not simply an expert but a moral and political agent.[18] In Conrad's words, the social control aspect of medicine refers to 'the ways in which medicine functions (wittingly or unwittingly) to secure adherence to social norms; specifically, by using medical means to minimise, eliminate, or normalise deviant behaviour' (1979:1).

Conrad suggests medical social control takes three general forms: medical technology (mainly surgery and drugs); medical collaboration with other authorities in the roles of 'information provider, gatekeeper, institutional agent, and technician' (1979:5); and medical ideology or the use of 'medical authority by way of language', and the imagery and vocabulary of disease and illness (1979:6). These forms of control are applied not only to generally recognised and agreed physical symptoms of disease, but also to mental, emotional and psychological states that are experienced and/or perceived as disturbed, disordered or abnormal in some way. 'The medical model' or approach is also considered appropriate for a range of other conditions, including physical and mental handicaps and disabilities, pregnancy and childbirth, and various types of social behaviour such as maltreatment and abuse of children, alcohol and drug dependency, homosexuality, suicide, hyperactivity in children, adolescent female sexuality and delinquency, ageing, political radicalism, and so-called 'suburban neurosis' in middle-aged women.

The process by which various categories of individuals and behaviour are redefined as forms of 'illness' is described as 'medicalisation' and this trend towards the expansion of medicine into new areas has been extensively discussed in the sociological literature. We will examine this process and its social implications as well as medicine itself in detail in a later chapter.

The 'social control system' in modern western societies is more complex and diverse than the simple division into 'law' and 'medicine' would suggest. One further distinction that can be made is between civil and criminal law and the corresponding sets of mechanisms. Spector (1981) in fact treats civil law or 'tort' as a separate 'method of control' and approach to problem and conflict resolution, one which preceded criminal law in the western world, but continues to exist in modern times. A number of writers, from the marxist,[19] sociology of deviance[20] and feminist[21] perspectives, claim that a third major system of social control in capitalist patriarchal countries is the welfare sector of society and in particular the modern welfare state. Collective arrangements for the maintenance and containment of various types of dependency became part of the responsibilities of the state gradually and mainly during the twentieth century. (It is important to remember that the state has not been and is not now the sole source of welfare benefits and services, and that 'welfare' and 'the welfare state' should not therefore be taken as synonymous.)

Some writers (and marxists especially) use the term welfare state to describe the mid-twentieth century capitalist state and they interpret all its structures and functions as part of the process of maintaining order and ensuring the reproduction of the conditions necessary both for capital accumulation and the legitimation of the system. Offe (1975), for instance, looks at the steady expansion of state involvement in all areas of society—economic, political, social, ideological—by both negative and positive mechanisms and policies. Gough defines the welfare state more specifically as 'the use of state power to modify the reproduction of labour power and to maintain the non-working population in capitalist society' (1979:44–5). Others take the term 'welfare' in a somewhat narrower sense and apply it to services, cash benefits and transfers directed at certain categories of 'need', specifically in the areas of housing, education, health, social security and personal social services (Walker, 1981:226). Others again restrict the notion of welfare spending to various types of social insurance or direct relief expenditure (Griffin et al., 1983:331); expenditure on crime control would thus fall outside the welfare category when defined in this way.

In the broadest sense, then, 'the welfare state' includes not only provision in cash and kind for dependent groups, but also public medical and health care services and even the judicial and correctional institutions and processes responsible for handling law-breaking and criminal deviance. It hence subsumes all three of the major 'formal' modes of social control characteristic of modern industrial society. For some purposes, considering these as part of a single control apparatus may well be adequate. But where, as here, interest lies in exploring the complexities, diversities and interconnections of different modes and mechanisms of social control, it is necessary to treat welfare, medicine and the law as separate regulatory instruments.

Although we may find little difficulty in drawing distinctions between the three control systems at the level of identifiable organisations and practices, there are not three separate and distinct control ideologies that correspond with the three sets of structures. As suggested earlier, the medical and the legal/judicial systems do adopt different approaches to the treatment of the individuals with which they deal, based on whether they see the deviance as respectively, involuntary or voluntary, as 'sickness' or 'wickedness'. Despite the fact, however, that the welfare sector constitutes a distinct area and form of social control, the provision of welfare benefits and services is not matched by a distinctive 'welfare' ideology. The 'therapeutic ideal' implies the sole use of the 'sickness' model, but in practice judgements are made about who 'deserves' assistance that seem to indicate elements of the 'wickedness' model. Though it makes sense in this study to devote our attention to each of these three systems separately and in considerable detail, in the social world they, and indeed other major institutions such as the education system, the family and the media,[22] are all involved in interrelated ways in control work. Some of the most interesting recent research on social control has explored the ways in which the range of control agencies and ideologies combine to manage perceived threats to social order, a prime example being the account by Hall et al. (1978) of the societal reaction to mugging in England in the 1970s.

Trends and shifts in patterns of social control

Under this heading we will include both the changes in social control that occurred from the late eighteenth century onwards with capitalism and the 'rationalisation' of the western world, and the patterns that have developed more recently, and particularly since the 1960s, which appear to reverse the general direction of some earlier trends.

It is a widely accepted fact (for sociologists, marxists and feminists alike) that with respect to social control the dominant trend which has accompanied industrialism and capitalism in western societies has been from private to public institutions, from informal to formal social processes and practices, from family, church and community to professional experts, specialised control agencies and the state. As Weber, Foucault and (many) marxists have observed, this involved not merely a shift in the location of power (and control), but a fundamental change in forms of power and authority, in modes of exercising control, and in the targets and objectives of that control.

For Marx, the mechanisms of 'subjection of the labourer to the capitalist' and to the factory system are the most important mechanisms of control. Though Marx discusses the role of the police and the law in supporting ruling class interests, he also claims it was essential that capitalism develop 'a working-class which by education, tradition, habit, looks upon the conditions of that mode of production as self-evident laws of Nature' (Marx, quoted in Melossi, 1980:387). To explain this, some marxists have examined the methods of organising labour and the productive process, and the role of political parties and parliamentary democracy, as well as the critical contribution of the state. Others have combined elements from marxist theory with the work of Foucault. Melossi (1979) and Melossi and Pavarini (1981), for example, draw a parallel between the prison and the factory, and point to common patterns of organisation and discipline.[23]

Weber characterises the underlying process as one of increasing 'rationalisation'. By this he means a movement from 'traditional' to 'rational-legal' bases of authority and legitimacy for social and political domination, from rule by patriarchal monarchs and feudal lords (in an often uneasy alliance with the church) to the bureaucratic forms of administration, run according to the criteria of calculability, impersonality and technical efficiency, that are found in both the political (and to a considerable extent in the economic) systems of the modern western world.[24]

Spitzer sees the 'rationalisation of social relations', the depersonalisation and the regimentation that capitalism brought as responsible for changes in the basic nature of control.

> While slavery-based, feudal, and monarchic structures of domination were dependent on extensive, indirect, and ceremonial forms of coercive regulation, capitalism was able to transform relations of production and domination in such a way that controls could become far more intensive, direct, and banal. (1979:190)

As Weber and others have shown, rationalisation and bureaucratisation of government and administration were paralleled by a transformation of labour and the productive process by attention to the principles of accounting, cost-effectiveness and maximisation of profit, which meant a rigid separation of tasks and division of labour, and the development of new methods for the training and control of the workforce (Spitzer, 1979:197–8).

> The management of domestic populations... had to become intensive and based on the concept of sound investment. The need to distinguish between 'good' and 'bad' investments in human capital stimulated a further development, the emergence of screening, sorting and classifying institutions for people processing, e.g. schools, welfare systems, therapeutic facilities, prisons, etc. And as capitalism continued to dissolve the traditional institutions of socialisation, integration, and social regulation, i.e. the family, church, community, etc., bureaucratic institutions became more and more important as mechanisms to differentiate and supervise categories of 'worthy' and 'unworthy' human material. (1979:198)

Over the period from the early nineteenth century a diversification of types and agencies of social control accompanied the proliferation of forms of socially recognised and societally regulated deviance. Foucault points to a mass of 'disciplinary mechanisms' and establishments (1977:211), including schools, factories, hospitals, the army, and even the family.[25] For Foucault, 'discipline' and 'training' are the characteristic forms taken by control in nineteenth century Europe. They involve particular modes of organising space, time, activities and environments along functional and hierarchical lines and the continuous classification, examination and assessment of individual performance that this entailed. 'Discipline' he describes as 'a diagram of a mechanism of power' (1977:205) or a 'set of physico-political techniques' (1977:223). Whereas in the model of the 'disciplinary society' control operates through a multiplicity of regulatory bodies or centres of observation and surveillance (1977: 212), the alternative approach requires the removal of problem categories of the population to special treatment places such as prisons and mental asylums.

Under capitalism social control becomes both more extensive and more intensive: it involves both dispersal and centralisation, apparently, but not necessarily, contradictory trends. In particular, this means that, during the nineteenth century and even more since, the state has steadily increased the nature and range of its institutions, expanded its functions, enlarged its scope, and diversified its activities. Also its methods have become more diverse, more subtle, often indirect and not easily visible. While there was never a period of total 'laissez-faire', the state until well into the last century had a relatively modest role to play in relation to the social control of industrial society,[26] even in the areas of crime, punishment and the law. From then, the state has assumed more and more varied powers and over more aspects of social life, and its objectives are not only or mainly prohibition and punishment of criminal acts but the regulation and management of society as a whole.

Important in this general process are, on the one hand as marxists have argued, the pressures on the capitalist state increasingly to assume overall responsibility for ensuring the necessary social conditions of production and, on the other, the emergence of ideologies of control (both within the penal area of crime control and with respect to other forms of deviance) that talk in terms of 'treatment' and 'welfare'. These inspired greater control efforts but enabled the control, and particularly its more coercive elements, to be disguised and justified as 'scientific', progressive' and 'humane'. (This kind of observation reminds us of the value that lies in maintaining an analytical distinction between methods and ideologies, that is between the technical and the moral aspects of social control.)

> Our current system of deviancy control originated in those great transformations which took place from the end of the 18th to the beginning of the 19th centuries: firstly the development of a centralized state apparatus for the control of crime and care of dependency; secondly the increasing differentiation of the deviant and dependent into separate types each with its own attendant corpus of 'scientific' knowledge and accredited experts, and finally the increased segregation of deviants and dependents into 'asylums', mental hospitals, prisons, reformatories and other such closed, purpose-built institutions for treatment and punishment. (Cohen, 1979a:341)

Others have stressed the importance of the new scientific discipline of medicine, of a new medically-based 'treatment' approach to control, and of psychiatry and the concepts of 'mental health' and 'mental illness'.[27]

The analysis of changes in patterns of social control can be conducted in several different ways. Either we can examine the overall control system and discover how the dominant institutions or modes of social control have altered (for instance from sin and tort, to crime, to illness and disease) as western capitalist society developed. Or we can focus on changes in methods of defining and dealing with a given problem or form of deviance over time (we could take, for example, 'madness'[28] or alcoholism[29] or, a feminist area of concern such as female sexuality and sexual relations[30]). Or we can monitor variations in the nature, scope and importance of particular modes or systems of social control, such as medicine[31] or prisons and corrections.[32] All three approaches will be used here.

Social control during the nineteenth and early twentieth centuries can be characterised by an increasing emphasis on rationality and discipline, the application of science and technology to diagnosis, management and treatment, the extension of the scope of state direction, supervision and administration, the supplementation of law and criminal justice as the major deviance control system by medicine, psychiatry and welfare, and bureaucratisation and professionalisation as organisational principles.

One deviance theorist, Little (1983:261), compares the images of and approaches to deviance and social control in the early and later periods of capitalism (and contrasts these with feudal society). Another, Cohen (1985:16–17), also gives a picture of what he describes as 'master changes in deviancy control' over three periods—pre-eighteenth century, from the late eighteenth century into the twentieth century, and from about the middle of the twentieth century. He describes in considerable detail changes in a number of aspects of control, including the roles of the state and of the professions, and the places, foci, modes and underlying philosophies of control.

A more marxist account would highlight particularly changes in the form, functions and apparatuses of the state in response to changes in the capitalist mode of production from the simple commodity form, through competitive, industrial capitalism, to monopoly or corporate capitalism (but without necessarily implying a causal relationship).[33] The three forms of the state can be described as 'liberal individualist' or 'laissez-faire', parliamentary democratic or 'protective', and 'welfarist' or 'interventionist'.[34] Roe talks of the 'changing theoretical functions of "social" policy—from residual to regulatory to redistributive' (1976: ix). The period during which the movement occurred from the first to the second form covers the nineteenth and early twentieth centuries, while the transition from the second to the third dates from the 1920s (and is related to particular events, namely the two world wars and the Great Depression).

Different apparatuses (and hence modes and mechanisms of social control) are available to the state in these three different situations. In the 'liberal' state, these were primarily laws and government statutes dealing with private property, contracts, trade, civil rights and the

Diagram 4.1: Broad historical trends in western images of deviance and the practice of social control

Historical period	Pre-industrial, feudal (pre-1500)	Mercantile/early industrial capitalism (1500–1900)	Advanced welfare state capitalism (1900–present)
Dominant groups/institutions	Church, clergy monarchy, and nobility	Landed gentry, merchants, and industrial capitalists	Industrial capitalists and state technocrats
Image of deviance identification	Sin/evil	Crime/illegal	Sickness/madness/ crime
Responsibility	Individual in relation to God and Sovereign	Individual in relation to the Law and the State	Individual denied responsibility
Social control practitioners	Clergy, monarchy, and nobility	Judges and courts	Medical, psychiatric, and social scientists, helping professionals and courts
Legitimation of authority	Tradition/Divine right/moral	Legal/rational/ moral	Technical/ rational/moral
Mode of response	Retributive/ corporal/capital/ penance	Restitutive/ incarceration/ capital/ banishment	Rehabilitative/ drugs or surgery/ repressive/ incarceration or capital
Image of the limits on human action	Supernaturalistic determinism/ original sin	Free will/Utilitarian, rational choice	Naturalistic determinism/ Bio-Psycho-social causes

Source: Little (1983:261)

protection of free competition and market forces, and the use by the state of legitimate force to keep order. As the state increasingly assumed a protective or servicing role on behalf of industry and business, it expanded its spheres of activity, increased the number and variety of bodies directly or indirectly under its administrative and/or financial control, and extended the range of services supplied both to cover areas which though essential were inappropriate or unprofitable for private enterprise (such as roads, energy, transport) and to provide for special categories of the population outside the normal work-force (the old, the sick, the mad, the bad, etc.). In the modern period, welfare and interventionism by the state have become so central to the maintenance of the capitalist system that it is hard to draw a distinction between the state and the economy or 'civil society'.

In earlier times, social control (by state or private bodies such as charities) was largely coercive and repressive and even the provision of state support was accompanied by overt and unambiguously negative moral judgements about poverty and dependency. During the nineteenth century, though it did not disappear, this moralism gave way to a more social utilitarian concern with improving the quality of the human resources of society (and particularly its labour force), with the state taking responsibility for ensuring minimum standards of housing, public health and so on and for providing education, training and exposure to discipline and authority. This replaced a previous preoccupation with punishment, segregation and incarceration for its own (moral) sake. There was an overall trend, from 'hard' to 'softer' modes of control or, in Gramsci's (1971) terms, from 'force' to 'persuasion and consent'. This was reflected in new policies and orientations in all three major control areas of welfare, psychiatry and mental health, and criminal law, justice and corrections.

Phase 1: Nineteenth to early twentieth centuries

We do have some historical material that illustrates how social control changed during the nineteenth century and into the twentieth, particularly in the areas of welfare, mental health and crime that increasingly became the responsibility of the state in western countries.

We are concerned here with major structures and processes of social control in Australia in the post penal settlement phase. However, the fact that white Australia started as a convict colony is of obvious importance, particularly in view of the responsibility this gave the state, first British and later Australian, over the maintenance of order, over the supply and discipline of labour, and over general economic management and development. Force, repression and the military were all seen as essential and officially sanctioned.

> From the moment of first occupation, force was applied on two fronts, against convicts and blacks—controlling the white workforce by the lash and the gallows, and creating the space within which the settlement could grow. Though official policy towards blacks had an element of sympathy and conciliation, which at times predominated in the governors' counsels, in normal practice the government supplied military support to white settlers at the frontier, and often enough, troops and police took the lead in skirmishes and massacres. . . This permanent imbalance of military power was the most decisive fact about the early settlements: it was the frame within which everything else happened. (Connell and Irving, 1980:32)

Connell and Irving (1980) provide a detailed account of the role of the state and the use of physical force in early Australian history and at the beginnings of colonial capitalism, and of its subsequent contraction when transportation ceased, free labour replaced convict, and market capitalism became established from the mid-nineteenth century.[35] Australia experienced from the start a high degree of 'official' and 'public' administration and regulation, which during the nineteenth century gradually gave way, for the white population, to 'private', 'civil' and local community-based modes of social control. The state also assisted in the development of a less punitive criminal justice and corrections system, and, as the century progressed, different approaches to the treatment of physical and mental illness and to welfare problems and dependency emerged, as they did in Europe over the same period. But its early penal settlement phase makes Australia untypical of western countries at the time.

Crime control was a fundamental part of the public, official obligations recognised by governments in industrialising countries in this early period.

> Many troublesome behaviors have been defined as crimes for so long that it is difficult to think of them any other way; yet crime is a fairly recent method of social disapproval... Until the eighteenth century, the state left many troublesome behaviors to religion and to the private dispute settling system. National governments had not developed an extensive system of social disapproval based on crime. The criminal law did exist, but it covered fewer troublesome behaviors than it does today. (Spector, 1981:130)

It is often not realised that a public administered and financed civilian police force only got established in England in the first half of the last century.[36] Until then, crime control was largely a private matter and to a considerable extent was organised along business lines, with both policing and the running of gaols and houses of detention offering profitable sources of income (Spitzer and Scull, 1977a; Stevenson, 1977). Law and order in England was maintained by a combination of the military and deputies and constables appointed by wealthy individuals, financial bodies and local communities, and assisted by thief-takers (Rock, 1985). O'Malley discusses a similar trend in the development of policing in Australia. The landowning and pastoralist groups tended to control the constabulary and the courts over most of the country; where substantial numbers collected (mainly in the towns) who were seen to pose a threat to disorder the military would be called in. As urban centres grew and the urban middle class became more powerful, the 'militaristic' and 'oligarchic' modes of control, which arose under the conditions of a dispersed rural population and the problems of large numbers of convicts and ex-convicts, became less appropriate and there was pressure to bring policing under centralised state and civil control (O'Malley, 1983:52–7).

Significant changes in the principal modes of punishment also occurred from the late eighteenth century. Ignatieff (1978, 1985) has produced a detailed analysis of the nature and historical development of the 'penitentiary' in England between 1770 and 1840. He gives a useful summary of the common elements in his account and those of Foucault (1977) and Rothman (1971). He lists the following:

> (1) The decline of punishments involving the public infliction of physical pain to the body...

> (2) The emergence of imprisonment as the pre-eminent penalty for most serious offences . . .
> (3) The penitentiary came to be the bearer of reformers' hopes for a punishment capable of reconciling deterrence and reform, terror and humanity . . .
> (4) As systems of authority, the new prisons substituted the pains of intention for the pains of neglect . . .
> (5) The new prisons substituted the rule of rules for the rule of custom and put an end to the old division of power between the inmate community and the keepers . . .
> (6) The new institutions enforced a markedly greater social distance between the confined and the outside world. (1985: 79–82)

When looking at imprisonment in this period, Shank (1979) points out that, although discipline continued to be the prevailing method of control for both workers and criminals, the actual mode of organisation in the prison and in the factory increasingly diverged. For Australia, Grabosky (1977:Chapters 6 and 7) provides evidence of a shift during the nineteenth century from punitive, violent and coercive methods for controlling crime and running penal institutions to a more moderate sentencing policy and a more orderly and disciplinary penology for New South Wales, though significant changes did not appear until the end of the century. For most of this period 'retributive incarceration remained the dominant correctional strategy' (Grabosky, 1977:173).

Most of the analyses of prisons and of the institutions of disciplinary societies are couched in fairly general terms and in particular they ignore gender differences in approaches to punishment and types of penal institution and regime. However, we do have some insights into how men and women have been differentially treated historically by the criminal law and justice system. In the second half of the mineteenth century, a number of American states established separate correctional facilities for women. They justified legislatively the use of indeterminate (which typically meant longer) sentences for convicted women, on the grounds that women's psychological makeup and hence rehabilitative capacity was different from men's, and the alleged moral and sexual 'depravity' of criminal women was usually mentioned (Armstrong, 1977; Feinman, 1979; Temin, 1973). Rafter's (1985) detailed study of the historical development of the Albion Women's Reformatory, New York, showed a clear perception of the gender-specific requirements of such an institution: to provide a morally-based training for the 'true good womanly life' (1985:291), seen in terms of the traditional domestic female role.

During the nineteenth century in America, separate facilities for delinquent youth were set up by private organisations and by the states, with the purpose of reforming children, mainly those from lower class and immigrant groups, and a whole range of 'needs' and 'problems' among youth was recognised as requiring official societal action. Liazos (1974) has described the function of juvenile justice in the last century as primarily 'class oppression', girls being prepared for domestic service and motherhood, and boys for manual trades and farm labouring. Though in the later part of the century the concept of juvenile delinquency was broadened, and despite the reformism of the child savers' ideology and the move to separate the administration of juvenile justice from that of adults by setting up special courts, the correctional orientation of the programmes continued and was extended to cover the existing and new categories of delinquent urban youth.

Though it was male delinquency that preoccupied the public and the authorities, female delinquency (which was much smaller in quantity) attracted the deeper moral concern. As Schlossman and Wallach express it, 'boys' delinquencies were roundly condemned but were rarely, as was often the case with girls', regarded as indications of innate moral perversity' (1978:69). These authors concentrate on how this moral concern with 'the crime of precocious sexuality' led to an expansion of government involvement in the control of female delinquent (and especially immigrant) youth and to 'discriminatory treatment of women and girls in juvenile courts and reformatories' in the 1910–20 'Progressive Era' (1978:70), and they produce convincing evidence for their thesis. Many (for example Riback, 1971; Rogers, 1972) have criticised the juvenile justice system's paternalism and discrimination with respect to girls. Others have shown how powerful the nineteenth century philosophy of rescuing girls from 'moral danger' and the traditional type of institutional regime still remain and how 'protectionism' continues to justify gender stereotyping, differential sentencing, limited training and educational opportunities, and general restrictiveness that characterise the court and correctional systems not only for the young but for adult women as well (Chesney-Lind, 1974, 1977; Feinman, 1979; Gold, 1971; Kress, 1979).

A comparable pattern appeared in Australia. Similar changes affected legislation, juvenile and adult justice and correctional institutions during the nineteenth and into the twentieth centuries. The state steadily took over more control. The categories of cases to be covered under juvenile statutes increased and there was a gradual shift at least at the level of official rhetoric from punishment and detention towards welfare, training and reform especially with respect to youth. Differential perception and evaluation of male and female crime and delinquency resulted in differential and discriminatory treatment of women and girls, and there was the same preoccupation in programmes and institutions with controlling female sexuality and with the necessity of inculcating traditional feminine virtues and skills.[37]

Though we have limited historical data on the criminal justice system and the control of women specifically in the post-convict period, there has been some research done on the characteristics and treatment of convict women and particularly on the treatment of prostitutes. Convict women, Summers (1975:Chapter 8) claims, provided virtually all of the white female population of Australia in the early period of colonisation and they were subjected to officially sanctioned and condoned economic and sexual exploitation in which the (male) authorities played a major role. Feminist historians have given us detailed accounts of women's position in colonial Australia and the way they were subject, as convicts and later as immigrants, both to the harsh conditions, low status and poor employment prospects, and to physical and sexual abuse by the administration and by men generally, at least until the middle of the nineteenth century. Daniels (1984) and others (for example, Alford, 1984:Chapters 4 and 5) have questioned the extent to which the situation of convict women and of those defined as prostitutes[38] can be generalised to the rest of the female population (even excluding the ruling class) especially after transportation ceased (in New South Wales in 1840). Summers in fact argues that the 'God's police' role was just as much a social and moral constraint on women's lives (though one which women themselves helped to enforce) as was that of 'damned whore' (1975:Chapter 9). Especially relevant here is a vivid account, based on original documents and records, given by Barbalet (1983) of the (sexual) moralism, the preference for rural and traditional patterns of life, and the emphasis on domestic service and motherhood for girls under the 'care' of the state, as wards in South Australia between 1887 and 1940. The 'boarding out' system, she says, was intended to create the middle class perception of the working class ideal child (1983:195). Though this system dealt officially with 'needy' rather than delinquent children, the attitudes and patterns of control, and sometimes also the institutions, were much the same (Barbalet, 1983; Weatherburn, 1979; Willis, 1979).

Changes in the structures and mechanisms of crime control, particularly in penal institutions, were paralleled by alterations in the models and methods favoured in the treatment of 'madness' or 'mental illness' during the course of the last century. For Foucault (1977), control in the form of 'discipline' and 'surveillance' constituted a general approach that was highly adaptable to a variety of situations. He shows (1967) how, from the seventeenth century on, the religious conception of madness as possession by demons or uncontrollable passions declined, to be replaced by a medical model which reflected both increasing rationalisation, secularisation and scientisation in western society and the rising influence of the professions of physician and later psychiatrist.[39]

Warren (1981:163) observes that the early 'asylums' were urban institutions and to be seen as a response to problems of crowded urban living, mobility, immigration, and the incapacity of families and communities to care for those members who were unable or unwilling to work, or otherwise in an unwanted category. The state entered the field by both legislating with respect to involuntary commitment and by setting up some of the mental institutions. Scull (1977a) argues that explanations for the 'rise of the insane asylum' in America and Britain which focus simply on the process of increasing urbanisation and industrialisation are inadequate. His thesis is that, as capitalism developed, an institutionally-focussed, centrally regulated system of social control for problem sections of the population (and specifically this meant the lower classes) was sought by more powerful classes as a means for looking after troublesome elements of the unemployed and unemployable poor. Scull also describes an alteration in the basis on which asylums were defended during the nineteenth century from 'fear of the threat posed to life, property and the orderliness of social existence' to a 'new-found conviction about the redemptive power of the institution' (1985:133), which reflected both a general shift in moral consciousness and the particular efforts of psychiatrists and reformers.

Garton (1983) provides a useful and interesting analysis of developments in prisons and mental asylums from 1880–1920 in New South Wales and in another article (1982) he gives a related account of psychiatry up to 1940, which in his view can be explained neither by economic conditions nor as a simple response to threats of disorder. Both systems of incarceration were almost entirely state or government controlled (by contrast with America and Britain) which, he points out, 'made incarceration practices particularly sensitive to conflicts over state policies' (1983:90). One half of commitments to asylums came through police prosecutions and the courts and had hence also passed through the criminal justice system. Inmates of both types of institutions were predominantly male (even more so in prisons) and lower class (men were labourers and women housewives and domestic servants), and immigrants and individuals from rural areas were also over-represented (1983: 93–4). He finds evidence of the kinds of changes discussed earlier, such as attempts within the sentencing and the prison systems to narrow the categories sent to gaol (by, for instance, excluding juveniles and drunks) and to introduce a more effective disciplinary (and hopefully reformative) regime. Apprehensions and court commitments to asylums of urban dwellers increased over the period Garton was examining, indicating a greater concern with what was happening in metropolitan Sydney. At the same time, private psychiatry also expanded.

Evans (1976) gives a bleak picture of life in social control institutions during the post-convict period in colonial Queensland and shows clearly how powerful and persistent were the moral condemnation, social rejection and punitiveness that characterised societal responses not only to criminals but to the chronic sick, the disabled, the aged, infirm, insane, alcoholics and prostitutes, all those who fell into the category of 'permanent indigent' or 'incapacitated paupers' (1976:80). In his view, the 'crime' model continued to prevail in the treatment of these groups into the twentieth century, because of what he sees as the dominant male community attitude of 'fear of the incurable and...distrust of the useless' (1976:90). Though he finds over this period some differentiation and separation of these various categories his account suggests these processes were slower to occur in Australia than in England or America.

Australia's welfare history has some distinctive features (Dickey, 1980:Chapters 1–3). Having started as a penal settlement, central administration played a central role at the start in regulating all aspects of the colony's life, including illness and dependency as well as crime. It was only in the post-convict era that welfare was left to non-government, private and mainly charitable bodies. No equivalent of the English Poor Law system was ever introduced in Australia, any proposals meeting with strong opposition; and unemployment overall was not a problem until the 1980s depression (Kewley, 1973:19–26). Apart from an exceptional early penal phase, the nineteenth century in Australia was a period of reliance on private sources and types of welfare, with some government financial support. 'The States only assumed full responsibility from the beginning for the insane and for the criminal, although increasingly for rejected children' (Roe, 1976: 13). It was not until late in the last century that the state began to move into the welfare area. Changes in welfare provision involved a wider acceptance of a welfare (as opposed to a legalistic, moralistic or charitable) orientation to social problems, dependency and need. Modern writers on the state reject the liberal interpretation that early welfare initiatives and later 'the welfare state' were the results of 'commonsense, benevolence, practical economics and consensus politics' (Watts, 1982: 225). Writers agree that a complex and changing set of social conditions forced the state from the late nineteenth century to take on an increasingly major role in financing and supplying most of the social services required by an industrialised, urbanised, mobile, privatised and longer-living society.[40]

Generally, changes in the nature and requirements of capitalism, the establishment of parliamentary democracy and the extension of suffrage, and the increased power of the union movement and organised labour are regarded as the main determinants of the quantitative and qualitative changes in the role of the state over time in the welfare field (Gough, 1979:Chapter 4; Higgins, 1978; Jones and Novak, 1980). As in the other control areas, this was accompanied by the displacement of private bodies by government, and by licensed and statutory agencies. Whereas 'welfare' in the nineteenth century meant 'charity and correction', in the twentieth century it came to represent the collective effort of governments to meet all kinds of human needs (Kennedy, 1982: 2–3).

Stedman Jones (1976, 1977) and the contributors to Donajgrodski (ed.) (1977)[41] provide valuable insights into the various mainly private methods and agencies of social control which characterised 'welfare' in mid-nineteenth century England. They stress the importance of control over the working classes and the diversity of 'moral' or 'social police', and the ways the middle classes generally attempted to regulate the leisure and social life of the poor, particularly in the cities. Social and economic conditions in the larger cities produced a major problem of 'demoralisation' among the casual poor and various strategies 'to induce thrift, regularity and hard work' (Stedman Jones, 1976: 271). Stedman Jones emphasises in this context the importance of the division between 'deserving' and 'undeserving' poor; the former deemed worthy targets of philanthropic organisations and the latter, 'the residuum', left dependent on the meagre and punitive provisions of the poor law (1976: Chapters 15–17); others have commented on the importance of this distinction in the treatment of poverty in Australia (Conley, 1982; Higgins, 1978:138).[42]

A comparable collection of historical writings to those in the Donajgrodski volume is a book edited by Kennedy (1982), *Australian Welfare History*. Kennedy (1982:Chapter 3) describes the range of provisions for the poor and indigent in nineteenth century Victoria, where though there was no poor law, there were still institutions for special problem groups (such as lunatics, juveniles, and inebriates, as well as criminals) and private charities (hospitals, orphanages, homes for the blind), as well as some provisions by private and religious bodies (for example, special schools for girls). Unlike the English volume, there is also some attention to the question of gender. Two authors, Windschuttle and Godden, trace women's relationship to philanthropy, both as recipients and organisers of welfare efforts. Here and elsewhere Windschuttle (1980) argues that a major part of Australian ruling class women's 'public role' was philanthropy and that their activities were inspired more by moral than by social concern about lower class families and especially their female children.

There were 'paradoxical elements' in nineteenth century Australian attitudes to the place of the state: 'a powerful demand for State action to promote development and, later, to regulate the collective conditions of labour, combined with some reluctance to accept direct State action to relieve individual need' (Kewley, 1973:7). Governments in Australia had, because of its particular history, always carried out a wider range of functions than in other western countries, in providing land and labour to new settlers and some infrastructural services such as roads. At the same time there was strong resistance for the major part of the nineteenth century to the state taking responsibility for various categories of dependency and 'need', on the grounds that this would undermine individual self-reliance and effort.

In New South Wales,[43] as Kewley (1973: Chapter 1) shows, the state's involvement, therefore, mainly took the form of financial assistance (which in some areas of need was substantial) to a variety of voluntary welfare and charitable organisations, a leading example being the Benevolent Society set up in 1818 (Dickey, 1980:20–7). These offered both indoor (i.e. places in institutions) and outdoor (cash, food, clothing, etc.) relief to a whole range of 'needy' groups—orphans, destitute women and children, deaf, dumb and blind, aged and infirm, sick—and provided hospitals and institutions for orphaned, neglected and destitute children. The able-bodied unemployed were largely excluded from such provisions and usually catered for by governments who employed them on public works for a wage. Overall these charitable organisations and the friendly societies coped with the problems of those who were unable to care for themselves. Although in the early part of the century, institutions such as the Sydney Benevolent Asylum accepted all sorts of needy people, later some degree of differentiation between categories and more specialised institutions began to appear. The state in New South Wales took over institutions for the destitute aged and infirm, leaving the 'asylums' to cater for mothers and children.

In the later part of the last century, and especially as a result of the 1890s depression and the power of organised labour (in a situation of chronic shortage of skilled workers and the needs of expanding industrial capitalism), there was increasing pressure for the state to take a more direct role in the welfare area. At the same time universal free schooling was being introduced and in the industrial area legislation was being passed regulating hours, wage rates and conditions for various categories of workers—this included the institution of the arbitration system. Early in the life of the new Commonwealth Government which was established in 1900 (and following the initiative of New South Wales where an old age pension scheme was introduced in 1901) legislation for non-contributory old age and invalid pensions for white Australian residents was passed (in 1908), followed by maternity allowances (in 1912).[44]

The pensions in particular marked a significant change in the approach to welfare and social security in Australia which did not substantially alter again until the 1940s. The state at this time took the major responsibility for social security provision only for the aged and invalids, while maintaining its indirect role as a major source of funds for a wide range of institutions, services and benefits provided by non-government bodies in the health and welfare area, and thus:

> It brought about a change from the haphazard and discretionary relief giving, characteristic of the poor law, to the provision of fixed rates of benefit to which there was a statutory and clearly defined right. This also marked a revolution in social policy which, in turn, reflected a new understanding of the causes of poverty and a new attitude to collective responsibility. (Kewley, 1973: 563)

Overall, we have a picture of a society which, as it moves out of firstly its penal settlement and later its colonial phases, progressively replaces the rule of a relatively centralised British and then colonial administration with a similar range of control institutions, agencies and mechanisms to those found in nineteenth century Britain and America.

By the turn of the century 'the state' (by which now we mean various State governments) has assumed more powers and is developing a new role, mainly in the form of the financing and supervision of special institutions and facilities for deviant and dependent groups (the mad, the bad, the old, the young, etc.) and meeting certain basic welfare or social security needs, a role which was maintained and later greatly expanded, particularly after 1940 when the Federal Government gained extended constitutional powers. Alongside the state (or more precisely working with it and through it) were the structures and ideologies of class, male domination and white supremacy which were major forces throughout the western world over this period and continue to be so.

Phase 2: 1940s–1980s

The 1940s and 1950s are generally regarded as the period of establishment of 'the welfare state' in Britain and in other western countries, as well as a period of development and expansion of a substantial range of welfare-oriented policies and services in Australia, and this process is linked both to the war and the need for popular support for the war effort, and to the subsequent period of economic prosperity. It is from this time that the description of the modern capitalist state as 'interventionist' or 'expansionist' also applies. We will cover here relatively briefly the major recent trends in the primary social control spheres of welfare, criminal justice and medicine/psychiatry.

Gough suggests that the period of 'the welfare state' from the 1940s to the early 1970s, which seemed at the time to mark a new phase or form of capitalism or industrialism, now looks more like an 'atypical or abnormal' phenomenon (1979:x). Gough provides figures for the United Kingdom which show a rise in state social services expenditure (in particular education, health, housing and social security) from around 4 per cent of the Gross National Product in 1910 to 16 per cent by 1951 and 29 per cent by 1975, while the state's total social expenditures (which includes also transport, environment, industry, justice, the military and debt interest) increased from 13 per cent to 45 per cent to 58 per cent over the same years (1979: 77). He identifies four major 'immediate' reasons (1979:84–92) for the rise, stressing especially the last two: rising relative costs, population changes, new and improved services (more people in need and more categories of need) and growing and changing social needs, and notes the trend from private to public sector provision of services.

Jones compares figures for Britain and Australia which indicate a similar overall increase in the two countries in welfare spending (income maintenance, health and education) from the early 1960s to the mid-1970s from 12.6 per cent to 16.7 per cent of the Gross Domestic Product in Britain and from 9.6 per cent to 12.8 per cent in Australia

(1980:46). He (1980:48) comments that in the 1970s under the Labor Government there was a notable shift in Australian public spending towards services, whereas previously 'welfare' had chiefly meant social security cash benefit schemes, though he concludes that even now compared with Europe, the Australian welfare state is relatively 'underdeveloped' (1980:5).

In *In and Against the State*, the London Edinburgh Weekend Return Group (1980:52) points out that commonly the 'welfare' part of the modern capitalist state is described as its 'good' side, where it attempts to remedy inequalities, injustices and deficiencies caused by the capitalist system, to be contrasted with the 'bad side' (defence, law and order, aid to business). It is this combination or intermixture of 'care' and 'control' that it is important to recognise as being a fundamental feature of the modern state in the western world. A number of other processes are relevant to an analysis of the modes and mechanisms of social control in modern industrial societies. These are the processes of rationalisation and bureaucratisation, professionalisation, the increasing importance of science and technology, medicalisation, and the emergence of welfarism and the 'therapeutic ideal'.

For Kittrie the 'therapeutic state' represents the 'merger of the newly broadened public welfare role of the state with the reforming drive of the social and behavioral sciences' (1971:11). He looks at mental illness, juvenile delinquency, psychopathy, drug addiction, alcoholism, and the use of surgical, biochemical and psychological methods for 'treating' particular categories such as the sterilisation of sexually violent men and mentally defective women. Kittrie and others (Pearson, 1975) are critical of many of the consequences of this process.

Others have focussed on the progressive (not necessarily in both senses of this term) 'medicalisation' of an increasing range of socially undesirable or problem categories of individuals. Ehrenreich and Ehrenreich make the important point that though medicalisation involves an 'expansion' of medical social control, medicine also operates in an 'exclusionary' way: the aim of the former being 'to encourage people both to enter sick roles and to seek professional help in a variety of nonsick situations' and of the latter to 'discourage entry into sick roles' (1974:29) and they relate the two types to class and gender. The middle and upper classes and women in particular were the targets of the expansionary activities of the medical system especially in the late nineteenth century, while 'disciplinary control. . .was aimed at the not-yet sick, the working poor' (1974:30).

Overall the medicalisation trend has caused considerable concern. What appears to be a move towards 'nicer', 'softer' and subtler forms of social control is seen as potentially dangerous from the point of view of individual freedom, civil rights and personal responsibility and of the power it gives to the medical profession and medical institutions over health, health care, individuals' lives and society. A major source of anxiety is the fact that the activities of medical personnel are largely beyond public scrutiny or direct government regulation. The individualisation and depoliticisation of human problems and social conditions that a 'medical model' entails are also regarded as undesirable.

While there has been pressure to decriminalise in some areas, (reflecting both the so called 'permissiveness' of the 1960s and the policy implications of labelling theory)[45] there has been, and continues to be, in others an increase in state regulation of individuals' lives and intervention in what were previously regarded as the 'private' spheres of personal relationships and organisational behaviour including both such issues as environmental protection, health, safety, discrimination and harassment in the work-place, and relationships within marriage and the family. In the family, for instance, the rights of parents and husbands have been redefined and to some extent curtailed as a result of pressure for the law to be used more effectively to protect children and wives especially from domestic violence.[46] The state also exercises control over marital breakdown, divorce and the associated custody and property settlements. In both these cases, state intervention can take a variety of forms: civil or criminal court hearings, imposition of penalties, voluntary or compulsory counselling, social worker investigations, etc., and involves a whole range of more or less obvious types of regulation of marital, familial and sexual relationships.[47] As a result there has been a further blurring of the division between public and private spheres (Sumner, 1983:133, 136).

In the 1970s there was a demand that the criminal law move into areas of deviant behaviour involving privileged sections of the community and/or enforce existing legislation more vigorously. Various interest groups, marxist sociologists and critical criminologists alerted us to what Little (1983) calls 'elite deviance', Box (1983) terms 'corporate crime', Pearce (1976) describes as 'crimes of the powerful' and Quinney (1977:50–1) categorises as 'crimes of domination'. Business, white-collar, organisational and professional 'crime' and a whole range of government 'sins of omission and commission', it was claimed, were not being defined as immoral or illegal nor being prosecuted as criminal because of the way wealthy and influential groups and organisations escaped the attention of the criminal law. In so far as western governments have made some limited attempt to meet this kind of complaint, they have in the main invoked the civil law and utilised various types of administrative and regulatory machinery, on the whole, their critics contend, ineffectually.[48] Cohen (1979b) discusses this 'moral mixture' of 'nihilism' and 'absolutism' in his excellent analysis of the criminal justice debate among American and British academic sociologists and radical criminologists during the 1970s.

The 1960s also saw a move towards what Cohen describes as the 'destructuring' of social control on a number of dimensions. As he puts it:

> We appear to be at the peak of a profound destructuring impulse. Those deep structures of the late eighteenth century—so beautifully and (to my mind) convincingly exhumed by Foucault—are alleged to be fracturing. The rhetoric of reform became abolitionist. The slogans are literally destructive: deinstitutionalization, decarceration, deprofessionalization, delegalization, demedicalization, anti-psychiatry, decentralization, deformalization, decriminalization, etc. And when all those walls began to crumble, so new, looser, and so much *nicer* arrangements would be set up; community control, informalism, neighbourhood justice, mediation, self help, the culture of civility. (1984:83, original emphasis).

Within this area , then, Cohen encompasses what others have identified as deinstitutionalisation or decarceration, but much more besides. The institutional approach to the management of a whole range of problem categories was being seriously reassessed. A number of alternative methods and approaches were being proposed which would avoid segregation, physical removal from the rest of the community, an over-regulated and artificial environment, and consequent stigma and difficulty in reestablishing a 'normal' life. This was the rhetoric and behind this were the facts that the previous measures did not seem to work and that the new methods would bring financial savings to governments. 'Care in the community' was so obviously cheaper, as well as being more socially acceptable in the current climate of opinion. This also involved the 'dispersion' or 'diversion' of social control, meaning more agencies and modes of social control and more diffuse and subtle forms of social control the effect of which, it was argued, would be to bring more people within the control 'net' but this fact would be disguised by the accompanying rhetoric.

A number of authors in the field have examined this phenomenon both as a proposed major policy change (with all sorts of ideological and other justifications) and in terms of what has actually happened during the 1970s and early 1980s. 'Destructuring' involves the replacement of control strategies based on exclusion by ones which assume inclusion and containment within the community (Cohen, 1985:76–83; Spitzer, 1982: 188–9). For Cohen, the whole process is captured in the concept of 'reintegration' (which replaces the previous master theme of 'reformation'), and the related notions in the crime control area of 'reparation, restitution, repayment and reconciliation' (1985:77).

A major feature of this shift in control ideology is the 'decarceration' or 'deinstitutionalisation' of criminals and mental patients. Scull's (1977) basic thesis, in his classic account of the nature, sources and consequences of this movement in Britain and America, is that the whole process was initiated for economic not ideological reasons; the main cause was the 'fiscal crisis' of the welfare state. His analysis has been variously criticised.[49] Scull has revised his position (1981a, 1981b, 1983, 1984) and now recognises that somewhat different elements and results are involved in respect to the treatment of mental illness, as compared with the criminal justice and corrections field. Specifically, as Cohen (1985:104–5, 131–2) also argues, deinstitutionalisation has gone further in the mental health sector of the social control system, one major factor being a lesser level of public concern over psychological and emotional disorders than over law-breaking.

Careful examination of policies and programmes in the crime and delinquency control area has revealed that decarceration has not resulted in the anticipated shift from punitive institutional sentences to treatment oriented, community based alternatives. Austin and Krisberg (1981) conclude from their evaluation of the realities and effects of six current policies in America—deinstitutionalisation, diversion, decriminalisation, deterrence, increasing due process, just deserts—that, despite their 'reform' potential (which is clear in all cases except deterrence), there has been instead an expansion and intensification of state intervention in crime control and management.[50]

In their attempt to capture the nature of social systems and patterns and the consequences of changes in social control, various writers (including Cohen, 1979a, 1985) have employed the highly appropriate and illuminating metaphor of 'nets'. For Austin and Krisberg (1981), whether intended or not, the consequences of current developments in social control (which they also illustrate from the criminal justice field) are 'wider, stronger and different nets'.

Critical observers of the current control strategies of the capitalist state conclude that, whatever the public rhetoric and the reasons given, these measures result in an overall increase in the number and range of types of control, a proliferation of control agencies and mechanisms, the reappearance of private (including profit making) organisations, a widening of the scope of control systems and a broadening of the definitions and categories of deviance to be brought under official control. American writers have identified some of the specific processes associated with this general trend: see Warren (1981); Abel (1982); Spitzer and Scull, (1977b); Scull, (1981a). Using different arguments, Bottomley (1979) and Bottoms (1983) point to counter trends in the current criminal justice and correctional fields: on the one hand, a disenchantment with rehabilitation and reemphasis on punishment, and, on the other, a continued reliance by the English courts on dispositions that are non-disciplinary (in Foucault's sense) and non-treatment, such as the fine.

Others have drawn attention to the gap between rhetoric and reality. The policy of community-based care for such groups as the aged, the mentally ill and those with a chronic illness or disability is still more an idea than a reality. Feminists particularly have pointed out the implications of such proposals where insufficient attention and funding is given for the adequate development of alternative services. This means in effect families, and specifically women, not 'the community' end up with the responsibility for caring for any members who come under these categories of dependency (Finch and Groves (eds), 1983; Mowbray and Bryson, 1984; Wilson, 1977).

The overall effects of these general processes are that traditional distinctions upon which sociologists have relied between public and private spheres and between formal and informal institutions and methods seem no longer to be meaningful or useful in the current circumstances,[51] and the boundaries between state and non-state agencies and mechanisms become blurred.

The current 1980s situation in industrial capitalist countries is in marked contrast to the earlier post-war pattern. The changes date from the mid-1970s when significant public expenditure cuts occurred following what O'Connor (1973) has termed 'the fiscal crisis of the state' and what others see as a complex and inter-related set of economic, political and ideological crises confronting modern western capitalist society. Graycar reports a levelling out of overall social expenditure by the Australian Commonwealth Government from the mid-1970s, after a rise from 12 per cent of Gross Domestic Product in 1963/4 to 14 per cent in 1972/3 and 21 per cent by November 1975 (when Whitlam lost power). Though overall Commonwealth Budget expenditure rose between 1975/6 and 1981/2, only social security and welfare spending increased proportionately more, while education, health, housing, urban and regional development all expanded at a lesser rate (1983:4), and Graycar gives figures which reveal that the increases were largely in unemployment and sickness benefits which can be attributed to the effects of economic recession (1983:6). This in his view constitutes the evidence for a 'retreat from the Welfare State'.

State expenditure overall on human services or 'welfare' in the broadest sense has been redirected rather than reduced (Taylor, 1981: 29–31) despite the public pronouncements of monetarist governments. Though the contribution to the 'social wage' has diminished, rising unemployment, increasing numbers in and levels of poverty, and greater concern over real or imagined problems of law and order have all demanded the state's attention and increased allocations of revenue. This suggests not a 'dismantling' but a 'restructuring' of the welfare state (Gough, 1979:138) in the direction of a 'stronger', 'tougher' and 'harsher' state, with a correspondingly greater emphasis on the use of physical force, coercion, surveillance and repression both domestically and in foreign policy (Held, 1984; London Edinburgh Weekend Return Group, 1980:Postscript; Ratner and McMullan, 1983).[52] The signs, one writer notes, include:

> . . . the number of police rapidly increasing, their technological and quasi-military capacities shamelessly strengthened, their discretionary powers of apprehension, interrogation, detention, and arrest liberally extended, and new prisons built or old ones

> extensively refurbished (all with money the government claims the country has not got to maintain existing standards of education, health, unemployment welfare, and social services). (Box, 1983:1)

This pattern of development has been particularly noticed by writers whose primary interest is the crime, law and justice area. They have expressed concern from both liberal and radical standpoints at current trends which seem either more extreme or at least more apparent in Australia (Boehringer et al., 1983). Cohen comments that 'the relationship between formal and informal is not cyclical or complementary (one contracts while the other expands) but additive: by "dislodging", the formal institutions increase their capacity. . . The state remains the only legitimate form of authority and grows, rather than contracts, by "delegation and devolution"' (1985:138–9). The overall pattern is one of 'redistribution from the soft to the hard edge of the system' (Cohen, 1985:133), or what Sumner describes as the state resorting to 'closure, repression and evasion' (1983:147). This has also been referred to as the 'rise of the exceptional state' (Ratner and McMullan, 1983) and is accompanied by an increase in the power of the Right.

In presenting an analysis of this kind emphasising the move towards repressive forms of social control and state intervention, we need to guard against the danger of falling into overly reified and deterministic ways of thinking about what the state is and does, and how social control works. Many modern writers, including some of those who are most concerned with and critical of current trends, argue on theoretical and political grounds against monolithic conceptions of the state and in particular its control apparatuses and functions. They prefer a different model of power and social structure and a conception of the state as a set of social relations and practices. In their view, the state not only reflects and responds to but also contains within itself the social divisions, conflicts, crisis and contradictions of modern society: the state is a major arena of struggle. This is well expressed in the title of the book produced by and for state employees who are also socialists, *In and Against the State*. Through a variety of mechanisms, including both well-established democratic institutions and methods of representation and more direct and less conventional tactics of protest groups and the 'new social movements', resistance and opposition is expressed and alternatives presented and fought for. The real issue from this perspective is not how to reduce, overcome or remove the state but how to modify and use its stuctures and procedures to bring about the kinds of social change that are desired.

To summarise, from this examination of changing patterns in the forms and levels of social control during the nineteenth century and since, the overall trend has been towards an increase in the number and scope of officially sanctioned control institutions and mechanisms. In practice until late in the nineteenth century control even of crime and certainly of dependency and other forms of deviance, as well as the regulation of most aspects of everyday life in democratic, industrialising societies, was primarily the responsibility and the concern of a whole range of 'private' agencies, organisations, groups and individuals. From the middle of the century social control, first in America and Europe and later in Australia, became increasingly specialised and professionalised and the state steadily increased its involvement in all forms and areas of control. Over the twentieth century these trends have continued and there have been further increases in the role of the state in social control that can be linked to, among other things, two world wars. Though there are important differences in control orientations, mechanisms and ideologies at different times over the period since the second world war, neither the first 'welfare state' phase, with its recognition of more categories of need, its provision of more services for more people and its emphasis on a more caring and humane approach, nor the second phase which saw attempts at 'destructuring', the moves for decriminalisation and normalisation, and the 'permissive society', nor the current phase of 'the strong state' (combined with state encouragement of a return to privatisation in some areas) have produced any decrease in formal, official modes and techniques of social control or any overall reduction in state activity in the control field.

5 The legal–judicial system

To those living in the modern world, there seems little doubt that the most serious and direct threat to social order comes from crime and the most important and obvious mechanisms of social control are those associated with the law, criminal justice and corrections.

Definitions of crime and the law present a classic example of the circular logic characteristic of much of the thinking, academic as well as popular, in the field of deviance and social control. Crime is conduct that the law prohibits and the law is the authority by which particular types of deviant and anti-social behaviour are designated crimes. However, although it is certainly true that in all societies authoritative judgements are made about what are to be considered unacceptable forms of conduct and sanctions are applied to those who transgress established norms, crime as a particular categorisation of deviance and the criminal law as a particular institutional mechanism for dealing with deviance are relatively recent and historically specific phenomena.

> Far from being a universal response to trouble, crime became a popular method of disapproval only in the late 18th century and was the dominant method of control for the next one hundred years. (Spector, 1981:129)

Spector points out that, prior to the development of a specific criminal law in western Europe, religion and the civil law (with provision for private compensation for wrongs or torts) were the principal control mechanisms. As we learned in the previous chapter (and as Spector briefly documents), in modern industrial societies the two major institutional approaches to social control are those of law and of medicine, usually operating separately, but sometimes in conjunction and sometimes in competition. Since the last century, though the criminal law and justice system continue to operate as major control agencies the medical or 'therapeutic' model has progressively extended its jurisdiction over a diverse range of social problems, including some previously defined as crimes, a process that is now widely described as medicalisation.

The other significant development in the social control field, which started somewhat later, is the expansion of state regulatory agencies functioning independently of the traditional criminal justice system and affecting particularly those areas such as industry and commerce and the family, areas that have conventionally been perceived as 'private' and relatively free of government interference. Such measures do involve legal or quasi-legal techniques and procedures, including provision for penal sanctions. These are rarely used, as on the whole civil remedies (conciliation and compensation) for infringement of government regulations are the preferred strategies for dealing with business and the corporate sector, as a recent Australian book on the subject shows clearly (Grabosky and Braithwaite, 1986).

The kind of analysis of social control we are undertaking here sees social control institutions and methods as social products and therefore as historically and culturally variable. We are interested primarily in the main public or formal systems that are responsible for handling the kinds of social problems that confront modern western societies. In this and the two subsequent chapters, we will look in turn at three such systems, the legal, the medical and the welfare systems.

In each of these three chapters, a similar structure for organising and presenting material will be adopted. We will start with some discussion of what is meant by each of the terms, then move on to a detailed examination of how each system operates (taking into account the different contributions made by the four perspectives we have identified), and conclude with an overall assessment of the control aspects of each system and its operations.

Conceptions of the law, criminal justice and corrections

For obvious historical reasons, of the three systems of control with which this book is concerned, only law and its related institutions were treated by the early social theorists as a major topic of sociological interest. Marx, Durkheim and Weber all devoted considerable attention to the law in its social context.

Durkheim saw the law as part of the basic normative order of both traditional and modern societies. The law represents the collective conscience: it is the 'visible symbol' of social solidarity, which is in itself 'immaterial' in character (1964:64). In his view, what was significant was the change from repressive to restitutive forms of law and approaches to control that accompanied the shift from mechanical to organic solidarity, a thesis which is now widely disputed empirically (de Espinosa, 1980; Schwartz and Miller, 1964; Spitzer, 1975b). In spite of an often insightful discussion of the nature and role of different types of law and legal sanctions, Durkheim's basic proposition that 'law may safely be treated as an undistorted reflection of society's collective morality' (Lukes and Scull, 1983:6) prevented him from recognising the variable and often problematic nature of the relationships between law, morality, custom and society.

Marx and Weber were interested particularly in law in its distinctively modern western form and they linked this with the rise of the state and the development of capitalism and industrialism. Both theorists also asked questions about the interconnections between legal forms, institutions and procedures and the economic, political and class structures of contemporary Western European society. Weber stressed that modern law differs from custom or convention in that it is based on rationality rather than tradition. It is formalised and codified, it is administered by specially designated and trained staff, and it derives its authority ultimately from the coercive power of the state.

Marx also focussed on the relationship between the law and the state, but for him both these institutions are primarily expressions of and serve as instruments for class control. Marx and Engels and most later marxists (Pashukanis being the notable exception) see law and the state as institutions found not only in capitalist society but also in all class societies (including ancient civilisations and feudalism). Most of their writing, however, concerns the nature and role of these institutions under capitalism. In the marxist view, law operates both directly as an instrument of repression based on its use of force and indirectly through its ideological representation or misrepresentation of social relations and class interests (this distinction between repressive and ideological techniques of state control was taken up and developed by Gramsci and Althusser among others and was discussed more fully in Chapter 3). The apparently universal character of bourgeois notions such as citizen, property, equality, justice and rights disguises the real nature of class relations.

Marx also recognises the diversity of forms of legislation and legally-based state regulatory instruments that can be employed in the interests of capital; these include not only the criminal law, and laws relating to property, contract and economic transactions, but also a range of measures concerned with the factory system, with unions and with the control of labour and the labour process generally. As Cain and Hunt (1979) argue in the excellent commentary that accompanies their extensive collection of extracts from the writings of Marx and Engels on the law, the account given of the law (and ideological forms generally) by these writers was not a simple economic determinist one (and this was particularly true of Engels). In the transition from feudalism to capitalism and in established capitalist societies,

> Legislation is both an active agency in historical processes and at the same time, it records and encapsulates the balance between social forces at particular historical moments and the ideological forms in which these struggles are fought out. (Cain and Hunt, 1979: 65)

Our concern here lies with the forms and functions of the law and of those institutions responsible for the formulation, interpretation and administration of the law that are characteristic of western industrial societies. Though something that we may call law exists across a whole range of types of society,[1] sociologists interested in the study of the law draw a major distinction between 'traditional' and 'modern', pre-industrial and industrial, or 'acephalous' (stateless) and 'state' societies (Michalowski, 1981 and Pfohl, 1981), and concentrate their attention on the latter. The organisational features of modern societies which, following Marx and Weber, are seen as critical for the kind of law and legal—judicial system that has developed in the modern western world are a particular type of political system (the bourgeois or rational state), a particular mode of production (capitalist or industrial), a complex division of labour and stratification system, bureaucratisation and secularisation.

Tigar and Levy (1977) see modern law as unique in form and content but argue that its origins can be traced back some eight hundred years (to the first signs in Europe of the emergence of cities, trade and commerce and a bourgeoisie). Weber also describes in some detail the development of the categories of legal thought and the set of administrative norms and procedures that make modern rational law distinctive (Rheinstein, 1954). As Spitzer (1979:187) has put it: 'historically-specific forms of legally-based coercion which have emerged over the last two centuries represent both a reflection of and a basis for the progressive rationalization of social life in capitalist societies'. In the previous chapter, we looked at the analysis by Spitzer and Scull (1977a) and others of the process by which crime control became in the eighteenth century a private profit-making business and only during the nineteenth century did the state gradually take over the responsibility (and they comment on the current trend towards reprivatisation in this area). According to their definitions:

> By public crime control arrangements we mean those which are characteristically supported by taxation, organized on a bureaucratic basis, and operated directly by full-time employees of the state. Private forms, by contrast, are predicated on a market or contractual relationship. (Spitzer and Scull, 1977a: 267)

What is distinctive about the law as a form of social control in the modern western world is its formal, public and official nature. This is reflected in the way laws are presented as sets of uniformly applicable, impersonally administered, rule-governed regulations and procedures and by the fact that the source of their legitimacy lies in the centralised authority of the state with ultimately the resort to the use of physical force. The law is used to add extra institutional authority to the prescriptions of custom and morality, to adjudicate between competing claims from members of society (which usually means reinforcing the position of dominant groups) and, in accordance with pre-existing principles, to enforce its own decisions. This means the law is implicated in all the major areas of social life, both public and private (though in the past, the state has often exercised its control by non-interference in key private sectors like the family and the workplace and/or by legislation that upholds the rights of the powerful in such settings). The modern state employs a whole range of institutions, mechanisms and procedures to help it rule and it works through private and semi-private as well as public agencies. Indeed a much stressed feature of the 'welfare' or 'interventionist' state of the mid-twentieth century is the proliferation of regulations and regulatory bodies on which government increasingly depends, all of which enjoy legal status. Though some important recent work on this aspect of governmental social control will be discussed in this and a later chapter, our main focus here is on the criminal law and related institutions as primary mechanisms of social control. The criminal law is distinctive in that:

> It defines behavior which is deemed intolerably disturbing to or destructive of community values and prescribes sanctions which the state is authorised to impose on persons convicted or suspected of engaging in prohibited conduct. (Goldstein, 1960: 544)

Under 'the law' must be included both ideas and institutions. By the law most obviously is meant the whole body of accumulated norms, rules, principles and doctrines and here writers draw a distinction between procedural and substantive aspects of the law: the former referring to the rules governing the organisation and operation of those institutions responsible for the administration of the law, and the latter to the rules setting out the guidelines for acceptable behaviour generally in society. However, 'the law' is employed also as a broad term covering both what is contained in statutes (the law 'in theory') and what legal bodies actually do (the law 'in practice'). It involves the whole range of mechanisms and procedures, personnel and organisations engaged in the interpretation and implementation of the law.

Since we are interested primarily in the forms of control that western societies have developed to deal with those types of deviance that are considered 'crimes', we will be dealing with the criminal law and the criminal justice system. What this involves is the study of the form and content of particular legislation, and the processes of detection and investigation of crime, arrest and charging of suspects, prosecution and trial, the determination of guilt or innocence and sentencing, and various forms of punishment. A number of institutions participate in these processes—law enforcement agencies, courts and prisons—and different categories of personnel—police, lawyers, magistrates, judges and correctional staff. All of these need investigation and analysis if we are to produce a sociological account of the legal, judicial and correctional systems in countries like Australia.

Briefly, then, our focus is on the criminal law and on the main subsystems of the criminal justice system, the police, the courts and corrections. Earlier, we looked at changing approaches to policing, and to punishment and corrections in Western Europe from the early nineteenth century. In this chapter we will concentrate mainly on contemporary aspects of the administration of criminal justice and we will draw on the various bodies of sociological theory and research that are currently available to help us understand these phenomena.

As one would expect and as we shall see, there are substantial differences among different theoretical schools in their views of the relationship between the law and social and moral norms and the role played by the legal-judicial system with respect to the maintenance of social order. At a very general level, however, there is substantial agreement among sociologists over the main features of this system in its modern western form—its rationality, formality, universalism, specialisation, professionalism, reliance on penal sanctions[2] and, what Kennedy (1976:37) calls its 'politicality' (that is its direct connection to government or the state).

Of the theoretical perspectives in which we are particularly interested in this volume, only structural functionalism, and specifically Parsons (1951, 1962), seems to accept the classic liberal conception of law and justice as a neutral technical means for achieving collective ends (in particular social integration) by providing mechanisms for reinforcing morality and for discouraging and containing deviance and conflict. His analysis is entirely in terms of law as a 'normative' device operating within a consensual situation and, given his general model of society, there is no allowance for the possibility of law serving sectional interests or being confronted with fundamental social divisions and disputes between competing groups.[3] The other three perspectives, though to differing extents and in different ways, all assume a conflict model of society and the importance of exploring the links between the power and interests of various organisations and groups and the nature and functioning of the law and the criminal justice system. A common characterisation of the legal system, one not specific to any single perspective, is that its primary task is the management of potential and actual disputes and conflicts (though of course functionalists and non-functionalists interpret this differently). Bredemeier (a functionalist) talks of the 'orderly resolution of conflicts' (1962:74), Rock (an interactionist) of the need 'to restrain the opportunities which men [sic] enjoy to hurt one another' (1979:78), Black (1984:7) of 'grievances' being expressed and redressed, and Christie of the 'prevention and solution of social conflicts' (1971:358). Galanter (1974) constructs a whole typology of types of litigation based on the characteristics of claims and parties to claims. Black (1976:4), Christie and Galanter (and indeed many other writers) stress the distinctive feature of legal-judicial modes of conflict regulation and social control as being adversarial or accusatory (whether this takes a criminal or civil form and has a penal or a compensatory outcome).

Much of the work done in the fields of the sociology of law and criminal justice up to the mid-1960s was conducted from either a liberal/empiricist or a functionalist/consensus standpoint. Then various forms of conflict theory (first interactionism and labelling theory, and interest group theory, and later a renewal of interest in the perspectives of Marx and Weber) took over the field. At the same time there has also been an increasing recognition of the significance of the gender dimension and of the relevance of feminist versions of conflict theory. By the 1970s, as O'Malley puts it, 'rapid theoretical and research expansion within the "conflict" approach had the double effect of opening up major cleavages within its ranks and of pushing consensualist theories to the sidelines' (1983:4).

Turk has summarised what he regards as the fundamental differences between consensus and conflict approaches in this field: 'conflict-coercion defines law as power, conflict as ubiquitous struggle, and order as the balance of power, while integration-consensus theory defines law as authority, conflict as unnecessary struggle, and order as voluntary association' (1976:282). Subsequently, he and Grimes (1981: 252–3) suggest that only those who take a marxist position adopt a 'neutral' (by which they mean a non-positive) conception of the law, whereas interactionists, like functionalists, they claim, work with a 'normative' definition of the law, as a 'good thing', though, unlike functionalists, they take a relativist view of deviance. Similarly Quinney (1974:Chapter 1) argues that the crucial difference between the two main bodies of writing on the sociology of criminal law, the one empirically-oriented (and in this he includes interactionism) and the other based on marxist theory, is the critical stance that is associated with the latter.

Commentaries and assessments of theory and research in this area by those committed to a conflict or marxist approach (like Turk and Quinney) tend to disregard the differences between empiricism, functionalism and interactionism and to categorise all these schools together as taking a non-critical and consensual approach which they then contrast, unfavourably, with their own. Some, however, acknowledge significant differences, not least on the issue of consensus, between functionalism and the labelling/interactionist perspective. They see the latter as constituting a third alternative to the straight consensus/conflict polarisation. Michalowski and Bohlander (1976), for example, call this position 'pluralist' and locate it in between the other two. Others perceive the 'new' deviance writers as moving away from pluralism as well as from functionalism, in particular in respect of their treatment of power as a structural dimension of social order (Grimes and Turk, 1978; Hall and Scraton, 1981). Common to all these accounts is, nevertheless, the notion that no perspective can deal adequately with the phenomena of deviance and control, law and order, without recognition of the centrality of structural bases of division and conflict in society and of the importance of the treatment of power and class in the analysis of the nature of legal, political and other forms of social control, and it is on these criteria that labelling theory and interactionism are found wanting.[4]

Though there are some insights to be gained from general comparisons of this kind between categories of theories, neither marxism nor interactionism/labelling theory, as we discovered in earlier chapters and as Turk and Grimes (1981) themselves concede, can be reduced to single homogeneous theoretical entities, nor can key figures in the field, such as Quinney and Turk, whose positions have changed over time, be easily assigned to a single perspective. To do justice to the material produced by sociologists working in the areas of law, criminal justice and corrections from the 1960s on, we need to recognise the differences between the various perspectives which claim to be taking a conflict approach and this includes differences within as well as between the major perspectives.

An alternative basis for comparison to the consensus/conflict division is the distinction between micro and macro levels of analysis in the study of law and criminal justice. For McBarnet micro is identified with interactionist sociology and macro in its old version with positivist social administration and in its new version with marxism. This division she claims is related to the split between those interested in 'the law in action' and 'the law in the books' (1978:25–6). Her basic thesis is that all such dichotomies need to be overcome as both dimensions are equally necessary, and closely inter-related. (McBarnet's work calls for some fundamental rethinking of the nature of 'the law' and of the relationship between legal rules and legal practice and will be discussed more fully later in the chapter.)

Traditional texts in this area all followed a similar pattern. Typically they started with a discussion of particular pieces of legislation and of the general relationship between norms, values and the law, which led on to an analysis of the institutions responsible for the administration and enforcement of the law and for the punishment of offenders, and then sometimes some assessment of the effectiveness of the system in countering crime. Essentially, their analyses reflected a basically liberal value position: that laws are for the equal benefit and protection of all right-minded people, that the administration of justice is fair and impartial, and that crime is the product of personal pathology, or of inadequacies in the family or community. From this standpoint, the workings of the criminal justice system are perceived to have few problems, and any that occur are attributed to deficiencies in personnel or resources.

By contrast, the studies that were conducted from the 'new' sociology of deviance perspective in the 1960s and 1970s rejected the liberal ideology surrounding the nature and operations of the law, criminal justice and corrections. The characteristics of labelling theory and interactionism were described in an earlier chapter. Basically they propose that social control involves the imposition of rules and sanctions by those with more power on those with less, and that deviance is the result of the processing of individuals by particular agencies and their personnel and of the social and organisational conditions under which they work. Those applying this approach to the study of the criminal law and the justice system asked questions about how and why particular laws were made, by whom and in whose interests, how the various enforcement agencies operated and what the system did to deviants, and attempted to answer some of these questions through empirical research. Social and organisational factors and processes (both formal and informal) were shown to be responsible for the patterns of law enforcement and for variations in such patterns.

Differences between the accounts given by functionalists (and most legal scholars prior to 1960) and by those taking a pluralist or non-marxist conflict approach (such as interactionists) are to be found over several basic issues: whether the law (and specifically particular laws) reflects the collective good or sectional interests; whether the descriptions given of legal and judicial institutions are of their formal structures and official procedures or are empirically-based analyses of the actual operations of agencies and personnel; whether inconsistencies and imperfections in the administration of the law are interpreted as exceptional cases or as inherent in the structures and processes; and whether the whole legal system is taken on its own terms or viewed from an external and critical standpoint.

Gradually during the 1970s, with the development of the 'radical' and 'critical' schools of criminology and penology, conceptualisations of power and conflict and of the relationship between crime, the law and other institutions and processes in society became increasingly marxist. Initially the kind of model that was being used was a relatively simple class conflict one, which entailed an instrumentalist view of the law, though later work shows increasingly the influence of structuralism.[5]

Though there are fundamental differences between the labelling/interactionist perspective and marxism, some of the ideas advanced by the sociology of deviance school (in particular their questioning of the objective status of the law and of crime and deviance as unproblematic categories, and their suggestion that the law, criminal justice and social control generally are not impersonal systemic processes but the products of the interests and actions of identifiable groups and organisations) provided a useful basis on which 'critical' theories of crime and the law could build. Quinney (1970, 1974, 1977) is a prime example of a writer in this field who started from a position which combined elements of interactionism and interest group theory with a model of society as 'politically organised' around the interests of key institutions and segments that goes beyond a simple pluralist conception and whose thinking during the 1970s moved consistently in a marxist direction.

With the reemergence of marxism in western sociology, analysis moved from a generalised treatment of power and conflict between groups and subcultures to a model of society in which there are specific dominant agencies and centres of power—the ruling class and the state—whose power derives from their position and function in the capitalist system. Given the place occupied by the law in its role as a major instrument of class repression and ideological control in the work of Marx and Engels and later marxists, not surprisingly the focus of interest shifted from social deviance (a concept covering a wide and diverse range of phenomena that had meaning only within particular sociological frameworks) to crime, an apparently more concrete category, and one with greater theoretical significance. For most, the appeal of marxism lay in its capacity to provide an overall structural theory within which the substance and operation of the law could be interpreted and in a more satisfactory way than previous alternative perspectives seemed to be able to do. One response that led to considerable debate among marxists working in this area was to argue that crime is no more legitimate a Marxian notion than deviance and further, that empirical studies of crime and the law are useless and there could be no such thing as a marxist theory of crime and the law (the issue is discussed by Hirst, 1975; Sumner, 1976; Taylor, Walton and Young, 1975). While the majority took a less extreme view, there was a general preference particularly in Britain for theoretical rather than empirical work, with the aim of producing a more complex understanding of both the dependency and the 'relative autonomy' of the legal order and the state in capitalist society (for example, the edited collections by Bankowski and Mungham, 1980; Carlen and Collison, 1980; Fitzgerald et al., 1981; Sugarman, 1983).

The 'critical' orientation in marxism and the 'relativist' or 'sceptical' (Cohen, 1971:14) element in labelling and interactionist theory meant that neither school accepted the law and the criminal justice system were what they claimed to be. However, because of the fundamental theoretical differences between these perspectives their analyses and the subjects they chose to study, though not necessarily incompatible, were rather different. The labelling/interactionist school produced a whole range of careful empirical investigations of the actual workings of different parts of the criminal justice system, often exposing major discrepancies between rhetoric and reality. Where such writers took sides, the position they aligned themselves with was that of the 'underdog'; almost invariably this involved viewing institutions and processes from the standpoint of the criminal (though Skolnick's (1967) study of the police from an empathic 'action' perspective was a notable exception).[6]

Marxists start from the premise that the law and its administration are part of the political and ideological apparatuses necessary for the preservation and legitimation of the capitalist system. Classic examples are studies of the way particular kinds of legislation and law enforcement procedures contributed to the historical development of capitalism (Pashukanis, 1978: Renner, 1949). More recent marxist work in the area reflects the theoretical developments in western marxism generally (Jessop, 1980[7]). Emphasising the ideological aspects of law and the criminal justice system over the coercive, and postulating a complex pattern of mutual reinforcement and contradiction between legal, political and ideological institutions, the class structure and the capitalist mode of production, current marxist thinking rejects earlier instrumentalist and economic reductionist conceptions of the relationship between the law, the state and capitalism.[8] One example of this kind of analysis (which draws on the work of Weber as well as on that of Marx and modern marxists) is O'Malley's (1983) book on the Australian legal order which we will look at in more detail later in the chapter.

Meanwhile, in this section of the chapter we have one more perspective to consider. It is a serious indictment of much of the so called 'new', 'radical', and 'critical' work in the sociology of the law, criminal justice and corrections that has appeared since the late 1960s that women and the gender dimension are treated as peripheral issues except where the authors were women. This is despite the acknowledged fact that throughout the western world women are significantly less criminal than men in terms of numbers, frequency and seriousness of offences and that both their offence patterns and their treatment by the legal-judicial system suggest gender-specific social factors and processes are at work. From the early 1970s, there has been a series of publications in the United States (Babcock, 1973; Chesney-Lind, 1974; Nagel and Weitzman, 1971), and a little later in Britain (Smart, 1976) and Australia (Scutt, 1976, 1978, 1979a), drawing attention to the neglect of women and the limitations of academic attempts at the explanation of criminality and of the workings of the criminal justice system that are based solely on material relating to men. Typically, the gender issue is dealt with descriptively by including some empirical material on women or sex differences where they appear to be especially relevant or controversial (the 'add on women' technique). Only rarely do male or non-feminist writers attempt to deal with gender divisions and inequalities as fundamental structural features of society or to build gender relations into their overall theoretical frameworks.[9] Even the (male) marxists, who in the 1970s were busy exposing other sources of ideological bias in sociological theorising, exhibited a remarkable degree of gender-blindness and androcentrism, and this has persisted into the 1980s.[10]

In an earlier chapter (Chapter 3), we examined various feminist theories of male domination and the gender order, and of the patriarchal nature of the modern capitalist state, and feminist analyses of mechanisms of social control, including the legal-judicial system. In the following section of this chapter, we will look at some feminist accounts of how the law, and the law enforcement and correctional agencies work in ways that systematically differentiate between, and in the process frequently also discriminate against, women whether as victims or offenders, or simply as citizens. Here we are referring not only to the differential treatment of females by the criminal law but also to feminist analyses of how women were and are constituted formally as legal subjects as compared with men. A strong feminist case has been made that, far from operating on neutral, universalistic principles as it claims, the law (like the state) represents the perspectives and interests of the dominant gender (and racial, ethnic and class) groups in society.[11] In the past, this meant that the law discriminated entirely negatively against women and girls. At the present there is some pressure on it from women to discriminate positively in their favour (for example most dramatically, in equal opportunity and affirmative action programmes but also in respect of wives/mothers in divorce and custody settlements, teenage girls' rights of control over their own sexuality, fertility and contraception, and the needs of women generally for protection from rape, domestic violence, sexual harassment and so on).

Sociological analysis of the law, criminal justice and corrections

It is not possible in a volume such as this to give an account of the full range of regulatory instruments, procedures and agencies based on the use of the law that are in operation in modern capitalist patriarchal societies. In deciding to concentrate on those whose object is crime control, we are excluding civil law (which is used by 'private' individuals to regulate the conduct of other individuals in areas such as marriage, divorce and the family, commerce, business and industrial relations). In addition, only brief reference will be made to an expanding and increasingly important area of state regulation over the activities of corporations and other non-public bodies through the use of agencies with statutory powers and responsibilities, whose work in three significant respects at least (namely the reliance on specialist staff, the investigative function and the authority to impose penal sanctions) parallels that of the conventional law-enforcement agencies.

An interesting recent Australian book by Grabosky and Braithwaite (1986) is worth mentioning here. In it they report the results of their major study of the regulatory provisions and practices of 96 public agencies working in the following fields: corporate affairs, consumer affairs, environment and radiation protection, food standards, anti-discrimination, occupational health and safety, transport safety, drugs and medical devices, and fraud with respect to medical benefits, tax and customs. These agencies are provided with a full armoury of enforcement measures, ranging from economic incentives for self-regulation, through encouragement of civil litigation, licensing and adverse publicity, to prosecution, issuing injunctions and directives, and seizure of goods (1986:183). The authors' overall finding was that, despite the existence of judicial and penal enforcement measures, 'none of the above enforcement tools are regularly used on a day-to-day basis in any but a handful of the agencies' (1986:190), and they mention specifically here the Trade Practices Commission, the Federal Taxation Office and some State Health Departments. The prevailing perception in the agencies of the problems with which they had to deal was of 'substandard practice' not of a 'criminal offence' (1986:191) and the preferred strategy was cooperative negotiation (particularly with the large companies), rather than recourse to more punitive techniques (and various explanations are put forward for these findings).

Our focus will be on the criminal law and the criminal justice system. Unlike the special regulatory machinery described above, a distinctive characteristic of the criminal law in its modern western form is that the 'crimes' with which it is concerned are acts committed by identifiable individuals against other identifiable individuals (Michalowski and Bohlander, 1976:101). The state's role is to intervene directly on behalf of the victim(s) and indirectly on behalf of society or a section of society. It has already been made clear that acts committed by individuals on individuals are typically what get considered 'crimes' and a whole range of 'covert institutional activities' (Liazos, 1972) in which social injuries are inflicted by various organisations (corporations, professions, unions) and by the state itself, so-called 'crimes of domination', are not treated as crimes (though they may be subject to other forms of regulation). Although there are practical difficulties and high costs associated with the detection and prosecution of the often very complicated and technically specialised types of dishonesty and exploitation occurring in such organisations, marxists and others concerned to expose this bias in the criminal law discount these as the real explanation for special treatment. Rather they regard the selectivity of the criminal law as an unavoidable feature of societies dominated by a capitalist class and capitalist state (Braithwaite, 1979; Pearce, 1976: Part 2; Quinney, 1977: Chapter 2).

The issue of bias in the criminal law has also been raised by feminists. Though in general laws are phrased in gender-neutral terms, feminists and others have drawn attention to the fact that some laws are discriminatory against women and girls. Smart distinguishes between 'sex-specific' and 'sex-related' offences. Sex-specific laws are ones which 'exclude the members of one sex by legal definition' (1976:6) either in the original statute or in accumulated case law and subsequent interpretation: infanticide and, up to recent times, adultery are examples. Sex-related offences are defined as those which 'may be committed by either sex but which in practice appear to be committed more by one sex than by the other' (1976:8). A better basis for distinction (which Smart mentions only briefly) lies between offences which are prohibited for members of one sex because the activity in question is presumed to be linked to biological differences between men and women (such as rape, homosexuality and prostitution) and offences related to gender-roles (shoplifting, child stealing and teenage sexual promiscuity). Many authors have drawn attention to the presence of discriminatory elements in juvenile statutes in the United States. Riback (1971), for example, focusses her attack on the vagueness and broadness of juvenile morals statutes, which provide plenty of scope for subjective and sexist interpretations and for differential and discriminatory enforcement given the prevailing double standard of sexual morality. An Australian study of Victorian legislation relating to juveniles and of the treatment of young males and females by the police and the courts, which was undertaken precisely to clarify this issue, found that gender discrimination occurred not in the framing of the statutes but in their implementation (Edwards Hiller and Hancock, 1981).

Scutt (1981) discusses a less visible aspect of sexism with respect to the criminal law. She suggests the law reflects dualistic notions of women and a double standard. In some instances (laws relating to infanticide, the traditional doctrine of couverture, and domestic violence) women are not considered as independent legal subjects,[12] while for other purposes women are held to be capable of exercising will and hence of taking responsibility for their own actions: in the case of prostitution, they alone are guilty of a crime; and in rape, the woman's behaviour is a critical factor in determining whether the event constitutes rape or consensual sexual intercourse. Edwards' (1981) investigation of rape laws in England reveals a dualistic notion also of women's sexuality which leads to an inconsistency in treatment: the statutes presume female sexual passivity, and court procedures an active role of offence-precipitation, on the part of women.

Before moving on to the detailed analysis of legal-judicial institutions as mechanisms of social control, we should perhaps discuss the meaning and appropriateness of the term 'system' in the context of the law, criminal justice and corrections. Sallman and Willis (1984) talk of criminal justice *systems*, by which they mean separate systems in each of the Australian States and in the Territories, as well as the one serving the Commonwealth. Other writers in the field express the theoretically-based reservation that the notion of 'system' carries functionalist overtones, emphasises formal over informal organisational features, and assumes a high degree of coherence and integration between the various institutions and functions (Baldwin and Bottomley,

1978: Introduction; Garland, 1983:x; Hogg, 1983:8). They prefer the conception of criminal justice as a complex set of interrelated processes rather than as a 'structure' or a 'system'. Certainly the concept is problematic (and not only with respect to the law and criminal justice, but also for medicine and welfare, the other control apparatuses we will be considering), but the term may still on occasion be a useful shorthand description of sets of institutions, personnel and practices with a common sphere of activity or area of responsibility.

Academics and practitioners working in the field of criminal law commonly draw a distinction between agencies and mechanisms concerned with lawmaking and those dealing with law enforcement, and divide the law enforcement further into three parts—investigation, adjudication and corrections. Sallman and Willis (1984) then point to an overall lack of clearly specified and uniform principles and goals to guide criminal justice policy and practice in Australia. This means the links between different parts of the process are *ad hoc*, pragmatic and related to administrative convenience, which, as we shall see, has important implications for the kind of social control that can be exercised.

There is a tendency for Australian books on criminal justice (except those designed for a narrow specialist legal readership) to include only material on the interpretation and implementation of the law and not to cover the laws themselves in any detail and their history not at all. This may partly be due to the scarcity of studies of the social origins of particular pieces of legislation (and this applies in Britain and America too) and partly be the consequence of the predominantly descriptive and empirical approach taken by most of the writers on the subject (for example, Biles, ed., 1977; Chappell and Wilson eds., 1977; Sallman and Willis, 1984).[13] Though this kind of orientation has been a significant tradition in British and American criminology and penology, and indeed continues up to the present date, much of the current work being produced by British criminologists (see Baldwin and Bottomley, eds, 1978) does provide a basis for a broader theoretical understanding of the administration of criminal justice, and is used extensively by Australian writers like Sallman and Willis. Much of the overseas work of sociologists and others in this area since the 1960s has, however, in general a far more theoretical character and books in which either a labelling/interactionist or a marxist perspective is adopted have usually attempted to provide material specifically on lawmaking, as well as on law enforcement (Box, 1971; Chambliss, 1969; Greenberg, 1981; Quinney, 1970, 1974; Rock, 1973b; Schur, 1971).

Feminists in their analyses of the law and criminal justice as they affect women have examined all aspects, including the circumstances surrounding the enactment of specific legislation and the phrasing of statutes, as well as how the various law enforcement agencies and personnel use the legislation and with what effects. Australian examples of such work are the previously mentioned study of differences in the processing of male and female juveniles, which looked both at the relevant legislation and at police and court practices (Edwards Hiller and Hancock, 1981) and Scutt's work on the law and its application with respect to rape (1979b, 1979c) and spouse assault (1980).

It was when various types of conflict approach began to emerge in the 1960s and offered a challenge to the previous consensus explanations for the existence and operation of the law that sociologists started to undertake analyses of particular pieces of legislation, drawing on interest group and elite theories and including ideas such as those of 'moral entrepreneurs' (Becker, 1963), 'symbolic crusades' (Gusfield, 1963) and 'moral panics' (Cohen, 1973). Famous American examples include studies of alcohol Prohibition (Gusfield, 1963) and drugs. With respect to the latter, although aspects of the interpretations vary, the accounts given by Becker (1963), Dickson (1968), Duster (1970) and Lindesmith (1965), and summarised in Chambliss (1976:87–90), and by Galliher and Walker (1977), of the laws controlling opiates (particularly the 1914 Harrison Act) and marihuana (the 1937 Act), all emphasise the crucial role played in the administration of what was originally a tax measure by the key law-enforcement agency in the field, the Federal Bureau of Narcotics, which was established in 1930. A third, American case reported by Roby (1969) concerns legislative changes relating to prostitution in New York, where various interests—welfare and civil liberties groups, bar associations, police and business—were all engaged in the struggle. Though no comparable sociological analysis is yet possible, the legal regulation of prostitution is currently undergoing change in Victoria, with the introduction of a licensing system for brothels and proposed legislation (following a special inquiry resulting in the Neave Report, 1985) for a considerable degree of decriminalisation of prostitution in the State.[14] Though not in the criminal law area, Hopkins' (1978) work on trade practices legislation in Australia provides an interesting example of how competing interests and groups (both political and economic) influence the development of legislation.

By the mid to late 1970s a more complex model of the law (and the state) as a mechanism for dealing with structural contradictions as well as social conflicts within capitalism was being advanced (what Chambliss, 1976, 1979 terms a 'dialectical' approach). A good illustration of this is the collection of papers published by the National Deviancy Conference in 1980 which looked critically at recent changes in the way the criminal law was dealing with a range of 'victimless crimes' (abortion, homosexuality, prostitution) and with the young. The mainly marxist authors, (such as Clarke, Greenwood and Young, Hall) argue there is an uneasy coexistence between competing, if not contradictory, control ideologies and policies: those of permissiveness and of intervention, of decriminalisation and criminalisation, of private and public forms of social regulation.

There are problems however, with attempts to treat the content of legislation separately from its application. The 'law' is both statute and implementation, a set of formal provisions and a whole collection of procedures and practices that develop over time. Any adequate analysis of criminal justice must, therefore, recognise the multiple levels on which the various systems and subsystems operate and on which they can be viewed by the sociologist: as formally constituted and legally defined; as culturally and ideologically perceived by politicians, legislators, their own personnel, the community in general, and others; and as produced and reproduced in the everyday actions of their members in their dealings with each other and with the 'clients' of the system—criminals and their victims. Although, as we shall discover, empirical research reveals as much inconsistency as it does consistency, as much independence as interdependence, between the different parts or subsystems, sociologists from each of the major perspectives have offered interpretations and explanations of the dominant forms and functions of the criminal justice system as a whole.

Bredemeier (1962), a Parsonian, examines the court system, as the embodiment of the law at a very general level, in relation to the functional prerequisites of the social system. Parsons himself (1951, 1962) talks only of the law and the role of the lawyer as professional and specialist and again in highly abstract theoretical terms. The characterisation of criminal justice and corrections that emerges in the work of labelling and interactionist writers is of control agents and agencies with their own ideologies, objectives and interests using their powers (both formal and informal) to impose their perceptions, evaluations and decisions on deviants. Law enforcement is seen as being as much a product of individuals and agencies' values and priorities as it is the result of formally prescribed procedures and policies.

A marxist conception of criminal justice is summarised (in an admittedly somewhat bald manner) by Michalowski and Bohlander:

> In the U.S. the legal order serves the interests of the capitalist ruling class by (1) facilitating the pursuit of capitalist goals, (2) legitimizing the repression of the economically and politically disadvantaged classes which must exist to maintain a capitalist distribution of wealth and who threaten capitalist interests through criminal activity, and (3) creating and maintaining a definition of 'crime' which guarantees the continued enjoyment of the first two benefits. (1976:100)

This is achieved through both ideological and the more obvious, directly repressive means. Modern marxists give considerable weight to the former, citing in particular bourgeois liberal notions of the individual, of property, of justice itself and of the neutrality of the law and law enforcement (Bankowski and Mungham, 1976; Clarke, 1978; Sugarman ed., 1983), as well as a whole range of cultural preconceptions and values about youth, the work ethic, the traditional family, the need for law and order, and so on that are consistent with and supportive of legal ideology (Hall et al., 1978). Recently, marxists have developed more sophisticated theoretical analyses of the relationships between the law and criminal justice, the ruling class and class conflict, and the state in contemporary capitalist society (de Sousa Santos, 1980).

Feminists also have particular theoretical constructions they put on the workings of legal, judicial and penal institutions in the modern western world. Adler vividly captures what many see as the essentially sexist character of the legal-judicial system:

> Woman throughout the ages has been mistress to the law, as man has been its master. Sometimes pampered, sometimes reviled, and always misunderstood, she has been the object rather than the subject of legal decisions. (1975:205)

Rafter and Natalizia (1981:84) identify two main forms of the sexism which they perceive as fundamental in the bourgeois moral code that underpins the law in capitalist society: 'paternalism, the restriction of women through enactment of "chivalrous" statutes ostensibly aimed at their protection', and an 'almost total failure to respond to issues of concern to women' (such as wife abuse or unsafe contraceptive techniques).

Before turning to a presentation of empirical material on the administration of the law and criminal justice, certain key conceptual notions and categorisations that have general relevance for our understanding of these processes need to be considered. These are the concepts of 'due process' and 'discretion' and various characterisations of current trends in social control.

In the previous chapter, the changing patterns of social control generally and crime control in particular since the nineteenth century were discussed and some contradictory aspects of recent trends were noted. On the one hand, there are the processes associated with what Cohen (1985) terms the 'destructuring movement' (decarceration, decentralisation, deprofessionalisation, diversion and the development of alternative community-based agencies and programmes). On the other, there are demands for a return to 'tough' policies and a 'strong' state with an emphasis on deterrence and just deserts rather than on rehabilitation. We also found that the reality is often very different from what official control philosophies and public rhetoric imply. Not only have custodial institutions like prisons remained a major component of the control apparatuses of capitalist societies in the 1980s, but in many cases increasing funds have been allocated to them and more use made of longer sentences.

The notion of 'due process' as one model of criminal justice has been described by Packer (1964, 1968) and contrasted with a 'crime control' model. The 'due process' model, which essentially embodies the 'liberal' conception of the role of law, stresses the importance of upholding the freedom and rights of the individual and of limiting state power. Thus, it seeks to maintain a balance between the need for effective strategies of crime control and respect for individual rights and other basic social values. The 'crime control' model takes the repression of crime as its unquestioned and overriding objective and preoccupies itself with considerations about means, placing primary emphasis on uniformity, efficiency and speed. Importantly, an underlying assumption made by those taking this approach is that, if properly operating, mistakes cannot occur and there is little need for the system to be concerned about protecting the rights of a suspect throughout all the stages of the criminal justice process. In this it differs markedly from the 'due process' model which observes the principle of innocent until proved guilty. The images Packer chooses to capture the basic elements of the two approaches are of 'an assembly line conveyor belt' (the 'crime control' model) and 'an obstacle course' (the 'due process' model).

When these models are used as descriptions of criminal justice, however, 'due process' being taken as the formal ideal and 'crime control' as representing the reality of how the system is used and abused for pragmatic and political purposes, problems arise. McBarnet (1978, 1979) has argued convincingly, and with supporting evidence, that the dichotomy breaks down between formal and informal aspects, between law and its practice. As she puts it:

> If we bring due process down from the dizzy heights of abstraction and subject it to empirical scrutiny, the conclusion must be that due process is *for* crime control. (1979:39, original emphasis)

For, as she says, 'a good many of the practices in criminal justice described as informal perversions of the formal rules are in fact allowed, facilitated or upheld in the formal rules of statute and precedent' (1978:30).

The basic notion of 'due process' as a set of guiding principles on which institutional mechanisms of social control are based can also be contrasted with a 'welfare' or 'therapeutic' orientation. The formal legalistic (or 'due process') approach assumes free will and rational intent on the part of the offender, and it recognises an obligation to protect the rights of (even criminal) individuals within an essentially punitive system. The 'welfare' approach starts from the assumption that deviant individuals have problems (of personality or environment) and offers treatment based on an individualised assessment of need. Under the legalistic model, predetermined rules and procedural guidelines are applied to decision-making and, as far as possible, the process takes place in public or semi-public settings (e.g. courts). In order to ensure that the system conforms with the standards set for it, the importance of legal representation and the right of appeal are recognised as essential components. The welfare model, by contrast, relies on experts and their professional knowledge and judgement and on the collection of detailed personal and background information about individuals. The decisions are reached typically in closed and private meetings at which the subject of the discussion is not usually present and little opportunity is offered for the individuals concerned subsequently to challenge the recommendations made.

The areas where debate over the relative merits of these two approaches is most likely to be found in the contemporary context are juvenile justice (and especially in the case of girls[15]) and rehabilitation programmes within the corrections system.[16] By the 1960s, the welfare orientation seemed to have become so dominant in many areas of social control within and outside the traditional territory of the criminal justice system that considerable concern was being expressed particularly in the United States by lawyers, academics and others about the consequent erosion of civil rights (Kittrie, 1971).[17] Subsequently, the movement back towards a more traditional approach to 'the crime problem' and disenchantment with the treatment approach (Ingraham et al., 1978) has led to a reemphasis on discipline, punishment and deterrence, but without any reduction or dismantling of the state's overall control apparatuses and hence, despite the rhetoric of the Right (especially in Britain), without any signs of a return to the 'smaller' state. However, useful though these categorisations may be at the general theoretical level, they are abstract types and social reality cannot be expected to correspond directly with one or other model. In fact, it seems criminal justice as it actually exists in societies like Australia and Britain at the present time is a combination (and in some respects an uneasy coexistence) of the two orientations and sets of procedures and practices (Garland, 1983).

'Discretion' is another key concept in this field, and has come to be regarded as a fundamental component of criminal justice in modern industrial societies. Pound has provided the classic definition of discretion as:

> . . . an authority conferred by law to act in certain conditions or situations in accordance with an official's or an official agency's own considered judgement and conscience. (Pound, cited in LaFave, 1962:105, n.1)

Two main sources and types of discretion have been identified. Where decisions follow the directions of the system, specifically its formal, established rules, this can be described as 'judicial' discretion, but where decisions are made independently of official legal rules and guidelines, it is more appropriate to talk of 'individual' or 'personal' discretion (LaFave, 1962:929–30).

Discretion was first discussed in America in the legal literature in the 1950s and early 1960s, where it was seen as a feature of the pre-arrest and prosecution stages of the criminal justice process (Goldstein, 1960;

LaFave, 1962; Kadish, 1962; Newman, 1956). At the time, the exercise of discretion by police in their law-enforcement work was perceived by legal scholars as rule-breaking and was attributed to deficiencies in the way individual officers performed their role. Packer, for instance, condemned the practice for being 'lawless' in the literal sense (1968: 290), meaning outside the law. LaFave (1962:112–6), however sees certain aspects of the law and criminal justice (ambiguity in the formulation of legislation, inadequate resources for enforcement, and the individualised treatment principle) as making some degree of discretion on the part of the police unavoidable. Skolnick, who conducted a major study into police practices, argued that it was not so much a question of individuals being good or bad policemen as that their behaviour was determined by the 'premises and design of the system in which they find themselves' (1967:5).

Some authors talked of police discretion resulting in the under- or over-enforcement of laws, with the implication that some objective standard for measuring 'proper' levels of enforcement exists. In fact, any such assumption was explicitly rejected by the interactionist and phenomenologically-oriented sociologists who took considerable theoretical and empirical interest in the phenomenon (see Cain's useful (1979) survey of sociological studies of police work). They argued that the law allows for, even requires, police, for example, to make judgements about priorities and probabilities in order to do their job. They have to choose which crimes to investigate, whom to pursue as a likely suspect, whether the evidence justifies making an arrest and on what charge. These are not purely individual decisions but are shaped by shared normative expectations and understandings, and by established organisational and occupational practices, which constitute everyday social reality for the people concerned as much as, if not more than, the formal requirements of the law.

Discretionary practices were also observed to affect the administration of law at the prosecution stage. Bargaining and negotiation over the charge and plea were first reported by Newman (1956) as a significant feature of the American court system. Newman related 'bargain justice' to its social context and, though some cause for concern, explained it as 'a natural, expedient outgrowth of deficiencies in the administration of our "trial-by-combat" theory of justice' (1956:790). Similarly, Sudnow's famous (1965) account showed how the public defender's office expedited the processing of 'normal crimes' by means of obtaining guilty pleas, thereby avoiding a trial.

Current sociological thinking is that discretion is a fundamental element of the legal, judicial and correctional systems. It occurs at most stages of the criminal justice process and at all levels of the system(s). It seems to have become an essential component of investigative and prosecution work, of court proceedings concerned with determining verdict and disposition, and of the execution of sentences, especially where these involve probation, supervision or institutional confinement. A whole range of criminal justice personnel (police, lawyers, magistrates and judges) exercise discretion to a greater or lesser degree, and much of this discretion is a product not of personal idiosyncrasies but of organisational and structural aspects of the system under which they work. Discretion then need not mean 'decisions are arbitrary or capricious, or even discriminatory' (Louthan, 1985:17).

We turn now to what has to be a selective treatment of aspects of the criminal justice and corrections system, seen against this broad theoretical background. Important to our understanding, as we have seen, are both structural theories (like marxism and feminism), which focus on the way the administration of the criminal law reflects and reinforces the divisions and inequalities of class and gender, and the work of the labelling/interactionist school which has shown how significant an influence on the process of law enforcement are such factors as organisational objectives, resources and constraints, professional ideologies and situational contingencies.

The criminal justice process is generally regarded as comprising a number of elements or stages. The main ones are the following: criminal investigation (essentially the task of the police, but requiring public assistance); pre-court decision-making with respect to arrest and charge or release, with or without a warning (this involves police, lawyers, prosecutors, and the suspect); court proceedings in which determination of a *prima facie* case and decisions about bail are made, the guilt or innocence of the defendant established and sentence passed (here the participating personnel are magistrates, lawyers, judges, juries, police and the accused); and correctional measures and services, including both custodial (imprisonment) and non-custodial penalties (fine, probation, community service order, etc.).

One useful way to represent the notion of criminal justice as a series of stages is in the form of a flow chart. Box, for example, produces the diagram shown overleaf.

Given the number of separate sectors and processes and the range of different categories of personnel involved in the administration of criminal justice (each with its own extensive literature), it is clearly impossible to give a comprehensive coverage of all aspects. It will be necessary to be highly selective and provide only a description of general patterns with some illustrative case material, where available using Australian sources. The focus will be on stages and aspects of the criminal justice process rather than primarily on personnel. This is partly because, though there has been much overseas writing and research on the police, lawyers, magistrates, judges and juries, there is still very little comparable Australian material (with the partial exception of Tomasic's work on lawyers[18]).

The most recent book on the Australian criminal justice system is by Sallman and Willis (1984) and the discussion here relies heavily on this

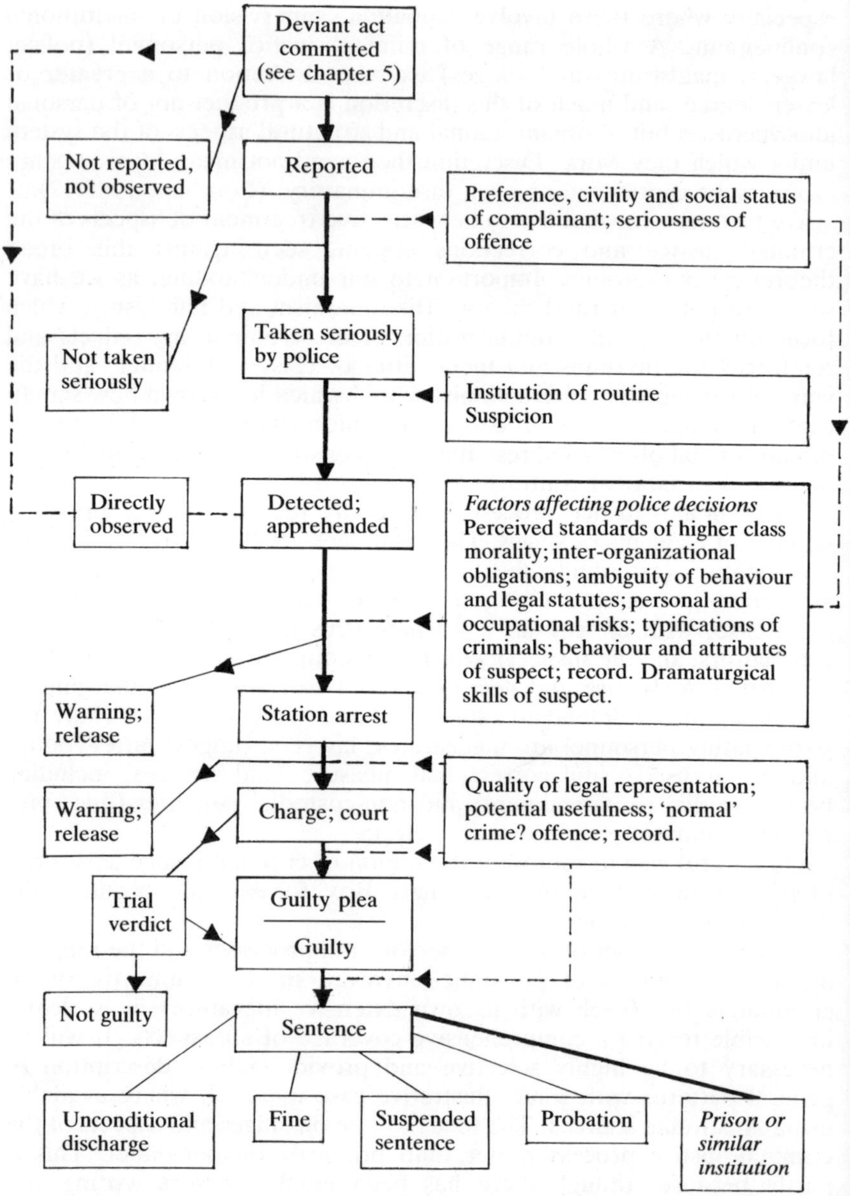

Figure 6.1 The social construction of official statistics on crime and criminals
——— Into official data; ——— out of official data;
– – – – – – – factors affecting community or official decisions.
Source: Box (1971:209)

and the earlier book by O'Malley (1983). These authors give a comprehensive account of the various aspects of criminal justice with respect to the Australian system and they base much of their analyses on certain, mainly British, sociologically-informed studies which have appeared over the past ten or so years. They also draw on the same theoretical traditions (except that they ignore feminism) that have contributed to the development of the perspective on social control from which this book is written.

The process of implementation of the criminal law starts with the observing or reporting of events of a potentially criminal nature. At this stage the public plays a major part in crime detection. As, for example, Chatterton (1976) has shown in an English study of patrol personnel and detectives, much of police work is 'reactive', it is a response to information supplied by others, and more arrests depend on public- than on police-initiated actions. The public includes not only victims and witnesses, but other types of control agents such as head-teachers, store detectives and works managers (Baldwin and Bottomley, 1978:38). A substantial part of the social reaction to crime, therefore, involves 'citizen' discretion.

The investigative work of the police with respect to most categories of crime is predominantly reactive and this is particularly the case with the more serious crimes. Police are required to establish that an offence has occurred, to locate one or more suspects, and to acquire the information necessary for bringing a charge and preparing a case for prosecution. All this involves evaluation of priorities and probabilities and a selection between alternative courses of action. The opportunities for and areas of discretion are affected by such factors as the nature of the crime, the level of public concern expressed, the type of neighbourhood or community, and so on. Many authors (Goldstein, 1960; LaFave, 1962; Skolnick, 1967) see visibility as a key factor influencing police work and they point out that visibility is substantially lower for the police than for other (court-based) law enforcement personnel. In particular they have demonstrated how extensive are the opportunities for discretion and the non-invocation of the law in the case of victimless offences (i.e. those where there is no member of the public as victim or complainant and the investigation is police-initiated).

Cain (1979) compares the various approaches to the sociology of police work and particularly to the phenomenon of police discretion. She points out that, whereas early legalistic interpretations saw it as a problem of individual cases of police 'deviancy', later sociological accounts of the exercise of discretion link it to the broader organisational and environmental context in which police operate. Classic American studies in the interactionist tradition (Bittner, 1967; Bordua ed., 1968; Cicourel, 1968; Piliavin and Briar, 1964; Skolnick, 1967) and more recent British research (Holdaway ed., 1979), interested in investigating the nature and extent of police discretion and the reasons for it, describe how occupational norms and informal procedures develop in response to certain specific aspects of lower level police work. They show also how particular geographical areas and sections of the population (lower classes, minority groups, young males) come to be the main targets of police attention and to figure prominently in police reports and crime statistics.

Although there is little comparable Australian material on the police, O'Malley (1983:62–8) has a useful survey of some of the issues in the Australian context and two of the contributors to Findlay et al. (eds) (1983) discuss the role of discretion in police work generally and the considerable opportunity presented for its exercise in street and public order offences legislation. Here, as they show, charges are typically police-initiated (often involving alleged offensive language, interpreted as disrespect for police authority), are made overwhelmingly against young males and, in New South Wales, against Aborigines in particular (Ronalds et al. and Travis). At the same time, women and feminist groups in Australia, as overseas, complain that police avoid responding to calls from female victims of assault when this involves domestic violence (Scutt, 1980).

Police, however not only initiate the law enforcement process but take an active part in determining whether and how cases will be presented to the courts. Therefore, the circumstances surrounding apprehension of a suspect and what happens during police interrogation have a crucial influence on the criminal justice process.

Evidence from studies of court proceedings shows that the great majority of defendants in Britain and Australia (including those charged with more serious, indictable offences) are dealt with in the lower courts and their convictions in most cases are the result of pleading guilty (McConville and Baldwin, 1981:6–7; Sallman and Willis, 1984: 16).[19] A critical aspect of such cases is the role played by confessions, obtained during police interrogation of suspects (McConville and Baldwin, 1981). A study in a New South Wales district court by Stevenson (1982) found in over 90 per cent of criminal cases that confessions had been obtained by the police and that this was a key element in the prosecution and subsequent conviction. The relationship between confession, guilty plea and conviction was also confirmed in a study of Melbourne magistrates courts. The researcher (Douglas, 1982) drew attention to the fact that in these cases, mainly traffic and public order offences, little attempt has been made (even where a non-guilty plea was entered) to refute the prosecution evidence and he attributes this to the circumstances of apprehension—the suspect was readily identifiable and/or the police themselves were the witnesses or complainants. In McBarnet's words, 'incrimination', in these sorts of cases (and many fall into this category) is 'simply not a problem' (1981:27). 'Indeed the three analytical stages of incrimination, assembling a case, and convincing the court collapse into one' (1981:35). Bacon and Lansdowne (1982) found a similar situation when they interviewed female homicide offenders and discussed aspects of their interrogation by the police and the question of admissions and confessions. (Though the crime was certainly not a routine, minor one, with respect to the identification of the accused and much of the evidence, the cases are not so different.) Put in simple terms, this means that 'in a real sense, the determination of guilt antedates the trial' (McConville and Baldwin, 1981:28). Since there is also evidence that the rights to silence and legal advice when charged are often not observed, and that police-suspect interviews are not recorded (by audio or video tape), the low visibility and therefore the problem of accountability of this stage of the criminal justice process causes concern to these and other writers. Kirby (1979) gives a very detailed analysis of the investigation and interrogation stages of the criminal justice process and considers a range of new controls, but his standpoint is very much that of the legal-judicial expert, in whose view injustices are the result of mistakes and misconduct by individual officers and can be remedied by technical means.

Many authors discuss the question of overlap between the pre-court and court phases of criminal justice and particularly the police role in this. Police are not only responsible for producing a suspect and deciding the charge, but as a result of these and other actions they also make a significant contribution to the course justice will take.

> The importance of the defendant's initial encounter with the police can scarcely be overstated for, in the great majority of cases, what takes place at that stage can critically influence what happens at later stages of the criminal process. (Baldwin and McConville, 1977:105)

Not surprisingly, having located a suspect and having decided they have the evidence to bring a case, police are convinced of the correctness of their judgement that the suspect was indeed responsible for the commission of the offence. As Bottomley (1979:99) points out, their view is that, once an arrest has been made, the criminal has been found and the determination of guilt is taken to be only a formality. Many of the procedures of the courts (specifically 'due process' provisions) are, therefore, regarded by the police as frustrations and obstacles to what they perceive as efficient and expeditious administration of justice (Skolnick, 1967:Chapter 9).

This situation is further compounded in countries like Britain and Australia where in the lower courts the police are also responsible for conducting the prosecution. This results in a 'considerable amalgamation of powers in the police' (Laurie, 1978:103). But this cannot be seen as a simple extension of police duties. It necessarily forces on the police a fundamentally 'paradoxical role' (McConville and Baldwin, 1981:18). For, as these writers go on to say the police

> are required under the adversarial approach to pursue partisan and fearless prosecution, yet at the same time to make dispassionate decisions about whether a prosecution is justified. (McConville and Baldwin, 1981:18)

In so far as law (or 'due process') and order (the 'crime control' model) are in conflict, the multiple roles of the police make this conflict an everyday personal one in police work.

> The actual requirement of maintaining social order under the principle of legality places an unceasing burden on the police as a social institution. Indeed, the police is *the* institution best exemplifying the strain between the two ideas. (Skolnick, 1967:9, original emphasis)

Thus, instead of the court hearing operating as a separate stage in the process, where police and other evidence is presented and weighed up by independent judicial officers, there is a merging of the tasks of obtaining sufficient evidence to bring a charge and of presenting a convincing prosecution case. Studies (some of which we have mentioned) have demonstrated that this occurs firstly, because at the interrogation stage many suspects decide or are persuaded to admit guilt and provide a confession, and, secondly, because the police prosecution case is often presented in such a way that the court is either unable or unwilling to reach any other decision than a conviction. McConville and Baldwin, as a result of their detailed analysis of the prosecution process in English courts,[20] came to the overall conclusion that what they observed to be a 'persistent exercise of discretion' by the courts in favour of the police was partly due to the fact that 'when courts are asked to adjudicate on unlawful searches, oppressive interrogation techniques, improper refusal of access to a solicitor, and the like, they are almost invariably faced with searches and interrogations that have proved successful in producing incriminating evidence' (1981:209), and hence the bases for a conviction. The result for many of those processed through the courts is that what they experience is 'a system of justice without trial' (Skolnick, 1967:13). Various aspects and implications of this situation, both for the rights of the accused and for the satisfactory operation of the Australian criminal justice system as currently constituted, are seen as problems needing attention (Lane, 1982; O'Connor, 1982; Sallman and Willis, 1984: Chapter 3).

In most respects the adjudication stage of criminal justice can be seen as a marked contrast to the previous stages. Unlike the investigation process, particularly the dealings with suspects, and the preparation of a case (which occur in relatively 'closed' contexts, often in private conversations, with the maximum opportunity for the exercise of discretion if not discrimination), adjudication takes place in the public and formal setting of the court. The court procedures are conducted in ways that are highly ritualised, the language is technical and specialised, and all the personnel apart from the defendant are regular participants and are able to establish routine patterns of relationship with each other, all of which reflect and reinforce the physical and social gulf between the accused and the system that is to decide his or her fate.

By far the most penetrating sociological observation and interpretation of the form judicial proceedings take for the overwhelming majority of people (whose cases are settled in the lower courts) is that provided by Carlen (1976) in her study of London magistrates' courts. Here, without the aid of costume and ceremony attached to a full jury trial and often with limited if any scope for lawyers' rhetoric, coercive power rests largely on formal ritualistic settings, and the use of specialised and mystifying forms of language and rules of conversational practice. Her basic argument is that justice, far from being the straightforward application of abstract legal rules, is more like a dramatic production, constructed around a whole range of technical props and complex strategies by court personnel. Critical for the maintenance of an image of justice and the law as absolute, unproblematic and consensual, in a situation where the defendant presents a constant challenge, is the 'transformation of the ritual display of justice into the socio-legal technology of coercion' (1976:38). McBarnet (1981:Chapter 7), though agreeing with much of the description of what happens, comes to a different conclusion. In her view, the lower courts are not applying 'justice' in the same way as the higher courts do or as the ideology implies: summary justice, unlike adversarial justice, has a form and function in which due process plays little part (and her particular thesis is that this is done quite legally).

The court hearing serves two functions: the determination of guilt or innocence and the passing of sentence. In Britain, the United States and Australia (but not Europe) an adversarial model is the model adopted for the adjudication of contested criminal cases. The prosecution case (handled by a Crown officer in the higher courts and in Australia by the police in the lower courts) and the defence (usually represented by a lawyer where a non-guilty plea has been entered) offer alternative accounts of the events in question and challenge each other's evidence,[21] which, depending on the type of case and court, magistrates or a judge and jury have to choose between.

Court officials and those responsible for the prosecution, Chambliss (1969:207) suggests, have both to fulfil a public expectation of effective performance and to produce a steady flow of cases through the system with whatever are perceived as adequate conviction rates, and to decide on the appropriate course of action for the cases which have to be processed so as to yield maximum benefit for minimum resource outlay. It is this context that writers use to explain the emergence and widespread utilisation of various forms of plea and sentence bargaining. Newman (1956) gave the earliest empirical account of what is now regarded as a routine practice in American courts. A recent major study undertaken in an English Crown Court using the same technique of investigating defendants who changed from a not-guilty to a guilty plea before trial, that of Baldwin and McConville (1977), established its existence in Britain. Of their sample (10 per cent of all guilty pleas entered during the research period) 70 per cent of defendants gave reasons for changing to a guilty plea that indicated the possibility of a plea bargain, 40 per cent claimed their change of plea was a direct response to lawyers' advice and 30 per cent reported that, through the efforts of the barrister, a bargain had been struck, involving either explicitly or tacitly an expectation of sentence reduction (1977:28). There is no Australian research comparable to that of Baldwin and McConville, but one Melbourne study of magistrates' court cases (a far less serious category of offenders than those in the English study) found evidence of bargaining over the number and types of charges and a relationship between bargains, pleas and legal representation, though this had no apparent effect on type of sentence received (Douglas, 1983).

These practices mean that the pre-court and the court phases of criminal justice are linked through the activities of police, lawyers and sometimes also the judge in influencing whether or not the accused pleads guilty and on what charge. The now well-documented incidence in Australia and elsewhere of plea-changing and plea-bargaining, and sentence discounting (described in Sallman and Willis, 1984:Chapter 3) lead to a higher incidence of guilty pleas (even in the Supreme Court this can amount to over 50 per cent of cases), which are negotiated often through lawyers on the basis that the charge will be for a lesser offence than the original and/or with the expectation of a lighter sentence (which may or may not be realised). This means that a substantial majority of convictions for indictable offences follow a guilty plea, and hence the possibility of a trial is avoided. Consequently, as the early American writers on the subject pointed out, criminal justice does not fit the 'formal combative' model of a defended trial, but rather a conviction represents an 'informal' or 'compromise' resolution of the case (Newman, 1956:788), and apart from a brief, largely predetermined hearing, the cases which come under the category of 'normal crimes' are handled almost as private matters (Sudnow, 1965). A further concern, and one strongly expressed by Baldwin and McConville (1977:63, 67) is that 'induced or negotiated pleas' may result in inaccurate and unjust determinations where, for various reasons, individuals fail to take advantage of the opportunity to contest the case. As O'Malley comments (1983:129), this results in the 'pre-emption of adversary procedure' and of the jury trial in particular. McBarnet expresses the basic issue as she sees it, in these terms (and her study of Scottish courts and the law was designed to provide a broader understanding of how and why this can occur):

> The conviction process in the legal sense poses a problem for explanation because it raises a strange paradox. All the rhetoric of justice we are so familiar with presents a picture of the system of criminal justice bending over backwards to favour the defendant rather than the prosecution. . . Why then the paradox that the vast majority of cases processed through a criminal justice system so geared to favouring the accused results in a finding of guilt? (McBarnet, 1981:1, 2)

Although a trial with lawyers, judge and jury (and a whole legal/judicial apparatus designed to protect the rights of the accused) is the popular image of how criminal justice operates, in reality this is a rare occurrence. The picture that emerges is rather one of 'routinised justice' (Bottomley, 1979:104), a method of administering the law and criminal justice which meets the professional and organisational requirements for efficiency and predictability of police and court officials in the context of an overwhelming volume of cases to be processed and the relatively trivial character of many of them. The majority of defendants in English and Australian magistrates courts are still appearing without legal representation (Bottoms and McLean, 1976:137; Cashman, 1982: 195). It seems, therefore, that far from taking the form of a contest or conflict, the administration of justice involves an extensive network of interrelationships of negotiation, alliance and exchange between the various parties, even including the defendants, with the common goal of 'settlement by a plea of guilty' (Feeley, 1973:416). Commentators such as Feeley (1973), McBarnet (1981) and McConville and Baldwin (1981) reject the previously advanced explanation that case overload and resource limitations are responsible for this situation and argue instead that we need to look at fundamental aspects of the law itself and of its application.

There is no implication in this analysis that police, lawyers and court officials in general are using their power illegitimately nor that the high proportion of hearings that (because of guilty pleas) can be resolved in the magistrates courts constitutes a subversion of justice. However, the situation does reveal significant, and for some observers worrying, aspects of the treatment most criminal suspects receive at the hands of law enforcement agents.

The second function of the court is the sentencing of the convicted criminal. McConville and Baldwin found that overall 'the adversarial model of justice was not much in evidence'; rather 'the main purpose of open-court adjudication related not to questions of guilt or innocence but to sentencing those who had already pleaded guilty' (1981:28). At this stage of the process, though the law prescribes particular penalties for offences, there is room also for judicial discretion. In part this is because allowance has to be made for variations in the circumstances and seriousness of the offence and in the prior record of the offender, and in part it reflects the fact that, to some degree, the notion of differential treatment according to the needs (and rehabilitative potential) of the individual has become accepted as a consideration in modern correctional policy. This points to the existence of alternative approaches to sentencing and punishment: on the one hand, the legalistic tariff principle, reflecting concern for uniformity, standardisation and formal equality of treatment of like cases; and, on the other hand, an individualised 'welfare' approach, according to which justice (in a substantive rather than a formal sense) requires that the different personal and social circumstances and needs of each offender merit a different type of penalty or treatment.

Judicial, academic and popular conceptions of treatment and punishment are an important influence on the policies and practices of the courts and, as we discovered earlier, there have been some significant shifts in this area since the last century and particularly over the past twenty or so years. The focal point of the corrections system in the nineteenth century was the prison, which was expected by providing a disciplined and moral environment to 'reform' the criminal. Garland (1983) gives a complex account of how in the twentieth century for a variety of reasons, including the emphasis given to an individualised conception of punishment and treatment, the expansion of services and professions engaged in the business of social regulation in the community, and the failure of prisons to prevent recidivism or deter crime, a range of alternative sanctions to imprisonment came to play an increasingly major role. Particularly important were non-custodial forms of surveillance and supervision (specifically probation and prison aftercare or parole) which relied heavily on social work, and the fine (which can be regarded as retributive, restitutive and/or deterrent in character, but is in no sense a 'reformative' or 'disciplinary', in Foucault's sense, measure).

The fine has become by far the most common penalty for less serious offences (especially traffic offences) and is frequently used in indictable offence cases in Australia and in England (Daunton-Fear, 1977:389). In both countries a proportionate decrease in the use of imprisonment (when measured by the percentage of convicted offenders given prison sentences) has resulted in the greater application of the fine (Bottoms, 1983). Biles (1983) gives figures to show a reduction in the imprisonment rate (which he calculates as the number of prisoners per 100 000 population) in Australia since 1960 though he notes there has been an increase in the actual number of prisoners. He also maps the relationships between crime rates and imprisonment rates which are markedly different in England and Wales and in Australia. Chan and Zdendowski (1986:67–90) in an attempt to examine empirically the evidence for decarceration in the various Australian States, present a detailed analysis of recent trends in imprisonment as compared with community based alternatives to prison (probation, community services order, parole) and excluding fines. They find there has been an increased resort to non-custodial options in the 1980s, but without 'appreciable effect on the use of imprisonment' (1986:81).

Turning to what is involved in the process of sentencing itself, the law provides for a considerable degree of discretion in determining the penalties for offences. Fox and O'Brien (1977) give a full account of the Australian situation in this respect, and comment on the extent to which increasingly the adversarial principle is applicable at the dispositional as well as the adjudication stage of court proceedings. However, empirical research (much of it done by criminologists) has produced evidence of 'disparities' or inconsistencies some of which cannot be accounted for by legally or judicially recognised factors relating to offence and the previous criminal record of the offender. Hood and Sparks (1970:Chapter 5) give an excellent summary of the state of knowledge of this issue at the time and propose an elaborate model of the sentencing process in courts presided over by a judge, to aid analysis of judicial discretion in decision-making. Variations in sentencing practices between courts and particular sentencing personnel may be explained as a result of the choice the system offers to magistrates and judges between alternative, and somewhat incompatible, penal philosophies and sentencing objectives (general or individual deterrence, reform, retribution, compensation). These work on two levels: they provide broad strategies for handling the problem of sentencing generally and they suggest ways of dealing with the disposition of particular cases (Sallman and Willis, 1984:Chapter 4). At the same time, in making their decisions, magistrates and judges are expected to be sensitive to prevailing community attitudes and concerns and to what is currently perceived as 'the public interest'. Alternatively or additionally sentencing decisions may be related to more personal factors (individual beliefs, attitudes and values) which influence perceptions and evaluations of particular offenders, offences and likely effects of the various dispositional options available. This situation is compounded by the fact that the sentence is supposed to fulfil two basically inconsistent roles or functions: to be a public demonstration of moral sentiment and to be an effective mechanism for changing behaviour (Weatherburn, 1983).

In one Australian study of magistrates courts, which looked at disparities in the conviction and disposition of shoplifters, the most significant single variable (where this data was available) was the magistrate; multivariate analysis also revealed interaction patterns between this variable and factors such as prior convictions, and legal representation (Grabosky and Rizzo, 1983). A similar finding was reported in another recent Australian study (Homel, 1983), which examined the sentencing of drinking drivers in magistrates courts in New South Wales. The research showed that variations were due to individual 'sentencing style' and that this was reflected in differential treatment of offenders according to class and age (which to some extent, the author argues, is justified or at least rationalised by the current emphasis on individualised penalties). A useful summary of the limited Australian data on sentencing patterns is given by O'Malley (1983:140–4), who concludes his discussion by pointing to current moves to make this area of decision-making more rational and technically sophisticated. He mentions specifically the use of pre-sentence reports supplied by probation officers and social workers and the shift in responsibility for determining type and length of custodial sentences served from the court to correctional authorities.

The kind of criminal justice that is experienced by different categories of the population (as victims and as offenders) is, of course, neither uniform nor randomly variable. Rather, it is systematically related not only to the criminal history and current offence of a suspect or defendant, but also to social and demographic factors such as class, race/ethnicity, age and gender. We have already considered the question of how dominant groups and sectional interests influence lawmaking. Here we are more interested in the administration of justice and in an exploration of how and to what extent the law is differentially enforced, with respect to different types of offence and categories of offender. The most frequently discussed social factor that is believed to be associated with differential law-enforcement policies and practices is class (or some measure of socio-economic status),[22] but the largely empirical emphasis of most of the overseas literature and the relative dearth of systematic Australian data[23] suggest this is an inappropriate topic to pursue here.

In the current Australian context, race and ethnicity invite attention. In particular the treatment of Aborigines by the criminal justice and corrections systems has become an increasingly important topic of academic, legal and public concern, as has the issue of special laws relating to Aborigines, some of which (for example land rights) seem to represent attempts at positive discrimination, while others (relating to conduct on reserves and to behaviour in public places) are obviously negative in their effect.[24] There is now plenty of evidence to show that Aborigines are over-represented in a number of offence categories (especially the more trivial, such as drinking, but also in a range of typical criminal offences like assault, breaking and larceny) and in the prison population (Milne, 1983).[25]

However, in order to make the best use of the feminist perspective which underlies and informs the analysis of social control in general and of the particular control systems with which this book is concerned, the significance of sex/gender in respect to the way criminal justice operates will be the main focus of interest. The fact that the criminal law contains some provisions that treat male and female experiences and behaviour differently (criminalising prostitution and female sexual 'delinquency' and formulating rape laws in ways that deny women in many cases the full benefit of legal protection and redress[26]) has already been stressed, and attention drawn to the possibility of the criminal law disadvantaging women as victims of criminal offences and/or as offenders themselves. At this point our interest lies in the administration of the law and in the various accounts of the nature and sources of sexism and gender discrimination in the criminal justice and correctional systems.

Even before we consider the relevant empirical evidence, it is important to acknowledge that providing a definition of and criteria for measuring 'justice' or 'fairness' is not a straightforward matter and poses particular problems for feminists. The common practice of simply measuring the treatment of females at various points in the criminal justice process against that of males and describing any deviation as injustice is both theoretically and methodologically questionable. It entails, at the very least, a totally uncritical acceptance of the principles on which criminal justice as experienced by males is based and on the idea that, even though substantial differences of relevance to the criminal justice system exist between the sexes, justice is achieved when men and women receive the same treatment. Recently this issue has been explored by a number of feminist writers interested in various aspects of the relationship between women and the law, most of whom have serious doubts about the possibility of the state and the law as currently constituted producing 'real' justice and equality for women.[27]

The basic features of the criminal justice system that have already been identified—the tension between 'legalistic' (or due process) and 'welfare' (or treatment) approaches to the management of deviance generally and to the determination of appropriate sanctions for convicted criminals, the scope for the exercise of police and judicial discretion, and the existence of differential law enforcement and sentencing practices for various categories of offenders—are all highly relevant to the analysis and understanding of the relationship between criminal justice and sex/gender. Though, as with other aspects of criminal justice in Australia, there is a shortage of theoretical writing and research on this topic, there is now a substantial body of feminist and sociological literature in Britain and the United States on which we can draw.

The fundamental issue around which most of the empirical and theoretical analysis is organised is whether women, as juveniles or adults, receive more or less favourable treatment from the criminal justice systems in comparison with men: relatively, do they encounter leniency or harshness from the police and the courts?

What has been termed the 'chivalry' thesis contends that paternalistic attitudes by law enforcement personnel (and society generally) result in females being more likely than males to receive a warning or a caution, to be charged with lesser offences, not to be held in custody pending the court case, to be acquitted, and, if convicted, to be given a less severe penalty. There are various supposed rationales for the preferential treatment offered to women. Steffensmeier (1980a) suggests five alternative inter-related factors: chivalry (referring to benevolent, protectionist attitudes); practicality (relevant particularly to custodial sentences which would leave children and domestic responsibilities untended); and the assumptions that women are less capable of crimes (what he calls 'naiveté'), commit less serious and dangerous types of crimes, and are less persistent and intractable in their criminality. Another manifestation of this kind of thinking is the reluctance to accord women the status of full legal subjects with responsibility for their actions. An instance of this, as Klein and Kress (1976:39) observe, is the way rape laws traditionally respected men's ownership rights over women, not women's rights over their own bodies.

The opposing thesis is that paternalism can equally well lead to greater judicial intervention in the lives of women than of men and especially in the case of juveniles, and, for those who come to the attention of the criminal justice and corrections systems, more severe treatment. Two alternative explanations can be suggested: either, that paternalism in the form of protectionism, operating in conjunction with a preference for the treatment approach to crime and a faith in rehabilitative philosophy (Armstrong, 1977), sees more need for and benefit from bringing deviant women into contact with the services associated with the criminal justice system than it does in the case of men; or, a more moralistic and punitive version of paternalism, which takes the view that, when a woman commits a crime, this is indicative of much greater wickedness than it is for a man (the 'evil women' notion), is much less understandable given women's nature and circumstances, and therefore demands harsher penalties. A greater readiness to sentence women and girls to institutional confinement and for considerable periods (which in the case of males is justified only where there is a long and serious criminal history) would be consistent with either of these two interpretations. Whichever form it takes, justice for women seems to imply a degree of suspension of the formal principles of equality before the law and due process, resulting in discriminatory treatment either of a positive or a negative kind. The denial of full and equal rights for women on the same basis as for men is socially legitimised through official and general public support for the 'sickness' model and the 'treatment' approach as methods for understanding and handling female deviance, including female criminality, rather than the 'wickedness' model and a legal-judicial approach (Hartz-Karp, 1981; Pearson, 1976; Phillips and DeFleur, 1982; Smart, 1976: Chapter 6).

The overseas research, which contains a number of inconsistent and inconclusive findings, nevertheless seems to support the idea that paternalism comes in different forms (Chesney-Lind, 1978: Chapters 6 and 7; Heidensohn, 1985:Chapter 3; Klein and Kress, 1976; Steffensmeier, 1980b).[28] It can mean a greater willingness to criminalise and a greater degree of severity of treatment for girls and young women and for females generally wherever sexuality is involved: in other words, 'chivalry' does not necessarily entail leniency. But at the same time, where women are engaging in conventional types of criminal activity (which for them are typically the less serious property offences, and this is still true even after some years of women's 'liberation'[29]), 'chivalry' does seem to imply leniency. Whether this is due to the sex/gender factor or to the greater likelihood that female offenders have fewer previous police contacts or convictions and that, for any given category of offence, their conduct takes a less serious form than is the case with males has often not been clearly established by the researchers. Comparisons of the conditions in penal institutions for juvenile and adult male and female offenders, especially in the past but continuing into the present, also give support to the notion that 'protectionism' may mean females are subjected to more restrictions, fewer opportunities and a relatively greater degree of deprivation than are males (Dobash et al., 1986; Feinman, 1979; Heidensohn, 1985: Chapter 4; Rafter, 1985;).[30] The effect of sexist ideologies on prison regimes for women can be summed up, in the words of Carlen and Tchaikovsky (1985:182), as 'Discipline, Infantilize, Feminize, Medicalize and Domesticize'.

Several recent overseas studies have found that type of crime (and to a lesser extent criminal history) is a major, if not the major, factor in influencing official responses to suspects and defendants at the police and court stages of the criminal justice process and that sex/gender (along with class, race and other such variables) has a far less important relationship to arrest, referral to alternative diversionary programmes, charge reduction (through plea bargaining), conviction and disposition (Bernstein et al. 1977: Eaton, 1986; Farrington and Morris, 1983; Fry and Miller, 1978; Nagel, 1981; Visher, 1983).

There is little Australian research on this issue, but with respect to juvenile offenders Hancock conducted a major study in Victoria in the mid 1970s. Her results (1980) showed that the majority of care and protection (or 'status offence') cases in the juvenile courts were female and the majority of female court appearances were on protection applications, while the vast majority of male court appearances were on criminal charges. Females were more likely than males to receive supervisory sentences (probation, supervision or institutional confinement). However, the overall figures conceal two distinct patterns: females convicted of criminal acts were treated more leniently than comparable males (and far more leniently than female non-offenders), while females who were in court for suspected or actual sexual 'misbehaviour' were treated more harshly. First offender female status offenders were more likely than were males to be placed in youth training centres than in community programmes, despite the fact that the offence histories of the girls were far less serious than those of the boys (Hancock and Chesney-Lind, 1985:240). Hancock explains this as the result of an underlying 'welfare' philosophy that encourages the police and the courts to intervene where a perceived 'need' for some official form of moral and social control is detected.

Particularly interesting in the research on this subject are indications that the kinds of factors that are taken into account in the exercise of police and judicial discretion, whether legalistic (i.e. previous record, type and seriousness of current offence) or social (such as class or family status) are interpreted and used differentially for males and females. Research needs to separate out gender *per se* from social factors with a high gender association e.g. family status (Kruttschnitt, 1984). (There is even the further suggestion, by for example Box and Hale, 1983; Farrington and Morris, 1983; and Kruttschnitt and Green, 1984, that the sex of the law enforcement officer may play an influence.) Several feminist authors are now proposing a complex theoretical interpretation of the role gender stereotyping plays at various stages of the criminal justice process. They build their case on a range of types of evidence. For example, the general observation that the kind of female deviance that attracts serious public attention is sexual in nature and, as Hancock found, in the case of juveniles, it is often parents that report their 'unruly' daughters. Or the finding, from a study of arrest decisions, that the greater importance of a range of demographic characteristics (age, race, demeanour) on the treatment of female suspects can be explained as an example of (male) law enforcement personnel responding favourably to women who 'display appropriate gender behavior and characteristics', according to traditional middle-class standards, and unfavourably to those who do not, such as suspects who are young, black or hostile (Visher, 1983:23). Or Edwards (1984) in her study of the pretrial and trial process for two 'typical' categories of female offenders, prostitutes and shoplifters, arguing that consistently the treatment of women (and she draws attention to the need to explore variations within the category 'women' as well as between men and women) reflects gender-specific conceptions of the motivations for and characteristic forms of criminal behaviour. Or, again, Kruttschnitt (1982), in attempting to account for variations in the sentences given to a variety of types of women offenders, focusses on the effect of 'dependency' on disposition, and specifically where dependency means residing in a marital or familial household (by contrast with having an independent source of income). She hypothesises that the presence of family members is taken by the courts as a sign that the woman already lives in a situation where she is under daily social control, thus making a supervisory or custodial sentence unnecessary.

Put simply, what this research suggests is the importance of making a distinction between rule-breaking and role-breaking behaviour with respect to female deviance and criminality. This then helps us understand differential responses to the various categories of female crime and the punitiveness with which the criminal justice system deals with 'unfeminine' conduct, and particularly in the sexual area, on the part of women, because this is seen as 'doubly deviant' (Heidensohn, 1985: 46–8), in departing from gender-specific as well as gender-neutral expectations. As Schur (1984) puts it, gender is more of a 'master [sic] status characteristic' for women than it is for men, and deviance for women is defined in terms of gender norms as well as in terms of general legal or moral standards. Heidensohn (1986:292) further suggests that the fact that women's deviance attracts particular kinds of informal as well as formal sanctions puts women in a situation of 'double jeopardy'.

The wider implications of this thesis are explored by Eaton in her major study of a London magistrates court. Based on a variety of sources of evidence (the grounds cited in pleas of mitigation, the information in social inquiry reports, and magistrates' talk), she suggests that the apparently equal weight given to 'family ties' as the critical factor in determining the treatment received by both male and female defendants, disguises the fact that 'the family' is experienced differently by men and women. The model of the family that court officials held recognised neither gender nor class variations in the meaning or content of 'the family'. Specifically, Eaton argues, the family is a mechanism for the social control of women in a way that it is not for men and, because it contains the same gender divisions and power relations as exist in society generally, placing a similar 'emphasis on the family for defendants of both sexes is an example of a practice which seems impartial but which actually perpetuates inequality' (1986:57).

It is theories of this kind that demonstrate the importance of locating the law and criminal justice in their broader societal context and of exploring the inter-relationships between such formal, official and public systems of social control and other more informal control mechanisms and agencies.

The criminal law, justice and social control

The law is widely regarded as the main regulatory mechanism of state and societal control in the modern world and is seen as relying primarily on coercive power. In deliberately choosing here to focus on the criminal law and criminal justice, it might seem that the only forms of social control that would be likely to be exposed are those specifically associated with coercion and repression. Whereas, had we considered some of the alternative types of law—administrative or civil, for instance (Feeley, 1976)—and other methods of delivering justice such as 'informal' or 'collective' (Abel, 1982; Cain, 1985), we would be more likely to find the full range of modes or 'styles' of social control discussed by Black, for example. Black himself (1976:4–6; 1984:8–10) explicitly makes a connection (though not a rigid or exclusive one) between types of law and types of social control. In his view, the 'penal style' is exemplified by the criminal law, with an emphasis on guilt, the 'compensatory' by tort and contract law, dealing with debt and obligation, and the 'conciliatory' by international law and marital disputes, with a concern for conflict resolution; the 'therapeutic style' is illustrated by psychiatry, whose task is to provide 'help' and 'care' for those 'in need'. Certainly, concentrating on the criminal law necessarily restricts to some extent the range of ways in which the law can be seen to exercise control in society. Feeley (1976) argues that the popular conception of law (which is shared by some socio-legal scholars) as a set of 'commands' or 'direct orders' neglects forms of law and government regulation aimed at what he describes as the 'manipulation of the field or environment' of entire populations, which are far less visible and political in their mode of operation. McBarnet (1984) makes a similar point by contrasting the 'oppressive' and the 'facilitative' aspects of law.

What the analysis in this chapter has shown is that the undoubtedly important and empirically demonstrable association between a 'penal' orientation, and criminal law and criminal justice can tell us relatively little about the specific criminal laws that a given society institutes or about the form and functioning of particular legal, judicial and correctional systems. 'Penal' may well serve as a description of the overall 'language and logic' (Black, 1984:8) of criminal justice, and punishment may well constitute one of its ultimate objectives, but 'penal' or 'repressive' measures are only some of the possible control ideologies and techniques that societies have developed for dealing with crime and deviance. According to Garland and Young (1983:22–23), the same applies to the correctional system and specifically to the so-called 'penal' institutions themselves: social relationships and modes of control can take a variety of forms, including legal and physical, but also economic and even sexual. They, with their treatment of the notion of 'penality' imply, and Chan and Zdendowski (1986:72), with the idea of a 'correctional continuum', explicitly state, that repression, coercion and punishment are variable dimensions rather than discrete attributes of a social control system.

So we could expect to find that criminal justice has a number of control functions and objectives (of which punishment is only one) and that it draws on a range of control mechanisms and strategies. It is not simply a matter of using coercive and repressive methods of restraint and sanction, backed by a barely concealed reliance on physical force and the power of the state. Indeed, it must be acknowledged that, even if a consensus model is rejected, to a varying extent laws rest on moral authority and social support in the community as much as they do on the resort by governments to armed force. Many writers have emphasised also the less obvious but important ideological aspects of the law and criminal justice, not least the significance attached to the basic notions of law, justice and 'the rule of law'. A comparative analysis of different control systems reveals that the simple equation of the law (seen as a punishment-oriented control instrument) with repressive means and medicine (a treatment-oriented instrument) with non-repressive, 'therapeutic' means totally misrepresents the diversity and complexity of the control mechanisms and ideologies employed by the personnel and institutions in each of these two systems.

It is unquestionably true, however, that criminal justice is explicitly and visibly about social control in a way that the other major institutions and structures like education, welfare and medicine (at least on the surface) are not. The criminal law (through statute and case law) specifies what are prohibited acts and the procedures that are to be followed whenever such acts occur. It consists essentially of directions as to how people should behave, both law-abiding citizens and law enforcement personnel. Law enforcement entails the authorisation of involuntary intrusion into the lives of suspects and the imposition of penalties that deprive individuals who are alleged to have committed criminal offences of 'life, liberty, dignity or property' (Goldstein, 1960: 545). The imposed nature of legal/judicial interventions is also related to the way in which these systems encounter those who are the primary targets of their control efforts. Such individuals do not identify themselves as being in need of the systems' services.

Because it is recognised that law enforcement is necessarily intrusive and coercive, the law contains instructions and regulations about when and how it should be applied. It is through the specification of procedural rules that the law operates as a control over those officials and institutions who collectively make up the criminal justice system. At the same time, through its substantive provisions, the law stipulates what are to be considered as unacceptable forms of behaviour by society as a whole. Although the generality and universalism of the proscriptions of the criminal law might be expected to mean that individuals from all sectors of society would have an equal chance of finding themselves the objects of criminal justice proceedings, in fact, because of selectivity in the definition and interpretation of what constitutes a 'crime', and because of the differential likelihood of members of different social categories being apprehended and convicted, certain types of people (young, male, lower class, minority group members, and petty offenders) are heavily over-represented in the criminal population.

Consequently, the legal-judicial system does have some quite distinctive characteristics: its publicly acknowledged and officially legitimised coercive mode of intervention; its 'penal' orientation and the involuntary nature of the treatment it metes out; its direct and formal links with the state; and the fact that, though all members of society have some dealings with and derive some benefit from the criminal justice system, those with whom the system is chiefly concerned—those being processed by the police or the courts for alleged offences—are drawn from specific and highly selective sections of society. In one or more of these respects, this system of social control differs markedly from the others, and from medicine, welfare (and education) in particular.

However, many of the factors and processes that have emerged in the course of the examination of the legal-judicial system are common to other systems. All those systems that are responsible for managing problematic categories of people or problematic aspects of everyone's lives (specifically we are thinking of the law, medicine and welfare) ultimately derive their authority from the state. They are officially assigned an area of jurisdiction and the responsibility for carrying out certain tasks. They all have the basic attributes of formal organisations: positions and activities are internally differentiated, hierarchically ordered and rule governed, and there is a clear demarcation and power imbalance between organisational personnel (who have the advantages of official status, superior knowledge and other resources) and the clients or consumers of their services.

The forms and functions of these systems are also influenced by such general features of modern western societies as rationalisation, bureaucratisation, division of labour and distribution of power, professionalisation, and structural divisions based on sex/gender, class, race and ethnicity. At the same time, research has revealed the presence of other less 'official', 'public' and 'formal' aspects of the structure and functioning of such institutions and organisations (such as working rules and routine practices) and discovered that these contribute significantly to the way these systems operate . None of these is necessarily the same as or consistent with the formal organisational goals, requirements and definitions of roles and tasks. All these elements, both formal and informal, official and unofficial, affect the nature of social control in such systems and the ways in which it can be exercised.

In the literature we surveyed in this chapter, there were accounts of the criminal law and criminal justice which stressed the formal, official aspects of their nature and functioning, and others which exposed the informal, unofficial side of the law enforcement process. The criminal justice 'system' was seen as having a number of objectives and as being required to respond to a number of demands, not all of which were compatible. Although the repression of crime is obviously a primary goal, keeping the system running smoothly and fulfilling both these tasks without departing too far from the procedural rules laid down are also major concerns. That there is a problem in reconciling these different objectives is widely recognised. Criminal justice is seen as an unstable blend of direct and repressive and indirect and ideological forms of social control (a combination of the 'crime control' and 'due process' models).

The criminal justice system operates on a number of levels, some more 'public' and 'official' and others markedly less so. This is where the concept of 'discretion' becomes relevant. Discretion can be interpreted in different ways: it can be seen as an institutionally necessary component of an individualised justice system; or as an unavoidable, even desirable method of reconciling incompatible expectations; or again, it can be seen to mean that law enforcement personnel are acting from purely personal interests. Many writers have described the administration of criminal justice in terms of the contrast between the formal ideal—'the law in the books'—and the pragmatic reality—'the law in action'.

The literature in this field that we have looked at offers alternative interpretations and explanations for what criminal justice is and does, and why. This poses problems for our understanding of the nature and sources of social control exercised by the legal, judicial and correctional systems. Some of the points at issue are fundamental questions about the most appropriate perspectives and levels of analysis. The following are the main examples of differences in conception and treatment of criminal justice that have important implications for the nature and study of social control. First, writers may choose to deal with either formal or informal aspects of the institutions and activities of these systems. Secondly, they may treat criminal justice as simply the application of rules and procedures contained in legal statutes (supplemented by case law) or as an ongoing social enterprise, the complex product of social conditions and human actions. Thirdly, some may emphasise in their overall theoretical framework the conflict elements in criminal law and criminal justice, while others stress the 'exchange' and cooperation aspects.

It is in attempting to make sense of these competing accounts that McBarnet's (1978, 1979, 1981) work is so important. It is not in her view a question of choosing between rhetoric and reality, the law and its application, the formal and the informal. What is needed, she contends, is the integration of the different aspects of the law and its operation, and the different theoretical perspectives (she refers in particular to interactionist and structuralist approaches). Her own study of the legal as well as social contexts within which the police and courts function is an example of how she believes this can be achieved. Her general conclusion is expressed as follows:

> By examining the law not just in terms of the general principles of its own ideology, but in terms of the details of its specific structures, procedures and decisions, this analysis has tried to show that the law governing the production, preparation, and presentation of evidence does not live up to its own rhetoric. . . legal structure, legal procedure, legal rulings, *not* legal rhetoric, govern the legitimate practice of criminal justice, and there is quite simply a distinct gap between the substance and the ideology of the law. (1981:154, 155, original emphasis)

As she points out, this has the most profound implications for sociological understanding of criminal justice as a social control mechanism, and of the relationship between the law and criminal justice, the state and ideology; and, though it has not been our primary concern here, she discusses some effects in the policy area, with respect to issues like extension of police powers, protection of defendants' rights, and the law and order debate (issues which are taken up also by McConville and Baldwin, 1981:Chapter 10).

Finally, any discussion of criminal justice institutions and practices needs to recognise they form a part only of a complex network of social control mechanisms and processes. As earlier acknowledged, our focus on criminal law has meant that some features of the law as a regulatory device of the state are highlighted, while others are neglected. The expansion of the state's regulatory activities into new areas and its utilisation of conciliatory and compensatory rather than penal methods have already been mentioned. At the same time, as various writers have observed, policing, surveillance and security, with respect mainly to property, have increasingly been privatised, and a range of relatively 'informal' or 'popular' methods of resolving disputes and administering 'justice' have appeared.

More interesting and relevant, however, in view of our concern in this book with the comparative analysis of the alternative approaches to control and different systems of control to be found in modern industrial societies, are the trend towards increasing medicalisation of various forms of deviance and social problems (including some previously treated as crimes) and developments in the welfare field, involving changes in ideology and in the provision by the state of services and benefits.

6 The medical–psychiatric system

The case was earlier made for treating medicine as, in Zola's (1972) words, a major 'institution of social control', which can usefully be contrasted with the principal alternative control institution in the modern world—the legal–judicial system. It was also argued that the problems with which these two systems deal—illness and crime respectively—can for sociological purposes be defined as forms of social deviance. Parsons was the first sociological theorist to look at medicine and the law in this way and in *The Social System* (1951) he devoted considerable attention to medicine and 'the sick role', as part of western society's mechanisms of social control.

Having in the previous chapter examined the nature of criminal law and justice as approaches to the control of deviant behaviour, we turn now to a consideration of the medical-psychiatric system: that set of perceptions, practices and institutions that developed in western industrial societies from the nineteenth century on as the preferred method for identifying and managing disease and disability. As the authors of two early articles in which these two approaches were compared themselves noted (Aubert and Messinger, 1958; Stoll, 1968), there are important differences between the two. They mentioned the different images represented by 'the criminal' and 'the sick'.

Whereas the criminal law holds individuals accountable for their actions and for the consequences of their actions, western medicine's conception of disease is of a misfortune, caused by non-human (or 'natural'), physical factors. Parsons (1951) and Freidson (1970a) both contend that medicine, like the law (its main competitor) functions as a formal, official instrument of control. Medicine may be a less obvious control agent but by exercising its responsibility for regulating the entry into, conduct in and exit from 'the sick role', it plays a crucial role in the management of those types of deviance that involve incapacity to meet social expectations and norms because of illness or disability. Medicine's operation as a control mechanism has been concealed, by its characterisation as a science and as a clinical treatment mode, both from most members of society and, until about the middle of the twentieth century, from sociologists as well.

Some conceptions of social control place emphasis on the role played by a body of individuals or ideas in determining definitions of reality and morality in society and give more weight to the processes of construction and imposition of definitions than to the legal or administrative bases of codes of behaviour or systems of rules and regulations (Stoll, 1968). They thus highlight ideological more than institutional bases for the exercise of social control. Freidson (1970a:Chapter 10) and Conrad and Schneider (1980a) treat the 'medical model' as a social construction, a mode of understanding human behaviour and the natural and social worlds, and explore the meaning and implications of the shift in the last hundred or so years from a 'badness' to a 'sickness' approach to deviance. Conrad and Schneider see deviance definition and designation as political matters, as involving 'enterprise, strategy and struggle' (1980a:8), and in their view (1980a:20) the currently 'ascendant' social control paradigm is medicine; they describe it as 'the central retributive agent in our society' (1980a:33) and 'the most powerful extralegal institution of social control' (1980a:241).

Overall, the trend has been for more and more of the problems of human behaviour and social order to be regarded as best handled by medical and therapeutic forms of intervention. In some cases, this has resulted in a redefinition of what was previously considered a criminal matter. A therapeutic control philosophy has generally been welcomed as a sign of a socially progressive and 'civilised' society. This process of increasing medicalisation means that undesirable aspects of the human condition and problematic forms of human behaviour have increasingly been treated not as the result of intentional acts of will but as determined by events and factors (biological, psychological or environmental) beyond conscious human control and as appropriate subjects for scientific investigation and clinical treatment.

Medicine consists of a language for describing the nature of deviance (employing the metaphor of illness or sickness), a scientifically-based theory about the causes and appropriate remedies for such phenomena, and a set of procedures, trained personnel and institutional facilities for diagnosis and treatment, all of which have been given moral and social support and official political authorisation in western industrial societies. What then is meant precisely by the term medicine?

Conceptions of medicine

First, medicine in the sense in which we are using the term is a socially and historically specific phenomenon. We are talking here of modern western scientific medicine, which as a set of principles, procedures and personnel became an established discipline only during the late nineteenth century. The objects of its concern—pain, disease, disability, death, disorders and malfunctions of the body (and later of the 'mind')—were not of course new, but they were viewed in a new way, significantly different from the previous systems of beliefs and practices whether these were based on magic, religion or practical knowledge. Ackerknecht, who in the 1940s published a number of classic works on medicine in preliterate cultures, summarised the main difference as follows:

> . . . primitive medicine is primarily magico-religious utilizing a few rational elements, while our medicine is predominantly rational and scientific, employing a few magic elements. (1946:468)

Coe (1970:Chapter 5) distinguishes between primitive, folk and modern medicine, arguing that of the three only modern medicine combines the three principal characteristics of being scientifically based, institutionalised, and practised by specialists.

Modern medicine thus comprises a number of separate though interconnected elements: an empirically-based approach; its own way of thinking about human nature, disease and the world, and its own vocabulary; theories about the forms, defining characteristics, specific etiology and developmental pattern of diseases (both physical and mental); and an accumulated body of knowledge and related technology that determines the identification of symptoms, diagnosis of disease and application of appropriate, typically physico-chemical, remedies.

A number of writers[1] have stressed the distinctive characteristics of the medical approach or 'the medical model': its reliance on the analytical separation of body and mind; its mechanistic conception of the structure and workings of the human organism; an individualistic focus—reflected both in its conception of disease as lying within the organism and in its approach to treatment; and its 'rational', scientific, positivist approach to the investigation, explanation and treatment of disease.

Scientific medicine gradually moved from a conception of 'the whole patient (or whole person with a disease)' to a focus on 'the pathology or the disease process itself'; this entailed, first, the objectification of the diseased person, as a body from which the mind and the soul are separated, and later the 'fragmentation' of the patient as an organism into various component parts, processes and functions (Jaco, 1958:4). At the same time, medical science as it developed[2] moved from reliance simply on observation and measurement to research methods involving experiment, laboratory investigation and vivisection, assisted by, on the one hand, the depersonalisation of disease and, on the other, the kind of access to large numbers and types of disease made possible by the expansion of public hospitals for the urban poor in the nineteenth century (Waddington, 1973).

Foucault's (1976) analysis of changes in medical ideas in the late eighteenth and early nineteenth centuries traces the connections between the 'birth of the clinic', new concepts of patient and disease, and the emergence of a new scientific discourse. Jewson (1976) depicts three phases in the production of medical knowledge between the late eighteenth century and the end of the nineteenth, each with its distinctive 'system of cosmology'; he terms these 'Bedside Medicine', 'Hospital Medicine' and 'Laboratory Medicine' and in the process medicine shifted from 'a person orientated toward an object orientated cosmology' (1976:232). From then on, medicine has continued to be

> dominated by the belief that improvements in health must rely on an engineering approach, chiefly chemical or mechanical, based on an understanding of the structure and function of the body and the disease processes that affect it. This concept has been largely responsible for the significance attached to the work of the acute hospital and for the relative neglect of psychiatric, geriatric and some other forms of care; it has had a powerful influence on the direction of medical research. (McKeown, 1970:343)

Clinical medicine has also largely ignored the environment by contrast with preventive and, now, occupational medicine.

Basically modern medicine works with a biologistic conception of the nature and causation of disease, the presence of disease being inferred from the observation or reported experience of discomfort, pain, disability or a physical irregularity which are taken as 'symptoms' of an underlying pathological condition, 'an abnormality in function and/or structure of any part, process, or system of the organism' (Fabrega, 1974:132). In order to make the connection between reported 'symptoms' and a disease, scientific knowledge and systematic investigation are applied. Disease is seen as an undesirable disruption of the 'normal' healthy state and any effective measures that can remove or cure the problem and restore health are by definition to be desired. Medicine's interventions are expected to be beneficial and, therefore, in principle always to be encouraged. Medical knowledge, medical techniques and medical practitioners are seen as contributing positively to the improvement and prolongation of human life. Medicine, thus, has status and value in its own right because of its capacity to enhance human happiness and welfare both individually and collectively.

When talking of 'medicine' or 'the medical system', however, it is important to distinguish between medical ideas and medical practices. Recent historians of medicine have made attempts to disentangle rhetoric from actual practice in assessing its contribution to society and to do better than simply give a chronicle of 'medical discoveries and personalities' (Woodward and Richards, 1977:17).

Medical science as a perspective on reality, a secular approach to problems of human existence—birth, death, pain, disease—did certainly make a significant contribution to western understanding of human nature, health and illness in nineteenth century Europe, but various writers have been critical of traditional historical interpretations of medicine's role in society. Doyal (1979:Chapter 4), among others, argues that a fundamental limitation is that its impact was mainly at the level of ideas. Medicine in the form of clinical or curative medical practice did not become a general influence on health until well into the twentieth century, and even now access to and the benefits of medical care can be overestimated. Classic accounts portraying western medicine as the major factor responsible for substantial reductions in mortality in the nineteenth and early twentieth centuries have now been refuted. Writers such as McKeown (1976) for England and Wales, McKinlay and McKinlay (1977) for the United States, Powles (1973) and Taylor (1979) have produced convincing evidence that improvements in life expectation and health were due rather to better living standards and diet, and to changes in hygiene and sanitation. These were in turn the result of public health measures adopted in the urban centres of industrialising societies. Much of the decline in deaths from infectious diseases occurred prior to the mass introduction of antibiotics and effective immunisation campaigns. Also access to medical care was restricted to the upper and middle classes and to insured sections of the (mainly male) working population until health services became part of welfare state provision following the Second World War (Doyal, 1979).

Overestimates of the importance of modern medicine for human health and well-being were largely the product of a failure to distinguish between medicine at the level of knowledge and techniques, and general medical practice, between medical rhetoric and reality, and, the fact that greater weight was given to scientific and clinical medicine by contrast with developments in the public health field. Public health was a far less exciting and prestigious area of health care activity in the nineteenth century than was clinical medicine, and since the former was oriented to the improvement of community living conditions rather than individual treatment, the tracing of connections between intervention measures and health outcomes was far harder to see.

The history of medicine is not only a history of ideas but of practices and institutions or, as Freidson puts it, of 'medical work' as well as of medical 'discoveries', and Freidson's own work (1970a, 1970b, 1975) is largely concerned with an analysis of medicine 'as a profession' and of the process whereby it established its position of 'professional dominance'. Mechanic (1968/78), another major contemporary medical sociologist, is interested in the emergence of particular forms of institutional setting for the practice of medicine over the last century and how these have affected modes of medical care. We will look at these writers and others later in the chapter.

Historical and sociological accounts of the nature and development of medicine and of the medical profession reveal how socially and historically contingent modern medicine is and remind us that western medicine is only one recent and particular approach to healing. Field (1973) and Kennedy (1973) discuss different cultural responses—magic, religion, medicine, and pastoral care—to that category of human problems represented, in Field's terminology, by the five Ds (death, disease, disability, discomfort, dissatisfaction). He suggests that it is with these that any health system has to cope, medicine being one such system.

Idler attributes the equation of health care with medical care, to be found in most sociology of medicine (including the work of Parsons, Freidson and Mechanic), and a neglect of 'the subjective social reality of health and illness' and of 'indigenous lay health knowledge, beliefs and practices' (1979:725), to the acceptance by sociologists of the medical definitions of the phenomena. He and Field (1973, 1980) argue that the range of responses to illness and health care are more diverse, even in modern society, than a medico-centric orientation allows for.[3]

Several writers have sought to categorise the various sorts of medical and health care systems to be found across the range of human societies, past and present. Particularly important in characterising modern western systems are their relationships to the state and to business, and hence their methods of organising, supplying and financing health services. Terris (1978) has identified three types of modern health care system—public assistance, health insurance, and a national health service (corresponding to three different economic systems, precapitalist, capitalist and socialist). He regards most systems of Western Europe, (but not Britain) North America and Australia as examples of the insurance system model. Field (1980:401) has developed a somewhat more complex typology based on a number of characteristics of health systems. He describes four main contemporary types, distinguishing between 'pluralistic' (or free enterprise), 'insurance', 'national health service' and 'socialised system'.

Terris and Field disagree over where to place Australia in their typologies— in the (largely privately funded) insurance system category or in the national (and government financed) health service category—and hence over whether Australia is in the same category as the United States or Britain. Najman and Western (1984) draw a further distinction between a national and socialised health system, both of which have publicly funded medical care but which differ over whether some or all medical staff are state employed, and hence over the extent to which some degree of medical autonomy is retained. They then examine the various policy changes regarding medical and hospital service provision in Australia during the 1970s and into the early 1980s, and comment on the effect of these on the type of health care system Australia has had over this period, which at different times fitted the categories of both a private insurance-based and a nationalised services system.[4]

Current developments in medical care

The main characteristics of the health care systems of western countries are their continuously increasing size, scope and cost, financed through a combination of private insurance and government funds (in varying proportions in the different countries). In America, for example, total health spending has increased from 4.4 per cent of GNP in 1958 to 10.8 per cent in 1983 (Field, 1980:411; Rushing, 1985:297). One way of expressing the variation between countries in the relative contribution of governments to health care expenditure is the proportion that comes from public sources: in 1975, the range was 93 per cent in UK, 92 per cent in Sweden, 77 per cent in West Germany, 64 per cent in Australia[5] and 43 per cent in USA (Pollitt, 1984:120).

By the mid 1970s, medicine was 'the second largest industry in the country [USA], exceeded only by construction, and... the fastest growing' (McKinlay, 1977:462) though by 1980 it had been overtaken by agriculture (Field, 1980:411). An important recent development has been the appearance (in the late 1960s) and rapid increase in investor-owned, for-profit health facilities, accounting by 1979 for 25 per cent of personal health care expenses, and covering the full range of services and facilities, accompanied by a significant contraction of government programmes at all levels under Reagan (Salmon, 1984:144–5), though a sizeable proportion of the income received by the investor-owned health care firms comes from the federal Medicare and Medicaid schemes (Salmon, 1984:164). Salmon also supplies some evidence of an expansion of the private sector in insurance and in health care provision in Britain.

The concept of the 'medical industrial complex' conveys the idea of profit-seeking corporations and large-scale industry being engaged in the production and distribution of medical goods and services. McKinlay (1977:461) lists some of the main reasons why 'medicine is immensely profitable':

(a) there exists a large and often captive market;
(b) demand by the public for medicine is often given primacy over other commodity consumption and appears to be insatiable;
(c) the association with medicine facilitates a strategic control over a near total consuming public;
(d) it makes possible strategic control over valued technology, thereby enhancing competitive position;
(e) it is an arena where the state acts as a guarantor for profit; and
(f) it enables exploitive institutions to project a false image of conspicuous benevolence.

Capitalist enterprise and medicine's commitment to advancing scientific innovation and research are both implicated in the ever-increasing degree of bureaucratisation, specialisation and reliance on high technology in modern health care systems. Current forms of organisation of medical care, the role of corporations, and government policy are seen as major factors in producing what Waitzkin (1983:111–2) describes as the contradictory current state of health care in America where 'private expansion' coexists alongside 'public contraction'. The main features he identifies are high subsidisation of the private sector by government, reduction in public provision of services and institutional facilities (especially hospitals), the dumping of poorer and uninsured patients on the public sector by the private, and a substantial population for whom medical care is unavailable for geographical, economic or other reasons.

Most western health care systems are facing very serious problems. On the one hand, costs seem to be impossible to contain and, on the other, despite massive expenditures and modern technology there is no real evidence that the overall incidence of disease and disability has declined or that the general population enjoys better health or at least longer periods free from ill-health. It is largely accepted that everyone has a right to medical care, since everyone at some time or other will have the need of it and for reasons over which they have little or no control. At the same time medical care becomes more and more expensive. Since the occurrence of disease and injury continues to be relatively high, there is, in Mechanic's words, 'almost unlimited possibility for continued escalation of medical demand and increased medical expenditures' (1977:62–3). Unlimited demand and the fact that the use of services (which increasingly involve expensive drugs and/or diagnostic or treatment equipment and expertise) is determined by physician decisions about appropriateness, not by cost (either to the consumer or to the treatment facility). Even in a nationalised health service system, there is limited scope for regulation of the nature and use of medical techniques and services and hence of overall expenditure prediction and control.

We will look now briefly at the main features of the Australian health care system. As we have seen, compared with other countries, the proportionate contribution to health expenditure from the government was similar to that of the United States in the 1970s and lower than that of Western Europe. Australians depended on voluntary insurance until the introduction of Medibank in 1975, though as part of its welfare expenditure the state was financially involved with certain areas of medical care—pharmaceutical benefits, pensioners' health, school medical service and public hospitals (Kewley, 1973). Najman and Western (1984), in surveying the main changes in government policy regarding health care provision from 1970, comment on the absence of any direct or necessary relationship between spending on health care and more equitable distribution of or access to services and hence any bases for assessment of the benefits of increased public spending in this field. Following the change of government in November

1975, some modifications were introduced to the scheme. During the following period of Liberal government, health expenditure remained remarkably stable and even fell between 1977/78 and 1978/79 (Jones, 1983:242). Though health continued to absorb increasingly larger sums in absolute terms, spending on medical care stabilised at between 7 and 8 per cent of the GDP in the late 1970s (Jones, 1983:241). Compared with other social services areas such as education, personal services and housing, health like social security seems to have been somewhat less seriously affected by budget controls on public expenditure in Britain in the late 1970s (Gough, 1979:129–30). In Australia, it appears that the federal government was more effective in holding health (and housing) costs in the period than it was in other welfare areas. However, recent figures on health expenditure per head of population still show a steady increase throughout the 1970s and early 1980s, with a slight decline in the proportion coming from public sources in the 1980s, when there was a shift back to voluntary health insurance (Social Indicators, 1984:95).

Sociological analysis of medicine, psychiatry and the health care system

We are dealing here with a body of theoretical and empirical material loosely described as the sociology *of* medicine (Straus, 1957), in which medical perspectives, practices, organisations, and the deliverers and recipients of medical services are subjected to sociological analysis. The dominant tradition in medical sociology (found in the work of interactionists, some functionalists and more empirically-oriented sociologists) is to treat medicine as a composite social phenomenon with its own social characteristics, institutional features and modes of functioning: the focus of concern is thus the roles, relationships, factors and processes internal to this sector of society. This kind of medical sociology (and one should note that neither Freidson nor Mechanic, the two leading American medical sociologists in the 1960s and 1970s, can fairly be put in this category) has been heavily criticised for accepting a medical definition of the area of study and for treating the medical world as a discrete and separate entity capable of being analysed and understood as a (micro) social system in its own right. Dissatisfaction with the restrictive equation of health care with medicine led many sociologists during the 1970s to redefine their area of study as 'health and illness' rather than 'medicine' (for example, Stacey in her (1978) review article).

Placing medical practice and the medical profession in their wider social context leads to an extension of the range of perceived influences and constraints on modern medicine. Medical care is seen not simply as the disinterested application of the latest scientific knowledge and techniques by specially trained personnel to the diagnosis and treatment of disease, but a complex social phenomenon operating at a number of levels and in a number of ways—practical, technical, professional, moral, cultural, institutional—and at the same time reflecting and reinforcing the dominant institutions and values of the wider society. An adequate understanding of health, illness, medicine and health care means relocating these phenomena within the overall structures of society.[6] For marxists these are the economic, the political, and the ideological structures of capitalist society (McKinlay, 1977; Navarro, 1976; Renaud, 1975). Thus critical determinants of health and medical care are the state and the institutions and interests of modern capitalism. Feminists would add as a separate or underlying set of societal forces the gender order, a complex network of institutions, factors and processes reflecting and reinforcing an overall structure of male domination (Barrett and Roberts, 1978; Broom, 1984; Doyal, 1979:Chapter 6). Having acknowledged that it is a limitation, the analysis here will be confined to the specifically medical system (a more manageable project in this context), though without the narrow focus that was characteristic of traditional medical sociology.

'The medical system', however, is interpreted as covering medical conceptions and treatment of mental as well as of physical disease. This is justified on three main grounds: (a) psychiatry by contrast with psychology and psychoanalysis is a specialist area within medicine, its practitioners belong to the medical profession, it follows the clinical model of disease diagnosis, etiology and treatment (though as we shall see this is contentious), and it has its own place in the officially recognised medical institutions; (b) as the traditional division between mind and body and hence western conceptions of disease as being either mental or physical are being increasingly questioned, it would seem appropriate to consider the whole range of diseases and treatments to which the medical model is applied; and (c) our principal interest being the social control exercised by certain types of institutions and occupational groups, the medical specialty with the most overt and generally acknowledged role as a social control agency has been psychiatry. Psychiatry does provide a particularly clear example of the contradictory position occupied by social control institutions, being:

> both part of the ideological and coercive mechanisms of industrial society and at the same time...committed to the resolution of the very tensions and strains which that society and its institutions produce. (Penfold and Walker, 1983:v)

Though in this chapter we talk mainly about 'medicine' in general terms, for certain purposes we accept the well-established but increasingly questionable division between 'physical' and 'mental' disease and a distinction between the definitions, categories of personnel, treatment methods and settings characteristic of medicine as a whole and those found in psychiatry. Indeed, Leifer comments that psychiatry is 'so deeply-permeated' with medical 'terminology', 'rhetoric' and 'habits of thought and language' that it is hard to separate the two (1969:11). The facts that we speak of mental 'illness' and mental 'pathology', that psychiatry is a recognised medical specialty, and that mental 'patients' are 'treated' in mental 'hospitals' all indicate the existence of a wide-spread acceptance in modern society of the notion that dis-eases and dis-orders of the mind and of the emotions may be considered analogous to diseases of the body, and hence the authority to deal with them has been gradually officially transferred to members of the medical profession.

Foucault (1967) offers what is now the classic account of the process by which 'madness' came under 'disciplinary' control in Western Europe, first as 'unreason' in the form of idleness and later as an illness. He notes that the separation of physical from psychological aspects of human nature and the recommendation of different treatment locations and regimes occurred relatively late (i.e. in the nineteenth century). As was the case with physical illness, mental 'illness' in the modern view was assumed to be the product of forces outside individual control and not therefore subject to reason or will.

Ingleby (1985) suggests there were two main periods and three revolutionary changes in the development of modern psychiatric methods of dealing with mental illness. The initial period was the first half of the nineteenth century in which we see 'the rise of the asylum as a remedial institution, and the capture of this domain by the medical profession'; this was followed by a second medical consolidation phase including 'the broadening of the concept of "mental illness", together with the addition of new functions of control and surveillance of the non-hospitalised population; and the development of new therapies and professional alliances, notably with psychology'. The first revolution, in his view, was the work of Turk and Pinel in laying 'the foundations of rational and humane treatment of the insane'; the second was 'the invention of psychoanalysis'; and the third was '"the drug revolution" and the emptying-out of the mental hospital population' (Ingleby, 1985:145). Grob (1973), Rothman (1971) and others have provided detailed historical accounts of the emergence and significance of the 'asylum', as the place of segregation, observation and treatment in nineteenth century western society.

A number of writers have discussed the applicability of 'the medical model' to non-physical illness. Taber et al. (1969) identify four key features of a disease model that would need to be substantiated for the model to cover mental conditions; these are—nosology (that symptoms exist and can be identified as specific entities and that they provide evidence of an underlying condition); pathology (that the illness process represents abnormality in an organism and/or in the functions of the organism that persists over time); etiology (that specific causes can be found for specific conditions); and therapy (that appropriate and effective treatment exists for each condition).

Ingleby (1985:162–3) describes key characteristics of the medical model as applied to physical conditions which also apply to the handling of 'mental illness'. These include the following: the legally conferred authority of the doctor to take over responsibility for those believed incapable of managing their own lives; the representation of this power and of medical knowledge as being technical not moral in character; particular social attributes of the sick role as isolating, discrediting and dependency-producing; and the perception of the problem as lying inside the sick person and hence of treatment as needing to take no account of external environmental factors. He stresses that a powerful link between psychiatry and the rest of medicine is the prominent role given from the nineteenth century on to physical modes of treatment for 'mental' as well as physical disease, of which the modern reliance on drugs is only the latest instance (1985:165).

These authors and others (for example Klerman, 1977; Leifer, 1970/1; Manning, 1976; Sedgwick, 1982) have cast doubts on whether the objective scientifically-based medical model does indeed fit diseases of the mind as well as those of the body. They contend that, rather than acting simply as the most suitable technique for classifying, explaining and dealing with certain types of problems given our current state of knowledge, the medical model when applied to 'mental illness' operates more as a socially-imposed moral construction or ideology which falsely claims (or is claimed) to have an independent scientifically justified status—issues which will be discussed later in the chapter.

A sociological conception of 'the medical system' sees it as containing at least three components: medical ideas, medical personnel and their practices, and institutional settings. Medicine is not only a science, a philosophy, a professional activity or a specialised technical occupation, each with its own characteristic form and dynamic; it is also an example of rational bureaucracy, of industrial technology and applied science, of capitalist enterprise, of a control ideology, and of a social organisation based on class and gender divisions.

In an examination of medicine as an institution of social control, various features of the medical system and aspects of its relationship with the broader society will be considered in turn. They consist of the following: (a) medical science and technology; (b) medicine as ideology; (c) professionalism; (d) rationalisation and bureaucratisation; (e) capitalism; and (f) gender and patriarchy. In the process, we will be drawing on the theoretical ideas contributed by sociologists from a variety of perspectives and we will find, not surprisingly, that the various features identified above receive unequal treatment from the different theoretical schools. Dealing with the medical system in this way necessarily involves some degree of simplification for analytical purposes of what is in reality a highly complex and interconnected set of institutions, factors and processes, no one of which alone can possibly provide an adequate basis for understanding the structure and workings of the whole system.

Science and technology in medicine

Though there has been some debate over whether the best overall characterisation of medicine (in its modern clinical mode) is that of a science, an art or a business (Carlson, 1975:31–6; Dubos, 1968:113–9), there is little dispute that medicine perceives itself as a science, and this is reflected in its system of education and training and is the basis of its claims to professional status. In its approach to the identification and explanation of disease, in its acquisition and communication of knowledge, in its development and application of treatment methods, and in the preference given to cure over care, medicine follows, albeit imperfectly, what is generally regarded as an empirical science model, and indeed demonstrates there is considerable overlap between medical and biological sciences. The development of medicine historically was linked to that of science. Parsons sees science as an important determinant of medical practice and indeed regards medicine as an 'applied science' (1951:432), but rejects any idea that science is value-free, regarding both modern science and modern medicine rather as cultural phenomena (1951:Chapter VIII).

Medicine in its applied science role has traditionally favoured an '"engineering approach" chiefly chemical or mechanical' (McKeown, 1970:343) to health and illness. This is reflected in medicine's attachment to an individualistic, biological model, in its continuing reluctance to take seriously the role of environmental determinants of disease. This affects the kinds of research and etiological theories produced and limits the strategies for managing disease by emphasising treatment and cure rather than prevention.

The physical science or engineering orientation means that the sick are turned into 'research objects' and 'laboratory artefacts' (Jaco, 1958:4), to whom investigative tests and physico-chemical procedures are applied and who are marginally if at all implicated in diagnosis, treatment or recovery. The medical view has been accused of 'scientization' (Waitzkin, 1983:33–4), 'miniaturization' (Carlson, 1975:37) and 'reductionism' (Dubos, 1968:66). In the words of White:

> ...[That] most diseases can be regarded as things that mechanistically 'attack' otherwise healthy individuals and that usually can be 'cured' by pills, potions, or procedures is an unwarranted extension of contemporary space age solid state semantics. (1978:5)

We must also question the assumptions that physical diseases are all potentially amenable to 'natural' scientific methods of investigation and explanation, and that much of the knowledge necessary for the identification, classification, diagnosis, treatment and prognosis of diseases has already been provided by the biological and medical sciences.

The state of our knowledge is imperfect. New diseases appear, new patterns of association between symptoms and antecedent factors emerge, new causal theories are suggested and new remedies are found. However, the imprecision and uncertainty in medical knowledge and practice is believed by some radical writers to indicate an inherent problem with the subject and not something which can or will be overcome with time and effort.[7] We need to acknowledge the idealised nature of the prevailing images of science in general and of medical science in particular and allow for the presence of considerable diversity within medicine with regard to the degree to which the scientific approach adequately captures the essential character of medical research and medical practice (Carlson, 1975:Chapter 7; Illich, 1975; Powles, 1973).

There are differences between various categories of personnel, conceptions of illness and types of treatment approach in the extent to which they conform to a strict scientific model. Freidson draws a distinction between a 'scholarly' and a 'consulting' orientation within the professions generally and within medicine, and suggests a number of elements that he believes make the 'clinical mind' different from the 'scientific' (1970a:168–9, 73–5). We have already noted the distinction between clinical, curative medicine and public health, as reflecting the division between the use of knowledge for individual diagnosis and treatment, and collective preventive measures, a distinction that was particularly relevant in the discussion of the history of scientific medicine and its contribution to health in the nineteenth and early twentieth centuries.

Similarly, the split between generalist and specialist branches of modern medicine, which developed in the nineteenth century, (Waddington, 1977) is of interest at this point for the light it sheds on our understanding of the relationship between medical care and the general scientific orientation of medicine, with consequent effects on the relationship between physician and patient, and on the types of personnel, the sorts of treatment methods and settings, and the modes of social organisation characteristic of the complex modern medical system. Here we are primarily concerned with assessing the relative importance of a particular type of scientific and technological focus for its influence on professional socialisation, the division of labour and work attitudes and practices. Were we attempting at this stage to offer a full sociological interpretation of medicine (as for example Mechanic does in his 1968/78 book) we would need to examine other sources of influence on typical patterns of medical practice, various forms of medical organisation, and alternative versions of 'the medical model' and to draw also on insights from the sociology of organisations and work (Davies 1979; Stacey, 1978).

It is a commonplace that modern western medicine is high technology medicine. Increasingly the various stages of medical intervention (identification, diagnosis, treatment) rely not only on scientific knowledge but on complicated and expensive machinery and drugs. The conditions that attract money, status and research effort are those amenable to research experimentation and spectacular technological innovation (transplant and coronary surgery, prematurity, infertility), while many common diseases remain uninteresting to medical science and relatively untouched by advances in medical knowledge and technology.

Specialisation within medicine, the bureaucratisation of medical practice and treatment settings, and the division between primary level general practice and high technology specialties provide evidence of a split between 'care' and 'cure', between 'social' and 'technical' aspects of treatment, and between a holistic person-centred medical approach and modes of medical intervention that conform with a mechanistic scientific model.

As Mechanic and others have noted, modern medicine is increasingly determined in its types of services and organisational settings by its reliance on ever more complex and costly technology. They claim the high degree of functional differentiation, specialisation and hierarchical ordering of specialties are a product of the domination of modern medicine by knowledge and technology. (Marxists would give as much emphasis, if not more, to the influence of economic factors, specifically capital concentration and accumulation, on the organisation and main forms of medical care.) Taylor in a recent Australian book (1979) discusses the nature and role of 'high technology' used for investigative, diagnostic and treatment purposes and the creation of 'superspecialists'. Like Illich (1975), he is deeply critical of technology in modern medicine, which he sees as 'out of control'.[8] The commitment to high technology involves in his opinion a confusion between what is possible and what is desirable with the result that much of what medicine does is 'counter—productive, ineffective...wasteful...inhumane...socially destructive' (1979:105). The powerful influence of technology in medicine has a number of social consequences, including what Taylor terms 'patientization'. All the aspects of modern medical care to which he draws attention have implications, as we shall see, for the kinds of social control exercised by the medical system.

However, consideration of the theories of causation and treatment applied to 'mental illness' as compared with physical disease does suggest some important differences between the relationship of psychiatry to the scientific approach and that of general medicine to science. Without misrepresenting physical medicine as a uniform and consistent set of ideas and practices or ignoring the influence of non-technical, non-scientific considerations in helping to determine the form and content of medical care[9] (and hence falling into an attitude of 'irreverent myopia' (Sedgwick, 1982:27) towards physical medicine), there are some broad points of contrast between the nature and application of medical science to 'mental' as compared with physical illness. Recognition of this does lead to the raising of serious questions as to the scientific status of psychiatry and the relevance of the disease model to mental and psychological disorders.[10]

In the first place, 'mental illness' requires the making of a social judgement about the appropriateness, acceptability and comprehensibility of a person's behaviour. It is therefore a question not of clinically-defined pathology but of social deviance. Definitions and classifications of mental 'diseases' and 'disorders' and diagnoses in particular cases basically involve imposing one set of interpretations and evaluations (based on allegedly objective criteria) on human behaviour, when what is being assessed is not a directly observable and describable physical phenomenon but rather an individual's thoughts, feelings, words and actions the meanings of which are specific to the individual, the situation and the wider cultural context.

Secondly, as a body of empirically substantiated knowledge, psychiatry is far less advanced than the other branches of the biomedical sciences. For example, schizophrenia, in the view of many, the archetypal modern psychiatric disorder, has no commonly agreed symptomatology, etiology and prognosis or knowledge-based, effective treatment within Australia (Fulcher, 1975), let alone cross-culturally. Related to this is the fact that, though treatments are available for most psychiatric conditions, there is a lesser degree of professional consensus in this than in other medical specialties and those treatments that are effective are mostly palliative rather than curative. This may be because there is in many instances no direct theoretical link between knowledge about the 'disease' and recommended therapies, or perhaps (as some sociologists would claim) because the scientific theories and 'the medical model' itself are wrong about the nature and causes of 'mental illness', which should be regarded as a social condition not a psycho-physiological one.

Thirdly, the technological advances in the treatment of many physical conditions have not been matched in the case of 'mental illness'. There is no equivalent in the treatment of psychological and psychiatric disorders to the removal of a diseased organ, organ replacement, corrective surgery, or the restoration of 'normal' functioning by the curing of infection by antibiotic drugs. Certainly, biochemical substances have come to play the major part in managing a wide range of psychotic and neurotic conditions, but in most cases the effect is to moderate the degree of the disturbance or to alleviate some of the associated symptoms, not to cure the underlying problem. Psycho-surgery (lobotomy) and physical remedies (such as electro-convulsive or shock therapy) have had variable rates of success and negative side-effects, and even where apparently effective, these measures worked on the symptoms rather than on the underlying causes. In many cases these were not well enough established to provide guidance as to appropriate treatments, and the value of such procedures has been increasingly questioned from a scientific and practical as well as moral standpoint. Behaviour modification, aversion therapy and conditioning techniques have also been the subject of public and professional concern. But where voluntarily requested or where the methods involve no serious or long-lasting physical or psychological damage and where there is a relatively high probability of the distressing or disabling symptoms being removed, these methods seem to have their place (for instance, phobias are overcome, smoking habits broken), but not when directed at changing orientations or behaviour (e.g. homosexual or aggressive) that happen to fall outside the prevailing norms.

Of major importance in the treatment of mental and emotional problems, and this is true of those defined as 'illness' as well as those designated psychological or social rather than medical, is the range of non-physical forms of therapy—individual and group counselling, psychoanalysis and an array of psychological techniques[11]—and various socially-oriented mechanisms. These supposedly work on feelings, perceptions and attitudes with the objectives of gaining insight and control over oneself and/or modifying interaction patterns within relationships and groups (and particularly in the family). Regardless of how effective these psycho-social methods are and of how they relate to the various theories about the causes of cognitive, emotional and behavioural disorders, the significant point to make here is that they are certainly not usually considered to be primarily or specifically 'medical' modes of treatment: they are tenuously if at all connected with the kind of scientific knowledge that forms a basis for the medical approach to physical health and disease. Their practitioners do not require prior medical training or expertise nor the facilities of hospitals or other types of medical settings for treatment. Indeed, insofar as the medical system has incorporated such therapies into its repertoire, this can be seen more as a concession to the whole person approach to illness, and a recognition of the multi-causal nature of disease and of the necessity for a correspondingly comprehensive and varied range of services and remedies, than as surrendering medicine's overall dominance of the professions and treatment methods operating in the health care field.

At this point, we are only interested in establishing in a general way what are the prevailing medical conceptions of the causes of various types of disease and of appropriate methods for treating them. Analysis and assessment of the social characteristics and conditions of the modern medical system and of the social and moral implications of medical models, medical practices and increasing medicalisation will be presented in the following sections of the chapter.

Medicine as ideology

Though the concept 'ideology' is defined in a very specific sense (meaning a biased and often false representation of social reality but one consistent with the selective interests of a particular, and typically dominant, section of society) by certain types of theorists, mainly those who favour a marxist or some 'radical' or critical theoretical perspective, it has also been used to refer to the particular mode of thinking about the world and their place in it that is shared by the members of a group or an organisation, such as an occupation or profession.[12] Stimson and Webb, for example, who studied the doctor-patient relationship from a basically subjectivist or interpretive perspective, offer the following definition of the professional ideology of doctors: 'the "system" of ideas that doctors collectively hold about the nature of man, disease, and the treatment of disease' (1975:136).

A number of writers, including Parsons, recognise that medicine does not function simply and solely on a technical level, as an applied science based on a well-established and objective body of knowledge, in this case knowledge about the human body and disease. Without denying the importance of the connection between scientific knowledge and methods and medical practice, medicine cannot be understood only as a rational or scientific set of ideas and activities. Kleinman (1973) suggests that only recently have medicine's dual roots in culture and human science as well as in the biophysical sciences been treated seriously. He puts forward the view that medicine is also a 'symbolic' system, which mediates between the biological and the psychosocial levels of reality, represented respectively by science and culture. In his words:

> A given medical system in its socio-cultural context does considerably more than name, classify and respond to illness. . . In a real sense, it structures the experience of illness and, in part, creates the form disease takes. Disease occurs as a natural process. . . But the experience of illness is a cultural or symbolic reality. (1973:208–9)

He argues that comparative studies of illness and responses to it reveal this non-scientific aspect of medicine. From this point of view, medicine is seen as having cultural elements and functions as well as objective, practical, scientific ones. Writers talk of it as a moral and social world view or 'cosmology' (Jewson, 1976) with its own language, imagery, philosophical assumptions and preferred values.

Parsons (1951:Chapter X and 1958) identified a number of prevailing cultural values that can be seen as reflected in the ways in which medicine defines and manages health and illness in contemporary American society. He is thereby indicating that medicine cannot be understood merely as a value-neutral scientific discipline nor as a straightforward technical exercise (and indeed the very idea of science as a value-free activity also becomes untenable). On the contrary, Parsons claims, medicine starts from a fundamental value judgement that ill-health is undesirable and that resources should be mobilised against it (1958:177). The recourse to science means that certain values and assumptions must be taken on at the same time as the technical approach to the problems of disease (associated with particular scientific knowledge) is adopted. He argues that medical practice has to deal with technical limitations—with uncertainty, and unpredictability—while also being expected to be competent and effective (1951: 447–51). For these and other reasons, the treatment of illness contains emotional and social aspects that are reflected in the way the roles of physician and patient come to be defined. Other authors have claimed that medicine is considerably more complex than Parsons suggests. For them, medical services have some partly contradictory characteristics: they consist of both a specialist knowledge and technology component (the 'cure' aspect) and a set of social attitudes, expectations and relationships (the 'caring' aspect). As Waitzkin and Waterman put it, there is both a 'medical expertise' ideology and a 'helping' ideology (1974:88–9). Strong expresses this as a tension between 'medical dominance' and 'medical gentility' (1979b:205).

The medical model (in all its various forms) is precisely that: a model, a paradigm, a social construction of reality. Whether it is applied to organic, psychological or behavioural phenomena, the assumption is made that a 'disease' or 'disorder' model is the most appropriate framework within which to conceptualise the nature and sources of problems and to determine social strategies for their management and the right choice of personnel to 'treat' them. The principal characteristics of a medical construction are that medicine's objects of concern are 'natural' phenomena (Strong, 1979b:212), the source of the trouble is located within the individual organism, and there is a 'clinical non-recognition' of social factors (Stark, 1982:138–9), all of which contribute to reification of the problem.

Much sociological analysis of medicine and particularly the trend to medicalisation (the politically and culturally sanctioned extension of 'the medical model' to an increasing range of individual and social 'problems') focusses specifically on its ideological aspects. Medicine in general and psychiatry in particular were seen by sociologists who took the interactionist or labelling approach as a powerful and persuasive source of influence on societal definitions of and responses to various types of human and social problem. They argued that illness was a social status or role, not an objective condition. The most obvious basis on which medicine could be seen as ideological was in its exclusive authority to define health and illness and to determine what should come under such headings.

> In the sense that medicine has the authority to label one person's complaint an illness and another's complaint not, medicine may be

said to be engaged in *the creation of illness as a social state which a human being may assume*. (1970a:205, original emphasis)

Freidson devotes considerable attention to the 'social construction of illness' as a form of deviance, and argues that, like 'law and religion, the profession of medicine uses normative criteria to pick out what it is interested in, and that its work constitutes a social reality that is distinct from (and on occasion virtually independent of) physical reality' (1970a:206).

Conrad and Schneider (1980a), who have published the major text on 'deviance and medicalization' are, along with Freidson, leading examples of writers who interpret the role of medicine as a defining agency for social problems and deviant behaviour, from what they call a 'social constructionist' perspective, that combines interactionism and conflict theory (1980a:xi, 17). From this standpoint, social control is based in control over ideas, over moral and social judgements about human beings and their behaviour, and how to deal with them. Their emphasis on the importance of 'the politics of deviance designation and definition' (1980a: 25, 22), and their use of terms such as 'medical paradigm' and 'hegemony of medical definitions' (1980a:28) demonstrate clearly how central to social control are the ideational or ideological aspects of social institutions and practices in their view and how important is the ideological role of medicine. Ideology for them is one of the three forms of medical social control, along with 'medical technology' and 'medical collaboration' (1980a:242).

They discuss the shift from a 'badness' to a 'sickness' designation and the way this has transferred power from religion and the law to a state-legitimated medical system (1980a:17). They point to the effects of a general tendency to prefer medical definitions and redefinitions of phenomena such as drug and alcohol addiction, sexual and emotional problems, some forms of interpersonal violence (for example, child abuse), and so on. In their book they include a historical analysis of the role of medicine and medicalisation in the treatment of major contemporary social problems. They examine how the individuals involved perceive themselves and their situation, how causality and responsibility are attributed, and what kinds of remedies and changes are advocated. They list a number of effects, both positive and negative, of medicine's central role in the social control field (1980a:246–52). Negative effects of a clearly ideological nature include the following: dislocation of responsibility from the individual; misrepresentation of the definition as morally neutral and of treatment as merely an expert technical matter; depoliticisation of the nature, resources and implications of the problem; and the exclusion, at an overt or acknowledged level, of moral judgements about good or evil in relation to either the intentions or consequences of actions.

Zola, in his classic paper on 'medicine as an institution of social control' (1972) focusses particularly on the power of medicine as a set of social and moral beliefs but adds some other features of the ideological character of medicine. He describes four aspects of what he terms the 'medicalizing' of everyday life: (i) 'the expansion of what in life is deemed relevant to the good practice of medicine'; (ii) 'the retention of absolute control over certain technical procedures'; (iii) 'the retention of near absolute access to certain "taboo" areas'; and (iv) 'the expansion of what is deemed relevant to the good practice of life' (1972: 492–7). He stresses the privileged access granted to medical authorities over highly personal ('taboo') areas, such as ageing, death, pregnancy, birth and sexuality, and argues that, by subsuming these matters under the categories of illness and health care, what would otherwise be regarded as invasion of privacy is allowed, even encouraged; medicine gains control over areas previously under the jurisdiction of the church and/or the monarch.

It was also in the mid-1970s that Illich published a powerful critique of medicine for its social implications that emphasised primarily the cultural or ideological aspects. His analysis of what he terms 'social' and 'structural iatrogenesis' is essentially concerned with what he sees as the disastrous psychological and cultural effects of the widespread misrepresentation of medicine in the modern industrial world as the solution to all forms of human suffering, pain and discomfort as well as to disease, resulting in a general state of human dependency and powerlessness or 'medical nemesis'.

> Medical nemesis...is the expropriation of man's coping ability by a maintenance service which keeps him geared up at the service of the industrial system...It is a symptom of the moral sickness of medical civilization. (1975:160)

Illich's case, which rests primarily on his analysis of industrial society, will be examined in more detail later in the chapter. Crawford (1977, 1980) too sees 'the medicalization of everyday life' as currently taking over yet further aspects of health care. Though partly arising out of general middle-class dissatisfaction with the traditional medical model, contemporary life-style and self-care movements, which he collectively describes as 'healthism', still work on the same individualistic and psychologistic assumptions, while at the same time extending moral and ideological coverage over a wider range of dis-eases.

Psychiatry and the medicalisation of psychological and emotional distress and disorder were also major targets of attack for those sociologists and others in the 1960s and 1970s who were questioning traditional academic assumptions about the nature of social order and social deviance. Following the work of Lemert (1951), they argued for a shift of focus from the causes of deviant behaviour to the processes of definition and to the effects of labelling and social reaction on the self-concept, social relationships and future conduct of the deviant.

Using this approach, Goffman (1961), Scheff (1966) and Szasz (1962), who made significant contributions to this topic, all emphasised the power of psychiatry as a method of defining and regulating certain personality types and forms of social behaviour. These writers disputed the validity and morality of a disease model when applied to non-physical conditions. Their basic thesis is that 'mental illness' consists of those socially inappropriate cognitive, emotional, verbal and behavioural responses which are upsetting, troublesome or threatening to others, and which are not readily explicable or predictable as within the 'normal' range of social expectations. Goffman, among others, points out that the first level of social reaction to 'problem' behaviour comes from family, friends and personal contacts and for them, a perception of 'the problem' as a form of illness is only one of the various alternatives (including, in many cases, normalisation, denial or accommodation). However, should such a possibility be seriously entertained by the person in question and/or significant others, a formal assessment may be sought from the relevant authorities, in this case a member of the medical profession, and thus a second phase of the deviance designation and control process is entered.

Those taking a sociology of deviance or anti-psychiatry position are not so much questioning whether the individuals concerned accept the medical diagnosis of the problem as 'mental illness' or whether they derive benefit from the treatment prescribed. They are rather examining with a critical eye the extent to which a medical conception of what Szasz calls 'problems in living' has become pervasive and powerful in the modern western world and asking what are the social and political consequences of this particular model. As Leifer argues, this is an example of medicine exercising an ideological function: 'psychiatry is social action disguised as medical treatment' (1970–1:20). In employing the disease model or 'metaphor', the impression is given 'that the psychiatrist functions as a physician rather than a social controller, a socializer, a spiritual guide, an educator or a social reformer' (1970–1:17). The ideological nature of medicine and psychiatry is masked by the 'tendency to think of medicine as above culture, politics and beliefs—as rooted in the "scientific" structure of the world rather than in human designs and purposes' (Leifer, 1969:54–6). Horwitz (1984) examines the particular characteristics of the 'therapeutic' mode of control over mental illness as being a focus on personality rather than conduct, reliance on persuasion rather than coercion, and the importance of language and shared understandings, all of which highlight the ideological aspects of this form of social control.

Leifer and others are particularly concerned to point out that the individualising, psychologising and depoliticising effects of a medical model are far more serious and morally and socially undesirable when applied to the definition, explanation and treatment of human beings' personalities, their experiences, their behaviour and their relationships, than when relatively objective biochemical and organic symptoms of an individual's physical condition are the target of attention. They also express considerable disquiet at the way in which the application of the 'disease' model in psychiatry leaves unrecognised and untouched the social conditions, pressures and constraints which ultimately produce the difficulties, frustrations and tensions which are then experienced and expressed as individual 'deviance' and 'disorder'.

Though not as interested specifically in psychiatry as are the sociologists of deviance, marxists also offer an analysis of medicine in its broad societal context, but they stress the links between medicine and an inegalitarian and oppressive socio-economic system. They reject Illich's analysis, arguing that the problem is capitalism rather than the cultural and moral aspects of industrial society; indeed, Navarro contends that industrialism itself is an ideology (1976:103). They look both at the role and content of 'the medical model' and at the part played by medical personnel as scientists and professionals in relation to the maintenance of the dominant ideology (with its concern for individualism, achievement, self-reliance, and materialism). This, they contend, is achieved directly by categorising and treating people's problems as 'diseases', thereby isolating those individuals from each other, locating the problem within the person and attributing no more than minor significance to environmental factors.

> Medicine as a therapeutic or clinical science locates the problem of disease in the human body. (Disease locates itself in the individual body and thus creates the need for a healing response to that individual experience. It is this fact that underlies the ideological problems being discussed.) (Crawford, 1980:371)

But medicine functions as an ideological force (and here they agree with the deviance theorists) by focussing public attention on its more dramatic technological accomplishments, and on the altruism and the 'caring' aspects of medical practice, therefore concealing the economic and political interests of doctors and of the medical institutions from general view. This then reduces the likelihood of discontent developing into a full-scale attack on the medical system and on the power structures that lie behind it. As Navarro puts it,

> the social utility of medicine is measured primarily in the arena of legitimation. Medicine is indeed socially useful to the degree that the majority of people believe and accept the proposition that what are actually politically caused conditions can be individually solved by medical intervention. (1976:208)

For Navarro, the medical and health care system, and this includes both public and private sector involvement, helps to reproduce bourgeois ideology—specifically the values of liberalism and individualism—as well as the major structural divisions of class and gender (1977:275–6): he claims the 'ideological aim of capitalist medicine is to reduce a collective phenomenon to an individual one' (1977:277). In one paper (1980), he discusses the way medicine is used generally to serve capitalist interests in the work sector. Elsewhere he (1977) mentions three current examples of health problems (psychosomatic conditions, occupational diseases, and cancer) whose structural causes are successfully obscured.

Marxists, and other critical and radical theorists, who have a clear view of cultural and moral systems as emerging and then being maintained in order to protect the interests of the ruling class and of the capitalist system, have developed a particular understanding of science, professionalism and the caring ethic as ideologies.[13] A major aspect of medicine is therefore that, like other institutions for handling deviance of various sorts, it is a complex socio-political instrument, operating ideologically on at least two levels. On the first and more obvious level medicine offers a particular construction of the nature of human beings and of certain types of problems, in terms of a disease model. On a second and more subtle level, in claiming a scientific, empirically-tested, value-free basis for its ideas, it disguises the fact that it also rests on social and moral assumptions and beliefs, and supports the collective interests and power positions of certain groups and institutions against those of others. In taking science as the basis of its authority, medicine (and psychiatry) from a marxist perspective not only conceals that there is a moral and social dimension to what it does but also disguises or denies that science itself is a historically-specific social phenomenon. As Figlio points out, invocation of science means that medicine as a symbolic system is rendered 'apparently autonomous from its social roots' (1978:170).

We should recognise at this point that those accounts of medicine which stress its moral and ideological power can be vulnerable on the question of how pervasive and persuasive medicine as a system of ideas actually is (Bury, 1986:157–9). Similar doubts can be raised about the empirical validity of marxist theories of ideology to those about functionalism's assumption of normative consensus. Pluralist theorists and interactionists dispute the extent to which ruling ideas actually do rule.[14]

Feminism is another theoretical perspective that has a contribution to make in exploring the ways in which medicine operates as an ideological agency on behalf of powerful values and interests in society. Feminists have drawn attention to the sexist, androcentric nature of much of the knowledge and underlying philosophy of western medical science, and of its concepts of health and illness, and consequently to sexist elements in medical practice and the organisation of medical care.[15]

Ehrenreich and English (1973) mount a persuasive case for the proposition that since the nineteenth century there has been the strong presumption in western medicine that women are uniquely susceptible to disease and pathology of a sex-specific kind: women's physical and emotional nature is determined by their body, and specifically by their reproductive organs. They and other feminist sociologists (Scully and Bart, 1973) use medical writings, gynaecology textbooks and other historical sources to document the extent to which physicians' analysis of women's disorders and their recommendations for the treatment of women patients reflected and still reflect dominant cultural perceptions of gender and gender roles rather than systematic empirical research. Smith-Rosenberg (1972) has pointed to the affinity between the nineteenth century concept of the 'hysterical woman' and the prevailing stereotype of femininity. Women (and middle class women specifically) were portrayed as innately frail, weak and sickly, this image being based on a reductionist and determinist biological argument, the ideological effect being to conceal the mediating role of culture in the characterisation of the relationship between sex and gender with respect to women (see also Smith-Rosenberg and Rosenberg, 1973).

Thus women were and are subjected in a quite special way to moral and social constraints and restrictions which are presented as being medically advisable and which are justified as being essential given women's biological constitution. The recourse to biologically-based arguments for treating women differently from men is a particularly strong ideological weapon (and one extensively used by the medical system), since having explained the necessity for certain social practices as deriving from 'nature' and not 'culture', it is much harder to find grounds on which such practices can be challenged and alternatives proposed (Smart and Smart, 1978:2).

The medical profession during the course of the last century also claimed exclusive authority over those bodily functions and processes that were uniquely female, even where no disease or malfunction had occurred. This meant medicine taking over control of women's fertility and sexuality, pregnancy and childbirth, the history of which has been well documented in the feminist and medical sociology literature. By the mid-twentieth century many of the cruder forms of this kind of social and medical thinking had apparently disappeared, but evidence for the sexualisation of women by medicine is still to be found (Roberts ed., 1981). The right for women to control their own bodies continues to be opposed on technical medical grounds, and this is seen in the cases of abortion, contraception, home-births, treatments for breast cancer, and gynaecological problems.

At the same time, the main focus of a biologically based gender differentiation with respect to diagnosis and medical treatment has shifted from physical to psychological and emotional forms of ill-health and dis-ease (Doyal, 1979:219). Various writers have commented on current tendencies to define 'women's disorders' that cannot readily be attributed to organic causes, as 'psychosomatic', with a consequent reduction in the importance attached to women's illnesses (Lennane and Lennane, 1973).

Many feminists have drawn attention to the particular ways in which modern psychiatry exercises ideological control over women. Penfold and Walker (1983), for instance, look critically at the sorts of problems that are presented by women to psychiatrists and the kinds of interpretations and responses women typically meet. Others comment on the close fit between the social construction of 'the sick role' and the expectations of passivity, dependency and obedience to the instructions of the relevant authorities in its occupants, on the one hand, and, on the other, the cultural stereotype of femininity. The famous American study by Broverman et al. (1970) revealed that mental health personnel (psychologists, psychiatrists and social workers) operated with gender-differentiated concepts of the healthy person; in terms of the traits chosen, healthy adults were by definition male, and females whose traits necessarily differed from those of males were therefore seen as less healthy. In some subsequent studies (including one in Australia by Anderson, 1975) similar findings were reported, but other researchers have questioned whether perceptual differences are any guide to treatment practices (e.g. Zeldow, 1978). Chesler (1974) claims that the frequency of psychiatric 'symptoms' in women and their willingness to adopt the 'patient role' in mental hospitals are to be understood as results of their cultural conditioning. 'Feminine' traits include

> mistrusting their own perceptions, feeling inferior, helpless and dependent. Just as schizophrenia is no entree into power for women, neither are 'female' diseases such as depression, paranoia, frigidity and suicide-attempts. Such 'disorders', whether hospitalised or not, constitute female role-rituals, enacted by most women. (1974:47)

She goes on to observe that given the ideological stereotypes of women and the way psychiatry operates in the modern world, whatever women do is potentially 'sick' behaviour.

> Women who fully act out the conditioned female role are clinically viewed as 'neurotic' or 'psychotic'. . . Women who reject or are ambivalent about the female role frighten both themselves and society. . . Such women are also assured of a psychiatric label. (1974:53–4)

The ideological role of psychiatry from this standpoint is that it both lends its authority to cultural constructions of femininity and, by operating a 'double standard of mental health' (1974:110), sanctions women, whether or not they conform to the approved stereotype. Psychiatry itself is accused of being a fundamentally sexist discipline and profession (Levine et al., 1974). Psychotherapy, according to an Australian critic (Homer, 1977), performs much the same function. The general practitioner's response to a distressed woman patient—a suggestion of 'mental illness' and the prescription of a psychotropic drug—means

> a further erosion of her capacity for self realization. . . The socialized values—an unhappy wife and mother must be sick—are reinforced,

> and the woman's confidence in her ability is further undermined—making her even less able to find pleasure and reduce stress. (Homer, 1977:127)

This mode of control is not, however, successful either in returning women to a state of 'health' or in lending sufficient support to traditional gender roles to prevent such 'problems' arising. It is now well-established that women's deviance is more likely to be defined as a form of sickness and dealt with by the medical system, while male deviance is more commonly treated as a criminal matter. Women's different biology, their emotionality and their allegedly lesser degree of rationality and psychological maturity are adduced as the reasons for their (apparently) higher incidence of physical and mental illness. Feminists explain this by linking their analysis of psychiatry, medicine and psychotherapy as ideological instruments of women's oppression to their overall theories about the role of the medical system in male dominated or patriarchal society, with which we will deal later in this chapter.

Medicine as a profession

The treatment of medicine as a particular type of occupation, enjoying a position of sole authority over a specialist area of activity, its mandate legally recognised, in other words a profession, is an important feature of the medical sociology literature and the central focus of one of its major contributors, Eliot Freidson (1977, 1985). For Freidson, medicine is 'an identifiable occupation which has gained the exclusive right to practice medicine by virtue of the support of the state and its own occupational organization' (1970a:47). Three preconditions he saw as necessary for an occupation to claim the status of a profession, conditions which only started to be met in the case of medicine in the later part of the nineteenth century, are: a recognised knowledge or expertise base; internal control over education and training and over entry criteria; and the state's underwriting of the profession's claims to exclusive rights of practice and self-regulation (1970a:10–11, 23–4). Weisz (1978) elaborates on these and produces a list of five elements of professionalisation, which he uses to describe the different routes to professionalism followed in the United States, Britain and France.[16]

Recently Willis (1983) has analysed the process by which doctors achieved professional dominance in Australia. He distinguished three phases in the relationship between the state and the medical profession (1983:29–30). Until 1900 the state left most of the health field to market forces and private bodies, while giving increasing official recognition to medical practitioners as a collective group.[17] The period from 1900 to the 1940s was the high period of state support for medical autonomy and dominance. More recently the state has become more involved in the health sector and, finding itself in conflict with the medical profession, has attempted, mostly unsuccessfully, to curb some of its power. Using a combination of marxist and sociological perspectives, Willis gives an account of the establishment and 'reproduction of medical dominance' and then examines the three 'modes' of subordination, limitation and exclusion used by doctors against respectively the occupations of midwifery, optometry and chiropractic in order to maintain their dominant position in the health care field. He points not only to medicine's capacity to define and regulate the internal division of labour and stratification within the health care system,[18] but also to the way a predominantly male profession manages to preserve the gendered nature of health occupations and the subordinate status of those occupations where women are numerically in the majority.[19]

Among the various historical accounts of the rise of medicine as a profession, most emphasise the significance of acquiring state sponsorship and the role of economic and class factors in the doctors' struggle for autonomy and control. Despite the fact that authors assign different weightings to the various aspects of professionalism, all agree that the particular combination of market control, state authorisation, specialist expertise, self-regulation, public demand, social status and moral worth, not to mention its class and gender characteristics, put medicine as an occupation in the modern world in a uniquely powerful position. This has important consequences both for its general role in society and for the nature of the relationship between professional service-provider and client or service-recipient (in this case between doctor and patient). As Krause using Weberian concepts argues, the medical profession enjoys multiple bases of power and authority incorporating the traditional, the charismatic and the rational-legal (1977:226); these can be illustrated respectively in the institutional character of medical settings, in the popular faith in doctors, and in the way the organisation of modern medicine reflects technical and scientific rationality and bureaucratic administrative forms.

Within the substantial body of sociological literature on medicine as a profession, some writers concentrate on medicine and its position within the field of health care, while others (following Parsons' work on 'the sick role') focus on the specific relationship between doctor and patient. Others again are more interested in exploring the links between medicine as a licensed monopoly occupation and the institutions of a patriarchal, capitalist, industrial society. Freidson and Mechanic are leading examples of writers who fall into the first category. They emphasise professionalism as the principal determinant of the doctor-patient relationship and of the medical system as a whole. Though, as Stacey (1978:289–90) acknowledges, Freidson's approach is 'structuralist' rather than interactionist, his analysis is limited, as various marxists have observed, by his choice of focus (the medical profession rather than society) and his conception of power (essentially pluralist). Although in later articles (1977, 1985) he debates some current trends, such as proletarianisation, with his marxist critics, his focus remains firmly on the profession and on how changing social conditions (mainly those internal to medicine) affect medical organisation and the power of doctors.

In Mechanic's major book (1968/78) he devotes a chapter (1978: Chapter 14) to a consideration of the factors that shape medical practice (specialisation, degree of group organisation, and system of remuneration) of which the first two are internal to the occupation, the third being to some extent influenced by market forces and the government. In another chapter (Chapter 11) he examines alternative forms of medical care system and describes the shift from an earlier system which was market-oriented, individualistic and entrepreneurial to a more formal, official and bureaucratic one, in which the government plays an explicit and direct role.

Both Mechanic and Freidson recognise a diversity of settings and types of medical practice within the modern system, some of which still allow an almost total degree of professional medical autonomy, but others of which are under increasing external control, from business interests or the state.[20] What the two writers have in common, by contrast with the marxists, is their emphasis on the internal characteristics of the medical profession and the medical system, even though they agree that considerable constraints are now being placed on the medical profession from outside sources. An interesting article looks at a recent American development in self-control by physicians at a time of considerable loss of public confidence, rising numbers of malpractice suits and increasing pressure for state regulatory activity. The author (Stimson, 1985) discusses one particular response by the profession, a proactive programme for identifying and treating 'physician impairment' which—predictably applying 'the medical model'—presents 'physician deviance' (caused by drugs, senility or disability) as stress-related disease.

Much of the current discussion and evaluation of medicalisation also contributes to our understanding of the occupational and professional characteristics of medicine. Medicalisation as a concept has already been discussed. What is relevant here is to assess the extent to which, being a licensed professional occupation, doctors as an organised group are able to exercise an influence over society. The fact that several of the authors who express concern over the undesirable if not dangerous effects of medical dominance or 'medical imperialism' (Strong, 1979a) offer deprofessionalisation as a solution is a clear indication of the importance they attach to professionalism as the foundation of medical power.

Fox (1977), for instance, in her discussion of 'demedicalisation' (which so far she sees as occurring only at the level of institutional structures without as yet affecting cultural values and beliefs) mentions pressures towards deprofessionalising various aspects of medical care. Conrad and Schneider (1980a:255), commenting on Fox's article, point out that she is mistaken in describing what are in fact moves towards deprofessionalisation as signs of demedicalisation, the latter being a much more fundamental and complex process. Illich (1975) shares Fox's view that professionalism is an essential component of a medicalised society and that deprofessionalisation must be a major priority in any attempt to curtail the 'hubris' of modern medicine and restore autonomy and self-reliance to the individual. We will take up Illich's thesis in the following section of the chapter.

The kind of orientation taken by the writers discussed so far in this section can be contrasted with that of other writers, marxists and feminists in particular, who locate medicine in its broader societal context and explore the structural factors lying behind and the social effects of the medical profession's position of dominance. Marxists, such as McKinlay (1977), Navarro (1985) and Stark (1982), criticise the weight given by Freidson and others to professionalism. McKinlay suggests more attention should be paid to the 'business of doctoring' and to the influence both of capitalist enterprise and of the activities of the capitalist state in furthering the interests of capital. Navarro rejects the limited conception of power which in his view characterises the thinking of both Freidson and Illich, among others, and argues instead for a marxist approach to the analysis of power and social structure. Stark advocates a broadly defined materialistic perspective in order to avoid the overestimation of the cultural bases of medical power found in non-marxist critiques of medicine.

Though marxists do discuss the significance of the professional character of medicine, their main concern is to explore the interconnections between, on the one hand, the occupation of medicine, medical ideology, the division of labour within the health care system and current developments in the organisation and provision of medical care, and, on the other hand, key features of capitalist society. Feminists seek to link what happens within the medical system to gender relations and to the wider structures of patriarchy. We will turn to a consideration of the insights offered by these two perspectives in subsequent sections of the chapter.

Medicine, rationality and bureaucracy

We have already noted that Mechanic (1977, 1978) characterises the predominant current trend in western health care systems as being towards the rational-bureaucratic form, partly as a result of changing technology; and Krause employed the same terminology to describe an important basis and expression of modern medicine's power. Though primary care is still organised on less formal lines, increasingly the medical diagnosis and treatment setting is the hospital or specialist clinic. Decision-making is influenced as much, if not more, by organisational, administrative and economic considerations as by technical and professional judgements. Hospitals in the modern world are highly functionally differentiated, hierarchical, impersonal, rule-governed organisations—rational-bureaucratic in the classic Weberian mode. It is with hospital-based medicine[21] that those writers concerned with the causes and consequences of the trend to bureaucratisation chiefly concern themselves. It is perceived as a logical development of the process that started in the late nineteenth century towards a disease-centred, laboratory-based, engineering approach to the treatment of illness.

Our interest in the hospital[22] here is not so much for the purposes of describing a particular sector of the health care system (usually seen by medical sociologists from a sociology of organisations perspective, Davies, 1979) but rather in order to understand how modern medicine is being shaped by the fact that it is practised in particular types of settings, which can loosely be described as bureaucratic, and how this affects the forms of control exercised. In this respect, medicine (both medical science and medical practice), like most other areas of social life, has come under the influence of the processes of rationalisation and bureaucratisation, which in Weber's view were the principal determining characteristics of western industrial society. Clinical medical practice is 'rational' to the extent that, given the overriding goals of cure or at least alleviation of symptoms, the investigation and treatment methods that are employed are those which on technical grounds are the most appropriate and efficient available and are followed regardless of the personal beliefs or preferences of doctor or patient. In theory, the more complicated or unfamiliar the problem, the more technical the knowledge and the more specialised the staff and skills required, the more dependent on complex modern technological aids, and the more objectified and dehumanised the sick role becomes. Consequently, the treatment setting and process is necessarily more formal, impersonal and bureaucratic, medicine is more preoccupied with cure than with care, and the experience of the patient is further removed from ordinary life situations and everyday patterns of interaction.

Parsons (1951:454–65) also makes an explicit connection between Weber's notion of rationality and the kinds of values he identifies as characteristic of professional occupations such as medicine in modern American society. These are, in his words, achievement, universalism, functional specificity, affective neutrality, and collectivity orientation (this last in Parsons' view distinguishing professions from business). Strong (1979b:Chapter 6) who conducted an empirical study of the 'bureaucratic mode' in a number of medical settings, found Freidson's analysis in terms of professional medical dominance useful but was critical of Parsons for, in his view, an over-general and entirely theoretically-derived characterisation of the doctor-patient relationship as simply a reflection of wider cultural patterns.

In medical care institutions of the bureaucratic kind, typically hospitals, responsibility for decision-making and positions of authority are increasingly likely to be given to management experts often without any medical training, rather than to physicians. Like businesses (which anyway they also are) planning, accounting, efficiency and productivity are all-important. Since the main considerations in running a hospital or specialist health care centre are administrative and financial, and medical knowledge and expertise though relevant on some issues (such as for example, the selection of technical medical equipment) are often not the primary determinants of organisational policy,[23] there is no longer any rational basis for medical dominance overall in such organisations. As McKinlay (1977) argues, this provides one major reason for questioning whether the traditional distinction in organisational studies between goods producing and human service organisations is still valid. He maintains that a marxist framework which focusses on the importance of capital and the capitalist state is better able to explain the structure and functioning of all types of large-scale organisations. In another paper concerned with the proletarianisation of physicians, McKinlay and Arches (1985) examine the contribution bureaucratisation makes to this process, but their basic contention is that it is not primarily a technological or organisational matter but rather that both processes are the products of the constant pressure within capitalism towards accumulation.

One of the best known critiques of modern medicine and one which attacks it precisely on the grounds of its formal and rational character is that mounted by Illich in his book published in 1975 under the title *Medical Nemesis: The Expropriation of Health* and renamed later more modestly *Limits to Medicine*. Illich's principal thesis (set out in summary form in his Introduction) is that the 'medical establishment has become a major threat to health' (1975:11). His indictment of scientific medicine forms (along with his equally famous book on 'deschooling') part of a sustained attack on the institutions and values of modern western society. He sees them as undermining personal and community autonomy and encouraging in the population a 'disabling' dependency on professional and expert authority and bureaucratic structures, accompanied by an unquestioning (but 'illusory') faith in the need for and the benefits of progress. Central to his analysis is the concept of iatrogenesis which he utilises to describe the 'sickening' impact of modern medicine. 'The undesirable side-effects of approved, mistaken, callous or contra-indicated technical contacts with the medical system' he calls 'clinical iatrogenesis' (1975:25–6). 'Social iatrogenesis', which constitutes a second-level of impact, is represented by various types of 'social over-medicalisation', which increase patients' sick role dependency. 'Structural iatrogenesis', as part of a general socially induced reliance in this industrialised world on goods and services, both of which are treated as commodities to be consumed, 'consists in the paralysis of healthy responses to suffering...when people accept health management designed on the engineering model' (1975:27). Thus, in his view, medicine under industrialism has appropriated for itself a role elsewhere assumed by the culture of each society to define, interpret and find ways of coming to terms with the threats to human existence posed by pain, disease and death.

The solution to the ever-increasing medicalisation of life and of suffering and death, according to Illich, is deprofessionalisation, which in his words 'means the unmasking of the myth according to which technical progress demands an increase in the specialisation of labour, increasingly arcane manipulations, and increasing dependence of people on the right of access to impersonal institutions rather than on trust in each other' (1975:121). This entails curbing the relentless pursuit of industrial and economic growth by the political imposition of criteria of equity and effectiveness on the industrial mode of production (1975:155) and consequently a reemphasising of personal autonomy and of each individual's power to cope with life, the essential precondition of health (1975:150). Though Illich identifies as key elements in the 'medical colonisation' of life a 'professional and physician-based health care system' and a dominant set of ideas and beliefs about disease and suffering (he does not use the term ideology), he sees these as manifestations of the impersonal and over-organised state of an 'over-industrialised civilization', this being the underlying source of the problem (1975:12). As we shall shortly see, it is over the issue of precisely what it is about modern industrial society that causes the problems, that Illich and the marxists differ.

Medicine and capitalism

Most of the theoretical writing in sociology about the nature and role of modern medicine has taken either a pluralist/interactionist or marxist orientation (with the exception of the Parsonian tradition which confined itself largely to the roles and relationships of physician and patient). Those following the former approach tend to stress the cultural and ideological aspects and the importance of professionalism and bureaucratisation in their analysis, while the marxists explore the interrelationships between medicine and the capitalist mode of production. Having dealt with the former in earlier sections we will turn now to the latter. Though this aspect of the sociology of health and illness is not our subject of concern here, the question of how social conditions, specifically those associated with capitalism and industrialism, contribute to the production and distribution of disease (and not only to the medical management of illness once it has occurred) is also important. Marxists who have written about the political economy of disease include Doyal (1979:Chapters 2 and 3); Eyer (1984); Krause (1977: Chapter 9); Navarro (1985); and Waitzkin (1983:Chapter 3).

Earlier in this chapter the existence of some significant variations between the health care systems of the western world was discussed. The main contrast lies between systems based on the state provision (out of taxation revenue) of free or subsidised health services and those based on the fee-for-service principle in conjunction with a national health insurance scheme (usually financed by contributions from individuals, employers and sometimes also the state)—the typical examples of the two being Britain and the United States. However marxists regard all modern industrial societies as essentially similar in being primarily organised around capital accumulation and economic interests, class domination and a state which devotes its extensive powers and funds predominantly to the maintenance of capitalism as a system. Their starting point is that like any other section of capitalist society the health care system is an industry (and health care a commodity) which therefore means it can only be understood in terms of its economic and social functions for capital (Rodberg and Stevenson, 1977).

Waitzkin (1983:Chapter 2) separates out three main 'social structures of medical oppression'—class, monopoly capital and the state—which, along with medical ideology, he regards as the basic determinants of the medical and health care systems of capitalist societies. Ehrenreich and Ehrenreich (1974) in an important early article reinterpreted the analysis of Parsons and Freidson of medicine as a social control mechanism from a more radical class perspective. They sought to explain the existence of two alternative forms of social control, described by them as 'disciplinary' and 'cooptative', and which reflected respectively an exclusionary and an expansionary utilisation of medical services, as part of the apparatus of a class (and gender) divided social system. Renaud (1975) focussed on how the role of the state in serving the needs of continual industrial growth and commodity consumption affected health policy. Navarro in his numerous publications since the mid-1970s also pays attention to the interconnections between class, business and the state, as does McKinlay. For them, it is the special characteristics of capitalism rather than the rational, bureaucratic features of industrialism that explain the nature and functioning of modern medical systems.

A useful way to introduce the marxist perspective on medicine is to consider some of the criticisms made by marxists of the non-marxist writers discussed earlier in the chapter. Admittedly we are dealing with an almost exclusively American body of material, but one in which the debate between opposing intellectual traditions is at least openly conducted, as Navarro (1985) makes clear. As he puts it:

> A major methodological difference between non-Marxist and Marxist scholarship in the study of medicine has been that the former has focused on the behavior and motivation of power groups within medicine, while the latter has analyzed these groups as part of broader categories (such as class) whose conflicts are the organizing parameters of all other conflicts and their realization. (1985:532)

McKinlay and Navarro in their respective critiques of Freidson and Illich explicitly acknowledge their own preference for a marxist perspective and contend that it is precisely the neglect of the centrality of capital that weakens the analysis offered by these authors.

McKinlay, in an important article assessing the work of Freidson, argues for a conception of doctoring as business. He gives a number of reasons for treating medical institutions theoretically not as a separate case (which he claims Freidson does) but in the same way as any other productive enterprises in a capitalist society (1977:472–6). At least four separate levels of analysis are required, in his view, in order to provide an adequate account of the nature and functioning of what he calls 'The House of Medicine' (the neglect of the first two of which are a fundamental weakness of Freidson's work). These are briefly: (1) 'The Level of Financial and Industrial Capital'; (2) 'The Activities of the Capitalist State'; (3) 'The Level of Medicine Itself'; and (4) 'The Level of the Public' (1977:464).

Navarro (1976:Part II), in his evaluation of Illich, claims that their different analyses of medicine are a reflection of their respective theoretical perspectives: Navarro subscribing to a marxist interpretation of western society and Illich working with something closer to a Weberian model, involving differing conceptions, in particular, of structure and power. Illich thus talks of an 'over-industrialised society', which for him means undue reliance on specialists and professionals, on impersonal and often inefficient organisations and on progress. Navarro's own analysis of medicine and the health sector (1976:Parts III and IV, 1983, 1985) is in terms of the characteristics of the modern American economy (including trends to increasing size, concentration and corporatisation[24]), the role of the interventionist state (fiscal crises, legitimation crises and re-privatisation), the occupational and class structures (increasing specialisation and proletarianisation) and the dynamics of the class struggle. Navarro (1985), therefore, rejects a whole range of non-marxist interpretations and evaluations of modern medicine on the grounds that they over-emphasise technological, moral and cultural aspects of medicine and that their understanding of power (they work with pluralist and instrumentalist models) is inadequate because they ignore wider structurally-based power categories such as class, race and gender and the overriding influence of capitalism itself.

A number of other authors have contributed to critical and marxist writing in this field. Waitzkin and Waterman (1974) produced one of the earliest accounts of health care in capitalist society as exploitative (though it has been argued by one set of reviewers, Ozonoff and Ozonoff (1975), that their basic framework is functionalist, not marxist). Rodberg and Stevenson suggest it is useful to distinguish between various modes of production within the health care field (as in capitalism itself), such as 'the communal (pre-commodity), petty commodity (fee-for-service solo practitioner), capitalist commodity (industrialized high-technology, hospital-oriented), and "social" (planned, use-value-oriented)' (1977:106). They then identify a number of complexities and contradictions within the health care system and in the relationship between health care and capitalism (1977:108–14).

Waitzkin, in a recent book (1983) describes the current situation as one of 'private expansion and public contraction' with respect to hospitals and medical services in America with a high level of public financial subsidisation of the private sector through grants for hospital construction, tax exemptions for non-profit bodies, and public insurance schemes (Medicare and Medicaid) providing poorer patients with the means to afford private facilities. He sees private health care provision as necessarily characterised by expensive, high technology facilities, duplication and uneven geographical distribution and social availability, since neither need nor equality of access are the prime considerations. Whereas the majority of the population make use of this system, financed by their own insurance or through one of the state schemes, there is also 'dumping' of low-income and minority patients from the private to the contracting public system and some sections of the working poor who are ineligible for federal assistance may miss out altogether (1983: 119–25), the casualties of an economically-oriented private health care system.

Even in Britain where there is a nation-wide public system of health service provision, the private sector remains important. The government has left the manufacture of drugs, technology and equipment to private business and corporate interests. Alongside the public health system there exists a private system of medical care in which rich and privately-insured patients receive often speedier, but not necessarily better, attention from fee-for-service physicians, many of whom are working both in the private and public sectors (Doyal, 1979:Chapter 5). As Iliffe (1977) observes, nationalisation covered the impoverished areas, the profitable sectors stayed with private industry. Nor did nationalisation greatly affect the power of the medical profession or the alliance between capital and the profession (Iliffe, 1977:94–5). Australia, after over a decade of various combinations of state-financed insurance, state-financed and provided services and private provision now has a mixed system and suffers from the problems characteristic of both public and private systems.

A major concern of marxist writers is the issue of distribution and access as well as quality of medical and health care, and in particular the existence of substantial class differences with respect to availability and utilisation of services. The notion of an 'inverse care law' was introduced by Tudor Hart (1971) to describe a situation in Britain where higher socio-economic groups derived more value from national health service facilities, but lower groups had a higher simple service utilisation rate. Townsend, also talking about Britain, distinguished between extent of use and equality of service provision as between classes and between men and women (1974:1186–7). There is some evidence that it is where they have access to 'free' services (for example, public hospitals or a nationalised health system), that lower income groups become more frequent users; in the Australian context, Najman et al. (1979:62) and Taylor (1979:26–7) discuss this possibility.

This is part of the 'paradox' of health care in modern societies: namely that health services cost more and more, become more and more sophisticated, with no apparent increase in effectiveness or equity (Jones, 1983:245–7). Medicine is more invasive and pervasive, and thus there is more control without increased therapeutic benefit. For marxists this is readily explained by the fact that the health care in a capitalist society will reflect the dominant interests and concerns of such a society and specifically profitability. Thus one should not expect any necessary relationship between the services provided and the meeting of collective human needs (McKinlay, 1977:463). However, although economic factors are always treated as the fundamental determinants, modern marxists recognise that professional medical interests, political considerations, and class and community pressures also exert influence over the nature and mode of organisation of health care systems.[25] It is the relative weighting given to these various sets of variables, and others such as sex/gender, that enables us to differentiate between the various perspectives within marxism and between marxists and non-marxists.

Medicine, gender and patriarchy

The most obvious starting point for any discussion of sex/gender and the modern medical system is the simple observation that doctors are predominantly male, most nurses and many paramedical workers are female, and over one half of patients are women. The characterisation offered by Lorber (1975) of women and the medical profession as 'invisible professionals and ubiquitous patients' captured very nicely the situation to that time—the mid 1970s—and still has validity today. She points out that, although American women doctors do exist and indeed are an elite group (they come from upper middle class urban, professional and managerial families and are themselves in the top education and academic category), within their profession on average they occupy the lower ranks (they have lower incomes, fewer have hospital appointments, and they work in less prestigious specialties). She (1975, 1984) favours an explanation in terms of discrimination, a 'sexual tracking system', operating through medical training and in the workplace, and an underlying masculine medical mystique.[26]

Verbrugge (1985) provides a useful, up-to-date summary of the sex differences with respect to illness and illness behaviour in the American population. The broad picture is of men having higher mortality rates at all ages, but of women showing a higher incidence of the key acute conditions and of most non-fatal chronic conditions; they report too more restricted activity days and days in bed; and these differences persist even if reproductive conditions are excluded. In the young adult and middle age groups, women's rates of health service utilisation and prescription drug use are also higher. The exceptions to the general pattern of higher female physical morbidity are that men have higher injury rates and suffer more from serious life-threatening chronic diseases (1985:157–63). Others have provided evidence for a higher female incidence also of a number of psychiatric and psychological conditions, in particular neuroses, depressive psychoses and other inner-directed forms of emotional disturbance, males having higher rates of externally directed, aggressive and personality disorders and alcoholism (Busfield, 1983; Dohrenwend and Dohrenwend, 1976; Gove, 1978; Nathanson, 1975).

Comparable figures for Australia reveal a similar sex distribution in the health professional and patient populations. In 1981, out of a total number of doctors of a little over 27 000, approximately 80 per cent were male and 20 per cent female. Of over 160 000 nurses, however, 93 per cent were female and 7 per cent male. Overall, 27 per cent of health workers were men and 73 per cent were women (Social Indicators, 1984:94). Fett's (1974, 1976) study of Australian medical graduates since the 1920s showed higher proportions of male doctors than of female were in general practice and in specialist practice, were in the higher status specialisms (surgery, internal medicine, obstetrics and gynaecology) and had obtained post-graduate qualifications. Higher percentages (though not larger numbers) of female doctors were to be found in hospital work, in the less prestigious specialisms, like psychiatry and anaesthetics and in areas such as family planning, child welfare and public health.

The findings of the Australian Health Survey conducted in 1977/8,[27] show higher physician consultation rates for women than for men at all ages (the differential being greatest between the ages of 15 and 45): 20 per cent of the women in the survey and 15 per cent of the men had consulted a doctor in the previous two weeks (*Doctor Consultations*: 15). If children are excepted, women also reported higher rates of consultation in most age groups with all other categories of health professionals, apart from physiotherapists (*Consultations with Health Professionals:7*). More women than men also had had episodes in hospital in the previous twelve months (15 per cent:10 per cent) and on average had had more episodes and longer periods of stay in hospital, the exceptions being young children and the over 65 year olds; pregnancy and child-birth are likely to be relevant here (*Episodes in Hospital*:6). From the 1983 Survey, rates were also calculated for self-reported illness conditions in the two weeks prior to the survey which again showed women with the higher rates: 673 per 1000 compared with 572

(*Australian Health Survey*, 1983:49–50). On only one of the categories of conditions recorded was the male rate higher, that for injuries, though men also reported higher rates of accidents—521 per 1000 compared with 365 (1983:53). In addition, this survey provided information on medication usage and again the female rates were higher—74 per cent to 60 per cent, though the usage patterns of the two sexes were similar (1983:8); and the female survey members reported higher usage of both prescribed and non-prescribed types of medication (1983:46).

Over the past fifteen or so years, feminists and social scientists have devoted considerable attention to the empirical investigation and theoretical understanding of the observed relationships between sex/gender, physical and 'mental' illness, utilisation of medical services, and treatment by the health care system, relationships which pose problems for measurement, interpretation and explanation (Mechanic, 1978; Clarke, 1983). Marxists and some sociologists, as we have seen, have been examining the systematic way in which the medical system reflects and reinforces the fundamental class-based structure of modern capitalist society. Some, like Navarro (1983) and Stark (1982), do actually mention gender and race as bases of social division along with class, but these two authors both make it clear that they regard class as of overriding structural importance. Here we will consider writers who give sex and gender a central place in their theory and in research, though in certain respects at least some of the feminist analysis parallels that of the marxists. For instance, marxist and feminist authors focus on the division of labour within the medical care system, on the links between the medical profession and wider centres of power in society, and on the ideological significance of medical models and the medicalisation of deviance for the maintenance of the established institutions and values of society.

In the same way as marxists concentrate on class and capital-labour relations, feminists have attempted to expose gender divisions, and sexist attitudes and practices within medicine. They have explored the connections between medical knowledge and beliefs, medical services, and the activities of medical and health care personnel, and the incidence and experience of illness for men and women. Key themes and concerns in feminist theory in general are prominent in the feminist literature on women and medicine: in particular, the utilisation of science by male-dominated occupations and institutions as a means of concealing and/or legitimating androcentric beliefs and practices, and the importance of the control of women's bodies (and their sexuality and fertility) to men and to a patriarchal social order.

As was the case in the previous section of the chapter, our focus here is on the medical construction of and responses to illness rather than on society's contribution to the causes of disease, though there is now an extensive feminist (and general sociological) literature describing and seeking to explain what are believed to be 'real' differences between men and women in the relative frequency of a range of types of physical and mental disease.[28]

We have plenty of evidence that historically medicine, both as a scientific discipline and as an occupation, has been overwhelmingly male and masculine. A number of writers have described the process by which from the nineteenth century on, male physicians have assumed exclusive control not only of all kinds of physical and mental disease and disorder, but have redefined all phases of reproduction as a medical matter, thereby transforming pregnancy, delivery, and the immediate post-natal period into 'illnesses'.[29] Earlier mention was made of Willis' (1983) account of how in Australia the medical profession discredited midwifery and gradually took over the management of pregnancy and childbirth, convincing the population that these were serious and potentially dangerous conditions, that required the same kind and degree of professional medical attention as is considered necessary for the treatment of recognised illness.[30]

The assertion of medical dominance over these aspects of human life meant the replacement of a tradition of family and personal responsibility for health and health care and a reliance on folk knowledge and practical experience in this as in other areas, with some assistance where required by particular categories of community members, such as midwives. At the same time it brought in, under the guise and with the authority of scientific knowledge, a whole set of cultural beliefs and (mis-)understandings about women's bodies, their emotional and psychological nature and their vulnerability to reproductive and sexual disorders. This led to a new form of male domination over women becoming established, which was justified on the basis of claims to scientific status and a humanitarian concern for the welfare of a group whose health was perceived to be at risk.

Fascinating insights into Victorian thinking on this subject can be obtained from the work of several American historians on the subject, a number of the best of which are reviewed in Verbrugge (1976). The most quoted authors in this field are probably Ehrenreich and English (1973) who, in their book *Complaints and Disorders*, described the way medicine expressed, in the classic dualistic form, the prevailing idea of women as both innately frail and at the mercy of their bodies (the 'invalidism' of the middle and upper classes) while in the case of working class women not only were they denied the protection such an ideology would have afforded them against exploitation by employers and others, but also, given the influence of the germ theory of disease in the late nineteenth century, they were regarded as the prime source of danger to the physical health and moral welfare of the middle class family. They also offer an account of 'hysteria', for higher class women the only acceptable form of protest against their restrictive role, as, since it had no discernible organic basis, posing a challenge to the medical profession at the time which ultimately led to the development of psychoanalysis.

Verbrugge (1975, 1976) suggests some less well known writers have actually produced better analyses of 'sex, politics and sickness' and she cites especially the work of Gordon, Rosenberg and Smith–Rosenberg (1975:332). In attempting to trace the connections between medicine and sexism she argues, it is necessary to see medicine not as a discrete entity but as being at the 'interface between science and society' (1975:331). Sexism is a multi-dimensional phenomenon whose inter-relationships with the wider society take a number of forms and operate at a number of levels. Figlio (1978) claims medical concepts reflect and reinforce (capitalist) social relations, but in such a way as to make the 'social' appear natural, and this is particularly the case with so-called women's diseases.

Research has revealed other areas of women's lives where physicians and other (male) experts have taken responsibility for determining what is 'normal' and 'desirable' on the basis of their understanding of medical and scientific knowledge and then imposed their views, through books and professional advice, on women. Areas where this has occurred and which have been examined from a critical feminist standpoint include contraception and abortion (Gordon, 1977, 1979; Petchesky, 1986), pregnancy (Graham, 1977; Graham and Oakley, 1981; MacIntyre, 1977) and infant care and child rearing (which has been examined as an aspect of the 'rationalization of domestic life' in a fascinating account of changes in the Australian family between 1880 and 1940 by Reiger, 1985). Ehrenreich and English (1978) provide an overall examination of experts' advice to women 'for their own good', over the past 150 years.

Recent studies, mainly done in America, warn us against assuming that modern medicine has rid itself of ideological conceptions of women and their biology. In an attempt to investigate the particular character of medicine in areas where women as women are the objects of concern, Scully and Bart (1973) analysed the content of leading gynaecology textbooks in the post-war period. They found these contained a strongly paternalistic and traditionalist representation of women's nature, sexuality and proper role, and Scully's later (1980) study of the education and training of gynaecologists and obstetricians in the hospital setting in the mid-1970s left little room for hope that the 'medical maltreatment of women' (1980:236) might be on the decline (even if causal factors and the forms it takes are changing). Also of interest here is Emerson's (1970) ethnomethodological analysis of the gynaecological examination, a situation where definitions of reality are highly precarious, and the (typically male) physician has to take steps to ensure that what elsewhere would be perceived as a personal and sexual encounter remains safely and unambiguously technical and clinical. Significant in this, she suggests, is the preparation work done by (female) nurses and the gender-differentiated modes of interaction between female patient and female and male medical personnel. Links between the sexual division of labour among health professionals and physician bias with respect to women have been suggested by various writers (for example Bullough and Bullough, 1975).

The effects of sexism within medicine have been observed also at the level of general practitioner-patient interaction, and with respect to a much wider range of conditions than simply those associated with contraception and reproduction. Barrett and Roberts (1978), Roberts (1985) and Wallen, Waitzkin and Stoeckle (1979) present evidence that doctors perceive male and female patients in terms of gender and gender role stereotypes, and respond differently to complaints, particularly those they judged to be psychosomatic. Verbrugge (1984; Verbrugge and Steiner, 1981), who carried out studies in America specifically to test for physician sex bias, did report differences in diagnoses and care given (she found particularly the boundary between physical and mental conditions 'more blurred' and 'more permeable' for women patients than for men), but is hesitant about concluding this is proof of bias. An in-depth analysis of medical conversations between (predominantly) male doctors and female patients in a hospital clinic explores the ways in which 'medical domination in the form of sexism is enacted' and exposes the cultural assumptions that lie behind the process by which '*woman* emerges as the master status and overrides the status of *patient*' (Fisher and Groce, 1985:103, 344, original emphases).

Nathanson (1975, 1980) has surveyed much of the contemporary literature (by Gove and others) that attempts to account for the apparently greater degree of ill-health among women. She identifies three alternative lines of explanation based on various aspects of gender-role related differences: experience of and outlets for stress; cultural acceptability of illness behaviour; and degree of compatibility between the 'sick role' and other social roles (in both the family and employment spheres).

Broom looks beyond the gender-role based approach[31] and focusses on the differential significance for men and women of the body (and hence of institutional mechanisms for managing the body, such as medicine) in shaping 'social experience, life chances, and personal alternatives' (1983:264). She advances the proposition that materially and symbolically the body (and biology) as socially constructed constitutes a more critical locus and medium of influence over the identity and experience of women than of men, because of the greater opportunity society allows to men to move from the world of 'nature' into the world of reason and 'culture'. Another Australian author, Matthews (1984), extends the feminist analysis of the relationship between medicine and gender to cover the role psychiatry plays in reinforcing dominant (and oppressive) constructions of femininity (in a study of the recorded biographies of 60 women who had been psychiatric patients).

Feminist challenges to orthodox male-dominated scientific medicine start from the premise that the body (and particularly those functions and processes specific to women) is indeed of crucial importance to women. But feminists dispute current cultural conceptions of women's biology and of how their perceived psychological and social characteristics relate to their physical attributes and functions, and the conventional, preferred methods of defining and treating women with problems. Instead they recommend strategies by which women can 'reclaim their bodies', by learning to trust their own feelings, by acquiring knowledge about the workings of their bodies, by developing techniques for investigating and monitoring their own and other women's bodies, and by generally regaining a sense of embodiment and control over themselves as physical beings (Fee, 1975; Petchesky, 1986).

Earlier in the chapter some of the literature on the ideological aspects of medicine and psychiatry with respect to the sexualisation of women and their problems was presented. There is now a well-established basis for arguing that medicine functions as a particularly powerful agency for the control of women, and for the control of aspects of women's experience and existence (contraception, sexual and marital problems, parenting, role frustrations, etc.) not obviously or directly concerned with illness. The various studies that have been conducted, some of which have been reported here, show very clearly that one major source of sexism in western medicine are the particular cultural assumptions about and attitudes to women's fertility, sexuality and biology. Though these have undergone some modification and revision over the past 150 years, the underlying fact remains that men and male-oriented and determined perceptions and prejudices encourage and justify the medicalisation of many aspects of women's lives, and shape the medical beliefs and practices that determine women's treatment as patients.

Medicine and social control

From the preceding analysis of the characteristics, functioning and effects of the medical-psychiatric system, it is possible to identify some of the key aspects central to our understanding of social control as exercised by and through medicine. Of assistance are the distinctions between micro and macro (or interpersonal and structural) levels of operation and between formal and informal modes of control.

Some aspects of medicine at a micro level can be described as informal and unofficial (reflecting personal and non-professional elements in the doctor-patient interaction), while others derive from and are consistent with the recognised specialist occupational skills and state conferred authority of medical practitioners. Class, gender, ethnicity, religion and cultural values can all play a part in influencing the perceptions and practices of doctors and may be the critical variables in explanations of some at least of the variations in the diagnoses and treatment received by different categories of people. In particular such factors would be likely to come to the fore where no clear organic pathology can be found and/or where the symptoms reported suggest conditions which the individual can be seen as partly responsible for causing or exacerbating. Patients of a different class, race or gender from that of the doctor (who is typically white, male and middle or upper class) are more likely to provoke moral and social assessments of a negative kind than are patients who come from the same social groups, and, as we have seen, these judgements affect medical practice. What the individual typically experiences in medical encounters is the dependency that goes with patienthood.

Most of the writers whose work we have surveyed in this chapter, however, offer an analysis of medicine largely in terms of its societal role. It is the macro level of relationships between medicine, the economy, the state, bureaucracy, the class structure and the gender order with which we have mostly been concerned. Medicine and psychiatry are viewed as a 'system', made up of knowledge and ideas, personnel, and institutions for dealing with problems of health and illness.

Medicine has a relationship with all the members of society that is unlike that of the other two control systems. Everyone is affected by all three systems but a significant proportion of society's members are not and do not expect to become clients of either the criminal justice or the welfare systems. By contrast, birth, sickness and death are universal experiences and whatever institutional mechanism a particular society has for managing these events will necessarily have an influence sooner or later on every member of the society.

Furthermore, it is important to recognise that medicine is also different from the law and welfare in that its control aspects are not officially sanctioned or commonly perceived (Broom, 1984:50). The state and the community grant an extensive, though covert, range of powers to the profession. This means medicine and psychiatry have officially licensed authority for what they think, say and do. However the techniques and effects, and hence the control activities of medicine and psychiatry are not only of a formally approved or officially recognised nature. Feminists have, for instance, argued that some of the most important (and for them pernicious) aspects of medical social control for women relate to the subtler, moral or ideological messages being conveyed by (male) doctors to their (female) patients and to women generally, but which frequently accompany treatments of a legitimate and unambiguously medical kind.

The material presented in this chapter shows that, irrespective of the intentions and rationalisations of medical personnel, medicine is a powerful mechanism for the moral, ideological, political and general social control of all members of society, but most particularly of those belonging to minority, subordinate, deviant and problem groups. In conclusion, we must acknowledge that such an analysis of medicine as a social control system still leaves open basic questions about the relative importance of the various sources of its power and capacity to control. Specifically, are the most significant or powerful forms of social control exercised by medicine and psychiatry those based on or otherwise associated with its formal, official, institutional role as the agency responsible for health care and the management of illness (and with the scientific and technological resources provided for this task)? Or do they stem from its structurally-derived but not officially acknowledged ideological activities on behalf of the capitalist state or the capitalist economic system? Or do they relate to such factors as gender, class, professionalism or general moral authority—factors given greater scope as a result of the trend toward medicalisation of a range of problems that are not medical in the conventional sense?

7 The social welfare system

Welfare is not readily identifiable with any specific sphere of social action or set of social institutions. Indeed, it is not clear whether the term is or should be applied to particular structures and forms of social activity or to certain social objectives and functions.

'Social welfare' or 'social policy' need not be defined as specific institutions, programmes, or activities at all: for Titmuss the terms refer to 'all collective interventions to meet certain needs of the individual and/or to serve the wider interests of society' (1958: 42) and for Mishra to 'those social arrangements, patterns and mechanisms that are typically concerned with the distribution of resources in accordance with some criterion of need' (1981: xi). Apart from the likelihood that in any one society various institutions and organisations are involved in meeting whatever are socially recognised as legitimate needs, there are considerable differences between societies in how problems of dependency are dealt with. The definition of 'need', the acceptance of social or societal responsibility for the 'needy', the utilisation of particular institutional means for coping with the different categories of 'need', and the accompanying moral and ideological justifications for whatever welfare systems and policies a particular society favours, are socially conditioned and therefore historically highly variable.

At different times and places, welfare has been regarded as an individual and a group or collective responsibility, a 'private' and a 'public' matter, has been both formally and informally organised, and been made sometimes selectively and sometimes universally available. It has been treated at the individual, family or neighbourhood level, as a customary but discretionary element in a complex set of traditional rights and obligations that characterise patriarchal regimes, as an expression of humanitarianism on the part of more prosperous and well-endowed sections of society, as the moral duty of those enjoying advantages of birth, position, education and wealth, and as a generally accepted component of the modern state's apparatuses of administration and management of society.

> Thus the notion of welfare used here is more akin to broad social categories like religion, education, kinship or politics than to specific social organisations like the social services. (Mishra, 1981: xi)

Conceptions of welfare

In the modern western world, welfare has now come to be seen as a public, that is as a state, matter. Though the form and content of welfare provisions have varied over time and between countries, responsibility for a wide range of material and social needs and dependencies has been gradually assumed since the late nineteenth century by the governments of most capitalist democracies. In the earlier period 'welfare' commonly meant the economic dependency of the old, the chronically ill or incapacitated, and deserted mothers and children. During the 1940s and since, conceptions of welfare, of legitimate categories of 'need' and of appropriate levels and types of service and benefit provision, all expanded as did the role of the state. The major areas now considered to constitute 'social welfare' are health, education and training, housing, social security and income maintenance, and personal social services, though some extend the concept to cover also policies in the employment, the recreation, leisure, arts and the physical environment fields.[1] The result of a steady increase in the number, type and extent of coverage of services provided by government in western countries has been described as 'the welfare state'.

The increase in the range of types of dependency or need recognised by governments has been accompanied by a shift from primarily highly 'selective' or 'residual' methods of determining eligibility for services and benefits towards more 'universalistic' principles of access and distribution, as is the case in education, some sorts of pension (sickness, old age and supporting parent), unemployment benefits, and medical services in some countries. This in turn has been associated with a change in the social and moral evaluation of welfare and its recipients, such that the assumptions of 'pathology', 'problem', or 'deficiency' (seen as attributes of the individual) are replaced by notions of rights, justifiable demands and community obligations. However this trend has not been maintained. From the mid-1970s and continuing at the present time, Britain, the United States and Australia have experienced a 'retreat from the welfare state' (Graycar, 1983), a reemphasis on individual responsibility for self and family and on individual moral worth as the criterion of eligibility for government assistance, and a questioning of the desirability of meeting claims on public concern and money for any but the most extreme cases of 'need'.

We will look now at the historical development of the welfare institutions and functions of the modern state, mainly with reference to the Australian situation, and at what has come to be called the current 'crisis' of the welfare state (Gough, 1979; O'Connor, 1973; Mishra, 1984).

The main Australian references on the general history of welfare are Dickey (1980), M. Jones (1980/3), Kewley (1973, 1978), Mendelsohn (1979), and Roe (1976). Dickey gives a useful summary of the whole period of white Australian history from 1788 and describes changing conceptions of and provisions for certain key categories of dependency—the 'sick', the 'destitute', 'children' and the 'poor'. Kewley, Mendelsohn and Roe concentrate on the period from federation (1901) up to the mid-1970s. Jones gives a brief historical overview and then examines welfare services and policies in the post-Second World War period, and particularly in the 1970s. Graycar (1979: Chapters 2 and 3) and Scotton and Ferber (eds.) (1978, 1980) also focus on welfare and social policy development in the 1970s. Roe introduces her overview of social policy in Australia with a definition of her subject-matter as the 'creation and operation of public support systems—of social security systems and health and welfare programmes' (1976:viii) and includes in her edited book case studies dealing with the introduction and administration of particular services in various States over the period in question. Kewley provides a comprehensive and detailed account of the changing nature of the Australian social security system during the course of the twentieth century, focussing specifically on income maintenance and health benefits and provisions. Mendelsohn and Jones cover a wider range of welfare measures, including also employment, housing, education and training, and 'personal social services' and they examine some of the underlying welfare concepts and issues, associated with 'poverty', 'inequality' and 'social dependency'. Graycar's (1983) edited volume entitled *Retreat from the Welfare State* explores the current situation in a number of major welfare areas—child care costs and policies, non-institutional care of the aged, unemployment benefits, housing, taxation policy and, in the non-government sector, welfare organisations and occupational benefits.

As we established in Chapter 4, the state moved into the welfare and social security field relatively late in Australia compared with Western Europe. For various reasons, Australia achieved only 'a weak version of a new Welfare State' (Roe, 1976:220), one based on the principle of non-contributory public assistance rather than the insurance principle as in Britain (Kewley, 1973:563; Roe, 1976:223) and one which only administered services on a universal principle to a limited extent (mainly under the Whitlam Labor Government in the early 1970s). As M. Jones says:

> Australia refused to adopt the European style universal welfare state. . . . Our social spending seems low and we have only austere,

non-contributory benefits. We have generally believed in selectivity not universalism, and only the political power of the aged has forced a quasi-universal aged pension. The private sector still dominates health care and housing, and personal care services are poorly developed. (1983:310, 311)

Several phases can be discerned in Australia's welfare history. Following the earlier period of centralized political control that characterised Australia's penal origins, during the latter part of the nineteenth century such welfare provision as existed was almost entirely in the hands of private bodies, mainly charitable societies (though these received substantial if often concealed financial support from the States), the exceptions being institutions for the insane, and for neglected and orphaned children, and prisons (Roe, 1976:13). The first government initiatives in the welfare and social security field were old age and invalid pensions, introduced initially in New South Wales and Victoria on a non-contributory basis but with fairly strict criteria of eligibility (residential, racial, moral and financial) and for which the Commonwealth took responsibility in legislation passed in 1908 (with less restrictive conditions attached), and in 1912 a maternity allowances scheme (Kewley, 1973). Despite some attempts, no further social security measures were adopted by the Federal Government until the 1940s, although some legislation was passed dealing with aspects of public health and child welfare (Kewley, 1973:165–6), and the repatriation and war widows and child benefits schemes were introduced following the 1914–18 War (McDonald, 1976; Mendelsohn, 1979:215). In Britain, by contrast, between 1906 and 1914, the state had assumed responsibility for minimum standards in a number of areas—housing, education, health, nutrition and medical care, and unemployment (Robson, 1976: 21).

In Kewley's view, the factors that help account for the absence of any significant extension of social security provisions in this period include problems of the relationship between the Commonwealth and the States, general insistence by all but the Labor Party on the contributory principle, the Depression and World War I, and the weakness of the Labor Party at the federal level (1973:166). Castles (1985) offers a somewhat different and original account. Including along with the introduction of pensions, legislation covering wages and working conditions, which was also passed early in the present century, he puts forward the thesis that the successful establishment by a (male) wage-earning working class of a state welfare system based on wage security (rather than the more usual social security model) meant that any subsequent move towards more extensive and generous public welfare provisions would involve a radical alteration in the labour movement's whole approach to the problems of poverty and dependency.

Particularly important in the 1940s (in which many new welfare measures were introduced) were alterations to the taxation system which gave income taxes to the Commonwealth rather than the States and enlarged the powers of the Commonwealth Government. This permitted a significant expansion of pensions, allowances, benefits and services in the social security, income maintenance, medical and child care areas during and after the second war, assisted by the general community acceptance of increased taxation and greater central government powers necessitated by the war (Roe, 1976:221–2). Specifically, legislation was passed between 1941 and 1949 covering child endowment, widows' pensions, new maternity allowances and funeral benefits, unemployment, sickness and special dependency benefits, free medicines and hospital treatment in public wards, child and maternity benefits for Aborigines, and the setting up of employment and rehabilitation services and a federal department of social services (Dickey, 1980:Chapter 6; Kewley 1973:175–87; Roe, 1976:217–8). Further provisions followed in the 1950s, including in particular a medical and pharmaceutical benefits scheme and subsidies to institutions and programmes for the aged and handicapped (Dickey, 1980:Chapter 7; Kewley, 1973:188–9; Roe, 1976:314–5).

As in Britain, the major modern welfare developments came as part of post World War Two social reconstruction, though in Australia there was an additional period of extension and expansion under the Whitlam Labor Government in the early 1970s. This saw the introduction of a universal health scheme and supporting parent benefit, the abolition of the means test for old age pensions, child care and community and urban development initiatives, increased funds to education, and various responses to the rediscovery of poverty, including the Australian Assistance Plan (Dickey, 1980:Chapter 8; Kewley, 1973:381–9; Sweeney, 1983).

Mendelsohn (1979:51) adds together the categories of welfare and social security, education, and health to produce Total Welfare figures of 1.66 per cent of GDP in 1900/1, 6.93 per cent in 1930/1 and 10.16 per cent in 1969/70. In 1900/1 57.36 per cent of government welfare spending was allocated to education and 19.74 per cent to social security, but from 1920/1 onwards social security absorbed over 50 per cent, except for the final years for which Mendelsohn gives figures, 1969/70, when the proportion declined to 42 per cent and education and health together received the majority of government funds (Mendelsohn, 1979:52). Social security has been almost entirely funded from Commonwealth Government sources since 1910/11 (the States contributed only 3 per cent from the 1950s on); education shows almost the opposite pattern, though in 1969/70 the Commonwealth contribution rose from below 10 per cent to 16 per cent; and health since 1950 has drawn increasingly on federal funds so that in 1960/1 and 1969/70 the proportion coming from the States fell below 50 per cent (Mendelsohn, 1979:54).

Later figures show that spending in the social security and welfare category (excluding education and health) rose from 4.3 per cent of

GDP in the late 1960s to 8.5 per cent in 1977/8 but then fell to 8.0 per cent by 1979/80 (Social Indicators, 1984:329). Graycar provides figures on what he describes as overall social expenditure, including all welfare categories and also housing, urban and regional affairs, by the Commonwealth Government (figures which are therefore calculated differently from those given by Mendelsohn). The proportions he gives are 11.8 per cent of GDP spent on social welfare in the broader sense in 1963/4, 12.4 per cent in 1969/70, 14.3 per cent in 1972/3, 20.6 per cent in 1975 (when Labor lost office) and they 'have levelled out while the Fraser Government has been in power' (Graycar, 1983:4). Scotton (1980) gives figures on public social expenditure for the 1970s which show that after 1975/6 'budget austerities did no more than cut public expenditure growth back to the very low growth rates of the economy as a whole' and concludes that up to 1977/8 the pattern overall was one of stability or 'immobility' in levels of welfare spending rather than cutbacks. However, he notes, in some areas, principally health, education, housing and community amenities, there were reductions, while social security spending increased largely because of larger numbers of persons eligible for benefits (1980:7).

Mendelsohn observes that total welfare expenditure by government in 1970 compared with 1900 'was about 16 times as high' in real terms and 'per head it was about six times as high', while living standards were only 2½ times higher (1979:53). Later figures indicate a steady increase in government spending on social security and welfare throughout the 1970s, reaching a total of $12 032m in 1981/2 (Social Indicators, 1984:329).

Gough (1979:Chapter 5) identifies various contributing factors in his analysis of the sources of increasing post-war state involvement in welfare in Britain. Some are relatively deep-seated and structural, like organised pressure from the working class and labour/democratic governments, state support of capitalism, and the social upheavals associated with a major war (1979:64–69), while others are more 'immediate' reasons such as higher costs, population changes, and growing social needs (1979:84–92). At the same time, as Mishra (1984:6) observes, the 1950s and 1960s were regarded as a period in which 'social welfare looked like an eminently successful way of tempering freedom with security, enterprise with stability, economic growth with a measure of social concern and amelioration'. A commitment to ever-increasing levels of welfare provision was taken as a natural corollary of the increasingly humane and civilised character of mature capitalism or as Titmuss (1958:34) so nicely phrased it: a 'process of unilinear progression in collective benevolence'.

> The very idea of welfare, and hence of well-being tends to suggest that once the problems arising from misunderstanding or ignorance have been resolved then dispute, conflict or opposition will melt away. (Hall et al., 1975:8)

Welfare initiatives cannot simply be equated with progress. However, as Pinker observes:

> The welfare institutions of a society symbolise an unstable compromise between compassion and indifference, between altruism and self-interest. If men were predominantly altruistic, compulsory forms of social service would not be necessary; and if men were exclusively self-regarding, such compulsion would be impossible. (Pinker, 1971:211)

Welfare, as many marxist writers have argued, far from being a matter of commonsense or the expression of human altruism, is in fact 'a major ideological structure of our time' (Watts, 1977:138). The fact that, since the mid-1970s, governments have been under financial and social pressure to curtail their expenditure on welfare and social services, as the post-war period of expansion, prosperity and full employment comes to an end in most western countries, lends further support to this line of argument and suggests the previously popular interpretations of this period need revision.

A number of separate phases ought perhaps to be distinguished in the apparently smooth upward curve of welfare provisions from the mid-1940s on. In Australia, two of these (1941–9 and 1972–5), both times of Federal Labor Governments, might be characterised as relatively 'progressive' or welfare-oriented, while the period from the mid-1970s (which includes the Hawke Labor Government) has been widely depicted as one of 'retreat from' and attack upon the welfare state (M. Jones, 1983:55–61). Whereas Elliott (1978) sees substantial differences in the welfare policies of the two parties in government, Tulloch (1979:14) denies this and blames what she perceives as the fundamental allegiance by both parties to the 'liberal-capitalist' system. Without attempting to enter the debate over the nature and causes of the so-called 'crisis' of modern western capitalism in recent times, it certainly has had major and serious effects on welfare provision in all the countries affected. For example, in Australia since the mid 1970s only the social or income security category of social welfare expenditure (unemployment and sickness benefits, in particular) has continued to increase in real terms.

Mishra (1984:xiii) lists some of the main problems facing the welfare system in the west: stagflation and the end of economic growth; unemployment; the fiscal crisis of the state; cutbacks in social services; and a general loss of confidence in the social system of the welfare state. He points out that in recent years all the major areas of social service expenditure have come under constant and sustained political attack and not only from parties and governments with anti-statist and/or monetarist approaches to economic and social policy, but also from social democrat and socialist parties. Traditionally Rightist parties oppose extensive public welfare programmes on the grounds that they undermine individual initiative, responsibility and effort and that only a return to 'the small state' will permit the recovery of the free enterprise market economic system. While from a socialist or left perspective even massive public welfare spending cannot ultimately overcome the inequalities and injustices of capitalism, and hence a preoccupation with 'welfare' diverts attention from the real source of the problem. Further the welfare state's degree of centralisation, professionalisation and bureaucratisation poses threats to the freedom and self-determination of individuals at the same time as it provides for their material and social needs (Jordan, 1976:Chapter 1; Klein, 1980; Mishra, 1984:Chapters 2 and 3; Offe, 1982). However, there is a tendency to assume the general population shares the concerns of politicians, some state employees and academics about this. A recent English study found approval for extensive spending on state welfare services coexisting alongside support for privatisation (Taylor-Gooby, 1986) and in Australia similar results were reported by Smith and Wearing (1986).

Western governments' responses to 'the current crisis' cannot simply be described as the 'dismantling of the welfare state' (Gough, 1979:138). As M. Jones (1983:Chapter 5) demonstrates, there has been a substantial increase in federal government expenditure on income support in Australia since 1970 which is due not simply to changes in demographic composition (such as a higher proportion of aged people) but to 'new' forms of social dependency, sole parent families, and the sick and handicapped, as well as the unemployed, which reflect changing social and economic circumstances and new welfare initiatives. Income maintenance or social security expenditure has continued to rise. Since 1966, the number of pensions and beneficiaries as a proportion of the total Australian population has increased from 7.4 per cent to 10.4 per cent in 1974 and 16.9 per cent in 1985 (Jamrozik, 1986:32). The proportion of Commonwealth social security expenditure devoted to aged and veterans has decreased from 69 per cent in 1968/9 to 53 per cent in 1981/2, while the unemployed, sick and handicapped category accounted for 22 per cent in 1981/2 (and only 2 per cent in 1968/9) and the category of widows and sole parents has risen from 6 per cent to 12 per cent (M. Jones, 1983:106). Over this period the total expenditure on social security has increased from \$1128m to \$11 312m, from 17 per cent of total federal spending to 28 per cent or from 4.1 per cent to 7.7 per cent of GDP (M. Jones, 1983:108, 102).

M. Jones (1983:110) compares the demographic dependency ratio (persons under 16 and over 65 years per 1000 aged between 16 and 64 years), which decreased from 642 in 1969 to 584 in 1979, with the ratio of all categories of state dependency, which rose from 938 to 1055, an annual growth rate of 1.2 per cent. Not only did the proportion of the population on benefits increase but the numbers and level of benefits also increased proportionately, at a greater rate than the CPI and average weekly earnings during the 1970s (M. Jones, 1983:111). For example, in 1973 the supporting mothers' benefit was introduced (and altered to supporting parent in 1977) and the means test eased on old age pensions. Changes in the economy and in the incidence of family breakup have resulted in greater demands being made on public funds for income support and, on the whole, given the social climate, governments seem to feel unable or unwilling to deny these types of claims. At the same time rising levels of unemployment have made it economically difficult and/or politically inexpedient for governments to attempt to contain the levels of expenditure on income maintenance by altering the rates or conditions of eligibility for unemployment benefits.

The Poverty Inquiry of the early 1970s revealed that large families and those with a sole adult head were over-represented among the poor, and its highlighting therefore of the situation of many children makes any proposals for curtailing the various benefits to families (including the supporting parent benefit) highly unpopular. In fact, as Cass (1985:74, 83) has shown, the numbers and proportions of children in poverty have increased from 8 per cent to 15 per cent, much more relatively than have those of persons generally if data for 1981/2 is compared with that for 1972/3, and such children are now to be found in far higher proportions in two-parent families as compared with single-headed households.

A number of mainly marxist writers (and some feminists) have argued that defining welfare and the welfare state in the narrow sense ignores the vast and steadily increasing range of government activities and expenditures concerned with assistance to and support of the capitalist system through aid to identifiable groups and organisations not normally categorised as 'welfare' clients. The terms 'welfare state' and 'interventionist state' attempt to capture the complex forms and functions of the modern capitalist state, and in particular the nature and consequences of its extensive involvement in other than the traditional social welfare or human services spheres of operation (that is, those covering education, health and social security). In Titmuss' classic formulation (1958:Chapter 2), western governments, as well as being engaged in 'social' or, as Sinfield (1978) renamed it 'public', welfare (meaning the traditional social services, the most direct and obvious form of welfare), are also involved in what he calls 'fiscal welfare' or the various types of relief, allowances and deductions made through the taxation system. In addition to these two 'public' i.e. state welfare 'systems' (his words), Titmuss identifies a third welfare 'system' in western capitalist societies, an occupational welfare system involving provision in cash and kind made by employers for their workers but one which is publicly subsidised since these benefits can be claimed by employees as a deductible expense for taxation purposes. All three categories, Titmuss points out (1976:192), are essentially concerned with redistribution. A major feature of this social division of welfare is the differential visibility of benefits between the three systems (Sinfield,

1978:136), the principal effect of which is the perpetuation of the (mis)conception that only 'social' or 'public' welfare need be considered in any examination of welfare and the distribution of public resources in modern industrial society.

The continued and increasing allocations to business, directly in the form of goods, services and cash and through the taxation system, and the inability of governments to curb rising social security and other social service costs, suggest not so much a 'dismantling' or reduction of the modern state is occurring in the 1980s, but rather a 'restructuring' (Gough, 1979:138). Increasing government participation and expenditure in all aspects of the so-called free enterprise or market economy certainly do not support the idea of a move towards the 'smaller state' but instead a redistribution of government resources and a reordering of priorities for public funds. The extent and range of state involvement in welfare (in all senses of the term) makes the question of the nature, purpose and consequences of various forms of welfare provision one of central importance in modern capitalist societies. The analysis of welfare and/or social policy (collective measures concerned with the distribution of resources to various 'needy' groups) has become a significant topic in its own right for academics, politicians, and practitioners.

'Social policy' in Mishra's (1981:x) definition (and he uses the term interchangeably with welfare) covers the consideration of needs as well as of 'the structural patterns or arrangements through which needs are met'. It should not be confined to what goes on in the public or government sector but rather social policy should encompass, as Titmuss (1958:42) expressed it, 'all collective interventions to meet certain needs of the individual and/or to serve the wider interests of society'. From this point of view, the distinction between economic and social or welfare policy cannot readily or usefully be sustained, since all economic measures have social justifications and consequences, and all social measures entail economic costs, alter the balance of economic resources and interfere with free market forces.[2] This line of argument has been advanced by a number of writers in the field, and Walker, for instance, puts it as follows:

> The concept of social policy being formulated implicitly here rests on the *distributional* implications or outcomes of the decisions and activities of a wide range of social institutions and groups. This is not to imply that social policy should be concerned only with the distribution of income and wealth, but rather with the production *and* distribution of a wide range of *social resources*, including income, assets, property, health, education, environment, status and power. It is assumed that the extent to which these resources are distributed equally or unequally relative to need still determine the pattern of welfare in any society. Thus the essence of social policy is the social production and distribution of inequality and welfare. (1981:239, original emphases)

Following Titmuss, Mishra includes as 'welfare', social services (education, health, housing and income maintenance), occupational provisions and fiscal benefits, and he points out that occupational welfare is neither separate from nor independent of the government or the 'public' welfare system, since firms obtain tax deductions for the benefits they supply to their employees (thus depriving the government of some revenue) and, a further complication, the state is itself an employer and a source of occupational welfare. Nor is it redistributive in the same way as are state-provided payments and services, since occupational fringe benefits are part of the rewards structure of the enterprise and hence are allocated in direct proportion to wages (thus reflecting occupational rank and perceived merit, not need) (Mishra, 1981:106–8). An even greater conceptual problem, Rein (1981:9–13) believes, is that Titmuss' social division of welfare assumes the utility and validity of the public/private dichotomy and of the distinction between the state and the economy and between benefits and wages.

Though the focus of this chapter is primarily on those forms of welfare that are under direct state control, any assessment of their effects on redistribution requires a careful examination also of the other forms of welfare provision. No assumptions are made about social policies necessarily being beneficial to all or most people, nor about interests and intentions being benevolent or progressive, nor about outcomes all being planned and consistent with the objectives or justifications of policies (Walker, 1981:240–1).

> Social welfare is emphatically not simply about pity and concern for the less fortunate: it is about running an efficient as well as a caring society. (Mendelsohn, 1982:2)

Essentially, as Titmuss (1974:Chapter 10) has argued, all policy is about values and choices, and social policy is about needs, rights, justice and equity. Social policy, though it necessarily entails some redistribution of resources, is not inherently 'beneficial or welfare-oriented' (Titmuss, 1974:26) (i.e. it may not selectively favour disadvantaged minorities) nor does it automatically bring 'social development' rather than 'social retraction or retrenchment' (Walker, 1981:240).

Sociological analysis of welfare and welfare systems

In the literature there are a number of categorisations of the various models of welfare and comparisons of the different theoretical approaches to the analysis of welfare, welfare systems and the welfare state. We are interested here both in *social* constructions of welfare (the models of welfare that influence formulation, adoption and implementation of welfare policies in society) and in *sociological* constructions of welfare (alternative interpretive and explanatory frameworks—and here we will make use of the four theoretical perspectives outlined in earlier chapters). It is at this level of analysis that we can look at the relationship between systems and policies, in welfare theory and practice, and social control.

We start by considering some of the various models available in society of how welfare can and should be organised, to whom it should be given, in what form and for what purposes. Such models embody a mixture of technical aspects (what services, how arranged and delivered, and to whom) and moral or ideological beliefs and values (such as, how 'need' is to be defined).

Alternative principles or dimensions for welfare provision and allocation in modern western societies include the following interrelated pairs of alternatives, some representing dichotomies and others polar extremes on a continuum: public or private; free or fee-paying; cash or kind; free or tied; formally or informally organised and administered; selective or universal; bureaucratic or discretionary criteria of eligibility; individual or collective-oriented; needs or rights-based; minimum or maximum coverage; paternalistic/authoritarian or democratic/participatory modes of policy-making and administration; the aim of measures may be minor social adjustments or major structural change in the economy or society.[3]

The public/private distinction reflects the classic separation between government and non-government sectors of society. As we have noted earlier, in Australia as in other western countries welfare and social services and benefits have over the last one hundred years increasingly become a public, and specifically a government, responsibility, although, as Titmuss pointed out, occupationally-based welfare schemes which are located in the private sector are also significant. Some writers, for example Grønbjerg (1982), Kamerman (1983) and Rein (1981), reject any simple equation of private with profit-making and public with non-profit-making activities and raise serious doubts as to whether the public/private distinction itself retains meaning or value in the mixed economies of advanced capitalist societies and particularly the United States. Walker (1981:231–2) argues the distinction, though still given considerable importance and widely used, needs to be recognised as an ideological device rather than a real social division. Feminists also take this view, emphasising the ways dominant male interests and men as a group are served by the association between perceived gender differences and the public/private dichotomy, and the social restriction and subordination of women that this entails.

Selectivity (or exclusivity) and universalism refer to the kinds of criteria used for deciding on the allocation of welfare benefits. In the former case, restrictive criteria are imposed (which may involve economic, social or moral indicators of 'need'), the main purpose being to accept responsibility for as few categories of need and as small numbers of claimants as possible in order to keep the amount of welfare provision to a minimum and hence avoid what is perceived by those favouring this approach as undesirable interference with the workings of the free market economy and the individualist ethic. Selectivity may apply to the service or to the ability to pay for it (Jamrozik, 1983:180). By contrast, universal availability means that all who fit into prescribed categories have automatic entitlement to a given benefit or service.

Various commentators have observed that typically Australian welfare benefits have been allocated on the selective principle, often explicitly relying on the deserving/undeserving division of potential claimants, rare exceptions being family allowances, maternity allowances and child endowment, schooling, preschool care and aged pensions and for a time in the 1970s medical care (under Medibank) (M. Jones, 1983:310; Mendelsohn, 1979:34–5; Roe, 1976:106, 224). The needs/rights distinction is closely linked to selectivity/universalism and reflects the alternative justifications for a welfare claim. Where needs are the basis of the allocation of a benefit or service, claimants are assessed according to criteria selected by those providing or funding the welfare item and even successful applicants usually find the process stigmatising or demeaning. Where welfare is a right, the criteria tend to be general rather than personal, no moral or social inadequacy is implied, and the power relationship between service provider and recipient can be more equal (Titmuss, 1976:Chapters X and XI). Finally, welfare can be oriented to the improvement of individual circumstances or the enhancement of group or collective conditions (Walker, 1981:228), and may therefore cause very little or a considerable degree of structural and institutional change.

The classic formulation of alternative welfare systems that has been extended and developed is that of Wilensky and Lebeaux. They compare what they described as the 'residual' and the 'institutional conceptions' or 'ideologies' of welfare. The 'residual' conception, they claim,

> holds that social welfare institutions should come into play only when the normal structures of supply, the family and the market, break down . . . These are the preferred structures of supply. In such cases, according to this idea, a third mechanism of need fulfillment is brought into play—the social welfare structure. This is conceived as a residual agency, attending primarily to emergency functions, and is expected to withdraw when the regular social structure—the family and the economic system—is again working properly. Because of its residual, temporary, substitute characteristic, social welfare thus conceived often carries the stigma of 'dole' or 'charity'. (1965:138, 139)

The 'institutional' conception

> sees the welfare services as normal, 'first line' functions of modern industrial society . . . This definition . . . implies no stigma, no emergency, no 'abnormalcy'. Social welfare becomes accepted as a

> proper, legitimate function of modern society in helping individuals achieve self-fulfillment. The complexity of modern life is recognised. The inability of the individual to provide fully for himself, or to meet all his needs in family and work settings, is considered a 'normal' condition; and the helping agencies achieve 'regular' institutional status. (1965:138, 140)

Much of the subsequent discussion of welfare conceptions or models explicitly or implicitly accepts this basic categorisation and then extends or develops it.[4]

Wilensky, in a report on research into the structural and cultural underpinnings of the welfare state in western industrial societies points to the co-existence of competing value emphases even within the American culture (specifically he mentions economic individualism and the success ethic versus equality, justice and security) and hence the misleading nature of simple equations between individualism and the insurance principle, on the one hand, and, on the other, collectivism and non-contributory state welfare schemes (1975:39–42).[5] Pinker (1971:97–115) explores some of the complexities of the relationships between the various dimensions of the two main normative models of social welfare. He questions two common assumptions in the literature: (1) that selectivity is the sole or the main source of stigma (he posits instead the capitalist work ethic and reward system); and (2) that the 'institutional' approach is based on the universalism principle and that universalism (or collectivism) necessarily implies a relative definition of social need and the pursuit of the twin goals of equality and justice. He then proposes a third possibility as an alternative to the choice between residual and institutional models, which he develops in a later book (1979:Chapter 12), and describes as a mixed economy/welfare state or a form of 'mercantile collectivism' (1979:235) which entails a form of social system that is neither capitalist nor socialist.

Various historians and sociologists have relied implicitly or explicitly on the comparison between a residual and an institutional model to help them describe the changes in the nature of welfare provision in western societies since the late nineteenth century. Overall, they agree, governments have moved from being reluctantly reactive to adopting more positive and constructive redistributive policies. Wilensky and Lebeaux argued that, although welfare in America combines elements of both the residual and the institutional ideologies, in the post-Depression period, the latter has become more powerful. Mishra (1981:110) describes the general trend as a shift from the 'nightwatchman state' towards the 'welfare state'. Roe, writing in the mid-1970s, suggests that the 'theoretical functions of "social" policy' in Australia have moved from being 'residual to regulatory to redistributive' (1976:ix). Mendelsohn talks of a transition from welfare as a 'destitution net' (1982:18), in other words from being about 'pity and concern for the less fortunate', to a commitment to 'running an efficient as well as a caring society' (1982:2), though, in M. Jones' estimation (1983:4) the Australian public welfare system has remained 'selective' and 'austere' never achieving more than a 'residual' level of provision (Tulloch, 1983:255). Recently, however, with pressure for cutbacks in public welfare expenditure there have even been signs in some western countries of a return to the 'social charity' approach (Pinker, 1974:18).

Titmuss (1974:30–1) describes three alternative models of social policy: the 'Residual Welfare Model', the 'Industrial Achievement-Performance Model' and the 'Institutional Redistributive Model'; the basic characteristics of the three are, respectively, minimal intervention and only where needs are not being met through 'natural' channels (i.e. the family or the private market), public assistance where earned 'on the basis of merit, work performance and productivity', and a system 'providing universalist services outside the market on the principle of need'. Mishra (1981:14) suggests the residual and the institutional models should be contrasted with a third one which he calls 'structural' and which rests on a totally needs-based orientation to welfare, but such a 'structural' model he sees as being incompatible with capitalism. In his view this type of welfare system and alternative approach to the distribution of resources derives from a critical or marxist conception of society and offers the complete opposite of the residual model, the institutional model being located somewhere between these two extremes. Mishra criticises Titmuss among others for conducting the theoretical debate about alternative approaches to social policy within the framework of capitalist democracy with a consequent restriction of the range of possible options, the result being that:

> In short, liberal capitalism is taken for granted as the framework within which the see-sawing battle between capitalistic and welfare-oriented values is to be waged perpetually. (Mishra, 1981:18)

As Tulloch, who takes a more radical systemic approach, says:

> Arguments about the relative merits of poverty-reduction versus income-maintenance programmes, earnings-related versus flat-rate benefits, universal or selective payments are basically irresolvable. . . [We are limited by] the logic of a liberal capitalist economy. . . The search for fair and rational solutions to these problems can be likened to the attempt to produce sound living conditions in an unstable structure. (1979:17)

A number of writers have pointed to affinities between residual, institutional and more radical structural models of welfare and various politico-ideological perspectives, such as those represented by the classic liberal and modern conservative or New Right, the social democratic, and the marxist or socialist positions respectively (Bolger et al., 1981:Chapter 1; Graycar, 1979:Chapters 1 and 8; Mishra, 1984:

Chapter 6; Pinker, 1971:Chapter 3; Pinker, 1979:Chapter 12). Not surprisingly, those working with different socio-political philosophies perceive the form and function of welfare and of a 'welfare state' differently. The most obvious contrast is between the liberal 'progressive' interpretation, that assumes welfare is a question of civic rights, and marxist approaches, which talk explicitly in terms of social control (Rochefort, 1981; Schram and Turbett, 1983). Room (1979) and Mishra in his most recent book (1984) explore the relationship between alternative approaches to welfare and social policy, and the three major political 'paradigms' of liberalism, marxism and social democracy. Put simply, the residual model of welfare fits with the traditional laissez-faire liberal position, with its emphasis on the free operation of market forces, minimal state interference, and the values of individual freedom, enterprise and self-reliance. The institutional model is compatible with a social democracy perspective that works with a social engineering, reformist approach to change, one which does not see a radical transformation of any of the key institutions of capitalist society as either necessary or desirable. The structural model does presume a fundamental critique of capitalism as a socio-economic system and obviously the most appropriate political perspective is marxism or socialism in some form.

Bolger et al. (1981:Chapter 1) compare three alternative ideologies of welfare in the contemporary world: social democracy which assumes that the situation of the weak and poor can be significantly altered within capitalism and that the state provides a mechanism for controlling the market and economic forces; Thatcherism which regards the welfare aspects of the state as unnecessarily and undesirably restrictive of capitalism; and democratic socialism which sees welfare and the state as important to both the ruling and the subordinate classes and as a site of constant but constrictive struggle. George and Wilding (1976) offer a somewhat different categorisation of four ideological groupings of British social policy theorists; these are anti-collectivists (the modern equivalent of liberals), reluctant collectivists, fabian socialists, and marxists. The views of certain key members of each of the four groups are examined in relation to four issues—social values, societal organisation, the role of governments, and the welfare state. Various authors interested in the critiques of 'the welfare state' coming from the New Right observe that, despite the 'small state' rhetoric, the overall policies of Thatcher and Reagan are not in practice uniformly 'minimalist' or 'anti-interventionist' (along classic liberal lines) but in favour of a 'strong state' and the exercise of highly though selectively regulatory state powers (see, for example, Clegg, Dow and Boreham, 1983:35; McLennan, 1984:349–52)[6]. Mishra (1984) advances a case for an 'integrated' or corporatist[7] welfare state as a solution to the current crisis in preference to both the marxist-socialist and New Right alternatives. His model assumes full employment and extensive social services are possible within the context of a 'liberal market society' (1984:105).

Tulloch (1978:66) gives a complex and comprehensive diagrammatic representation of the different elements involved in what she identifies as four major normative (or socio-political) approaches to welfare and social policy: the conservative-liberal, welfare-liberal, radical-liberal, and socialist.[8] The distinguishing elements of the various approaches include preferences for either a residual or an institutional model, for individualism or collectivism, for selectivity or universalism, and for a hierarchical or egalitarian structure of society. She comments that, although freedom figures in both the conservative and radical-liberal perspectives, it takes on quite different meanings: in the former being associated with individualism and inequality, in the latter with collectivism and equality.

Though, like political philosophies and social ideologies, sociological theories and perspectives reflect particular sets of value assumptions about how the world is and how it might be, we are here primarily interested in their sociological content. We are considering only perspectives which assume 'the social' has to be given a position of central importance in any explanatory theory. Conceptions of what 'the social' represents, however, differ markedly as among the various perspectives on which I have chosen to draw.

The quantity and quality of work done on welfare from each of the four perspectives varies considerably. Though in the 1970s critical analysis of welfare drew on the interactionist and labelling perspectives in deviance and social control, at the present time marxism and feminism (in their various forms) seem to be responsible for much of the substantial volume of theory and research being produced, particularly on the welfare state and on the 'public' and 'fiscal' welfare systems in particular.

Several writers have commented on the a-theoretical nature of much of the analysis of social policy up until very recent times. Social administration seems to have been a largely empirically-oriented, if not empiricist, subject or field of study and can be contrasted with sociology which, from the nineteenth century 'founding fathers' on, established itself as a theoretical discipline (Pinker, 1971:Chapter 1). Although classical sociologists did not on the whole regard 'welfare' and 'social policy' as we understand the terms as key social institutions, they were centrally concerned with the social and moral problems facing urban-industrial society and with poverty and inequality. Their views of the sources of these problems and of the solutions to them followed from their evaluations of which were the major institutions and processes in society and how they operated, which in turn were based on a particular theoretical approach to the analysis of the social world.

Various commentators on the welfare and social policy literature have compared different perspectives on welfare and capitalist society, and specifically marxist and non-marxist perspectives; in the latter category are included various 'liberal' and 'individualist' modes of thought (in both economics and sociology) and 'social democrat' or social 'reformist' approaches (which range from Durkheim and Weber to social policy theorists like Marshall and Titmuss). For Room (1979: Chapter 2), the major differences lie in the way in which writers representing these two broadly-defined sociological traditions deal with three key features of 'capitalist market society', namely (a) the division of labour and the class structure, (b) capital accumulation and social change and (c) social integration. George and Wilding (1976:Chapter 1) follow the conventional practice of drawing a distinction between order and pluralist theories, on the one hand, and conflict and elite theories, on the other hand (giving as examples Parsons and Marx) and then compare their perceptions of power, the state, social problems and social policy. Mishra (1981) also sees value in a basic division into marxist and non-marxist theoretical approaches; he relates this to different conceptions of capitalist society and assessments as to whether the capitalist system could ever adequately provide for the welfare needs of its members or whether this could only be achieved under a socialist system. Taylor-Gooby and Dale (1981:Chapters 2–4) identify three bodies of theory which offer accounts of welfare and the welfare state: these they call 'individualist', 'reformist' and 'structural' or 'structuralist' (they do not discriminate between these two terms), the principal difference in their view being between the idealism which underlies the first two types of approach and some forms of structuralism such as functionalism, and the materialism that characterises systemic or structuralist theories of a marxist orientation.

From the various marxist and non-marxist perspectives we derive alternative interpretations of what welfare is and what it does, and what are its effects on society. Liberal individualist, pluralist and functionalist models of the social order give different accounts of the role of welfare institutions and ideologies and all these differ again from marxist explanations of the forms and functions of welfare. Explanations of how particular welfare institutions and systems originated and developed also vary according to perspective.

We have already questioned the notion that the existence of public systems of welfare benefits and services of a reasonably generous and comprehensive kind in modern western societies simply reflects a heightened moral consciousness. We have defined welfare as those social arrangements concerned with the distribution of resources according to 'need' and have noted that in modern western capitalism a principal organiser of these arrangements is the state. The key questions for the sociologist, therefore, are: Under what conditions do particular types of welfare arrangements emerge? What factors are responsible for determining perceptions of need and of welfare? What types of people and interests shape welfare policy? What are the processes which shape the role played by the state in the welfare field and in modern capitalist society generally?

Functionalism (and some forms of marxism which utilise functionalist logic) 'explain' the form a particular institution takes, how it operates, and why it operates in the way it does in terms of some general societal requirements or 'needs' that have to be met in order that the system as a whole may be maintained. Although Parsons and functionalism generally have not devoted much attention to welfare, the main function that welfare like social control is seen to serve is 'integration': in other words it helps to ensure that the parts of a society, whether they are institutions or individuals and groups, work together harmoniously and mutually supportively. Integration and order depend on the moral status of society being protected and reinforced so that it continues to be perceived by its members as a successful and desirable form of social organisation. Thus welfare, by taking care of the casualties and failures of a social system (western industrial society) without challenging the basis of that system, acts as a type of social cement and by invoking such notions as community, altruism, 'the social good', confirms the fundamental moral character of society. The fact that in modern societies the state is the main vehicle for the delivery of welfare services rather than the family or religion is explained in terms of the increasing differentiation and specialisation of institutions and functions that comes with development.[9]

There are similarities between the nature of functionalist accounts of welfare and its role in modern western society and so-called convergence theories which link modern developments in welfare and social policy as in other institutional areas to the process of industrialisation, and specifically to the requirements of technology. Convergence theories (such as that of Wilensky and Lebeaux, 1965) focus on the common characteristics of welfare in industrial societies, in particular the expansion of services, the greater proportion of expenditure devoted to welfare, the increasingly important role of the state and the rise of the professions. They interpret the rise of the welfare state as the outcome of more or less autonomous social processes and a reflection of common values and interests across industrial societies.[10]

Elements of the functionalist argument and a consensus approach are relatively common in the social policy literature in the form of general statements about welfare measures meeting community needs and reflecting shared values. Even Titmuss (as Hall et al., 1975:11–12 point out) shows such tendencies in his earlier work (for example, 1958:39) where he uses phrases such as 'socially recognised needs', 'society's will to survive as an organic whole' and 'essentials for the continued existence of the parts and the whole'.

Some marxists also employ functionalist language and logic. In their case, the 'needs' of the system refers to the conditions under which the capitalist mode of production can continue to operate satisfactorily (i.e. continue to accumulate capital). 'Welfare' is seen as one of several mechanisms for diverting attention from what is basically and unavoidably a competitive, exploitative and inhumane system by offering some limited forms of (usually material) compensation to some of the system's casualties, thereby weakening the basis of potential organised opposition but without displacing from its central position the capitalist work ethic and reward system. This kind of marxist analysis shares with consensus functionalism the view that a welfare system or state has a significant ideological role to play, and what Parsons describes as 'pattern maintenance and tension management' O'Connor, Gough and others have described as 'legitimation'. The state (and particularly its welfare activity) is explained in terms of meeting ideological, as well as more obvious material, requirements so that the social conditions on which capitalism relies can be reproduced. Both structural functionalists and marxist functionalists see the increasing size, importance, and public nature of the modern welfare system as a necessary part of 'mature' or 'developed' capitalism/industrialism and as making an important contribution to the smooth running of the system.

Because of the major dissimilarities between functionalism and marxism in their theoretical models of the bases of social order (idealist versus materialist) and their conceptions of the fundamental characteristics of capitalist-industrial society (progressive versus exploitative), they see welfare systems and social control generally quite differently: functionalists regard both as highly desirable and essential in all societies, and of individual and collective benefit; while marxists claim both would become unnecessary were capitalism to be abolished and believe that, like all other capitalist institutions, they work in the interests of the capitalist class and against the interests of all other groups.

Interactionist and subjectivist sociologies see social forms as the outcome of goal-oriented activities of individuals and groups. Their analysis rests on a pluralist conception of power and the political order. The different institutions and practices that societies develop, and the different methods of social control exercised in different times and places are consequently products of the individual and collective efforts of human agents. Sociologists taking an interactionist or pluralist perspective trace the origins of particular welfare schemes and measures to identifiable groups and interests, to pressure group politics, and to moral crusades on behalf of 'needy' groups by middle-class reformers and philanthropists, though they may also pay some attenion to the wider social and cultural contexts within which these campaigns occurred. Examples are Hall et al. (1975) and Graycar (1979) who link social policy to the political system and to pressure group politics.

An adequate sociological explanation, from this perspective, of the origins, nature and operation of a control institution or system such as welfare thus must take seriously the accounts given by the actors concerned, both those giving and those receiving a certain form of service. Of special relevance in the welfare field is the emphasis placed by interactionists on subjective definitions and perceptions. Pinker has stressed the gap in our knowledge of how individuals define their needs and why they define them as they do and hence our failure to link the essentially normative models used by social policy and social administration writers to 'the experience and subjective reality of the everyday life of ordinary people' (1971:104). He is arguing for much more input from sociological theory and research into discussions about social welfare and social policy.

Pinker (1971:Chapter 4) and others with a concern for the effects on individuals of welfare and social control institutions and personnel (and in particular the social and psychological effects of the moral judgements that often accompany their activities) have focussed attention on stigma and on devalued social statuses in general as a critical element in social control. Though the welfare state has on the whole replaced voluntary charity, the idea of some welfare claimants as being more deserving than others still continues and much welfare is still provided on conditional and selective grounds, which tends to mean that as long as welfare provision is made on the basis of official definitions of need rather than universally recognised rights it will carry some negative moral and social connotations.

The welfare literature rarely acknowledges explicitly the relevance of the contribution of sociology of deviance and the labelling perspective.[11] However the notion of deviance as a master status, the concepts of social control, labelling, deviant career and stigmatisation, the recognition of the inequalities of power and the reinforcement of feelings of inferiority and dependency that characterise the relationships between welfare staff and their clients, and the appreciation of the ideological nature of welfare concepts and policies, all clearly owe allegiance to the work of that school.

Matza, whose (1969) book *Becoming Deviant* became a classic deviance text, in an earlier paper on poverty (1971) discusses the social and symbolic significance of such a moral concept as 'disreputable poor'. He identified three separate, but overlapping, sources of 'disrepute'. These 'circles of poverty' attracted differing degrees of stigma. They were, firstly, poverty itself, secondly, dependency on welfare or public assistance (as distinct from insurance-based welfare schemes) and thirdly, special morally questionable 'disreputable' categories of the welfare population—such as unemployed able-bodied men, long-term recipients, and 'problem families'. He contrasts morally neutral (or minimally disapproved) forms of welfare and dependency and those characterised by 'demoralization' or 'maximum disrepute'. 'Demoralization [he says] should be understood in the double sense of the withering of conscientious effort and the decline of moral standards' (1971:612). Others have also pointed to the historical importance of distinctions such as that between 'decent' or 'deserving' and 'undeserving' poor, between 'the poor' and 'the pauper class', with differing degrees of blame attached to the various conditions. For instance, in a recent article Loewenberg (1981), drawing explicitly on Goffman's work on stigma, examines the changing relationship between stigmatisation and deterrence and assesses evidence from various areas of American welfare for a trend towards destigmatisation.

During the 1970s, a critique of welfare agencies and personnel and of social work in particular (along with the helping professions generally) began to develop which drew on interactionist concepts and insights. A typical example is 'Social Services as controllers', the title of a chapter in *Control Without Custody* (edited by King, published in 1976). In this, the author, Stevenson, a major figure in social work education in England, explores some of the ways in which social work in the modern welfare system influences the lives of a far wider section of the population than just 'the poor'. Others combined this approach with more critical structural perspectives. Pearson (1975), for instance, assesses the contribution of the new deviance theories, in his words the 'misfit sociologies', to contemporary psychiatry and social work. He concludes that, although they did succeed in raising important questions about the politics and morality of the therapeutic and welfare professions and of the welfare state itself, they fell short of being radical in practice (1975:203).

Jordan (1976:Chapter 5) also identifies interactionism as a significant intellectual influence on contemporary analyses of social work and social control, though he too finds this approach of limited value in his attempt to deal with the broad issues of 'freedom and the welfare state'. The earlier and widely quoted assessment of the sociology of deviance, and specifically of Becker's work by Gouldner is relevant here. In his article on 'sociology and the welfare state', Gouldner's principal charge was that the 'new underdog sociology', far from offering a real basis for moral and political opposition to and reform of the control structures of the modern state, is a 'sociology of and for the new welfare state' (1968:110). In locating the source of deviants' problems at the level of the encounters with caretakers, local officials and middle-level bureaucrats in welfare institutions, Becker he contends misrepresents the situation, since real power lies with 'top dogs' in government, administration and the private foundations. Though Gouldner at this time was not putting forward a case for structural or class analysis along marxist lines, with hindsight we can see he was moving in that direction, and it is to marxism we will now turn.

The idea that an understanding of social institutions, including social control institutions generally and welfare institutions in particular, requires some consideration of human agency, of individual and collective interests and actions, is to be found not only in interactionist sociology but also in some brands of marxism. An account has already been given of the diverse schools of thought in modern marxism and of the various ways in which marxists analyse the forms and functions of the capitalist state, in particular focussing on its 'welfare' and 'interventionist' characteristics. As we discovered in the general discussion of marxism in Chapter 3, some modern marxists work with a highly theoretical model, in some respects similar to the Parsonian systems model, while others prefer an approach which, though still materialist, does not assume economic, technological or some form of structural determinism and which gives weight to the part played by human consciousness, will and agency in the production and reproduction of the social world.

These writers reject both functionalist and structuralist models of society. They emphasise the presence of conflict and contradiction within social institutions and structures, including the welfare state itself and the capitalist mode of production. Explanations for the development of the welfare state, and for certain types of welfare policy over the last hundred years are couched more in terms of the class struggle than of the 'needs of capital'.[12] Tulloch (1983) gives such an interpretation of the Australian welfare system since Federation, attributing its overall 'residual' character even under Labor governments to the lack of an effective radical working class and the strength of ruling class interests. Castles' recent (1985) book on the development of welfare policy in Australia and New Zealand also addresses this question, though his particular interest is exploring the influence of the working class through party politics and the parliamentary system.

This type of marxist approach includes writers who see the state responding to problems and issues arising from the conflicts and divisions in society but not simply in the capacity of servant of the ruling class or of capital, and others who focus on internal contradictions and power struggles between competing groups and between sectors of operation within the state itself and its institutions and structures, which are not just reflections of struggles between external forces but are partly autonomous. Examples of the former are those (such as Castles, 1985; Corrigan (ed.), 1980; Roe, 1976; Tulloch, 1979) who, without denying the importance of overall structural considerations, attribute a number of government welfare initiatives to working-class pressure exercised through unions and political parties, which has the effect of restricting if not displacing free market forces and the primacy of the profit motive. Examples of the latter are those (for instance, Bolger et al., 1981; C. Jones, 1983; London Edinburgh Weekend Return Group, 1980; van Krieken, 1980) who look at the contradictory roles of state employees (and hence at contradictory aspects of state activities) because they are at the same time agents of the state and the ruling class, and hence part of the regulatory apparatus through which people's lives are controlled, and also workers and hence members of the 'oppressed' class.

Working 'in' and 'for' the welfare state also entails not only a contradictory class position but also exposure to other kinds of structural tensions, such as the conflict between professional identification and bureaucratic organisational requirements, between ideology and practice, and between 'care and control' (Jordan, 1976; Simpkin, 1983). For social workers in particular, their role in the welfare state contains contrary elements. Their job involves both taking a humanitarian, individualistic approach to the problems and needs of clients, and the application of predetermined procedural rules and the utilisation of one or other of a limited range of officially acceptable remedies. Despite a moral commitment to caring for the individual, the inevitable result is a high degree of supervision and management by social workers of those with whom they come into contact in accordance with the assumptions of their professional ideologies, the objectives of government policy and the wider constraints of societal priorities and resources.

These writers acknowledge fundamental dilemmas, therefore, facing marxists (and others) who have the ultimate aim of reforming and/or reorganising society. This is the fundamental question as to whether and to what extent the state can be a positive force on the side of the working class, and other oppressed groups, or whether, despite the best intentions and the apparent achievement of some short-term gains, the capitalist/industrial state (in its 'welfare' as well as its more obviously repressive capacity) is constrained to serve only the interests of capital, because of the relatively less powerful structural position occupied by the political system in modern western societies as compared with that of the economic system.

None of the commentators on the current state of theoretical knowledge about welfare and the welfare system (who are almost exclusively male) seem to recognise the existence and value of a feminist perspective. Although some comment on the particular characteristics of women as welfare clients and on the presence of sexist assumptions in welfare ideologies and policies, and acknowledge the contribution of the women's movement in exposing these aspects of the welfare system (C. Jones, 1983:92–3; Kennedy (ed.), 1982; London Edinburgh Weekend Return Group, 1980:83–4, 90–1; Jordan, 1976:57, 183–8; Pinker, 1974; van Krieken, 1980:25) they treat gender and sexism as theoretically unproblematic, as simply an extra dimension to the analysis of welfare.

The feminist perspective, however, goes beyond this and attempts to reconstruct theories and models to take account of the centrality of gender divisions and inequalities in the organisation of social life. Rose (1981:493–4) points out that social policy in England was first forced to accept a 'class division of welfare' and is now being confronted by the parallel notion of a 'sexual division of welfare'. It is not surprising that much of the feminist analysis of welfare and the welfare state draws on the marxist tradition (including the work of the modern structuralists, Althusser and Poulantzas[13]) and tends to favour theories which emphasise the importance of state institutions and policies for the maintenance of both social/ideological and material conditions for the persistence of the capitalist system. The focus is on the relation between the state, welfare, the family and women's position. Much of the work in this field comes from England and a useful overview is provided in a recent book by Dale and Foster (1986) entitled *Feminists and Social Welfare*. The analysis that developed in England during the 1970s from a feminist perspective is principally identified with the work of Land, McIntosh, Rose and Wilson.

Land (1976) claims that the post-war welfare system reflects the assumption of Beveridge that married women should be treated differently from men and single women because of their marital advantage in being supported by their husbands. She examined various welfare provisions and concludes that the key determinant of welfare provisions for women is marital status not motherhood. In a later article, Land (1978) argues:

> Social policies are *implicit* family policies because most, if not all, of them are based on certain assumptions about the pattern of 'normal' relationships between the sexes and the generations within the family. (1978:258 original emphasis)

She again contends it is women's position as wives and not principally as mothers that is reflected in welfare policies. She then demonstrates how gender roles and the sexual division of labour (which shape women's domestic responsibilities and their patterns of paid employment) are reinforced both as ideologies and as ongoing social realities by state intervention in family life. Land sees welfare policies and the domestic labour commitments of women as the main factors responsible for women's lower participation in the paid workforce. Lewis (1983) argues a similar case for the period 1870 to 1945. She too emphasises the way government policies rested on the assumption that dependency was women's normal state. Wilson, who wrote the first book giving an overall feminist analysis of 'women and the welfare state', talks of 'the State controlling the way in which the woman does her job in the home of servicing the worker and bringing up their children' (1977:40).

McIntosh (1978) traces the connection between the state and the dependency of married women on the male wage-earner through both the social security system and labour market policies. She identifies two separate dimensions (she calls them 'functions') to the state's regulation of women in the family sphere and in the paid work sphere: 'the reproduction of labour power' and 'the reproduction of relations of production' (1978:264). This involves women in looking after children and male workers, makes the household dependent on wage-earner(s) and hence ensures that women are a source of 'marginal' or 'reserve' cheap labour, thereby reinforcing their dependency. She examines not only the nature and effects of state family policies but also state measures that perpetuate a sex-segmented labour force and gender inequalities in wages and working conditions, thus limiting women's participation in paid employment. She also draws a useful distinction between three categories of women, defined by their relationships to men and children, who receive differential treatment from the welfare system; these are:

> (1) Women living with husbands or male sexual partners [who] are assumed by the state to be dependent upon them (and so either *are* dependent on them or are forced to work at, possibly, very disadvantageous rates of pay). (2) Women living with their children and without a man, and some other older widows, [who] are supposed to be allowed to depend on state payments without being expected to seek work. . . (3) Most other women [who] are required to seek work or prove disablement, as (almost) all men are, before they can get either contributory or supplementary benefits. (McIntosh, 1978:281, original emphasis)

Rose (1981), Wilson (1977) and, more recently, Finch and Groves (1983) and, in Australia, Bryson (Bryson and Mowbray, 1986; Mowbray and Bryson, 1984) have discussed how welfare cutbacks in human services areas and the deinstitutionalisation movement affect women, and specifically women in their traditional domestic role. Cass (1982:19) attributes the shift back towards the family as provider of services to 'contractionist economic policies and neo-conservative political parties' in Australia as in other western countries. Changes in the provision of welfare benefits and services with respect to the aged, invalids and the disabled (adult or child), which have meant female family members replacing paid trained staff, reflect traditional assumptions about gender roles and women as 'natural' carers. They thus extend and reinforce the sexual division of labour and women's dependency. These writers expose the hidden assumptions about the division of unpaid labour within the family and women's culturally assigned responsibility for 'caring work' that lie behind contemporary moves towards 'normalisation' and 'deinstitutionalisation' of the incapacitated aged, the disabled, the psychologically disturbed, and the chronically sick and the advocacy of 'community care' alternatives.[14] What Mowbray and Bryson (1984:261) describe as 'a tripartite transfer of responsibility towards more local, family-based and private provision' simply means extended obligations and more domestic duties for women (in addition to meeting their existing commitments to husband and children). This is work accorded no economic reward and little social value but which reduces such women's opportunities for participation in the paid workforce and increases their dependency on male wage-earners or state financial support. In addition, the ideological arguments for increased community care put by government officials and experts are not necessarily supported by members of 'the community'. Though there has been very little research on the views of the general public on this topic, one Scottish study (by West et al., 1984) found that (although for the majority residential care was the least favoured alternative) only a minority were in favour of family and informal care, and fewer women than men, and there was a preference for domiciliary residential day centre and professional care alternatives.

During the 1980s a number of publications on welfare and the welfare state have been produced by Australian feminists. Particularly important is the work of Cass and the collection entitled *Women, Social Welfare and the State* edited by Baldock and Cass (1983). In one article, Cass (1982) examines the effects on women of changing welfare and taxation measures and of the 'social wage', in the post-war period, and in another publication (1983), she traces the connection between population policies and family policies. Elsewhere, Keens and Cass (1982) acknowledging the value of Titmuss' threefold division of welfare, explore the relationship between the taxation system, the sexual division of labour, women and dependency, finding further evidence (for example in the dependent spouse rebate) for Land's proposition that it is women's marital status, not their family responsibilities, that determines their eligibility for various financial benefits from the state (1982:37). The subject of women and social work has also recently been examined from a feminist or what the Australian editors of the book call a 'gender perspective' (Marchant and Wearing, 1986).

A number of overseas and Australian feminists (for instance, Cass, 1985; Pearce, 1978; Scott, 1984) have drawn attention also to the relationship between gender and poverty. They argue that a significant contribution to the 'feminisation of poverty' is made by the state through the conditions for and levels of welfare services and benefits it sets and through the employment (and unemployment) policies it operates. In particular, they point to the situation of female-headed households, the underlying sources of whose poverty are a combination of domestic responsibilities (dependent children), lack of a male provider (through wages or maintenance payments), restricted access to paid work and, when obtained, low wages, compounded in some cases by the further disadvantages associated with migrant or black racial/ethnic status. However the immediate cause is the inadequate public welfare system and a basic approach which sees welfare posing a constant threat to the work ethic, and hence rejects any argument for raising welfare benefits above subsistence level even for women.

We will deal with this material and draw on the interpretations of the various perspectives—feminist, marxist and non-marxist—in our analyses of the social control aspects of welfare, the welfare systems and the welfare state in the following section of the chapter.

Welfare and social control

As we have seen, 'welfare' is a very broad concept. It covers not only public but private organisations and mechanisms for dealing with human needs outside the ordinary commercial system (where some of the same services are also available on an individual fee-paying, professional-client basis), though excluding such services when they are part of the 'caring work' done by women for family members and friends. As well as differences in the sources of welfare, there are wide variations in the kind of welfare 'goods' provided in modern western societies, the five major categories of service being health, education, housing, income maintenance and personal social services. Since we cannot deal adequately here with the whole of the welfare field, we will concentrate on 'public' or state forms of welfare provision and, given the overall concerns of the book, we will exclude education and housing and focus on the income maintenance, social security and taxation systems, and on the personal or caring services (that is principally social work). This will permit us to explore the diversity of 'means' by which the state intervenes; for Offe (1983:64), these include 'bureaucratic rules and legal regulations, monetary transfers and professional expertise of teachers, doctors, social workers, etc.'

The major sources of insights into the modes of operation and effects of welfare systems and of particular welfare measures are marxism, feminism and deviance theory. Functionalism is only concerned with welfare as one of a set of mechanisms whose contribution to the smooth running of the social system and the preservation of consensus through the control of 'deviance' is of more importance than any consideration of the specific details of the various institutions engaged in these activities. It is more interested in the general function being served (integration in this case). Nor does this approach take much account either of possible negative effects or of the subjective perceptions of and responses to welfare by its recipients. The other three perspectives (with the exception of the more determinist versions of functionalist marxism) treat welfare as a set of ideologies and practices of central importance in modern industrial society and as worthy of study in their own right.

All three perspectives perceive the welfare system and the welfare state as being essentially concerned with social control although, as we have seen, they conceptualise the how, why and for whom of social control differently. A recent assessment of the welfare state in advanced capitalist societies which draws mainly on marxist and feminist work states clearly at the outset that 'the central issue [is] control, the degree of control and in whose interests control is exercised' (Bryson, 1984:119).

There are at least two levels at which welfare can be described as an instrument of social control. Welfare, as a range of social policies and practices concerned with providing services to meet socially recognised needs, is in the process engaged in the management (or control) in various ways of dependent populations. At the same time, particular welfare measures have specific targets and utilise specific methods which involve to a varying extent the exercise of different kinds of social control. Just as welfare may take various forms—money, goods, services—so too does social control: it may be physical, material, financial, psychological, social, or moral/ideological.

A particular welfare policy may indeed have positive consequences (such as giving resources to the poor) but at the same time it contributes to a situation in which an unequal distribution of opportunities, wealth and power is maintained and, through its very existence and ideological representation as 'welfare', the power relations and dominance of some groups in society are obscured.

Discussion of the social control aspects of the welfare system will be confined here to a consideration of two areas of public welfare. The first is the personal social services (or social work) and the welfare issue of care versus control. The analysis will rely mainly on marxist and feminist oriented theory and research, though some ideas are taken from the sociology of deviance. The second is income maintenance, social security and taxation, and with a focus on the issue of welfare as poor relief or as progressive redistribution of resources. Relevant empirical material is derived from a number of sources, but the two principal ones are (a) official statistics and surveys (Census data, Budget figures and ABS publications) giving information on basic economic and social characteristics of individuals and households, and on the nature of government expenditures relating to welfare; and (b) research studies and government inquiries, with a specific area of welfare or category of the population (for instance, unemployment, poverty or single parenthood) as their focus of investigation. The Social Welfare Research Institute of New South Wales, a major producer of material on welfare in Australia, makes extensive use of both sorts of data.

Personal social services

These are the 'individualised, "personalised", helping services that do not involve the transfer of income or the provision of health care, formal education or public housing'; such services cover information, referral, advocacy, practical help, counselling and guidance, community centres, mutual aid and self help (Kamerman, 1983:9, n.6). As M. Jones (1983:273) observes, the family is the 'central caring agency in modern society'. Since the nineteenth century, however, 'personalised' or 'caring' services in which welfare entails giving primarily non-material assistance or responding to needs of an emotional or social nature have become an increasingly significant part of public and private welfare systems, to the extent of being categorised the 'sixth social service system' (Kahn and Kamerman, 1980:1). These services offer support and assistance of various kinds to all sections of the population and not only to special dependent or 'problem' categories. Among welfare users there are those who seek aid in the form of information, counselling or casework from voluntary or government agencies, as well as others who find that personal care services are a non-optional accompaniment of the adjudication and administration of other welfare claims, and particularly requests for state pensions and benefits. On the whole the middle classes, when requiring personal services, employ the skills of businesses or professionals in the private sector and enjoy the status of voluntary fee-paying clients or consumers. By contrast, the working and lower classes are the main users of publicly provided services, and those available (free) from charitable agencies; in either case the service tends to carry a degree of stigma, something which those who can afford to buy professional help can avoid. The classic Melbourne study of the use of personal services by McCaughey et al. (1977) compared three categories of families which they describe as the 'copers', the 'vulnerable' and the 'passive' (based on their attributes and resources) who differed markedly in their attitudes, resources and methods of dealing with life and its problems.

Although social work is commonly thought of as being about 'care' rather than 'control', posing these as alternatives can be misleading, since they are not mutually exclusive; nor is 'care' automatically good and 'control' bad (Simpkin, 1983:40–1).

The prime example in Australia of Commonwealth government involvement in personal social services is in the field of income maintenance (through the Department of Social Security), though the federal government to a lesser extent is also engaged in catering for personal service needs with respect to employment, Aborigines, immigrants and veterans, for all of whom it accepts primary responsibility (M. Jones, 1983:283–4). More specifically-oriented personal service provision (and this includes family services in particular) is largely under state administration (though with federal financial assistance).

The procedures and personnel employed to operate the Australian public welfare system are highly bureaucratised, but not based on specialist professional orientation or expertise. As M. Jones (1983:291) points out, unlike overseas countries, social workers here have less influence over the organisation and philosophy of welfare agencies. This means that

> the administrative philosophy has triumphed in Australian social welfare: there is no professionalised and monopolistic 'middle man' [sic] to compare with the doctors in health care, and the academics and school teachers in education. (M. Jones, 1983:282)

Wilensky and Lebeaux (1965:Chapter X) in their classic analysis of social welfare in industrial society identified bureaucracy as the characteristic pattern of welfare organisation and control, with, as its key components, routinisation of activity and formalisation of relationships between functionaries and clients, specialisation of function and clientele, and hierarchy; the disadvantages for users are segregation and stigmatisation, gaps between or duplication of services, division of responsibility for clients and their needs between agencies. They saw the role of the social work profession as the second major influence on welfare services in the modern world (Chapter XI). Kahn and Kamerman writing about social services across western industrialised societies identify social work as 'the central profession for the personal social services' (1980:371) but they note that social workers are usually a minority in their work settings and that personal social services are often an 'adjunct' to other welfare systems.

Within the welfare system social work as 'a form of state intervention... is distinguished by its highly intensive and personalised approach'; social work (particularly when families and their problems are the objects of concern)

> demands almost total immersion...in relationships, emotions and feelings; virtually nothing that occurs in these clients' lives is regarded as insignificant or irrelevant. (C. Jones, 1983:75)

In the earlier phase of the 'welfare state' in western societies (in the 1950s and 1960s), a therapeutic casework orientation with the objective of client self-determination[15] characterised the practice of social workers, including those employed by government. Since the 1970s, however, social workers, and especially now this affects those working in Britain for local authorities (where most personal services are located), have found themselves increasingly required to operate as a rationing mechanism (Simpkin, 1983:27–8) and as a 'servicing/dustbin agency of the state' (C. Jones, 1983:132; Jordan, 1976:Chapter 12). Their independent professional role and commitment to the client has become harder to maintain in the face of tighter administrative controls, reduced financial and other resources and a shift generally towards a tougher, more coercive and disciplinary state (C. Jones, 1983:146–8); London Edinburgh Weekend Return Group, 1980:126–9; Simpkin, 1983:25). This process has meant a change in the nature and bases of social control exercised by social workers.

Social work critics have pointed to the individualising and depoliticising implications of the traditional casework approach to human and social problems, with both the approved means and desired outcomes being defined in terms of personal characteristics and aspects of the relationship between professional and client (Corrigan and Leonard, 1978: Chapter 10; Pemberton and Locke, 1971). Social work practice in its classic form reflected class background, professional training, psychoanalytic orientation, and certain social values—consensus, cooperation and self-help—and traditional notions of gender and the family. More recently, developments in community work suggest different ideological influences, namely leftism and feminism (Creed and Tomlinson, 1984).

First deviance theory and later marxism exposed the power dimension in all forms of social work, whether power is manifested as humane personal concern, or as paternalistic authority or as professional assistance and technical advice. Pearson identified a basic ambiguity in social work focussed around its having simultaneously a relationship to the individual and to society and

> the question of whether social work represents a personal counselling service for active, free-willed human agents or a mopping-up operation for society's 'dregs'. (1975:130)

Pemberton and Locke (making use of both the functionalist concepts of pattern-maintenance and tension management and the sociology of deviance and social control) describe the social worker as

> a *double-agent*; while claiming to be working on behalf of the client, he [sic] is really an agent of socio-political control, bolstering the existing social order by reinforcing and interpreting moral, social and political rules. (1971:101, original emphasis)

Pearson suggests one factor that made this moral and social issue more acute in Britain from the 1960s was the incorporation of professional social workers into the public welfare system (1975:131). Jordan, writing about the same time, sees the addition of a range of supplementary forms of public assistance to the basic income maintenance and social welfare provisions of the post-war welfare state, which requires social workers to investigate and evaluate eligibility of applicants, as an important development. They thereby came to exercise a supervisory and surveillance function over claimants as part of the administration of discretionary benefits, which marked a significant shift in state modes of social control (Jordan, 1976:Chapter 9). He warns that:

> The trend seems to be not towards liberalisation of the controls on deviance, but towards the identification of a larger group of people who need to be closely watched, and the appointment of a larger number of social workers to watch them. New powers for social workers reflect a social philosophy which defines a certain proportion of the population as burdens or threats, so irresponsible as to be regarded as morally inferior, and therefore not to be trusted with the liberties that full citizens enjoy. (1976:165)

Thus the control elements involved in social work in the public welfare sector became more direct, more systematic and more intrusive. 'Policy-makers and administrators have committed the state to a massive protective yet infantilising provision for the needy; social workers translate this into actual relationships in which provision becomes a form of denial of citizenship, and of adult identity' (Jordan, 1976:167). By the 1970s, this had become apparent both to social workers themselves (which led to attempts by radical and marxist-inspired social workers to develop theoretical analyses and political strategies to deal with the situation) and to clients (some of whom formed their own pressure groups often in alliance with the organised working class or with the feminist movement).

More recently, as a result of the general restructuring of the welfare state, economic and political pressure for cutbacks in welfare spending and the increasing burden of dependency owing to unemployment, inflation and the economic policies of western governments, social work in the public sector has become even more enmeshed in state apparatuses and mechanisms of control over the working classes and other disadvantaged groups (such as women, youth and immigrants). Specifically, and this is particularly a concern of the British writers, social workers are given the tasks of determining access to state welfare resources, rationing public goods, regulating the lives of potential and actual clients, and providing social reinforcement for the prevailing ideologies of individualism, family life and the work ethic (C. Jones, 1983; London Edinburgh Weekend Return Group, 1980; Simpkin, 1983). Thus social workers in government departments concerned with the broad range of types of welfare are, whether they know it or not, exercising a variety of forms of social control on behalf of the state—social-psychological, moral-ideological, and material—in the process of regulating access to welfare services and benefits.

The effects of pressure to restrict welfare spending mean that social workers have

> bigger caseloads, with consequent alienation and heightened militancy. New 'techniques' of social work, such as 'crisis intervention' have been developed as justifications for social workers to spend less time with more clients, while traditional casework, which attempted to deal with problems in a more leisurely fashion approximating at times to psychotherapy, has fallen into disrepute. (Wilson, 1977:180)

Jordan (1976), as we have already noted, identified an increasing reliance during the 1970s by the state on social workers for the management of multi-problem welfare cases with an underlying paternalistic if not repressive orientation to welfare administration. For those sections of the population exposed to such critical supervision, there is even less accountability and protection of citizens' rights and freedoms associated with this form of state regulation than in the other areas of public welfare, namely housing, income maintenance, education and health care. C. Jones (1983:Chapter 7) comments on the resulting tension between the aims of professional social workers and current demands by their employer—the state—for them to 'police' the welfare system. The state is responding to this by replacing social workers with clerical staff and less highly trained welfare workers and by imposing a greater degree of control over its employees' activities through formal specification of tasks, higher caseloads and computerised record-keeping procedures. Australian commentators (such as M. Jones, 1983:288–92) point to differences in the degree of reliance on and power of social workers in the public sector welfare system as between Britain and Australia; in Australia there is no equivalent degree of local authority involvement in personal care services and any social work input to state welfare provision is at the point of service delivery not at the critical levels of general philosophy and policy formulation.

Marxists have mainly concentrated on the class aspects of social work as a major mechanism of state control (seeing social workers as state employees engaged in the disciplining of members of their own working class) and have attempted to devise alternative radical social work strategies for countering the power of the state and the ruling capitalist class (Bolger et al., 1981; Corrigan and Leonard, 1978; C. Jones, 1983; London Edinburgh Weekend Return Group, 1980; Simpkin, 1983). Feminists have extended the analysis to cover gender as well as class. They point to the fact that families are a major focus of social work practice, in both state and private or voluntary welfare organisations, which typically means clients are women in their roles as wives and mothers. Australian writers have commented on the high proportions of women in social work and the large numbers of women welfare clients (Roe, 1983; Turner, 1981; Marchant and Wearing eds., 1986). Women are especially over-represented in those client categories where discretionary benefits rather than statutory entitlements apply (for instance assistance for dependent children and family obligations, as compared with sickness or unemployment pensions which are based on national insurance or other universalistic principles).

Women's encounters with social services and social workers, therefore, often involve the application of official standards and assessments of the performance of female roles (in particular mothering) and the provision of material, practical and other forms of assistance may be made conditional on complying with official requirements (Marchant and Wearing eds., 1986). This has the result that women welfare clients are subject to gender specific forms of social control (Bryson and Edwards, forthcoming). Women are also more likely to be found in certain areas of social work, particularly individual casework, and the health and child welfare fields (Healy, 1982). 'Caring' or 'personal service' is traditionally perceived as a feminine quality or predisposition (Mowbray and Bryson, 1984:261; Finch and Groves (eds), 1983; Wearing, 1985). This is evident both in the composition and methods of the social work profession (charity and social work were historically female activities) and in the kinds of needs and situations characteristic of female welfare clients. It is also manifested in the current official preference for 'community care' over institutional and professional forms of care, which entails increasing numbers of women (in a family or voluntary capacity) bearing the extra load of caring for various special dependency groups—such as the elderly, the handicapped and the mentally disturbed. Adams (1971) describes the presumed feminine propensity for 'protecting' and 'nurturing' as a 'compassion trap' and she uses this notion to help account for the numbers and the preferred areas of activity of women in social work.

Various authors have documented both the initial dominance of women in social work in Australia and, as the demand for social workers increased, diversified and professionalised in the post-war period, the emergence of a gender division of labour within social work: men, though still a minority, take over the senior managerial and policy-making positions while women predominantly occupy the lower direct service and caretaker roles (Gumprecht, 1985; Healy, 1982; Kiel, 1982), all patterns which have been reported also overseas (Kravetz, 1976; Sutton, 1982). Gumprecht suggests the gender composition of the social work profession is partly responsible for the apparently 'relatively docile' characteristics of social workers as employees (1985:20), which is relevant to any understanding of the role of social workers as social control agents in the welfare institutions of the modern western state. More specifically, Turner draws attention to the contradictions in women's relationship to welfare processes which she sums up as follows:

> . . . women as caretakers have served to constrain women's autonomy through their adherence to conservative feminist ideologies, giving primacy to family values. State intervention, while guaranteeing minimum income security, has tended to reinforce women's identity as family-centred and dependent. The 'professionalization' of welfare services, which might have been expected to provide opportunities for expanded roles for women professionals, has served paradoxically to create a sexual division of labour in the welfare professions, with men occupying senior administrative positions, undercutting women's power and influence. (1981:177)

Academic writers and some social workers and client groups thus agree that personal social services under the modern welfare state operate as modes of social control. Social workers are required to act as moral and social control agents: they are gatekeepers and dispensers of society's welfare goods, supervisors of the lives of certain sections of the community and mediators and reinforcers of the dominant moral values and ideologies of society. Marxists and feminists contend that the way the personal or 'caring' services are currently organised and delivered (through state agencies and with the aid of social workers) has a powerful influence on class and gender divisions and inequalities. By focussing on the effects of welfare service provision rather than on the motives and intentions of welfare planners and providers, and without denying some short-term benefits to individuals, they expose welfare and social work in particular as a moral enterprise, and hence as a mechanism of ideological control.

Income maintenance, social security and taxation

Income maintenance or security generally covers:

> those measures where 'the object of public action' is to provide alternate income to persons whose normal private incomes have

> temporarily or permanently disappeared, or to remove from individuals and families the burden of more generally experienced changes in income. (Kewley, 1973:xi)

Tulloch (1979:17) defines 'income security' as 'a set of policies which are designed to protect minimum income levels and to maintain existing income levels during certain defined periods of increased financial outlay'. She distinguishes between 'poverty reduction' programmes (pensions and benefits to those with inadequate or no income) and 'income maintenance' programmes (support in the form of cash grants, tax rebates and allowances for particular types of expenditure, such as housing, health and child-rearing). Cash payments of this sort may be tied to particular expenditure items (housing, medical services or funeral expenses for example) or may be simply sums of money determined according to a scale of benefits for particular categories of welfare recipient. Income security payments take two main forms (Graycar, 1983:5): they can be (a) a substitute for wages (whether those of the recipient or of another, such as a husband, on whom the recipient has been dependent)—for instance unemployment, sickness and old age pensions, widows' pension, deserted wives' pension; or (b) additional or supplementary, where the main income comes from another source—this category includes family and maternity allowances, child endowment, and assistance to those caring for invalids, aged and handicapped children in their own homes. Cash transfers may come through the public welfare system as pensions and benefits or through the taxation system as allowances or rebates. In Australia, most state pensions and benefits are non-contributory and either means or income tested directly or included as part of taxable income (Cass and O'Loughlin, 1985:253).[16]

Income maintenance and social security provisions cannot be assessed in isolation from the taxation system, and in particular personal income tax, and from consideration of the labour market (as the principal determinant of income and hence benefits derived from the taxation system). Individuals' socio-economic circumstances are, therefore, both shaped by labour force participation (and the state of the employment market) and government welfare and fiscal policies, by both the presence and size of earned income and by 'the social wage' (Baldock, 1983; Jamrozik, 1986; Keens and Cass, 1982; Pearce, 1978). Within the capitalist system, dependency on welfare (in the form of reliance on income security schemes) is related not only to employment but to family situation. As Rein and Rainwater (1978:532) express it:

> Welfare at present seems to serve primarily as a way society copes with two of its problems, family disruption and labour market inadequacy.

In a period of economic recession, the effects of rising unemployment, which are not randomly distributed, are a direct cause of poverty, particularly for certain categories such as women, sole parents and youth.

As a broad generalisation, it appears that such redistribution as occurs though government taxation and expenditure patterns is largely of an intra-class and inter-generational character: there is no evidence of a significant overall redistribution of resources from the wealthy to the poor. A recent survey of post-World War II United States government policies found that increasing unemployment, economic growth and taxation favoured capital over labour, inflation had an equalising effect and only minimum wage provisions and some areas of government spending benefited labour more than capital (Devine, 1984)[17].

Head (1980) and Harding (1984) assess the effects of government policies in the form of personal tax and of cash transfers and public goods on income distribution in Australia.[18] Income tax on the whole, they find, has had only a limited progressive impact. Cash transfers (means-tested and selective) do seem to reach those most in need.

> Taxes paid by the young, the unmarried, and the employed, in effect subsidise the pensions paid to the elderly, the unemployed and the parents of large families. In other words, the flow of cash payments is largely a circular intra-class transfer rather than a flow from rich to poor. (Head, 1980:49)

They argue that since the mid-1970s, the taxation system has become less progressive owing to increasing avoidance and evasion (which inevitably confers more advantages on higher tax-paying groups) and to the diminishing proportion of government revenue derived from business profits compared with individual wage and salary earnings. Social services or 'public goods' have varying effects depending on the basis on which they are provided: social security and housing are redistributive, health less so, and education, being freely available to all, gives no particular advantage to lower income groups. Cass claims that the social welfare and tax systems since the 1940s have produced 'horizontal redistribution within classes to benefit the period of child-rearing' (1982:14). In other words, there has been some degree of inter-generational transfer (M. Jones, 1983:184) and a redistribution from income earners and taxpayers without children to people with children, but no real redressing of inequalities between classes (Cass, 1982:17). Graycar contrasts gains, for example, for 'homeowning elderly people with family supports' with a notable lack of improvement in the circumstances of 'female-headed families [and] unemployed teenagers' (1983:3). Cass (1982:30–3) comments that government responses to the less favourable economic climate since the latter 1970s have meant the diminishing real value of the social wage and of unindexed universal benefits like family allowances (at a time of rising unemployment) but have not affected fiscal and occupational benefits which advantage the higher income groups. Tulloch is pessimistic about the prospects of achieving any real redistribution through public welfare and taxation measures alone. In her words (1979:65):

> Universal benefits, unless accompanied by a reduction of inequality in the market place and the elimination of private insurance and superannuation schemes, will not. . .reduce poverty. When universalism in welfare but not redistribution of resources in the market is favoured, the consequences are bound to be regressive.

Keens and Cass (1982) examine the effects of personal income tax and of income situation on gender as well as class inequalities. They see the taxation systems as 'nominally progressive', but highlight a number of respects in which women are disadvantaged on gender grounds, because of their lack of or lower earned income (and hence eligibility for tax allowances and rebates), and/or because of their traditional domestic roles (responsibility for dependent children is unpaid but takes precedence over paid employment and thus denies women the right to certain income or tax-related benefits) and/or because government welfare policies assume equal collective sharing of family resources whereas the income from whatever source tends to be in the hands of the husband/father/principal earner.[19]

Shaver (1983:150–1) suggests that as tax becomes less progressive, women suffer since as a group they typically gain from redistribution of a progressive kind.[20] She describes the relationship between women and the welfare state as follows:

> To put it bluntly, when it comes to paying for the welfare state the system treats women as individuals, but in respect of virtually every benefit conferred back on them, social policy measures treat them as somebody's wife, or somebody's mother. The basic nexus of women's oppression—the link between family and labour process—is replicated almost literally in the structures of the welfare state. (1983:148)

Kamerman (1983, 1984) reports the results of a comparison of public provisions for female-headed families in eight industrialised countries, including Australia. Various policies were examined: family and child allowances; housing allowances; unemployment insurance; and other schemes. The situation of female-headed sole parent households is dependent on both general socio-economic and gender-related factors, and recent estimates suggest these families constitute a sizeable proportion, if not the majority, of the poor in western countries. Kamerman (1983:455) concludes that those countries with a social assistance rather than a positive family policy orientation (and Australia falls into the former category) make less generous provision for women and their children.

Cass and O'Loughlin (1985) analyse available statistical data on the effects of government policies on single parent families in Australia since 1974. Of those on government benefits (supporting parent benefits), over 90 per cent were women (including both separated and never married) and female sole parents were more likely than males to have little extra income, to require full benefits and to qualify for supplementary (rental) assistance. Their economic situation had worsened over the period owing to deterioration in job opportunities for women sole parents with dependent children and the failure of the government to index the supporting parent pension. A recently published study of female (non-aged) social security recipients in Melbourne identified three separate, though inter-related, aspects of these women's situation—their position as mothers, wives, and paid workers—that jointly contributed to their recipiency status. But they stressed that being in the position of sole carer for dependent children seemed to be the most critical factor (Montague and Stephens, 1985).

It is generally accepted that there are significant class and gender inequalities associated with the distribution of welfare. The fiscal and occupational systems tend to advantage the income earners, and particularly the wealthy and those on high salaries, and men; the public welfare system (and only parts of that) directs its resources relatively more towards the poor, the lower income earners and women. Clearly access to the labour market and, if employed, levels of income are directly related to the benefits available from the occupational and fiscal systems, while disadvantaged groups are forced to rely on the more meagre provisions of the public welfare system.[21] Given the principles on which the three welfare systems currently operate, lower income earners and less well-organised workers, and women suffer multiple disadvantages.

> It can be said that the social services compensate men for disservices which they experience in the economic market. Women, however, suffer a double disservice, firstly in their role as workers and secondly in their role as users of the social services. . . Sexual discrimination is the most evident offence against social justice in our society today since it cannot be defended by reference either to the ethics of the economic market or to those of social welfare. (Pinker, 1974:12)

Economic control is a fundamental feature of the modern industrial state both with respect to business and the general population. Taxation is an essential prerequisite of welfare programmes and a burden that increasingly falls on individual income earners, and the power to decide the relative financial contributions to public welfare to be made by different classes and sections of society lies officially with government. As Klein (1980:26–7) points out, a 'paradox of the mature Welfare State' is that increasingly more people, and particularly people in the middle and even lower income groups, 'have to be coerced into paying higher taxes in order to make what will be inevitably less of an impact on the distribution of income'. As we have observed, the fiscal and occupational welfare systems allocate benefits in direct proportion to earnings, while the public welfare system (though to a limited extent) seeks to compensate for the deficiencies and inequalities of the market and the sexual division of labour. By providing cash and services to those with demonstrated need, it attempts to increase the material resources of those disadvantaged by the capitalist/patriarchal economic system. The underlying principle of allocation in the fiscal and occupational fringe benefit systems is regressive (it parallels the reward structure of the occupational system itself), whereas the public welfare system is at least partially progressive in its approach to economic distribution. However, because of concern that living on government benefits might become more attractive than working for a wage, the level of welfare payments is strictly limited and rarely allowed to rise much above subsistence. Public welfare has always been regarded in capitalist societies as a potential threat to the work ethic and hence to the capacity of the system to generate profit and to provide the necessary basis for the expansion of the economy.

We have already discussed various marxist analyses of the role of the modern welfare or interventionist state in the management of the economy (specifically in ensuring the reproduction of labour power, helping to maintain the non-working sections of the population, and creating favourable overall conditions for capitalist enterprise and continued capital accumulation and legitimation of the system) and in devising methods for dealing with the economic, political and ideological crises that currently confront advanced capitalist societies. All see government as having primary responsibility for protecting the moral bases of the work ethic essential to the capitalist system (with its emphasis on competition, achievement, individualism, and self-reliance). The accounts differ in their estimates of the extent to which the state (and particularly the welfare sector) is responsive to working-class pressure as opposed to acting only in the interests of capital or the capitalist class, and hence take different views of the relative degrees of regulation and control exercised by the state over the economic circumstances of labour and capital.

Marxist feminists ask similar questions about the role of the state and welfare systems with respect to gender divisions and differences in the economic and social situations of men and women within the overall class structure. For them, most women's dependence on a male wage-earner and their marginal, intermittent or otherwise limited participation in the labour market (the result of the sexual division of labour and female responsibility for child care and household work) serve the interests of capital and of men (Baldock, 1983; Barrett, 1980; Cass, 1982; McIntosh, 1978). Although the 'family wage' notion is now out-dated and most married women expect to take paid employment, they are disadvantaged in various ways: on the one hand, by lack of access to and types of job training, and inferior occupational opportunities, wages and conditions, and, on the other, by insufficient financial or service provision for child care and domestic responsibilities.

Government social policy has so far failed adequately to redress these inequalities. Indeed Cass (1982:9) contends that, underlying the range of employment, welfare and taxation policies, is a government commitment to the traditional forms of marriage and the family and that 'family policy' continues to operate as a powerful mechanism of social control over the lives of women.

Not only has the tension between welfare and the work ethic produced only modest if not positively meagre levels of provision of services and benefits for dependent groups, but it is accompanied by a set of social attitudes towards welfare and welfare recipients (and the poor generally) that confers on them low status at best and at worst moral condemnation and social marginality.

> . . . in the 1960s we were forced to learn that the public welfare system in fact reached very few of the poor, and that it exacted penalties of intimidation and degradation from those few it did reach. With these facts laid bare, a new explanation began to emerge of public welfare not as a mechanism of state philanthropy, but as mechanism by which the state enforced work and the search for work on these people at the bottom, either by denying aid outright or by making the receipt of aid so degrading as to intimidate most of the poor into surviving as best they could given the vagaries and hardships of the low-wage labor market. (Cloward and Piven, 1977b:56)

As Jordan (1976:189) argues, under capitalism, the welfare state is one of the means whereby the society gets its work—paid and unpaid—done. Just as in the nineteenth century able-bodied pauperism posed a major problem for poor law relief schemes, so a constant anxiety about creating a category of 'dole-bludgers' and a climate of opinion in which paid work is no longer the unquestionably preferable alternative to dependency on the state, influences the nature and level of modern welfare state provisions. Pemberton (1980) gives an illustration of this concern in the current Australian context in his analysis of the Fraser government's response to dole fraud in the late 1970s. Rein and Rainwater (1978) contend that this fear is ideologically rather than empirically based; drawing on data derived from a major longitudinal study of welfare families in America, they found no support for the idea of a substantial 'semi-permanent welfare class' or for work and welfare necessarily being in opposition.

Various welfare writers have commented on the power and persistence of the deserving/undeserving moral distinction as applied to various classes of welfare claimants from the nineteenth century onwards and shown how 'worthiness' is linked to evaluations of capacity to work and social class (Dickey, 1980:226; Graycar, 1979:51; Mendelsohn, 1979:Chapter 8; Pinker, 1974). A recent survey of American income support schemes for families—the current Aid to Families with Dependent Children (AFDC) and its forerunners—traces the relationship between eligibility for welfare assistance and assumptions about capacity and suitability for paid work (Mason et al., 1985). Cass (1983) describes how the history of child endowment and family allowances in Australia illustrates the continual struggle between the claims of women and children to direct state support, and concern to preserve the incentive to work and traditional gender relations in marriage. Sweeney (1986) contrasts the child care approach (which works on the principle of universal rights) with the 'child welfare' orientation (which means targeting mainly working class groups with special needs) as these have affected policy in Australia since the 1960s. Others have exposed the contrast between the underlying moral assumptions associated with the residual and the institutional approaches to welfare, or between a system based on social assistance and one based on social insurance, or between a conception of welfare as a form of charitable relief to the needy few and one of welfare as a right of all citizens and a method of ensuring a more just overall distribution of resources.

Stigma and a devalued social status are attached to welfare recipiency under a reluctant or ideologically unsympathetic welfare state. A much-quoted example of this kind of control is the so-called 'cohabitation rule' enforced on women in receipt of sole parent benefits by social security departments who require detailed personal information and can exercise continual close supervision over the lives of claimants (Bryson, 1983; Fairbairns, 1985). Another instance of particular concern (e.g. Jordan, 1976) is the recent trend towards a dual level system of welfare provision whereby there is a minimal statutory benefit and additional but discretionary assistance. This gives maximum scope for social discrimination and manipulation by government officials and departments in the process of determining the relative needs and merits of welfare cases.

The importance placed by sociologists and feminists on the moral meanings given to 'welfare' and to the status of welfare recipient follows from their conception of welfare measures as a mechanism of social control. Traditionally the moral connotations of welfare have been a significant component in the social regulation of people's lives. Recent developments in the methods of record-keeping, monitoring and supervision of welfare claimants and the population generally by the state, which suggest technical and administrative criteria of eligibility are replacing more overtly moral ones (Bryson, 1984:133–4), may mean alterations in the primary modes of social regulation and surveillance, but bring no necessary reduction in levels of control.

Welfare and other social policies, as feminists have argued, help maintain gender roles and fundamental social differences between the positions of men and women. The full range of social policies affecting women—income maintenance, taxation, employment, child care provisions and the current preference for family and community care of dependent members of society—operate as both material and ideological regulatory devices, reflecting and reinforcing the sexual division of labour and gender inequalities and perpetuating female dependency. The theoretical and empirical work of marxists, feminists and others forces us to question whether welfare under present circumstances can make any significant contribution to social justice.

There are also 'radical' critics of the public welfare system and of the welfare state who are not so pessimistic about the prospects of any real progress in the direction of justice and equality within capitalism. They are more likely to emphasise the complex and contradictory nature of social work, welfare institutions and policies, and of the state itself. They therefore point to the opportunities such contradictions allow for key groups (and particularly those united by class and/or gender) to organise themselves and to work both from inside and outside for change by exploiting weaknesses, inconsistencies and conflicts within the system.[22] They prefer a less deterministic analysis of the economic and structural constraints on modern society and devote much of their efforts to the analysis of alternative social policies, their aims and implications, given particular sets of social conditions. Hence for this latter group, welfare and the welfare state are not only about social control in a negative sense but about possibilities for positive social change.

Endnotes

Chapter 1: Concept of social control

1 The American sociologist, Ross, is usually considered to have produced the first major work on the subject of social control; his book with that title was originally published in 1901. Other early American sociologists, such as Sumner, Cooley, Thomas and Park, seem also to have found the term or at least the idea of social 'control' or 'regulation' useful. Janowitz (1975:88–94) and Pitts (1968:382–3) both give brief accounts of the early history of the concept in American sociology. All three of the European 'founding fathers' of sociology (Marx, Durkheim and Weber) treated the problem of the maintenance of social order as one of their main concerns even though none seems to have made the specific term 'control' a key concept or dimension around which to organise their general theories.

2 For a full account of these as well as the later sociological perspectives in this field, see Davis (1975/80) and Pfohl (1985).

3 In his discussion of 'normal' and 'pathological' forms of social phenomena, Durkheim (1938:65–72) argues that certain levels of crime must be regarded as 'normal' and socially 'useful'. Modern writers who deal specifically with the issue of the functions of deviance include Box (1971:Chapter 2); Coser (1962); Erikson (1966:Chapter 1).

4 The association of socialisation with social control is not unique to the labelling/interactionist school of deviance writers. It is also a logical extension of Durkheim's conception of the basis of social order as lying in collective values, and, as we shall see in Chapter 2, socialisation and social control are explicitly discussed in these terms by Parsons (1951).

5 Hawkins and Tiedeman (1975) use these terms which they derive from Wilson (1970) in their categorisation of the various approaches to the sociology of deviance.

6 'Revisionist' is the description that has been given to historical explanations of the development of particular control programmes and systems that challenge 'reformist' accounts, and their uncritical acceptance of new initiatives in the control field as 'progressive'; see, for instance, Cohen and Scull (1985:1–4).

7 Stedman Jones is one of the most often quoted proponents of this view. Cohen and Scull (1985) include his original (1977) article and some papers defending the concept in their recent edited volume on social control. The issue is discussed further in Chapter 3.

8 One of the most prolific and significant contemporary social theorists, Giddens, who has not in general shown any particular interest in the social and sociological problems associated with deviance, nonetheless gives the concept of control a prominent place in his theory of structuration. In various works (1979, 1981, 1984) he explicitly discusses the nature and aspects of control and various forms of sanctioning, the links between control and power, and the use of violence as a form of control in the modern capitalist state. His theoretical analysis helped in the identification of key dimensions in the conceptualisation of social control, see Chapter 4.

9 The concept is not in itself a theory, though in various bodies of theory it has occupied a central position (in particular, functionalism and the labelling/interactionist school) and its importance has been explicitly recognised. Though its critics (particularly the marxist critics) imply the term 'social control' necessarily entails the use of one particular theoretical perspective or explanatory theory only, the major thesis of this book is that this is not so: that on the contrary, the concept has been and can be usefully employed within a range of differing sociological perspectives.

Chapter 2: Sociological perspectives and social control

1 Janowitz (1975:95–6) points out that from the 1940s American sociology tended to equate social control with socialisation and with establishing the normative bases of social conformity.

2 Davis' book in its original (1975) and revised (1980) editions and the latest addition to this literature, Pfohl's (1985) book, provide the two most comprehensive and insightful analyses of 'sociological constructions of deviance'. Pfohl's book is in fact entitled 'Images of Deviance and Social Control', but, like most of the literature on this subject, his characterisation and treatment of different 'deviance' perspectives centres around explanations of deviance. Overall 'images' and 'strategies' of social control (to use his terminology) are not considered theoretically to be important elements in their own right, nor seen as worthy of the same social and sociological attention as deviance.

3 This is the reason we are looking only at the Parsonian version of structural-functionalism, and his social system model specifically, since this does contain a theoretical treatment of social control as well as of deviance, whereas the other leading American functionalist in the field, Merton, puts forward his theory of anomie as an explanation of the social causes of deviant behaviour. The emphasis on what theorists have to contribute to our understanding of social control rather than the question of the etiology of deviance is the key criterion in the selection and presentation of material in this chapter and in the book as a whole.

4 This is what Hamilton (1983) describes as 'Parsons^2': the phase in which Parsons first develops his social systems model. Hamilton and others have commented on the shift of emphasis from the action to the system level of analysis in Parsons' thinking that occurred in the 1940s and 1950s.

5 The most useful general references for this section of the chapter are Davis (1975:Chapter 5), Douglas (1970), Gouldner (1970:Chapter 6), Hamilton (1983), Horton (1966), Parsons (1951:Chapter VII), Pfohl (1985:Chapter 6).

6 It is generally recognised that in *The Social System* Parsons is thinking primarily in terms of processes occurring at the macro level. However, and this is true of his chapter on deviance and social control (Chapter VII), he still also talks at times of interactions as more interpersonal and open-ended processes.

7 This part of his model is more fully developed in his later writings (see Hamilton, 1983:106).

8 Pitts, who wrote the entry on social control in the *International Encyclopaedia of the Social Sciences* (1968), elaborates on the Parsonian framework, listing five functions which social control processes can perform.

9 Wright and Hilbert (1980) dispute the commonly made assertion that functionalism is necessarily 'conservative' in its values.
10 Presumably, Parsons must also assume that social control usually if not always works, since otherwise he would seem to be suggesting that for one category of human beings, those who have committed deviant acts (and whose deviance was entirely the result of external social forces), society may not be all-powerful. Interestingly, at this point his view comes close to that of some marxists who perceive politicised criminals as the only 'true' revolutionaries in the modern western world (this view has been called 'left idealism', see Young, 1979).
11 The key references cited here are mostly secondary sources, which provide a comprehensive presentation and assessment of the diversity of ideas contained within this perspective; see, Edwards and Wilson (1975:Introduction); Downes and Rock eds. (1979) and particularly Chapter 4 by Plummer; Hawkins and Tiedeman (1975); Schur (1971); and Suchar (1978:Chapters 5–8).
12 Though Plummer comes to a somewhat different conclusion about the limitations, strengths, and potential of interactionism, especially with reference to the question of 'structure' and macro level theorising (1979:115–6).
13 Others who have contributed to the clarification of these philosophical issues are Manning (1975) and Rock (1973a, 1979).
14 What this value stance entails is the subject of a famous exchange between Becker (1967, 1974) and Gouldner (1968).

Chapter 3: Radical social perspectives and social control

1 Key references for this section are mainly those dealing with marxist theories of the state; particularly useful are Clark and Dear (1984), Gold, Lo and Wright (1975), Gough (1979), Jessop (1982), Lindberg ed. (1975).
2 'Radical' or 'critical' criminology need not be marxist, as, for instance, Hinch (1983) argues.
3 Ainlay (1975/6) compares radical criminology in England and in America in relation to the issue of 'anti-correctionalism'.
4 For a useful recent reconsideration of 'radical criminology' and its tendencies towards 'meta functionalism' and/or 'instrumentalism', see Spitzer (1980); see also Turk and Grimes (1981).
5 'Pluralist' is a term also applied to functionalist and integrationist models. Though there are obviously important differences between pluralist models, all share at least the view that differences between groups are not seriously divisive and can be relatively amicably settled through approved conventional democratic political channels in a societal context in which all parties subscribe to a core set of basic values and assumptions about the political process; see Alford (1975), Head (1983: Chapter 2), Offe (1972).
6 One exception to this was the passing of the Factory Acts. For a brief description of Marx's analysis of the significance of this legislation, see Corrigan (1977).
7 Modern theorists have extended Marx's analysis of capitalist control of the labour process, see Braverman (1974) and Burawoy (1985).
8 For a classic marxist account of the relationship of the family to capitalism, see Zaretsky (1976, 1982). As we shall see later in the chapter, feminists present somewhat different accounts.
9 Jessop also describes a third possible orientation that he calls 'discourse-theoretical' (1982:191–202) of which Foucault's work would be a prime example.
10 On this point Weberian and marxist analyses of the modern state converge. The Frankfurt School and Habermas in particular draw on both traditions.
11 Offe and Habermas (along with other members of the 'Frankfurt School') reject both the more orthodox economistic and the modern structuralist schools of marxism. However their work on the nature and problems of the modern western state, draws

on and contributes to contemporary marxist analysis. A useful summary of this work is by Pierson (1984), who describes Offe as 'post-marxist'.

12 Their thesis (advanced in this and later work, Cloward and Piven, 1977a) has provoked considerable, critical comment; see for example, Griffin et al. (1983); Isaac and Kelly (1981); Skopcol (1980).

13 Offe (1972, 1984) and Therborn (1983) place some considerable importance on the ideological and political significance of democratic political forms, processes and ideals in western capitalist societies, in particular their legitimating function for the activities of the state.

14 Other critics of 'social control theory', particularly as used by revisionist historians, include Bellingham (1986), Muraskin (1975–6), Sydney Labour History Group (1982), van Krieken (1986) and Weiner (1978).

15 Useful references which inform a discussion of feminist perspectives on social control include Barrett (1980), MacKinnon (1982, 1983), McIntosh (1978), Millman and Moss Kanter eds. (1978), Smart and Smart eds. (1978), Smith (1974, 1979).

16 The concept 'role' does not belong only to the functionalist perspective, but was a key concept in a very different tradition in American sociology going back to the 1920s and 1930s associated with the schools of symbolic interactionism and social psychology, see Edwards (1983).

17 Although early feminists favoured drawing a distinction between 'sex', by which they meant biological differences between male and female human beings and 'gender', which referred to socially perceived and enforced distinctions between men and women, more recently this practice has been reviewed. Given that the designations 'male' and 'female' and the categories 'man' and 'woman' are based on a complex combination of elements including relatively objective anatomical and physiological characteristics, and culturally variable perceptions, expectations and attributions, in most contexts it seems preferable to acknowledge this as a problem and use the two terms in conjunction (except in rare cases where one or the other obviously is appropriate). On this question, see Eichler (1980:Chapter 1), Jaggar (1983:106–13), MacKinnon (1983:635, note 1), Rubin (1975), and Person (1980:606).

18 The most commonly used categories in such typologies are 'liberal', 'radical' and 'marxist' feminism; others also found include 'cultural' and 'socialist'. See Elshtain (1981:Chapter 5), Jaggar (1983), Oakley, (1981:Chapter 16).

19 Jaggar (1983) argues that different conceptions of human nature provide the best criterion for distinguishing between the major schools of contemporary feminism and a basis for comparing their various approaches to women's liberation.

20 For a sensitive and perceptive account of the major weaknesses (as well as the strengths) of American radical feminism, see Cocks (1984); see also Eisenstein (1984).

21 Major references on this subject include the classic article by Hartmann (1979) entitled 'The Unhappy Marriage of Marxism and Feminism', which is discussed by the various contributors to Sargent ed. (1981); see also Barrett (1980), Beechey (1979), Eisenstein (1979).

22 An understanding of the intra-psychic and psychological aspects of the relationship between personality, subjectivity and social and cultural practices is also important for feminism; and psychoanalytic theory has made a contribution in this area, first with the work of Mitchell (1975), later Chodorow (1978) and recent French feminists.

23 Though the public/private and nature/culture dichotomies have been extensively used in feminist analysis, as noted above, they are products of western androcentric thought and hence should not be treated as unproblematic. On the public/private distinction, see also various contributors to Gould ed. (1984), and Siltanen and Stanworth (1974).

24 See Barrett (1980), Harrison and Mort (1980), McIntosh (1978, 1984), MacKinnon (1983), Peterson (1977), Smart (1982, 1984) for accounts of various ways in which the state operates as a 'male protection racket' (Peterson's term).

25 This was not true of Millett (1972) or of the feminists who were directly concerned

with campaigns against such obvious forms of male brutality as rape and wife battering, Griffin (1971) and Brownmiller (1976) among others.

26 For a more detailed examination of the changing views of different groups of feminists over the period 1970–85 with respect to male violence and the social control of women, see Edwards (1987).

27 Some relevant British and American references are Bowker (1978), Ehrenreich and English (1978), Heidensohn (1985), Klein and Kress (1976), Millman (1975), Rafter and Stanko eds. (1982), Smart (1976) and Smart and Smart eds. (1978).

28 For example Davis (1975, 1980), Liska (1981) and Orcutt (1983). The first case is especially surprising since elsewhere Davis (1977) has written about the influence of changing gender roles and the feminist movement on women, deviance and social control. Even in Cohen's recent work (1981:241; 1985:255–6; Cohen and Scull, 1985:11–12), though he agrees that gender as a significant social variable deserves more attention, the theoretical implications of feminist analysis for the study of social control are not apparently perceived or considered significant. Taylor's (1981) book on 'law and order' from a socialist position does much the same thing.

29 For relevant Australian material, see Baldock and Cass eds. (1983), Mukherjee and Scutt eds. (1981).

30 On 'victim precipitation' specifically, see Weis and Borges (1973); with respect to rape, see Edwards (1981) and Clark and Lewis (1977); on wife battering, see Breines and Gordon (1983), Dobash and Dobash (1977, 1981), and Stark and Flitcraft (1983); and on the treatment of female victims of male violence generally, see Klein (1981), Rafter and Stanko eds. (1982), Stanko (1985) and Tong (1984).

31 Smart (1985) discusses in some detail the relationship of Foucault not only to Poulantzas and modern marxism generally (and suggests some affinity with Gramsci), but also to Weber and the Frankfurt School of Critical Theory. In a recent article on the 'social constructionist' perspective in recent medical sociology, Bury (1986) claims the influences of Foucault and marxism are quite separate and in some respects contradictory.

32 See, for example, Adams and Minson (1978), MacKinnon (1982:526, note 22), and Plaza (1981).

33 Though in his later writing on class and the state in which he explicitly acknowledges the importance of Foucault's work, Poulantzas moves away from the notion of the state as an 'intrinsic entity', as either 'instrument' or 'subject' (1978:128–9), he refuses to accept Foucault's more extreme position that no central or organised structures of power (whether economic, political or ideological) exist or should be theoretically hypothesised (Hall, 1980; Smart, 1983).

34 Foucault's work, and especially his analysis of power, is far more complex and difficult than these few observations might suggest; see Minson (1980), Sheridan (1980), Smart (1983), Wickham (1983).

Chapter 4: The study of social control

1 This chapter draws extensively on Cohen's latest book (1985) and to a lesser extent on his other publications on the subject of social control (1979a, 1984; Cohen and Scull, 1985); his latest book deals with past and present 'visions of social control' and particularly programmes, policies and approaches in the crime control field.

2 Some interesting aspects of norms, the labelling of deviance and the social control process can be explored also through the study of 'exceptional' individuals whose behaviour or attributes surpass the 'normal' standards set for most 'ordinary' people. Cultures have provision for 'heroes' and 'saints' as well as 'fools', 'villains' and 'sinners' (Klapp, 1962). It is not necessarily the case either that 'excellence' is universally and unequivocally praised and rewarded (Posner, 1976) nor that deviants who have earned a negative label attract only negative sentiments and evaluations, as the creation of folk anti-heroes demonstrates.

3 This kind of circular reasoning and functionalist logic is not only to be found among sociologists who follow the Parsonian tradition but also among interactionists, marxists and feminists (Barrett, 1980:Chapter 1; Turk and Grimes, 1981).

4 This is a problem with a number of the marxist writers on the state, including some of those discussed in Chapter 3.

5 The importance of the visibility or privacy factor has been widely recognised in the sociology of deviance; a useful discussion is to be found in Ball (1975) and in Inciardi (1972).

6 Downes and Rock (1971) present a useful review of the factors affecting reactions to deviance both at the social and the societal levels.

7 Hawkins and Tiedeman (1975:Chapter 9), Plummer (1979) and Suchar (1978: Chapter 7) all show how complex the analysis of the nature and effects of labelling needs to be and what an adequate empirical investigation of the labelling process would need to cover.

8 See:Buckner (1971); Downes and Rock (1971); Hawkins and Tiedeman (1975); Lemert (1951, 1967); Plummer (1979); Rubington and Weinberg (1968); Schur (1971). The formal/informal distinction with respect to legal institutions and methods has recently assumed considerate importance—see Abel ed. (1982).

9 This is a long-established tradition in political philosophy, and reflects its liberal and (male) sexist assumptions about the nature of society; see Gamble (1981:Chapter 2) and Elshtain (1981).

10 Cohen (1985:Chapter 6) develops Foucault's ideas about exclusion and inclusion as alternative modes of social control and shows how important this distinction is in the analysis of 'visions' of control.

11 For an examination of the effects of both types of social control on the freedom of the individual in a welfare society, see Jordan (1976:Chapter 5).

12 The notions of protest, contest, struggle, negotiation and conflict are to be found in all the major perspectives except functionalism.

13 Piven (1981), in an excellent critique of much of the work in the deviance field, argues that sociologists have 'obliterated human agency', and 'force' as a mechanism of control, and produced as a result a 'theory of pure domination'.

14 This has been recognised as a significant modern phenomenon by writers with very different perspectives on social control and the nature of social order. For example, see Kitsuse (1980), Habermas (1981), and Schur (1980:Chapter 4).

15 Newman (1976) reports on an interesting study of cross-cultural consensus and dissensus with respect to a range of morally and legally 'deviant' acts. For empirical studies of the relative seriousness ratings of a whole range of criminal offences in America and other countries, see Pease et al. (1975) and Rossi et al. (1974).

16 With respect to 'crime' and 'the powerless', see Box (1983:Chapter 1); Michalowski and Bohlander (1976); Thio (1973); and Wilson and Braithwaite eds. (1978). Wilson and Braithwaite (1978:2) make the interesting observation that whereas in sociology the deviance paradigm is chosen when studying the powerless, an organisations or professions framework is regarded as the appropriate one for studying the powerful.

17 Quinney (1977:50–2) lists four categories of what he calls 'crimes of domination': 'crimes of control' (offences by law-enforcement agents), 'crimes of government', 'crimes of economic domination' (by corporations, professionals, businessmen and including state and business involvement in organised crime), and 'social injuries' committed by capitalists and the state that are not necessarily illegal acts.

18 Conrad and Schneider (1980a); Ehrenreich and Ehrenreich (1974); Freidson (1970a:Chapters 12 and 14); Zola (1972; 1975).

19 Corrigan (1977); Gough (1979); Higgins (1978).

20 Hawkins and Tiedeman (1975:146), for instance, describe the legal system, the therapeutic health system, and the social welfare system as the three 'spheres of formal social control' in modern America and include material on all three in their book on the creation and control of deviance.

21 Baldock and Cass eds. (1983); McIntosh (1978); Wilson (1977).

22 Though all these latter institutions have control aspects and functions, they do not have a specific 'deviant' section of the population as the targets of their control efforts (unless children are by definition 'deviant') nor are their activities primarily or predominantly the exercise of social control, in the way this concept is here employed.

23 This thesis has been criticised by Lea (1979) in particular, who argues that Melossi concentrates on the factory and the production system and ignores the role played by the market in regulating capital-labour relations.

24 For Weber's writings on 'The Types of Legitimate Domination', 'Economy and the Law', and 'Domination and Legitimacy', see Chapter III (Part I), and Chapters VIII and X (Part II) respectively in Roth and Wittich eds. (1978).

25 Foucault dates the start of this process from the end of the eighteenth century in Europe, but Garland (1983), in an important historical account of 'punishment and welfare' in Britain, argues that in that country at least the new approach developed much later, towards the end of the Victorian period. He relates it to the end of free market capitalism, an emerging new role for the state and the marginalisation of the lower classes.

26 The pre-capitalist economy in the west was by contrast highly regulated (Humphries and Greenberg, 1981:219–21).

27 Hawkins and Tiedeman (1975:344–51); Ingleby (1985); Kittrie (1971); Scull (1977: Chapter 2); and, of course, Foucault (1967, 1976, 1977).

28 This is a particularly well-researched topic, see Castel (1985); Foucault (1967); Ingleby (1985) and Rothman (1971): for an account of women and madness in England in the sixteenth and seventeenth centuries see MacDonald (1986).

29 Gusfield (1963).

30 Brophy and Smart (1981) and Smart (1982); Harrison and Mort (1980); Weeks (1981).

31 Conrad and Schneider (1980a); Foucault (1976); Freidson (1970a).

32 Cohen (1985); Garland and Young eds. (1983); Ingleby (1985).

33 Humphries and Greenberg (1981); Spitzer (1979); Spitzer and Scull (1977a, 1977b) discuss changes in crime control as capitalism developed. Taylor-Gooby and Dale (1981:Chapter 7), however, reject the idea of a direct relationship between changes in capitalism and modes of state intervention.

34 The analysis which is presented here draws on the work of, among others, Corrigan (ed.) (1980); Gough (1979); Jessop (1977, 1978); Offe (1975, 1982, 1984).

35 As well as Connell and Irving (1980:Chapters 2 and 3) see also the first three chapters in Wheelwright and Buckley eds. (1975) by Buckley, Dunn and Clark.

36 For historical material on policing in America, see Harring and Spitzer, both in Greenberg ed. (1981), which contains a range of mainly historical articles on different aspects of crime control.

37 Barbalet (1983); Daniels (1984); Edwards Hiller and Hancock (1981); Robinson, Weatherburn, and Willis in MacInolty and Radi eds. (1979); Salt (1984); Windschuttle (1981).

38 Daniels ed. (1984) contains a variety of accounts of the treatment of prostitutes in various States during the nineteenth and early twentieth centuries.

39 Ingleby (1985) provides an excellent overview and evaluation of the various historical and theoretical accounts of the development of 'mental illness' and the 'mental institution'; see also Castel (1985); Ignatieff (1985); Minson (1980) and Scull (1985).

40 The pluralist approach focusses on opportunities for different interest groups to influence policy in a democratic political system. There are various marxist alternatives: Griffin et al. (1983) identify three, the structuralist, economic and class struggle models, which they then test against data on welfare spending in the post second war era in America.

41 We earlier noted that Stedman Jones (1977) is highly critical of what he calls 'the social control approach' in history; but he does use the term himself (see his 'Outcast London', 1976).

42 Conley (1982:289) comments that there was by the 1940s a reversal of the nineteenth

century pattern, with the state now taking over the 'deserving' and the charities being left with the 'undeserving' category, whom they rejected in the earlier period, when moral character was as important to them as physical need. See also Roe (1976:106, 224) on the persistence of these notions.

43 There were significant differences between the States with respect to welfare provision; South Australia, for instance, had a centralised government relief system (Kewley, 1973:7; Roe, 1976:13).

44 See Kewley (1973:Chapters 4–7) for details of the original provisions and later modifications of these benefits up to 1939. Kewley points out that the Federal Government was restricted by the Constitution in what it could do in the welfare and social security area until the second war and the referendum of 1946.

45 A volume entitled *Permissiveness and Control* was published in Britain in 1980 which explored this issue; see, particularly, the chapters by Greenwood and Young and by Hall.

46 There is now a very substantial body of literature (professional, sociological and feminist) on the subject of domestic violence and how to deal with it; for a good up-to-date Australian account, see Scutt (1983).

47 Smart has published a book (1984) on the legal and social policy aspects of the current ways in which divorce is handled officially in England and Wales. See also the references given in note 30 above.

48 Boehringer et al. (1983) discuss current Australian responses by the state and sections of the community to various major problems not conventionally regarded as 'criminal' or not effectively prosecuted; in particular they discuss issues of importance to those concerned about state power that are raised by the tax avoidance debate.

49 See Matthews (1979); Melossi (1980); Sedgwick (1982:192–205); Speiglman (1979).

50 See also Cohen (1979a, 1985) and Van Dusen (1981).

51 Once again, Cohen (1985:131–9) provides an insightful analysis of what this involves.

52 The aggressive and punitive response of the Thatcher British Government to the riots in British cities (in 1980 and 1981) and to the miners' strike (1984–5), as well as Northern Ireland and the Falklands, provide further evidence of this trend.

Chapter 5: The legal–judicial system

1 The question of how to define law for the purposes of cross-cultural comparison remains a problem for sociologists and anthropologists; see, for example, Krygier (1980).

2 Goldstein emphasises the 'involuntariness' of such sanctions. As he points out, their essential characteristic is that they are 'imposed by the state presumably against, or at least without regard to, the wishes of the individual being deprived' (1960:544, n. 4). Feeley (1976) points out that negative sanctions may be characteristic of the criminal law but they are not essential components of other forms of law (of which he gives examples).

3 Parsons (1962:72) states the optimum conditions for law to operate effectively as a social control agent are those that prevail in a 'pluralistic liberal society', such as (in his view) the United States.

4 Melossi (1985), in an interesting recent paper, takes a different view again. He contends that marxism needs interactionism (particularly the Meadian variety) and labelling theory if it is to avoid falling back into economic determinism and a narrow legalistic conception of social control.

5 Turk and Grimes (1981) offer a brief general account of the move from instrumentalism to structuralism and of the changes over time in the work of writers such as Chambliss and Quinney.

6 As Young (1975, 1979) and other marxists have noted, there are echoes of this romanticisation of the deviant in critical criminology, though in the form of 'left

idealism'. This is associated with a tendency to overlook the fact that working-class people are also victims as well as perpetrators of crime.

7 Jessop's (1980) useful description of the various recent marxist developments in this field deals with marxist theory in more technical detail than is necessary here.

8 The much-quoted collection edited by Hay et al. (1975) is a good example of the more sophisticated interpretations of these phenomena.

9 One of the rare exceptions, (apart from Schur 1984, who was mentioned earlier) is Cousins (1980) who raises some difficult questions about concepts of 'sexual difference', of man-made law and of 'feminist criminology'. These issues have also been discussed by feminists; see, for example, Brown (1986); Greenwood (1981); Heidensohn (1985).

10 For example, Michalowski (1981); Taylor (1981).

11 On the fundamentally patriarchal character of the state, see MacKinnon (1983).

12 O'Donovan (1979, 1985) expands on the ways in which English laws relating to marriage and divorce historically prescribed different treatment for men and women according to their gender roles, with women being regarded as a 'male appendage'. Smart (1984) in a recent study confirms that gender ideologies are still a powerful influence on the law in this area.

13 This is not true of O'Malley, whose treatment of the law (1983:Chapters 2 and 3), though illustrated with empirical examples, is largely theoretical.

14 For an interesting recent analysis of the issues surrounding campaigns for the legalisation of prostitution in England, seen particularly through the eyes of PROS, an organisation of prostitutes fighting for reform of the laws relating to soliciting, see Dominelli (1986) and McLeod (1982).

15 Collison (1980); Edwards Hiller and Hancock (1981); Hogg and Brown (1985); Morris (1978); Morris et al. (1981).

16 Cohen (1985) provides a detailed and extensive coverage of the various policies in the juvenile justice and corrections areas; see also Garland and Young eds. (1983).

17 For a somewhat different evaluation of the 'justice model' and the 'treatment ethic' from a marxist standpoint, see Clarke (1978).

18 Tomasic ed. (1978); Tomasic and Bullard (1978).

19 Baldwin and McConville (1977:Chapter 2) discuss the main differences between the American and British judicial systems as these affect bargaining.

20 Their study is reported in three separate volumes, published in 1977, 1979, 1981.

21 Though the latter may be seriously impeded by the fact that the prosecution need reveal very little of its case before trial (Lane, 1982); for a more thorough analysis of the balance of advantage in favour of the prosecution in trials, see McBarnet (1981:Chapter 5).

22 As Chambliss (1969:85–97) points out, and this may to some extent be specific to the American situation, it is members of the lower classes, and in particular amateur, occasional and petty criminals who are the most vulnerable to law enforcement and the justice system, while the higher classes, and professional and white collar criminals are in a much stronger position to conceal their activities, to buy protection from the police and other authorities, and secure effective legal representation. Baldwin and McConville, who confirm from their English study of Crown Court defendants that the majority are 'relatively unskilled, ignorant and singularly unprofessional' (1977:5), nonetheless reported also that the professional criminals in their study and individuals from the higher classes did not seem to feel they had any advantage in dealing with the system (1977:96–7).

23 The only major Australian work apparently covering this topic (Braithwaite, 1979) in fact deals only with the incidence and forms of criminality as between class groups and areas and not with the workings of the criminal justice system.

24 The classic Australian study of Aborigines and the law is Eggleston (1976); more recent books which explore the wide range of aspects of this subject are Hanks and Keon-Cohen eds. (1984) and Swanton ed. (1984).

25 For a discussion of race, gender and imprisonment in Australia, see Donnelly (1984); Hartz-Karp (1981).

26 The handling of rape and prostitution is seen by several feminist writers (Edwards, 1984; Smart, 1976:Chapter 4) as revealing a consistent underlying pattern of gender stereotyping and discrimination.

27 See Gelsthorpe (1986); Heidensohn (1985, 1986); Scutt (1985); Smart (1986); Stang Dahl (1987); Thornton (1986).

28 For a summary of the overseas and Australian material relating to women, crime and criminal justice, see Edwards (1982).

29 A detailed statistical analysis of female and male crime rates in the United States is presented by Steffensmeier; see Steffensmeier (1980b) and Steffensmeier and Steffensmeier (1980). For a definitive analysis of the material on changes in the level and types of female crime in England and Wales since 'liberation', see Box and Hale (1983). The trends in crime rates for various Australian States from 1900 to 1976, according to sex and general offence category (person, property, good order) are presented in Mukherjee and Fitzgerald (1981).

30 For a broad survey of the issues relating to women and the prison system in both the United States and Australia, see Hatty ed. (1984). The equity issue with respect to the different conditions found in male and female prisons in Victoria was specifically addressed in a report edited by Hancock (1982) for the Community Services Department.

Chapter 6: The medical–psychiatric system

1 Carlson (1975:31–6, 195–215); Dubos (1968:Chapters 3 and 5); Figlio (1977:267–82); Foucault (1976); McKeown (1976:Chapter 1).

2 McKeown (1970:343–4) lists six separate tasks that medicine involves and gives different dates for when each began to be technically reliable.

3 It is important to recognise that lay people, typically family members, play a major role in health care (Graham, 1984) and that a number of non-scientific and folk remedies continue to be widely used alongside orthodox western medicine.

4 Other writers who discuss the Australian governments' relatively late entry into and recent policy changes in the health area are Dickey (1977); Jones (1983:Chapter 9); Mendelsohn (1982:Chapter 6).

5 This was the year in which the first version of Medibank started operation, but since it came in on July 1, its effects on government funding in the health area were not evident until the following year.

6 Though Parsons does see medicine as part of the total social system, not surprisingly, given his consensus model of society, the key structures and processes to which he relates medicine are those concerned with normative integration.

7 Parsons initially identified 'uncertainty' as a problem for medical science and medical practice. Later writers have argued that the extent of 'real' uncertainty and the strains it imposes have been overestimated and its usefulness as a collective strategy in dealing with patients has been neglected (Atkinson, 1977; Atkinson et al., 1977; Davis, 1972; Fox, 1980).

8 For an even more recent Australian account of modern medical technology and the problems it raises, see Bates and Lapsley (1985). Their provocative account includes both an assessment of medical technology under the headings of 'the beginning of life', 'maturity' and 'old age, death and dying' and a projection of likely future trends in health care.

9 For an interesting illustration of the presence of what the author calls 'magical elements in orthodox medicine', see Posner's (1977) description of the management of diabetes.

10 In the following account, we are drawing on the work of Bates (1977); Conrad and Schneider (1980a:Chapter 3); Klerman (1977); Leifer (1969, 1970/1); Manning (1976); Scheff (1966); Sedgwick (1982).

11 It is important to distinguish between psychiatry, which is a medical specialty, and

psychology and psychoanalysis which have their own (and different) theoretical understandings of the workings of the mind, but which do not require of their practitioners that they also have undergone a medical training.

12 For two interesting accounts of the conceptual problems in dealing with the relationships between (medical) professionalism, ideology and rationality, see Glasner (1979) and Young (1983).

13 Edelman in a classic article shows how the language of the 'helping professions' (with words like 'therapy', 'care' and 'help') often working on behalf of the state, 'structures perceptions of status, authority, merit, deviance, and the causes of social problems' (1984:296). He and Gerson (1976), like Foucault, argue for the importance of recognising the political nature of language and of the social processes of definition, explanation and treatment of illness.

14 An interesting recent study of the significance of medicine in the lives of ordinary people in London's East End is Cornwell (1984).

15 This is dealt with in more detail and references are given in the section of this chapter which specifically addresses the question of medicine's relation to gender and patriarchy.

16 There is an extensive sociological literature on professions and professionalism which we cannot cover here. The following provide historical accounts of the medical profession and the role of the hospital in Britain and the United States: Berlant (1975); Krause (1977:Chapter 1); Parry and Parry (1976); Peterson (1978); Starr (1982); Waddington (1973, 1978).

17 Though initially in convict days, medical treatment (such as it was) was supplied by penal administrations and indeed medical personnel were paid by the state (Gandevia, 1967), the States accepted responsibility only gradually in the latter part of the nineteenth century for the supervision as well as the financing of hospitals.

18 An important mechanism of control over health occupations in the modern context is the medical profession's capacity to supervise the employment and industrial conditions, as well as aspects of education and training for a range of 'allied' health workers (Brown, 1973).

19 The gender division of labour in medicine and other health occupations is discussed in a later section of the chapter.

20 The research by Horobin in the British context suggests the issue of medical autonomy is not simply a matter of either state control (where doctors are employees and/or working in hospitals) or colleague control (where they are self-employed or working in general practice); see Gill and Horobin (1972) and Horobin and McIntosh (1977).

21 It should be made clear at this point that the comments that follow apply more to the management of physical disease than they do to so-called 'mental illness', since high technology and institutional treatment are significantly less relevant to the latter.

22 And we should note Freidson's qualification in his discussion of the place of the hospital in modern medical care in the United States: where doctors are not full-time salaried employees of hospitals, he observes, 'the physician is not so much part of the hospital as the hospital is part (and only one part) of the physician's practice' (1970a:115).

23 For an interesting empirical investigation of where power lies with respect to decision-making about the adoption of technology in hospitals, see Greer (1984).

24 An Australian researcher who also questions the relative importance of the processes of industrialism and bureaucratisation as compared with the commercialisation and commodification of health and health care services is Egger (1978).

25 It is the relatively minor role given to these factors by Navarro that is a major source of criticism of his work; see, for instance, Freidson (1985), Reidy (1984).

26 Elston (1977) in England and Fett (1974, 1976) in Australia also discuss the nature and sources of male dominance (in numbers and in positions) of the medical profession. For an historical account of nursing in relation to the sexual division of labour, class and capitalism in Britain, see Garmarnikow (1978).

27 The 1983 Australian Health Survey obtained very similar results, but the 1977/8 figures are quoted here as the data presented on sex differences is more detailed in the earlier report. Unlike the data on the sex ratio of physicians, morbidity measurements suffer from major methodological problems. While many studies using a variety of instruments have confirmed the higher female rates, some (for an Australian example, Waddell and Floate, 1986, on the use of health care services in Perth) find no evidence of significant sex differences.

28 In America, since the early 1970s, when Gove published his original theory of 'sex, marital status and mental illness' (Gove, 1972; Gove and Tudor, 1973), the sociological literature on this subject has largely consisted of a steady stream of publications by Gove (and various colleagues) expanding on his thesis and a large number of empirical and theoretical articles carrying critiques of his work.

29 See Donnison (1977); Ehrenreich and English (1978:Chapters 2 and 3); Oakley (1984); Versluysen (1981).

30 Willis points out that, although the mainly male members of the medical profession have established a position of overall control over confinement, doctors continue to rely on the services of female nurses and midwives in caring for women during pregnancy, childbirth and the post-natal period (1983:122).

31 The limitations of role analysis in general and sex-role analysis in particular (with specific reference to Gove's work) are discussed in Edwards (1983).

Chapter 7: The social welfare system

1 Mendelsohn (1979:16) includes protective legislation covering workplace conditions and the industrial conciliation and arbitration system in his conception of welfare provisions. However, as Pinker (1971:148) points out, even the broader definitions of welfare usually exclude public amenities such as parks, libraries, etc. In this chapter, I am following what seems to be the most common practice of treating the five major service areas of health, education, income security, housing, and personal social services as constituting the public welfare sector.

2 The complex nature and different levels of state involvement in the economy at the present time in advanced capitalist societies makes any attempt to differentiate between social policy and economic policy even more futile (Klein, 1980:30–2; Mishra, 1981:170).

3 Rein (1970:xv–xvi) elaborates on these dimensions and raises a number of issues relating to conceptions of social policy, organisation and delivery of services, implementation of services, distribution and allocation of services, outcomes and consequences.

4 For example, Graycar (1979:Chapter 1); Jamrozik (1983); Mendelsohn (1979: Chapter 8); Mishra (1981:Chapter 6); Pinker (1971:Chapter 3); Room (1979: Chapter 8); Tulloch (1979:Chapter 3).

5 George and Wilding (1976:Chapter 6) argue that fundamental incompatibility between the basic values of capitalism and those required for a successful public welfare system is the principal reason for the failure of the modern welfare state.

6 The current state of the modern state was analysed in some detail in Chapter 4.

7 Corporatism in relation to welfare provisions is also mentioned by Pinker (1979: Chapter 12) and Taylor-Gooby and Dale (1981:250–3); corporatism was defined and discussed in Chapter 3.

8 The use of the term 'liberal' in this context can be confusing, since different writers give it different meanings and use it in different ways: for some 'liberal' refers to supporters of laissez-faire and individualist philosophy (of a nineteenth century kind), while for others 'liberal' means progressive or reformist.

9 See for example, the work of Smelser (1959, 1964), one of the few functionalists to take any substantial interest in welfare, who is also untypical in applying structural-functionalism to the analysis of historical change, specifically the industrial revolution.

10 Mishra (1981:Chapter 3) has an extended discussion of the industrialisation thesis regarding the emergence of public welfare systems. See also Habermas and Offe, whose approach to the analysis of crisis management by the modern capitalist state is discussed by Mishra (1981:Chapter 5) and in Chapter 3.

11 Exceptions are Jordan (1976:Chapter 5); Pearson (1975); Simpkin (1983:133–4); Sinfield (1978:143).

12 Adams (1985) offers a useful summary of different marxist accounts of the relationship between 'social policy and the working class'. For a theoretical assessment and empirical test of different kinds of marxist explanations of state welfare, see Skopcol's (1980) analysis of the American New Deal welfare programmes; Devine (1985) and Griffin et al. (1983) look at the determinants of state welfare expenditure in the United States in the post–war period, and compare the different marxist accounts.

13 The influence of these theorists is explicitly acknowledged by Barrett (1980) and Wilson (1977).

14 For a critical interpretation of the ideological implications of the usage of the term 'community', see Bryson and Mowbray (1981).

15 See Jordan (1976:Chapter 7); Reamer (1983).

16 See Mendelsohn (1979:Chapter 8) for an extended discussion of alternative approaches to income and/or social security. Mendelsohn (1979:203–4) defines social security in more restricted terms than Kewley (1973).

17 Similar patterns have been reported in Britain and commented on by various welfare writers; see, for example, Gough (1979:108–17); Mishra (1981:119–27); Rose (1981:495–500); Sinfield (1978:151–3).

18 See also Dickey (1980:Chapter 7); Encel (1978); Higgins (1982); Scotton (1980).

19 M. Edwards (1981a, 1981b) has provided convincing empirical evidence and theoretical argument for rejecting the assumption that 'the family' shares its resources equally and is therefore a satisfactory administrative unit for income and taxation purposes. She has subsequently argued strongly for taxation and welfare policies to take these facts into account and suggested mechanisms whereby state benefits and cash transfers which are intended to assist dependent family members actually do so.

20 There are additional disadvantages in countries like the United States and Britain where state benefits and pensions follow the insurance principle and are contribution-, and hence income- or earnings-related; see, for instance, Land (1976, 1983) on the British situation and Nelson (1984) on America.

21 In Britain, where there is a national insurance system, in which pensions are contributory and earnings-based, not only the fiscal and occupation systems but also public welfare is tied to employment status and to wage and salary levels. The nature and effects of such a system is relevant in the light of current Australian proposals for a state superannuation scheme of a comparable kind.

22 The following take this view of the state: Cass (1982:33–6); Cass and Baldock (1983); Gough (1979); London Edinburgh Weekend Return Group (1980); McIntosh (1981).

Bibliography

Abel, R.L. (ed.) *The Politics of Informal Justice* Vol. 1, New York: Academic Press, 1982.

——— 'Introduction' to Abel (ed.), 1982, pp. 1–13.

Ackerknecht, E.H. 'Natural Diseases and Rational Treatment in Primitive Medicine', *Bulletin of the History of Medicine* XIX(5), 1946, pp. 467–97.

Adams, M. 'The Compassion Trap' in V. Gornick and B.K. Moran (eds.) *Women in Sexist Society: Studies in Power and Powerlessness* New York: Mentor, 1971, pp. 555–75.

Adams, P. and J. Minson 'The "Subject" of Feminism' *M/F* 2, 1978, pp. 43–61.

Adams, P. 'Social Policy and the Working Class' *Social Service Review* 59(3), 1985, pp. 387–402.

Adler, F. *Sisters in Crime: The Rise of the New Female Criminal* New York: McGraw Hill, 1975.

Ainlay, J. Review of Taylor, Walton and Young, 1973, and Taylor, Walton and Young (eds), 1975 *Telos* 26, 1975/6, pp. 213–25.

Alford, K. *Production or Reproduction? An Economic History of Women in Australia, 1788–1850* London: Oxford University Press, 1984.

Alford, R.R. 'Paradigms of Relations Between State and Society' in L.N. Lindberg et al. (eds) *Stress and Contradiction in Modern Capitalism* Lexington: D.C. Heath and Co., 1975.

Allen, J. 'Marxism and the Man Question: Some Implications of the Patriarchy Debate' in J. Allen and P. Paton (eds) *Beyond Marxism? Interventions After Marx* Leichhardt: Intervention Publications, 1983, pp. 91–111.

Althusser, L. *Lenin and Philosophy* London: New Left Books, 1971.

Anderson, M.J. and The Feminist Psychology Group 'Sex Role Stereotypes and Clinical Psychologists: An Australian Study' *Australian Psychologist* 10(3), 1975, pp. 325–31.

Armstrong, G. 'Females Under the Law–"Protected" but Unequal' *Crime and Delinquency* 23(2), 1977, pp. 109–20.

Atkinson, P. 'The Reproduction of Medical Knowledge' in Dingwall et al.(eds.), 1977, pp. 85–106.

Atkinson, P., M. Reid and P. Sheldrake 'Medical Mystique' *Sociology of Work and Occupations* (4)3, 1977, pp. 243–80.

Aubert, V. and S.L. Messinger 'The Criminal and the Sick' *Inquiry* 1, 1958, pp. 137–59.

Austin, J. and B. Krisberg 'Wider, Stronger and Different Nets: The Dialectics of Criminal Justice Reform' *Journal of Research in Crime and Delinquency* 18(1), 1981, pp. 165–96.

Australian Health Survey: Consultation with Health Professionals Canberra: Australian Bureau of Statistics, 1977/8.
Australian Health Survey: Doctor Consultations Canberra: Australian Bureau of Statistics, 1977/8.
Australian Health Survey Canberra: Australian Bureau of Statistics, 1983.

Babcock, B.A. 'Introduction: Women and the Criminal Law' *The American Criminal Law Review* 11(2), 1973, pp. 291–4.
Bacon, W. and R. Lansdowne 'Women Homicide Offenders and Police Interrogation' in Basten et al. (eds), 1982, pp. 4–35.
Baldock, C.V. and B. Cass (eds) *Women, Social Welfare and the State* Sydney: Allen and Unwin, 1983.
Baldock, C.V. 'Public Policies and the Paid Work of Women' in Baldock and Cass (eds), 1983, pp. 20–53.
Baldwin, J. and A.K. Bottomley (eds) *Criminal Justice* London: Martin Robertson, 1978.
Baldwin, J. and M. McConville *Negotiated Justice: Pressures to Plead Guilty* London: Martin Robertson, 1977.
_____ *Jury Trials* London: Oxford University Press, 1979.
Ball, D.W. 'Privacy, Publicity, Deviance and Control' *Pacific Sociological Review* 18(3), 1975, pp. 259–77.
Bankowski, Z. and G. Mungham *Images of Law* London: Routledge and Kegan Paul, 1976.
Bankowski, Z. and G. Mungham (eds) *Essays in Law and Society* London: Routledge and Kegan Paul, 1980.
Barbalet, M. *Far From a Low Gutter Girl: The Forgotten World of State Wards, South Australia 1887–1940* Melbourne: Oxford University Press, 1983.
Barrett, M. *Women's Oppression Today* London: Verso, 1980.
Barrett, M. and H. Roberts 'Doctors and Their Patients: The Social Control of Women in General Practice' in Smart and Smart (eds), 1978, pp. 41–52.
Barry, K. *Female Sexual Slavery* Englewood Cliffs, N.J.: Prentice Hall, 1979.
Bartky, S.L. 'Towards a Phenomenology of Feminist Consciousness' in M. Vetterling-Braggin et al. (eds) *Feminism and Philosophy* Totowa, N.J.: Rowman and Littlefield, 1977, pp. 22–34.
Basten, J., M. Richardson, C. Ronalds and G. Zdendowski (eds) *The Criminal Injustice System* Sydney: Australian Legal Workers Group (N.S.W.) and Clayton, Vic.: Legal Service Bulletin Co-op. Ltd., 1982.
Bates, E. *Models of Madness* St. Lucia: University of Queensland Press, 1977.
Bates, E. and H. Lapsley *The Health Machine: The Impact of Medical Technology* Ringwood: Penguin, 1985.
Becker, H.S. *Outsiders: Studies in the Sociology of Deviance* New York: Free Press, 1963.
_____ 'Labelling Theory Reconsidered' in P. Rock and M. McIntosh (eds) *Deviance and Social Control* London: Tavistock, 1974: pp.41–66.
Beechey, V. 'On Patriarchy' *Feminist Review* 3, 1979, pp. 66–82.
Bellingham, B. 'Institution and Family: An Alternative View of Nineteenth Century Child Saving' *Social Problems* 33(6), 1986, pp. 535–57.
Berlant, J. *Profession and Monopoly: A Study of Medicine in the United States and Great Britain* Berkeley: University of California Press, 1975.
Bernard, J. 'My Four Revolutions: An Autobiographical History of the A.S.A.' *American Journal of Sociology* 78(4), 1973, pp.773–91.
Bernstein, I.N., E. Kick, J.T. Leung and B. Schultz 'Charge Reduction: An Intermediary Stage in the Process of Labeling Criminal Defendants' *Social Forces* 56(2), 1977, pp. 362–84.
Biles, D. (ed.) *Crime and Justice in Australia* Melbourne: Sun Books and Australian Institute of Criminology, 1977.

——— 'Crime and Imprisonment' *British Journal of Criminology*, 23(2), 1983, pp. 166–72.

Bittner, E. 'Police Discretion in Emergency Apprehension of Mentally Ill Persons' *Social Problems* 14(3), 1967, pp. 278–92.

Black, D. *The Behaviour of Law* New York: Academic Press, 1976.

——— (ed.) *Towards a General Theory of Social Control* Vol. 1 and 2, Orlando: Academic Press, 1984.

——— 'Social Control as a Dependent Variable' in Black (ed.), 1984, pp. 1–36.

Blackburn, R. (ed.) *Ideology in Social Science: Readings in Critical Social Theory* Chapter 11 'The Problem of the Capitalist State', London: Fontana/Collins, 1972.

Boehringer, G. et al. '"Law and Order" for Progressives? An Australian Response' *Crime and Social Justice* 19, 1983, pp. 2–11.

Bolger, S., P. Corrigan, J. Docking and N. Frost *Towards Socialist Welfare Work* London: Macmillan, 1981.

Bordua, D. (ed.) *The Police: Six Sociological Essays* New York: Wiley, 1967.

Bottomley, A.K. *Criminology in Focus* Oxford: Martin Robertson, 1979.

Bottoms, A.E. 'Neglected Features of Contemporary Penal Systems' in Garland and Young (eds), 1983, pp. 166–202.

Bottoms, A.E. and J.D. McClean *Defendants in the Criminal Process* London: Routledge and Kegan Paul, 1976.

Bowker, L.H. *Women, Crime and the Criminal Justice System* Lexington, Mass.: Heath and Co., 1978.

Box, S. *Deviance, Reality and Society* London: Holt, Rinehart and Winston, 1971.

——— 'Where Have all the Naughty Children Gone?' in National Deviancy Conference (eds.), 1980, pp. 96–121.

——— *Power, Crime and Mystification* London: Tavistock, 1983.

Box, S. and C. Hale 'Liberation and Female Criminality in England and Wales' *British Journal of Criminology* 23(1), 1983, pp. 35–49.

Braithwaite, J. *Inequality, Crime and Public Policy* London: Routledge and Kegan Paul, 1979.

Braverman, J. *Labor and Monopoly Capital* New York: Monthly Review Press, 1974.

Bredemeier, H.C. 'Law as an Integrative Mechanism' in W.M. Evan (ed.) *Law and Sociology* Free Press of Glencoe, 1962, pp. 73–90.

Breines, W. and L. Gordon 'The New Scholarship on Family Violence' *Signs* 8(3), 1983, pp. 490–531.

Broom, D.H. 'In Sickness and in Health: Social Policy and the Control of Women' in Baldock and Cass (eds), 1983, pp. 262–78.

——— 'Natural Resources: Health, Reproduction and the Gender Order' in D.H. Broom (ed.) *Unfinished Business: Social Justice for Women in Australia* Sydney: Allen and Unwin, 1984, pp. 46–61.

Brophy, J. and C. Smart 'From Disregard to Disrepute: The Position of Women in Family Law' *Feminist Review* 9, 1981, pp. 3–16.

Broverman, I.K., D.M. Broverman, H.E. Clarkson, P.S. Rosenkrantz and S.R. Vogel 'Sex-Role Stereotypes and Clinical Judgements of Mental Health' *Journal of Consulting and Clinical Psychology* 34(1), 1970, pp. 1–7.

Brown, B. 'Women and Crime: The Dark Figures of Criminology' *Economy and Society* 15(3), 1986, pp. 355–402.

Brown, C.A. 'The Division of Laborers: Allied Health Professionals' *International Journal of Health Services* 3(3), 1973, pp. 435–44.

Brown, D. 'Some Notes on the State of Play in Criminology' *Alternative Criminology Journal* 2(4) and 3(1), 1978, pp. 67–87.

Brown, P. and L.J. Jordanova 'Oppressive Dichotomies: The Nature/Culture Debate' in Cambridge Women's Studies Group *Women in Society: Interdisciplinary Essays* London: Virago, 1981, pp. 224–41.

Brownmiller, S. *Against Our Will: Men, Women and Rape* Harmondsworth: Penguin, 1976.

Bryson, L. 'Women as Welfare Recipients: Women, Poverty and the State' in Baldock and Cass (eds), 1983, pp. 130–45.

_____ 'The Welfare State' in J. Eastwood, J. Reeves and J. Ryan *Labour Essays 1984* Melbourne: Drummond, 1984, pp. 119–38.

Bryson, L. and A.R. Edwards 'Gender and Welfare: Correctional Services Versus Family Support' *Australian and New Zealand Journal of Sociology*, forthcoming.

Bryson, L. and M. Mowbray '"Community": the Spray-On Solution' *Australian Journal of Social Issues* 16(4), 1981, pp. 255–67.

_____ 'Who Cares? Social Security, Family Policy and Women' *International Social Security Review* 2, 1986, pp. 183–200.

Buckner, H.T. *Deviance, Reality and Change* New York: Random House, 1971.

Bullough, B. and V.L. Bullough 'Sex Discrimination in Health Care' *Nursing Outlook* 23(1), 1975, pp. 40–5.

Burawoy, M. *The Politics of Production* London: Verso, 1985.

Burton, C. 'Engels, *The Origin of the Family* and Feminist Theory' in N. Grieve and P. Grimshaw (eds) *Australian Women: Feminist Perspectives* Melbourne: Oxford University Press, 1981, pp. 3–14.

_____ *Subordination: Feminism and Social Theory* Sydney: Allen and Unwin, 1985.

Bury, M.R. 'Social Constructionism and the Development of Medical Sociology' *Sociology of Health and Illness* 8(2), 1986, pp. 137–69.

Busfield, J. 'Gender, Mental Illness and Psychiatry' in M. Evans and C. Ungerson (eds) *Sexual Divisions: Patterns and Processes* London: Tavistock, 1983, pp. 106–35.

Cain, M. 'Trends in the Sociology of Police Work' *International Journal of the Sociology of Law* 7(2), 1979b, pp. 143–67.

_____ 'Beyond Informal Justice' *Contemporary Crises* 9, 1985, pp. 335–73.

Cain, M. and A. Hunt *Marx and Engels on Law* London: Academic Press, 1979.

Campioni, M. and E. Gross 'Love's Labors Lost: Marxism and Feminism' in J. Allen and P. Patton (eds) *Beyond Marxism? Interventions After Marx* Leichhardt: Intervention Publications, 1983, pp. 113–41.

Carlen, P. *Magistrates' Justice* London: Martin Robertson, 1976.

Carlen, P. and M. Collison (eds) *Radical Issues in Criminology* Oxford: Martin Robertson, 1980.

Carlen, P. and C. Tchaikovsky 'Women in Prison' in P. Carlen (ed.) *Criminal Women* Cambridge: Polity Press, 1985, pp. 182–6.

Carlson, R.J. *The End of Medicine* New York: Wiley, 1975.

Cashman, P. 'Representation in Criminal Cases' in Basten et al. (eds), 1982, pp. 195–225.

Cass, B. *Family Policies in Australia: Contest Over the Social Wage* University of N.S.W. Social Welfare Research Centre Report No. 21, 1982.

_____ 'Redistribution to Children and Mothers: A History of Child Endowment and Family Allowances' in Baldock and Cass (eds), 1983, pp. 54–84.

_____ 'The Changing Face of Poverty in Australia: 1972–1982' *Australian Feminist Studies* 1985, pp. 7–89.

Cass, B. and C.V. Baldock 'Introduction' in Baldock and Cass (eds), 1983, pp. xi–xvii.

Cass, B., C. Keens and D. Wyndham 'Child-Rearing: Direct and Indirect Costs' in Graycar (ed.), 1983, pp. 13–24.

Cass, B. and M.A. O'Loughlin 'Single Parent Families and Social Policies in Australia 1974–1982' *Australian Journal of Social Issues* 20(4), 1985, pp. 247–66.

Castel, R. 'Moral Treatment: Mental Therapy and Social Control in the Nineteenth Century' in Cohen and Scull (eds.), 1985, pp. 248–66.

Castles, F.G. *The Working Class and Welfare* Sydney: Allen and Unwin, 1985.

Chambliss, W.J. (ed.) *Crime and the Legal Process* New York: McGraw Hill Book Co., 1969.

_____ 'Functional and Conflict Theories of Crime: The Heritage of Emile Durkheim and Karl Marx' in W.J. Chambliss and M. Mankoff (eds.) *Whose Law What Order? A Conflict Approach to Criminology* New York: Wiley, 1976, pp. 1–28.

_____ 'The State and Criminal Law' in Chambliss and Mankoff (eds), 1976, pp. 66–106.

_____ 'On Lawmaking' *British Journal of Law and Society* 6(2), 1979, pp. 149–71.

Chan, J. and G. Zdendowski 'Just Alternatives—Parts I and II' *Australian and New Zealand Journal of Criminology* 19(2) and 19(3), 1986, pp. 67–90, 131–54.

Chappell, D. and P.R. Wilson (eds) *The Australian Criminal Justice System* Sydney: Butterworths, 1977.

Chatterton, M.R. 'Police in Social Control' in J.F.S. King (ed.) *Control Without Custody*? Canberra: Canberra Institute of Criminology, 1976, pp. 104–22.

_____ 'The Supervision of Patrol Work Under the Fixed Points System' in Holdaway (ed.), 1979, pp. 83–101.

Chesler, P. *Women and Madness* London: Allen Lane, 1974.

Chesney-Lind, M. 'Juvenile Delinquency: The Sexualization of Female Crime' *Psychology Today* 8(2), 1974, pp. 43–6.

_____ 'Judicial Paternalism and the Female Status Offender' *Crime and Delinquency* 23(2), 1977, pp. 121–30.

_____ 'Young Women in the Arms of the Law' and 'Chivalry Reexamined: Women and the Criminal Justice System' (Chs. 6 and 7) in L.H. Bowker (ed.) *Women, Crime and the Criminal Justice System* Mass.: Lexington Books, 1978, pp. 171–96, 197–223.

Chodorow, N. *The Reproduction of Mothering* Berkeley: University of California Press, 1978.

Christie, N. 'Law and Medicine: The Case Against Role-Blurring' *Law and Society Review* 5(3), 1971, pp. 357–66.

Cicourel, A.V. *The Social Organization of Juvenile Justice* London: Heinemann, 1976.

Clark, A.L. and J.P. Gibbs 'Social Control: A Reformulation' *Social Problems* 12(4), 1965, pp. 398–415.

Clark, G.L. and M. Dear *State Apparatus: Structures and Language of Legitimacy* Boston: Allen and Unwin, 1984.

Clark, L.N.G. and D. Lewis *Rape: The Price of Coercive Sexuality* Toronto: Women's Press, 1977.

Clarke, D.H. 'Marxism, Justice and the Justice Model' *Contemporary Crises* 2(1), 1978, pp. 27–62.

Clarke, J.N. 'Sexism, Feminism and Medicalism: A Decade Review of Literature on Gender and Illness' *Sociology of Health and Illness* 5(1), 1983, pp. 62–83.

Clegg, S., J. Dow and P. Boreham (eds) *The State, Class and the Recession* London: Croom Helm, 1983.

Cloward, R.A. and F.F. Piven *Poor People's Movements: Why They Succeed, How They Fail* New York: Pantheon, 1977a.

_____ 'The Acquiescence of Social Work' *Society* 4(2), 1977b, pp. 55–63.

Cousins, M. '"Mens Rea": A Note on Sexual Difference, Criminology and the Law' in 4(4), 1979, pp. 651–69.

Cocks, J. 'Wordless Emotions: Some Critical Reflections on Radical Feminism' *Politics and Society* 13(1), 1984, pp. 27–57.

Coe, R.M. *Sociology of Medicine* New York: McGraw Hill, 1970.

Cohen, A.K. 'The Sociology of the Deviant Act: Anomie Theory and Beyond' *American Sociological Review* 30(1), 1965, pp. 5–14.

_____ *Deviance and Control* Englewood Cliffs, N.J.: Prentice Hall, 1966.

Cohen, S. (ed.), *Images of Deviance* Harmondsworth: Penguin, 1971.

_____ *Folk Devils and Moral Panics* St. Albans: Paladin, 1973.

_____ 'The Punitive City: Notes on the Dispersal of Social Control' *Contemporary Crises* 3(4), 1979a, pp. 339–63.

_____ 'Guilt, Justice and Tolerance: Some Old Concepts for a New Criminology' in Downes and Rock (eds), 1979b, pp. 17–51.

_____ 'Footprints on the Sand: A Further Report on Criminology and the Sociology of Deviance in Britain' in Fitzgerald et al. (eds), 1981. pp. 220–47.

_____ 'The Deeper Structures of the Law or "Beware the Rulers Bearing Justice": A Review Essay' *Contemporary Crises* 8(1), 1984, pp. 83–93.

_____ *Visions of Social Control* Cambridge: Polity Press, 1985.

Cohen, S. and A. Scull (eds) *Social Control and the State* Oxford: Blackwell, 1985.
Cohen, S. and J. Young (eds) *The Manufacture of News: Deviance, Social Problems and the Mass Media* London: Constable, 1973.
Colfax, J.D. 'Varieties and Prospects of "Radical Scholarship" in Sociology' in Colfax and Roach (eds), 1971, pp. 81–92.
Colfax, J.D. and Roach, J. (eds) *Radical Sociology* New York: Basic Books, 1971.
Collier, J.F. and M.Z. Rosaldo 'Politics and Gender in Simple Societies' in S.B. Ortner and H. Whitehead (eds) *Sexual Meanings: The Cultural Construction of Gender and Sexuality* Cambridge: Cambridge University Press, 1981, pp. 275–329.
Collison, M. 'Questions of Juvenile Justice' in Carlen and Collison (eds), 1980, pp. 152–77.
Conley, M. 'The "Undeserving" Poor: Welfare and Labour Policy' in Kennedy (ed.), 1982, pp. 281–303.
Connell, R.W. *Which Way is Up? Essays on Sex, Class and Culture* Sydney: Allen and Unwin, 1983.
_____ 'Theorising Gender' *Sociology* 19(2), 1985, pp. 260–72.
Connell, R.W. and T.H. Irving *Class Structure in Australian History: Documents, Narrative and Argument* Melbourne: Longman Cheshire, 1980.
Conrad, P. 'Discovery of Hyperkinesis: Notes on the Medicalization of Deviant Behavior' *Social Problems* 23(1), 1975, pp. 12–21.
_____ 'Types of Medical Social Control' *Sociology of Health and Illness* 1(1), 1979, pp. 1–11.
Conrad, P. and J.W. Schneider *Deviance and Medicalization: From Badness to Sickness* St. Louis: C.V. Mosby, 1980a.
_____ 'Looking at Levels of Medicalization: A Comment on Strong's Critique of the Thesis of Medical Imperialism' *Social Science and Medicine* 14A, 1980b, pp. 75–9.
Cornwell, J. *Hard-Earned Lives* London: Tavistock, 1984.
Corrigan, P. 'The Welfare State as an Arena of Class Struggle' *Marxism Today* 21(3), 1977, pp. 87–93.
Corrigan, P. (ed.), *Capitalism, State Formation and Marxist Theory* London: Quartet Books, 1980.
Corrigan, P. and P. Leonard *Social Work Practice Under Capitalism: A Marxist Approach* London: Macmillan, 1978.
Coser, L.A. 'Some Functions of Deviant Behavior and Normative Flexibility' *American Journal of Sociology* 68(2), 1962, pp. 172–81.
Coser, L.A. and B. Rosenberg (eds) *Sociological Theory: A Book of Readings* New York: Macmillan, 1966.
Cousins, M. '"Mens Rea": A Note on Sexual Difference, Criminology and the Law' in P. Carlen and M. Collison (eds.) 1980, pp. 109–22.
Crawford, R. 'You are Dangerous to Your Health: The Ideology and Politics of Victim-Blaming' *International Journal of Health Services* 7(4), 1977, pp. 663–80.
_____ 'Healthism and the Medicalization of Everyday Life' *International Journal of Health Services* 10(3), 1980, pp. 365–88.
Creed, J. and J. Tomlinson 'The Role of Ideology in Community Work: Contributions from Feminism and the Left' *Australian Journal of Social Issues* 19(4), 1984, pp. 273–83.

Dale, J. and P. Foster *Feminists and State Welfare* London: Routledge and Kegan Paul, 1986.
Daly, M. *Gyn/Ecology: The Metaethics of Radical Feminism* Boston: Beacon Press, 1978.
Daniels, K. (ed.) *So Much Hard Work: Women and Prostitution in Australian History* Sydney: Fontana, 1984.
Daunton-Fear, M.W. 'The Fine as a Criminal Sanction' in D. Chappell and P.R. Wilson (eds) *The Australian Criminal Justice System* Sydney: Butterworths, 1977, pp. 389–411.

Davies, C. 'Organization Theory and the Organization of Health Care: A Comment on the Literature' *Social Science and Medicine* 13A, 1979, pp. 413–22.

Davis, F. 'Uncertainty in Medical Prognosis, Clinical and Functional' in E. Freidson and J. Lorber (eds) *Medical Men and Their Work* Chicago: Aldine-Atherton, 1972, pp. 239–48.

Davis, N.J. *Sociological Constructions of Deviance* Dubuque, Iowa: Wm. C. Brown, 1st Ed. 1975/2nd Ed. 1980.

——— 'Feminism, Deviance and Social Change' in E. Sagarin (ed.) *Deviance and Social Change* Beverly Hills, Sage Publications, 1977, pp. 247–76.

de Espinosa, E.L. 'Social and Legal Order in Sociological Functionalism' *Contemporary Crises* 4(1), 1980, pp. 43–76.

Delmar, R. 'Working Again at Engels "Origins of the Family, Private Property and the State"' in J. Mitchell and A. Oakley (eds) *The Rights and Wrongs of Women* Harmondsworth: Penguin, 1976, pp. 271–87.

de Sousa Santos, B. 'Law and Community: The Changing Nature of State Power in Late Capitalism' *International Journal of the Sociology of Law* 8(4), 1980, pp. 379–97.

Devine, J.A. 'State and State Expenditure: Determinants of Social Investment and Social Consumption: Spending in the Post-War U.S.' *American Sociological Review* 50(2), 1985, pp. 150–65.

Dickey, B. 'Health and the State in Australia, 1788–1977' *Journal of Australian Studies* 2, 1977, pp. 50–63.

——— *No Charity There: A Short History of Social Welfare in Australia* Melbourne: Nelson, 1980.

Dickson, D. T. 'Bureaucracy and Morality: An Organizational Perspective on a Moral Crusade *Social Problems* 16, 1968, pp. 143–56.

Dingwall, R., C. Heath, M. Read and M. Stacey (eds) *Health Care and Health Knowledge* London: Croom Helm, 1977.

Dinitz, S., R.R. Dynes and A.C. Clarke (eds) *Deviance: Studies in the Process of Stigmatization and Societal Reaction* New York, Oxford University Press, 1969.

Ditomaso, N. '"Sociological Reductionism" from Parsons to Althusser: Linking Action and Structure in Social Theory' *American Sociological Review* 47(1), 1982, pp. 14–28.

Ditton, J. *Controlology* London: Macmillan, 1979.

Dobash, R.E. and R.P. Dobash 'Love, Honour and Obey: Institutional Ideologies and the Struggle for Battered Women' *Contemporary Crises* 1, 1977, pp. 403–15.

Dobash, R.P. and R.E. Dobash 'Community Response to Violence Against Wives: Charivari, Abstract Justice and Patriarchy' *Social Problems* 28(5), 1981, pp. 563–81.

Dobash, R.P. and R.E. Dobash and S. Gutteridge *The Imprisonment of Women* Oxford: Basil Blackwell, 1986.

Dohrenwend, B.P. and B.S. Dohrenwend 'Sex Differences and Psychiatric Disorders' *American Journal of Sociology* 81(6), 1976, pp. 1447–54.

Dominelli, L. 'The Power of the Powerless: Prostitution and the Reinforcement of Submissive Feminity' *Sociological Review* 34(1), 1986, pp. 65–92.

Donajgrodzki, A.P. (ed.) *Social Control in Nineteenth Century Britain* London: Croom Helm, 1977.

Donnelly, R. 'Infants and Aboriginal Women in Prison' in Hatty (ed.), 1984, pp. 163–9.

Donnison, J. *Midwives and Medical Men* London: Heinemann, 1977.

Douglas, J.D. 'Deviance and Order in a Pluralistic Society' in J.C. McKinney and E.A. Tiryakian (eds) *Theoretical Sociology: Perspectives and Developments* New York: Appleton Century Crofts, 1970, pp. 367–401.

Douglas, R. 'Case Structure, Participation and Verdict in the Melbourne Magistrates' Courts' *Australian and New Zealand Journal of Criminology* 15(4), 1982, pp. 195–206.

——— 'Pre-Trial Withdrawals: Trial, Bargain, or Pseudo-Bargain?' *Australian and New Zealand Journal of Criminology* 16(4), 1983, pp. 210–23.

Downes, D. and P. Rock 'Social Reaction to Deviance and Its Effects on Crime and Criminal Careers' *British Journal of Sociology* 22(4), 1971, pp. 351–64.

——— (eds) *Deviant Interpretations* Oxford: Martin Robertson, 1979.

Doyal, L. *The Political Economy of Health* London: Pluto Press, 1979.
Dubos, R. *Man, Medicine and Environment* London: Pall Mall Press, 1968.
Durkheim, E. *The Division of Labor in Society* Glencoe: Free Press, 1933.
_____ *Rules of Sociological Method* New York: Free Press, 1938.
Duster, T. *The Legislation of Morality: Law, Drugs and Moral Judgement* New York: Free Press, 1970.
Dworkin, A. *Pornography: Men Possessing Women* London: The Women's Press, 1981.

Eaton, M. *Justice for Women? Family, Court and Social Control* Milton Keynes: Open University Press, 1986.
Edelman, M. 'The Political Language of the Helping Professions' *Politics and Society* 4(3), 1974, pp. 295–310.
Edholm, F., O. Harris and K. Young 'Conceptualising Women' *Critique of Anthropology* 9 and 10, 1977, pp. 101–30.
Edwards, A.R. 'Women, Crime and Criminal Justice: The State of Current Theory and Research in Australia and New Zealand' *Australian and New Zealand Journal of Criminology* 15, 1982, pp. 69–89.
_____ 'Sex Roles: A Problem for Sociology and for Women' *Australian and New Zealand Journal of Sociology* 19(3), 1983, pp. 385–410.
_____ 'Male Violence in Feminist Theory: An Analysis of the Changing Conceptions of Sex/Gender Violence and Male Dominance' in J. Hanmer and M. Maynard (eds) *Women, Violence and Social Control* London: Macmillan, 1987, pp. 13–29.
Edwards Hiller, A. and L. Hancock 'The Processing of Juveniles in Victoria' in S.K. Mukherjee and J.A. Scutt (eds), 1981, pp. 92–126.
Edwards, A.R. and P.R. Wilson (eds) *Social Deviance in Australia* Melbourne: Cheshire, 1975.
Edwards, M. *Financial Arrangements Within Families* Canberra: National Women's Advisory Council, 1981a.
_____ 'Financial Arrangements Within Families: Empirical Results and Tax Implications' *Australian Child and Family Welfare* 6(3), 1981b, pp. 16–19.
Edwards, S.S.M. *Female Sexuality and the Law* Oxford: Martin Robertson, 1981.
_____ *Women on Trial* Manchester: Manchester University Press, 1984.
Egger, G.J. 'Medical Nemesis and Economic Health, or Economic Nemesis and Medical Health: The Modern Dilemma' *Australian Journal of Social Issues* 1978, pp. 287–301.
Eggleston, E. *Fear, Favour and Affection* Canberra: Australian National University, Press 1976.
Ehrenreich, B. and J. Ehrenreich 'Health Care and Social Control' *Social Policy* 5(1), 1974, pp. 26–40.
Ehrenreich, B. and D. English *Complaints and Disorders: The Sexual Politics of Sickness* New York: The Feminist Press, 1973.
_____ *For Her Own Good: 150 Years of the Experts' Advice to Women* New York: Anchor Press/Doubleday, 1978.
Ehrlich, C. 'The Unhappy Marriage of Marxism and Feminism: Can It Be Saved?' in Sargent (ed.), 1981, pp. 109–33.
Eichler, M. *The Double Standard* London: Croom Helm, 1980.
Eisenstein, H. *Contemporary Feminist Thought* Sydney: Allen and Unwin, 1984.
Eisenstein, Z. 'Developing a Theory of Capitalist Patriarchy and Socialist Feminism' in Eisenstein (ed.), 1979, pp. 5–40.
_____ (ed.) *Capitalist Patriarchy and the Case for Socialist Feminism* New York: Monthly Review Press, 1979.
Elliott, G. 'Two Steps Forward Two Steps Back: An Australian Welfare State?' in A. Graycar (ed.) *Perspectives in Australian Social Policy* South Melbourne: Macmillan, 1978, pp. 26–48.
Elshtain, J.B. *Public Man, Private Woman* Oxford: Martin Robertson, 1981.
Elston, M.A. 'Women in the Medical Profession: Whose Problem?' in Stacey et al. (eds), 1977, pp. 115–38.

Emerson, J. 'Behavior in Private Places: Sustaining Definitions of Reality in Gynecological Examinations' in H.P. Dreitzel (ed.) *Recent Sociology No. 2: Patterns of Communicative Behavior* New York: Macmillan, 1970, pp. 73–97.

Encel, S. 'Capitalism, the Middle Classes, and the Welfare State' in E.L. Wheelwright and K. Buckley (eds) *Essays in the Political Economy of Australian Capitalism Vol. 2* Sydney: Australian Book Co., 1978, pp. 148–68.

English, D., A. Hollibaugh and G. Rubin 'Talking Sex: A Conversation on Sexuality and Feminism' *Feminist Review* 11, 1982, pp. 40–52.

Erikson, K.T. *Wayward Puritans: A Study in the Sociology of Deviance* New York: John Wiley, 1966.

Ermann, M.D. and R.J. Lundman 'Deviant Acts by Complex Organizations: Deviance and Social Control at the Organizational Level of Analysis' *Sociological Quarterly* 19, 1978, pp. 55–67.

Evans, R. 'The Hidden Colonists: Deviance and Social Control in Colonial Queensland' in Roe (ed.), 1976, pp. 74–100.

Eyer, J. 'Capitalism, Health and Illness' in McKinlay (ed.), 1984, pp. 23–59.

Fairbairns, Z. 'The Cohabitation Rule—Why It Make Sense' in C. Ungerson (ed.) *Women and Social Policy* London: Macmillan, 1985, pp. 63–74.

Farrington, D.P. and A.M. Morris 'Sex, Sentencing and Reconviction' *British Journal of Criminology* 23(3), 1983, pp. 229–48.

Fee, E. 'Women and Health Care: A Comparison of Theories' *International Journal of Health Services* 5(3), 1975, pp. 397–415.

Feeley, M.M. 'Two Models of the Criminal Justice System: An Organizational Perspective' *Law and Society Review* 7(3), 1973, pp. 407–25.

——— 'The Concept of Laws in Social Science: A Critique and Notes on an Expanded View' *Law and Society Review* 10(4), 1976, pp. 497–523.

Feinman, C. 'Sex Role Stereotypes and Justice for Women' *Crime and Delinquency* 25(1), 1979, pp. 87–94.

Fett, I. 'Australian Medical Graduates in 1972' *Medical Journal of Australia* 1, 1974, pp. 689–98.

——— 'The Future of Women in Australian Medicine' *Medical Journal of Australia* 2, 1976, pp. 33–9.

Field, M.G. 'The Concept of the "Health System" at the Macrosociological Level' *Social Science and Medicine* 7(10), 1973, pp. 763–85.

——— 'The Health System and the Polity: A Contemporary American Dialectic' *Social Science and Medicine* 14A, 1980, pp. 397–413.

Figlio, K. 'The Historiography of Scientific Medicine: An Invitation to the Human Sciences' *Comparative Studies in Society and History* 19, 1977, pp. 262–86.

——— 'Chlorosis and Chronic Disease in Nineteenth Century Britain: The Social Constitution of Somatic Illness in a Capitalist Society' *Social History* 3(2), 1978, pp. 167–97.

Finch, J. and D. Groves (eds) *A Labour of Love: Women, Work and Caring* London: Routledge and Kegan Paul, 1983.

Findlay, M., S.J. Egger and J. Sutton (eds) *Issues in Criminal Justice Administration* Sydney: Allen and Unwin, 1983.

Fine, B. 'Labelling Theory: An Investigation into the Sociological Critique of Deviance' *Economy and Society* 6(2), 1977, pp. 166–93.

Fine, B. et al. (eds) *Capitalism and the Rule of Law: From Deviancy Theory to Marxism* London: Huchinson, 1979.

Firestone, S. *The Dialectic of Sex: The Case for Feminist Revolution* London: Paladin, 1972.

Fisher, S. and S.B. Groce 'Doctor-Patient Negotiation of Cultural Assumptions' *Sociology of Health and Illness* 7(3), 1985, pp. 342–74.

Fitzgerald, M. et al. (eds) *Crime and Society: Readings in History and Theory* London: Routledge and Kegan Paul and Open University, 1981.

Foucault, M. *Madness and Civilization* London: Tavistock, 1967.

______ *The Birth of the Clinic: An Archaeology of Medical Perception* London: Tavistock, 1976.
______ *Discipline and Punish: The Birth of the Prison* Harmondsworth: Penguin, 1977.
______ *The History of Sexuality, Vol. 1* New York: Pantheon, 1978.
Fox, R. 'The Medicalization and Demedicalization of American Society' *Daedalus* 106(3), 1977, pp. 9–22.
Fox, R.C. 'The Education of Medical Uncertainty' *Milbank Memorial Fund Quarterly/ Health and Society* 58(1), 1980, pp. 1–53.
Fox, R.G. and B.M. O'Brien 'Fact Finding for Sentences' in D. Chappell and P.R. Wilson (eds), 1977, pp. 277–315.
Freiberg, A. 'Reward, Law and Power: Toward a Jurisprudence of the Carrot' *Australian and New Zealand Journal of Criminolgy* 19(2), 1986, pp. 91–113.
Freidson, E. *Profession of Medicine: A Study in the Sociology of Applied Knowledge* New York: Dodd Mead and Co., 1970a.
______ *Professional Dominance: The Social Structure of Medical Care* New York: Atherton 1970b.
______ *Doctoring Together* New York: Elsevier, 1975.
______ 'The Futures of Professionalisation' in Stacey et al. (eds), 1977, pp. 14–38.
______ 'The Reorganization of the Medical Profession' *Medical Care Review* 42, 1985, pp. 11–35.
Fry, L.T. and J. Miller 'The Impact of Diversion on Adult Women' in M. Evans (ed.) *Discretion and Control* Beverly Hills, Calif.: Sage Publications, 1978, pp. 107–23.
Fulcher, G. 'Schizophrenia: A Sociologist's View of Psychiatrists' Views' in A. Edwards and P.R. Wilson (eds), 1975, pp. 75–89.

Galanter, M. 'Why the "Haves" Come Out Ahead: Speculations on the Limits of Legal Change' *Law and Society Review* 9(1), 1974, pp. 95–160.
Galliher, J.F. and A. Walker 'The Puzzle of the Social Origins of the Marihuana Tax Act of 1937' *Social Problems* 24(3), 1977, pp. 367–76.
Gamble, A. *An Introduction to Modern Social and Political Thought* London: Macmillan, 1981.
Gandevia, B. 'Medical History in its Australian Environment' *Medical Journal of Australia* 2, 1967, pp. 941–6.
Garland, D. *Punishment and Welfare* Aldershot, Harts.: Gower, 1983.
Garland, D. and P. Young (eds), *The Power to Punish* London: Heinemann, 1983.
Garmarnikow, E. 'Sexual Division of Labour: The Case of Nursing' in Kuhn and Wolpe (eds), 1978, pp. 96–123.
Garton, S. 'The Melancholy Years: Psychiatry in New South Wales, 1900–40' in Kennedy (ed.), 1982, pp. 138–66.
______ 'Bad or Mad? Developments in Incarceration in N.S.W., 1880–1920' in Sydney Labour History Group, 1983, pp. 89–110.
Gelsthorpe, L. 'Towards a Sceptical Look at Sexism' *International Journal of the Sociology of Law* 14(2), 1986, pp. 125–52.
George, C. and P. Wilding *Ideology and Social Welfare* London: Routledge and Kegan Paul, 1976.
Gerson, E.M. 'The Social Character of Illness: Deviance or Politics' *Social Science and Medicine* 10(5), 1976, pp. 219–24.
Gibbs, J.P. 'Conceptions of Deviant Behavior: The Old and the New' *Pacific Sociological Review* 9, 1966, pp. 9–14.
______ 'Social Control, Deterrence, and Perspectives on Social Order' *Social Forces* 56(2), 1977, pp. 408–23.
______ *Norms, Deviance and Social Control: Conceptual Matters* New York: Elsevier, 1981.
______ (ed.) *Social Control* Beverly Hills: Sage Publications, 1982.
Giddens, A. 'Functionalism: Apres La Lutte' *Social Research* 43(2), 1976, pp. 325–66.
______ *Central Problems in Social Theory* London: Macmillan, 1979.
______ *A Contemporary Critique of Historical Materialism* London: Macmillan, 1981.

——— *The Constitution of Society* Cambridge: Polity Press, 1984.

Gill, D.G. and G.W. Horobin 'Doctors, Patients and the States: Relationships and Decision-Making' *Sociological Review* 20(4), 1972, pp. 505–20.

Glasner, A.H. 'Professional Power and State Intervention in Medical Practice' *Australian and New Zealand Journal of Sociology* 15(3), 1979, pp. 20ff.

Goffman, E. *Asylums* New York: Doubleday-Anchor, 1961.

Gold, D.A., C.Y.H. Lo and E.O. Wright 'Recent Developments in Marxist Theories of the Capitalist State' *Monthly Review* 27(5), 1975, pp. 29–43.

Gold, S. 'Equal Protection for Juvenile Girls in Need of Supervision in New York State' *New York Law Forum* 17, 1971, pp. 570–98.

Goldstein, J. 'Police Discretion Not to Invoke the Criminal Process: Low Visibility Decisions in the Administration of Justice' *Yale Law Journal* 69(4), 1960, pp. 543–94.

Gordon, L. *Woman's Body, Woman's Right: A Social History of Birth Control in America* Harmondsworth: Penguin, 1977.

——— 'The Struggle for Reproductive Freedom: Three Stages of Feminism' in Z. Eisenstein (ed.), 1979, pp. 107–32.

Gough, I. 'State Expenditure in Advanced Capitalism' *New Left Review* 92, 1975, pp. 53–92.

——— *The Political Economy of the Welfare State* London: Macmillan, 1979.

Gould, C.C. (ed.) *Beyond Domination: New Perspectives on Women and Philosophy* Totowa, N.J.: Rowman and Allan Held, 1984.

Gould, M. 'The New Sociology' *Signs* 5(3), 1980, pp. 459–67.

Gouldner, A.W. 'The Sociologist as Partisan: Sociology and the Welfare State' *American Sociologist* 3(2), 1968, pp. 103–16.

——— *The Coming Crisis of Western Sociology* London: Heinemann, 1971.

Gove, W.R. 'The Relationship Between Sex Roles, Marital Status and Mental Illness' *Social Forces* 51(1), 1972, pp. 34–44.

——— (ed.) *The Labeling of Deviance* New York: Wiley/Halsted Press, 1975.

——— 'Sex Differences in Mental Illness Among Adult Men and Women: An Evaluation of Four Questions Raised Regarding the Evidence on the Higher Rates of Women' *Social Science and Medicine* 12B, 1978, pp. 187–98.

Gove, W.R. and J.F. Tudor 'Adult Sex Roles and Mental Illness' *American Journal of Sociology* 78(4), 1973, pp. 812–35.

Grabosky, P. *Sydney in Ferment: Crime, Dissent and Oficial Reaction 1788–1973* Canberra: A.N.U. Press, 1977.

Grabosky, P. and J. Braithwaite *Of Manners Gentle* Melbourne: O.U.P., 1986.

Grabosky, P. and C.J. Rizzo 'Dispositional Disparities in Courts of Summary Jurisdiction: The Conviction and Sentencing of Shoplifters in South Australia and New South Wales, 1980' *Australian and New Zealand Journal of Criminology* 16(3), 1983, pp. 146–62.

Graham, H. 'Images of Pregnancy in Ante-Natal Literature' in Dingwall et al. (eds), 1977, pp. 15–37.

——— *Women, Health and the Family* Brighton: Wheatsheaf, 1984.

Graham, H. and A. Oakley 'Competing Ideologies of Reproduction: Medical and Maternal Perspectives on Pregnancy' in Roberts (ed.), 1981, pp. 50–74.

Gramsci, A. *Selections from the Prison Notebooks* London: Lawrence and Wishart, 1971.

Graycar, A. *Welfare Politics in Australia* South Melbourne: Macmillan, 1979.

——— (ed.) *Retreat from the Welfare State* Sydney: Allen and Unwin, 1983.

——— 'Retreat from the Welfare State' in Graycar (ed.), 1983, pp. 1–12.

Greenberg, D.F. (ed.) *Crime and Capitalism: Readings in Marxist Criminology* Palo Alto, Calif.: Mayfield Publishing Co., 1981.

Greenwood, V. 'The Myths of Female Crime' in A. Morris and L. Gelsthorpe (eds.) *Women and Crime*, Cambridge: Cambridge Institute of Criminology, 1981, pp. 73–84.

Greer, A.L. 'Medical Technology and Professional Dominance Theory' *Social Science and Medicine* 18(10), 1984, pp. 809–17.

Griffin, L.J., J.A. Devine and M. Wallace 'On the Economic and Political Determinants

of Welfare Spending in the Post-World War II Era' *Politics and Society* 12(3), 1983, pp. 331–71.
Griffin, S. 'Rape: The All-American Crime' *Ramparts* 1971, pp. 26–35.
Grimes, E.M. and A.T. Turk 'Labelling in Context: Conflict, Power and Self-Definition' in M.D. Krohn and R.L. Akers (eds) *Crime, Law and Sanctions: Theoretical Perspectives* Beverly Hills: Sage Publications, 1978, pp. 39–58.
Grob, G. *Mental Institutions in America: Social Policy to 1875* New York: Free Press, 1973.
Grønberg, K.A. 'Private Welfare in the Welfare State; Recent U.S. Trends' *Social Service Review* 56(1), 1982, pp. 1–26.
Gumprecht, N. 'Women as Employers and Managers in Social Service Agencies' *Australian Social Work* 38(1), 1985, pp. 19–23.
Gusfield, J.R. *Symbolic Crusade* Chicago: University of Illinois Press, 1963.

Habermas, J. 'What Does a Crisis Mean Today? Legitimation Problems in Late Capitalism' *Social Research* 40(4), 1973, pp. 39–64; reprinted 51(1 and 2), 1984.
_____ *Legitimation Crisis* Boston: Beacon Press, 1975.
_____ 'New Social Movements' *Telos* 49, 1981, pp. 33–8.
Hagan, J., J.H. Simpson and A.R. Gillis 'The Sexual Stratification of Social Control: A Gender-Based Perspective on Crime and Delinquency' *British Journal of Sociology* 30(1), 1979, pp. 25–38.
Hall, P., H. Land, R. Parker and A. Webb *Change, Choice and Conflict in Social Policy* London: Heinemann, 1975.
Hall, S. 'Deviance, Politics and the Media' in P. Rock and M. McIntosh (eds) *Deviance and Social Control* London: Tavistock, 1974, pp. 261–305.
_____ 'Nicos Poulantzas: State, Power, Socialism' *New Left Review* 119, 1980, pp. 60–9.
Hall, S. et al. *Policing the Crisis* London: Macmillan, 1978.
Hall, S. and Scraton, P. 'Law, Class and Control' in Fitzgerald et al. (eds), 1981, pp. 460–97.
Hamilton, P. *Talcott Parsons* Chichester: Ellis Horwood and London: Tavistock, 1983.
Hancock, L. 'The Myth That Females are Treated More Leniently than Males in the Juvenile Justice System' *Australian and New Zealand Journal of Sociology* 16(3), 1980, pp. 4–13.
_____ (ed.) *Prisoner and Female: The Double Negative* Melbourne: Victorian Council of Social Service, 1982.
Hancock, L. and M. Chesney-Lind 'Juvenile Justice Legislation and Gender Discrimination' in A. Borowski and J.M. Murray (eds), *Juvenile Delinquency in Australia* North Ryde: Methuen, 1985, pp. 236–52.
Hanks, P. and B. Keon-Cohen (ed.) *Aborigines and the Law* Sydney: Allen and Unwin, 1984.
Hanmer, J. 'Violence and the Social Control of Women' in G. Littlejohn (ed.), 1978, pp. 217–38.
Harding, A. *Who Benefits? The Australian Welfare State and Redistribution* University of N.S.W.: Social Welfare Research Centre Report No. 45, 1984.
Harring, S. L. 'Policing a Class Society: The Expansion of the Urban Police in the Late Nineteenth and Early Twentieth Centuries' in Greenberg (ed.), 1981, pp. 292–313.
Harrison, R. and F. Mort 'Patriarchal Aspects of 19th Century State Formation: Property Relations, Marriage and Divorce, and Sexuality' in Corrigan (ed.), 1980, pp. 79–109.
Hartmann, H.I. 'The Unhappy Marriage of Marxism and Feminism Towards a More Progressive Union' *Capital and Class* 8, 1979, pp. 1–33.
Hartsock, N. 'Feminist Theory and the Development of Revolutionary Strategy' in Z. Eisenstein (ed.), 1979, pp. 56–77.
Hartsock, N.C.M. *Money, Sex and Power: Toward a Feminist Historical Materialism* Boston: Northeastern University Press, 1985.
Hartz-Karp, J. 'Women in Constraints' in S.K. Mukherjee and J.A. Scutt (eds), 1981, pp. 167–95.

Hatty, S.E. (ed.) *Women in the Prison System* Canberra: Australian Institute of Criminology, 1984.
Hawkins, R. and G. Tiedeman *The Creation of Deviance: Interpersonal and Organizational Determinants* Columbus, Ohio: Charles E. Merrill, 1975.
Hay, D. et al. *Albion's Fatal Tree* New York: Pantheon Books, 1975.
Head, B.W. 'Inequality, Welfare and the State: Distribution and Redistribution in Australia' *Australian and New Zealand Journal of Sociology* 16(3), 1980, pp. 44–51.
——— (ed.) *State and Economy in Australia* Melbourne: Oxford University Press, 1983.
——— 'State and Economy: Theories and Problems' in Head (ed.), 1983, pp. 22–54.
Healy, J. 'The Status of Women in the Australian Welfare Industry' *Australian Social Work* 35(3), 1982, pp. 19–26.
Heidensohn, F. 'The Deviance of Women: A Critique and an Enquiry' *British Journal of Sociology* 19(2), 1968, pp. 160–75.
——— *Women and Crime* London: Mcamillan, 1985.
——— 'Models of Justice: Portia or Persephone? Some Thoughts on Equality, Fairness and Gender in the Field of Criminal Justice' *International Journal of the Sociology of Law* 14 (3 and 4), 1986, pp. 287–98.
Held, D. et al. (eds) *States and Societies* Oxford: Martin Robertson and Open University, 1983.
——— 'Introduction: Central Perspectives on the Modern State' in Held et al. (eds), 1983, pp. 1–55.
——— 'Power and Legitimacy in Contemporary Britain' in G. McLennan, D. Held and S. Hall (eds) *State and Society in Contemporary Britain: A Critical Introduction* Cambridge, Polity Press, 1984, pp. 299–369.
Held, D. and J. Krieger 'Accumulation, Legitimation and the State: The Ideas of Claus Offe and Jurgen Habermas' in Held et al. (eds), 1983, pp. 487–97.
Higgins, J. 'Social Control Theories of Social Policy' *Journal of Social Policy* 9(1), 1980, pp. 1–23.
Higgins, W. 'State Welfare and Class Warfare' in G. Duncan (ed.) *Critical Essays in Australian Politics* Melbourne: Edward Arnold, 1978, pp. 135–63.
——— '"To Him That Hath...": The Welfare State' in Kennedy (ed.), 1982, pp. 199–224.
Hills, S.L. *Demystifying Social Deviance* New York: McGraw Hill, 1980.
Hinch, R. 'Marxist Criminology in the 1970s: Clarifying the Clutter' *Crime and Social Justice* 19, 1983, pp. 65–74.
Hirsch, M.F. *Women and Violence* New York: Van Nostrand Reinhold Co., 1981.
Hirst, P.D. 'Marx and Engels on Law, Crime and Morality' in Taylor, Walton and Young (eds), 1975, pp. 203–32 and 328–43.
Hogg, R. 'Perspective on the Criminal Justice System' in Findlay et al. (eds), 1983, pp. 3–19.
Hogg, R. and D. Brown 'Reforming Juvenile Justice: Issues and Prospects' in Borowski and Murray (eds), 1985, pp. 393–412.
Holdaway, S. (ed.) *The British Police* London: Edward Arnold, 1979.
Hollingshead, A.B. 'The Concept of Social Control' *American Sociological Review* 6(2), 1941, pp. 217–24.
Homel, R. 'Sentencing in Magistrates' Courts' in Findlay et al. (eds), 1983, pp. 109–25.
Homer, A.R. 'Women and the Politics of "Psychotherapy"' *Australian Journal of Social Issues* 12(2), 1977, pp. 120–9.
Hood, R. and R. Sparks *Key Issues in Criminology* London: Weidenfeld and Nicolson, 1970.
Hopkins, A. *Crime, Law and Business: The Sociological Sources of Australian Monopoly Law* Canberra: Australian Institute of Criminology, 1978.
Horobin, G. and S. McIntosh 'Responsibility in General Practice' in Stacey et al. (eds), 1977, pp. 88–111.
Horowitz, I.L. and M. Liebowitz 'Social Deviance and Political Marginality: Towards a Redefinition of the Relation Between Sociology and Politics' *Social Problems* 15(3), 1968, pp. 280–96.

Horton, J. 'Order and Conflict Theories of Social Problems as Competing Ideologies' *American Journal of Sociology* 71(6), 1966, pp. 701–13.
Horwitz, A.V. 'Theory and Social Solidarity' in Black (ed.), 1984, pp. 211–25.
Humphries, D. and D.F. Greenberg 'The Dialectics of Crime Control' in Greenberg (ed.), 1981, pp. 209–54.

Idler, E.L. 'Definitions of Health and Illness and Medical Sociology' *Social Science and Medicine* 13A, 1979, pp. 723–31.
Ignatieff, M. *A Just Measure of Pain: The Penitentiary and the Industrial Revolution* New York: Pantheon, 1978.
_____ 'State, Civil Society and Total Institutions: A Critique of Recent Histories of Punishment' in Cohen and Scull (eds), 1985, pp. 75–105.
Iliffe, S. 'A Marxist View of Primary Medical Care' *Marxism Today* 21(3), 1977, pp. 93–6.
Illich, I. *Medical Nemesis: The Expropriation of Health* London: Calder and Boyars, 1975.
Inciardi, J.A. 'Visibility, Societal Reaction, and Criminal Behavior' *Criminology* 10(2), 1972, pp. 217–23.
Ingleby, D. 'Mental Health and Social Order' in Cohen and Scull (eds), 1985, pp. 141–88.
Ingraham, B.L. et al. 'Discretion and Rehabilitation: Fads and Fixtures' in M. Evans (ed.) *Discretion and Control* Beverly Hills, Calif.: Sage Publications, 1978, pp. 89–106.
Isaac, L. and W. Kelly 'Racial Insurgency, the State, and Welfare Expansion: Local and National Level Evidence from the Postwar United States' *American Journal of Sociology* 86(6), 1981, pp. 1311–86.

Jaco, E.G. 'Introduction: Medicine and Behavioral Science' in Jaco (ed.) *Patients, Physicians and Illness* Glencoe: Free Press, 1958, pp. 3–8.
Jaggar, A.M. *Feminist Politics and Human Nature* Brighton: Harvester Press, 1983.
_____ 'Human Biology in Feminist Theory: Sexual Equality Reconsidered' in Gould (ed.), 1984, pp. 21–42.
Jamrozik, A. 'Universality and Selectivity: Social Welfare in a Market Economy' in Graycar (ed.), 1983, pp.171–83.
_____ 'Social Security and the Social Wage: Priorities and Options in Social Policy' in Jamrozik (ed.) *Social Security and Family Welfare: Directions and Options Ahead* University of N.S.W.: Social Welfare Research Centre Report No. 61, 1986, pp. 9–41.
Janowitz, M. 'Sociological Theory and Social Control' *American Journal of Sociology* 81(1), 1975, pp. 82–108.
Jessop, B. 'Recent Theories of the Capitalist State' *Cambridge Journal of Economics* 1, 1977, pp. 353–73.
_____ 'Capitalism and Democracy: The Best Possible Political Shell? in Littlejohn et al. (eds), 1978, pp. 10–51.
_____ *The Capitalist State* Oxford: Martin Robertson, 1982.
Jewson, N.D. 'The Disappearance of the Sick-Man from Medical Cosmology, 1770–1870' *Sociology* 10(2), 1976, pp. 225–44.
Jones, C. *State Social Work and the Working Class* London: Macmillan, 1983.
Jones, C. and T. Novak 'The State and Social Policy' in Corrigan (ed.), 1980, pp. 143–70.
Jones, M.A. *The Australian Welfare State: Growth, Crisis and Change* Sydney: Allen and Unwin, 1980.
_____ *The Australian Welfare State: Growth, Crisis and Change* Sydney: Allen and Unwin, (Rev. Ed.) 1983.
Jordan, B. *Freedom and the Welfare State* London: Routledge and Kegan Paul, 1976.

Kadish, S.H. 'Legal Norm and Discretion in the Police and Sentencing Processes' *Harvard Law Review* 75, 1962, pp. 904–31.
Kahn, A.J. and S.B. Kamerman *Social Services in International Perspective* New Brunswick: Transaction Books, 1980.

Kamerman, S.B. 'The New Mixed Economy of Welfare: Public and Private' *Social Work* 28(1), 1983, pp. 5–10.
_____ 'Policies and Female-Headed Families in Industrialized Countries' *Signs* 10(2), 1984, pp. 249–71.
Keens, C. and B. Cass *Fiscal Welfare: Some Aspects of Australian Tax Policy, Class and Gender Considerations* University of N.S.W.: Social Welfare Research Centre Report No. 24, 1982.
Kelly, J. 'The Doubled Vision of Feminist Theory: A Postscript to the "Women and Power" Conference' *Feminist Sudies* 5(1), 1979, pp. 216–27.
Kennedy, D.A. 'Perceptions of Illness and Healing' *Social Science and Medicine* 7(10), 1973, pp. 787–805.
Kennedy, M.C. 'Beyond Recrimination: Some Neglected Facets of the Theory of Punishment' in Chambliss and Mankoff (eds), 1976, pp. 34–65.
Kennedy, R. 'Charity and Ideology in Colonial Victoria' in Kennedy (ed.), 1982, pp. 51–83.
_____ (ed.) *Australian Welfare History: Critical Essays* Melbourne: Macmillan, 1982.
Kewley, T.H. *Social Security in Australia 1900–72* Sydney: Sydney University Press, (2nd Ed.) 1973.
_____ 'Social Security and Welfare: Legislative and Policy Changes' in Scotton and Ferber (eds), 1978, pp. 137–78.
Kiel, H. 'Women in Social Work: Caretakers or Policy Makers?, *Australian Social Work* 36(2), 1982, pp. 9–14.
King, J.F.S. (ed.) *Control Without Custody*? Cambridge: Cambridge Institute of Criminology, 1976.
Kirby, M.D. 'Controls Over Investigation of Offences and Pre-Trial Treatment of Suspects: Criminal Investigation and the Rule of Law' *Australian Law Journal* 53, 1979, pp. 626–47.
Kitsuse, J.I. 'Societal Reaction to Deviant Behavior: Problems of Theory and Method' *Social Problems* 9, 1962, pp. 247–56.
_____ 'Coming Out All Over: Deviants and the Politics of Social Problems' *Social Problems* 28(1), 1980, pp. 1–13,
Kitsuse, J.I. And Cicourel, A.V. 'A Note on the Uses of Official Statistics' *Social Problems* 11(2), 1963, pp. 131–9.
Kittrie, N.N. *The Right to be Different* Baltimore: John Hopkins Press, 1971.
Klapp, O. *Heroes, Villains and Fools* Englewood Cliffs, N.J.: Prentice-Hall, 1962.
Klein, D. 'The Etiology of Female Crime: A Review of the Literature' *Issues in Criminology* 8(2), 1973, pp. 3–30.
_____ 'Can This Marriage be Saved? Battery and Sheltering' *Crime and Social Justice* 12, 1979, pp. 19–33.
_____ 'Violence Against Women: Some Considerations Regarding Its Causes and its Elimination' *Crime and Delinquency* 27(1), 1981, pp. 64–80.
Klein, D. and J. Kress 'Any Woman's Blues: A Critical Overview of Women, Crime and the Criminal Justice System' *Crime and Social Justice* 5, 1976, pp. 34–49.
Klein, R. 'The Welfare State: A Self-Inflicted Crisis?' *Political Quarterly* 51(1), 1980, pp. 24–34.
Kleinman, A.M. 'Medicine's Symbolic Reality: On a Central Problem in the Philosophy of Medicine' *Inquiry* 16, 1973, pp. 206–13.
Klerman, G.L. 'Mental Illness, the Medical Model and Psychiatry' *Journal of Medicine and Philosophy* 2(3), 1977, pp. 220–43.
Krause, E.A. *Power and Illness: The Political Sociology of Health and Medical Care* New York: Elsevier, 1977.
Kravetz, D. 'Sexism in a Woman's Profession' *Social Work* 21(6), 1976, pp. 421–6.
Kress, J. 'Bourgeois Morality and the Administration of Justice' *Crime and Social Justice* 12, 1979, pp. 44–50.
Krohn, M.D. and R.L. Akers (eds) *Crime, Law and Sanctions: Theoretical Perspectives* Beverly Hills: Sage Publications, 1978.

Kruttschnitt, C. 'Women, Crime and Dependency' *Criminology* 19(4), 1982, pp. 495–513.
______ 'The Unresolved Controversy' *Research in Crime and Delinquency* 21(3), 1984, pp. 213–32.
Kruttschnitt, C. and D.E. Green 'The Sex-Sanctioning Issue: Is it History?' *American Sociological Review* 49(4), 1984, pp. 541–51.
Krygier, M. 'Anthropological Approaches' in E. Kamenka and A. Tay (eds) *Law and Social Control* London: Edward Arnold, 1980, pp. 27–59.
Kuhn, A. and Wolpe, A.M. (eds) *Feminism and Materialism* London: Routledge and Kegan Paul, 1978.

LaFave, W.R. 'The Police and the Non-enforcement of the Law, Parts I and II' *Wisconsin Law Review* No. 1 and 2, 1962, pp. 104–37, 179–239.
Land, H. 'Women: Supporters or Supported?' in D.L. Barker and S. Allen (eds) *Sexual Divisions and Society: Process and Change* London: Tavistock, 1976, pp. 108–32.
______ 'Who Cares for the Family?' *Journal of Social Policy* 7, 1978, pp. 257–84.
______ 'Who Still Cares for the Family? Recent Developments in Income Maintenance, Taxation and Family Law' in J. Lewis (ed.) 1983, pp. 64–83.
Lane, W.B. 'Fair Trial and the Adversary System: Withholding of Exculpatory Evidence by Prosecutors' in Basten et al. (eds), 1982, pp. 174–92.
Laurie, P. 'Negotiations Between the Defendant and the Police' in Baldwin and Bottomley (eds), 1978, pp. 91–4.
Lea, J. 'Discipline and Capitalist Development' in Fine et al. (eds), 1979, pp. 76–89.
Leifer, R. *In the Name of Mental Health* New York: Science House, 1969.
______ 'The Medical Model as Ideology' *International Journal of Psychiatry* 9, 1970/1, pp. 13–21.
Lemert, E.M. 'The Folkways and Social Control' *American Sociological Review* 7(3), 1942, pp. 394–9.
______ *Social Pathology* New York: McGraw Hill, 1951.
______ *Human Deviance, Social Problems, and Social Control* Englewood Cliffs, N.J.: Prentice Hall, 1967.
Lennane, K.J. and R.J. Lennane 'Alleged Psychogenic Disorders in Women: A Possible Manifestation of Sexual Prejudice' *The New England Journal of Medicine* 288(6), 1973, pp. 288–92.
Leonard, E.B. *Women, Crime and Society: A Critique of Theoretical Criminology* New York: Longman, 1982.
Levine, S.V., L.E. Kamin and E.L. Levine 'Sexism and Psychiatry' *American Journal of Orthopsychiatry* 44(3), 1974, pp. 327–36.
Lewis, J. 'Dealing with Dependency: State Practices and Social Realities 1870–1945' in J. Lewis (ed.) *Women's Welfare, Women's Rights* London: Croom Helm, 1983.
Liazos, A. 'The Poverty of the Sociology of Deviance: Nuts, Sluts and Preverts' *Social Problems* 20(1), 1972, pp. 103–20.
______ 'Class Oppression: The Functions of Juvenile Justice' *The Insurgent Sociologist* 5(1), 1974, pp. 2–24.
Lindberg, L.N. et al. (eds) *Stress and Contradiction in Modern Capitalism* Lexington, Mass.: D.C. Heath and Co., 1975.
Lindesmith, A.R. *The Addict and the Law* Bloomington: Indiana University Press, 1965.
Liska, A.E. *Perspectives on Deviance* Englewood Cliffs, N.J.: Prentice Hall, 1981.
Little, C.B.*Understanding Deviance and Social Control: Theory, Research and Social Policy* Hasca, Illinois: F.E. Peacock, 1983.
Littlejohn, G. et al. (eds) *Power and the State* London: Croom Helm, 1978.
Littlejohn, G. 'Introduction' in Littlejohn et al. (eds), 1978, p. 9.
Lloyd, G. *The Man of Reason: 'Male' and 'Female' in Western Philosophy* London: Methuen, 1984.
Loewenberg, F.M. 'The Destigmatization of Public Dependency' *Social Service Review* 55(3), 1981, pp. 434–52.

London Edinburgh Weekend Return Group *In and Against the State* London: Pluto Press, 1980.

Lorber, J. 'Women and Medical Sociology: Invisible Professionals and Ubiquitous Patients' in Millman and Moss Kanter (eds), 1975, pp. 75–105.

—— *Women Physicians: Careers, Status and Power* London: Tavistock, 1984.

Louthan, W.C. 'Politics of Discretionary Justice' in C.F. Pinkele and W.C. Louthan (eds.), *Discretion, Justice and Democracy* Ames: Iowa State University Press, 1985, pp. 13–18.

Low, C. 'The Sociology of Criminal Justice: Progress and Prospects' in Baldwin and Bottomley (eds), 1978, pp. 7–22.

Lukes, S. and A. Scull (eds) *Durkheim and the Law* Oxford: Martin Robertson, 1983.

McBarnet, D.J. 'False Dichotomies in Criminal Justice Research' in Baldwin and Bottomley (eds), 1978, pp. 23–34.

—— 'Arrest: The Legal Context of Policing' in Holdaway (ed.), 1979, pp. 24–40.

—— *Conviction: Law, the State and the Construction of Justice* London: Macmillan, 1981.

—— 'Law and Capital: The Role of Legal Form and Legal Actors' *International Journal of the Sociology of Law* 12(3), 1984, pp. 231–8.

McCaughey, J., S. Shaver, H. Ferber et al. *Who Cares*? Melbourne: Sun Books, 1977.

McConville, M. and J. Baldwin *Courts, Prosecution, and Conviction* Oxford: Clarendon Press, 1981.

MacCormack, C.P. and Strathern, M. (eds) *Nature, Culture and Gender* Cambridge: Cambridge University Press, 1980.

McDonald, D.J. 'The Australian Soldiers' Repatriation Fund: An Experiment in Social Legislation' in Roe (ed.), 1976, pp. 101–12.

MacDonald, M. 'Women and Madness in Tudor and Stuart England' *Social Research* 53(2), 1986, pp. 261–81.

McFadden, M. 'Anatomy of Difference: Toward a Classification of Feminist Theory' *Womens's Studies International Forum* 7(6), 1984, pp. 495–504.

McInolty, J. and H. Radi (eds) *In Pursuit of Justice: Australian Women and the Law 1788–1979* Sydney: Hale and Iremonger, 1979.

McIntosh, M. 'The Welfare State and the Needs of the Dependent Family' in S. Burman (ed.) *Fit Work for Women* London: Croom Helm, 1977, pp. 153–72.

—— 'The State and the Oppression of Women' in A. Kuhn and A.M. Wolpe (eds) *Feminism and Materialism* London: Routledge and Kegan Paul, 1978, pp. 254–89.

—— 'Feminism and Social Policy' *Critical Social Policy* 1, 1981, pp. 32–42.

—— 'The Family, Regulation and the Public Sphere' in G. McLennan, D. Held and S. Hall (eds) *State and Society in Contemporary Britain: A Critical Introduction* Cambridge: Polity Press, 1984, pp. 204–40.

MacIntyre, S. *Single and Pregnant* New York: Prodist, 1977.

McKeown, T. 'A Sociological Approach to the History of Medicine' *Medical History* XIV, 1970, pp. 342–51.

—— *The Role of Medicine—Dream, Mirage or Nemesis*? London: Nuffield Provincial Hospital Trust, 1976.

McKinlay, J.B. 'The Business of Good Doctoring or Doctoring as Good Business: Reflections on Freidson's View of the Medical Game' *International Journal of Health Services* 7(3), 1977, pp. 459–83.

—— (ed.) *Issues in the Political Economy of Health Care* New York: Tavistock, 1984.

McKinlay, J.B. and J. Arches 'Towards the Proletarianization of Physicians' *International Journal of Health Services* 15(2), 1985; pp. 161–95.

McKinlay, J.B. and S.M. McKinlay 'The Questionable Contribution of Medical Measures to the Decline of Mortality in the United States in the Twentieth Century' *Milbank Memorial Fund Quarterly/Health and Society* 55, 1977, pp. 405–28.

MacKinnon, C.A. 'Feminism, Marxism, Method and the State: An Agenda for Theory' *Signs* 7(3), 1982, pp. 515–54.

_____ 'Feminism, Marxism, Method, and the State: Towards Feminist Jurisprudence' *Signs* 8(4), 1983, pp. 635–58.
McLennan, G. 'The Contours of British Politics: Representative Democracy and Social Class' in McLennan et al. (eds), 1984, pp. 241–73.
McLennan, G., D. Held and S. Hall (eds) *State and Society in Contemporary Britain: A Critical Introduction* Cambridge: Polity Press, 1984.
McLeod, E. *Women Working: Prostitution Now* London: Croom Helm, 1982.
Manders, D. 'Labelling Theory and Social Reality: A Marxist Critique' *The Insurgent Sociologist* 6(1), 1975, pp. 53–66.
Manning, P.K. 'Deviance and Dogma' *British Journal of Criminolgy* 15(1), 1975, pp. 1–20.
_____ *The Sociology of Mental Health and Illness* Indianapolis: Bobbs Merrill, 1976.
_____ 'The Social Control of Police Work' in Holdaway (ed.), 1979, pp. 41–65.
March, A. 'Female Invisibility in Androcentric Sociology Theory' *The Insurgent Sociologist* 11(2), 1982, pp. 99–107.
Marchant, H. and B. Wearing (eds) *Gender Reclaimed: Women in Social Work* Sydney: Allen and Unwin, 1986.
Mason, J., J.S. Wodarski and T.M.J. Parham 'Work and Welfare: A Reevaluation of A.F.D.C.' *Social Work* 30(3), 1985, pp. 197–203.
Matthews, J.J. *Good and Mad Women* Sydney: Allen and Unwin, 1984.
Matthews, R. '"Decarceration" and the Fiscal Crisis' in Fine et al. (eds), 1979, pp. 100–117.
Matza, D. *Becoming Deviant* Englewood Cliffs, N.J.: Prentice-Hall, 1969.
_____ 'Poverty and Disrepute' in R.K. Merton and R. Nisbet (eds) *Contemporary Social Problems* (3rd Ed.) New York: Harcourt Brace Johanovich, 1971, pp. 601–56.
Mayer, J.A. 'Notes Towards a Working Definition of Social Control in Historical Analysis' in Cohen and Scull (eds), 1985, pp. 17–38.
Mechanic, D. *Medical Sociology* New York: Free Press, (1st Ed.) 1968/(2nd Ed.) 1978.
_____ 'The Growth of Medical Technology and Buraucracy: The Implications for Medical Care' *Milbank Memorial Fund Quarterly/Health and Society* 55, 1977, pp. 61–78.
_____ 'Sex, Illness, Illness Behavior, and the Use of Health Services' *Social Science and Medicine* 12B, 1978, pp. 207–14.
Melossi, D. 'Institutions of Social Control and Capitalist Organization of Work' in Fine et al. (eds), 1979, pp. 90–99.
_____ 'Strategies of Social Control in Capitalism: A Comment on Recent Work' *Contemporary Crises* 4(4), 1980, pp. 381–402.
_____ 'Overcoming the Crisis in Critical Criminology: Towards a Grounded Labeling Theory' *Criminology* 23(2), 1985, pp. 193–208.
Melossi, D. and Pavarini, M. *The Prison and the Factory System: Origins of the Penitentiary System* London: Macmillan, 1981.
Mendelsohn, R. *The Condition of the People: Social Welfare in Australia 1900–75* Sydney: Allen and Unwin, 1979.
_____ *Fair Go: Welfare Issues in Australia* Ringwood: Penguin, 1982.
Merton, R.K. *Social Theory and Social Structure* New York: Free Press, (Rev. Ed.) 1957.
Michalowski, R.J. *Order, Law and Crime: Introduction to Critical Criminology* Glenview, Illinois: Scott, Foresman, 1981.
_____ 'Crime Control in the 1980s: A Progressive Agenda' *Crime and Social Justice* 19, 1983, pp. 13–23.
Michalowski, R.J. and E.W. Bohlander 'Repression and Criminal Justice in Capitalist America' *Sociological Inquiry* 46(2), 1976, pp. 95–106.
Miliband, R. *Class Power and State Power* London: Verso, 1983.
_____ 'Poulantzas and the Capitalist State' *New Left Review 82*, 1973, pp. 83–92.
Millett, K. *Sexual Politics* London: Abacus, 1972.
Millman, M. 'She Did It All for Love: A Feminist View of the Sociology of Deviance' in M. Millman and R. Moss Kanter (eds), 1975, pp. 251–79.

Millman, M. and R. Moss Kanter (eds) *Another Voice* New York: Anchor Books, 1975.

Milne, T. 'Aborigines and the Criminal Justice System' in Findlay et al. (eds), 1983, pp. 184–99.

Minson, J. 'Strategies for Socialists? Foucault's Conception of Power' *Economy and Society* 9(1), 1980, pp. 1–43.

Mishra, R. *Society and Social Policy* London: Macmillan, (2nd Edn.) 1981.

______ *The Welfare State in Crisis* Brighton: Wheatsheaf, 1984.

Mitchell, J. *Women's Estate* Harmondsworth: Penguin, 1971.

______ *Psychoanalysis and Feminism* Harmondsworth: Penguin, 1975.

Molyneux, M. 'Beyond the Domestic Labour Debate' *New Left Review* 116, 1979, pp. 3–27.

Montague, M. and J. Stephens *Paying the Price for Sugar and Spice: A Study of Women's Pathways into Social Security Reciprocity* Canberra: Australian Government Printing Service, 1985.

Morris, A. 'Juvenile Justice: Where Next?' in Baldwin and Bottomley (eds), 1978, pp. 252–67.

Morris, A. et al. *Justice for Children* London: Macmillan, 1981.

Moulton, J. and F. Rainone 'Women's Work and Sex Roles' in Gould (ed.), 1984, pp. 189–203.

Mowbray, M. and L. Bryson 'Women Really Care' *Australian Journal of Social Issues* 9(4), 1984, pp. 261–72.

Mukherjee, S.K. and R.W. Fitzgerald 'The Myth of Rising Female Crime' in Mukherjee and Scutt (eds), 1981, pp. 127–66.

Mukherjee, S.K. and J.A. Scutt (eds) *Women and Crime* Sydney: Allen and Unwin, 1981.

Muncie, J. and M. Fitzgerald 'Humanising the Deviant: Affinity and Affiliation Theories' in Fitzgerald et al. (eds), 1981, pp. 403–28.

Muraskin, W.A. 'The Social-Control Theory in American History: A Critique' *Journal of Social History* IX, 1975–6, pp. 559–69.

Nagel, I. 'Sex Differences in the Processing of Criminal Defendants' in A. Morris and L. Gelsthorpe (eds) *Women and Crime* Cambridge: Cambridge Institute of Criminology, 1981, pp. 104–22.

Nagel, S.S. and L.J. Weitzman 'Women as Litigants' *The Hastings Law Journal* 23, 1971, pp. 171–98.

Najman, J.M. et al. 'Patterns of Morbidity, Health Care Utilisation and Socio-Economic Status in Brisbane' *Australian and New Zealand Journal of Sociology* 15(3), 1979, pp. 949–58.

Najman, J.M. and J.S. Western 'A Comparative Analysis of Australian Health Policy in the 1970s' *Social Science and Medicine* 18(11), 1984, pp. 949–58.

Nathanson, C.A. 'Illness and the Feminine Role: A Theoretical Review' *Social Science and Medicine* 9(2), 1975, pp. 57–62.

______ 'Social Roles and Health Status Among Women: The Significance of Employment' *Social Science and Medicine* 14A, 1980, pp. 463–71.

National Deviancy Conference (ed.) *Permissiveness and Control: The Fate of the Sixties Legislation* London: Macmillan, 1980.

Navarro, V. *Medicine Under Capitalism* New York: Prodist, 1976.

______ 'Social Class, Political Power and the State and Their Implications in Medicine' *International Journal of Health Services* 7(2), 1977, pp. 255–92.

______ 'Work, Ideology and Science: The Case of Medicine' *International Journal of Health Services* 10(4), 1980, pp. 523–50

______ 'Radicalism, Marxism and Medicine' *International Journal of Health Services* 13(2), 1983, pp. 179–202.

______ 'U.S. Marxist Scholarship in the Analysis of Health and Medicine' *International Journal of Health Services* 15(4), 1985, pp. 525–45.

______ *Crisis Health and Medicine: A Social Critique* New York: Tavistock, 1986.

Neave Report *Final Report of the Inquiry into Prostitution* Melbourne: Government Printer, 1985.
Nelson, B.J. 'Women's Poverty and Women's Citizenship: Some Political Consequences of Economic Marginality' *Signs* 10(2), 1984, pp. 209–31.
Newman, D.J. 'Pleading Guilty for Consideration: A Study of Bargain Justice' *Journal of Criminal Law, Criminology and Police Science* 46, 1956, pp. 780–95.
Newman, G. *Comparative Deviance: Perception and Law in Six Cultures* New York: Elsevier, 1976.

Oakley, A. *The Sociology of Housework* Oxford: Martin Robertson, 1974.
_____ *Subject Women* Oxford: Martin Robertson, 1981.
_____ *The Captured Womb* Oxford: Basil Blackwell, 1984.
O'Brien, M. *The Politics of Reproduction* London: Routledge and Kegan Paul, 1981.
O'Connor, J. *The Fiscal Crisis of the State* New York: St. Martin's Press, 1973.
_____ 'The Fiscal Crisis of the State Revisited: A Look at Economic Crisis and Reagan's Budget Today' (Working Paper of the) *Kapitalistate* 9, 1981, pp. 41–61.
O'Connor, K. 'Controlling Prosecutions' in Basten et al. (eds), 1982, pp. 151–72.
O'Donovan, K. 'The Male Appendage-Legal Definitions of Women' in S. Burman (ed.) *Fit Work For Women* London: Croom Helm, 1979, pp. 134–52.
_____ *Sexual Divisions in Law* London: Weidenfeld and Nicolson, 1985.
Offe, C. 'Advanced Capitalism and the Welfare State' *Politics and Society* 2(4), 1972, pp. 479–88.
_____ 'The Theory of the Capitalist State and the Problem of Policy Formation' in Lindberg et al. (eds), 1975, pp.125–44.
_____ 'Some Contradictions of the Modern Welfare State' *Critical Social Policy* 2(2), 1982, pp. 7–16.
_____ 'Competitive Party Democracy and the Keynesian Welfare State: Some Reflections on Their Historical Limits' in Clegg, Dow and Boreham (eds), 1983, pp. 51–71.
_____ *Contradictions of the Welfare State* London: Hutchinson, 1984.
O'Malley, P. *Law, Capitalism and Democracy* Sydney: Allen and Unwin, 1983.
Orcutt, J.D. *Analyzing Deviance* Homewood, Illinois: Dorsey Press, 1983.
Ortner, S.B. 'Is Female to Male as Nature is to Culture?' in Rosaldo and Lamphere (eds), 1972, pp. 67–87.
Ozonoff, V.V. and D. Ozonoff 'Steps Toward a Radical Analysis of Health Care: Problems and Prospects' *International Journal of Health Services* 5(2), 1975, pp. 299–314.

Packer, H.L. *The Limits of the Criminal Sanction* Stanford: Stanford University Press, 1968.
Parry, N. and J. Parry *The Rise of the Medical Profession* London: Croom Helm, 1976.
Parsons, T. *The Social System* London: Routledge and Kegan Paul, 1951.
_____ 'Definitions of Health and Illness in the Light of American Values and Social Structure' in Jaco (ed.), 1958, pp. 165–87.
_____ 'The Law and Social Control' in W.M. Evan (ed.) *Law and Society* Free Press of Glencoe, 1962, pp. 56–72.
Pashukanis, E. *Law and Marxism: A General Theory* London: Ink Links, 1978.
Pearce, D. 'The Feminization of Poverty: Women, Work and Welfare' *Urban and Social Change Review* 11(1 and 2), 1978, pp. 28–36.
Pearce, F. *Crimes of the Powerful: Marxism, Crime and Deviance* London: Pluto Press, 1976.
Pearson, G. *The Deviant Imagination: Psychiatry, Social Work and Social Change* London: Macmillan,1975.
_____ 'Women Defendants in Magistrates' Courts' *British Journal of Law and Society* 3(2), 1976, pp. 265–73.
Pease, K., J. Ireson and J. Thorpe 'Modified Crime Indices for Eight Countries' *Journal of Criminal Law Criminology and Police Science* 66(2), 1975, pp. 209–14.
Pemberton, A. 'Doing Something About Nothing : A Note on the Australian Government's Response to Dole Fraud' *Australian and New Zealand Journal of Sociology* 16(3), 1980, pp. 72–6.

Pemberton, A.G. and R.G. Locke 'Towards a Radical Critique of Social Work and Welfare Ideology' *Australian Journal of Social Issues* 6(2), 1971, pp. 95–107.

Penfold, S.P. and G.A. Walker *Women and the Psychiatric Paradox* London: Eden Press, 1983.

Person, E.S. 'Sexuality as the Mainstay of Identity: Psychoanalytic Perspectives' *Signs* 5(4), 1980, pp. 605–30.

Petchesky, R.P. *Abortion and Woman's Choice* London: Verso, 1986.

Peterson, M.J. *The Medical Profession in Mid-Victorian London* Berkeley: University of California Press, 1978.

Peterson, S.R. 'Coercion and Rape: The State as a Male Protection Racket' in M. Vetterling-Braggin et al. (eds) *Feminism and Philosophy* Totowa, N.J.: Rowman and Littlefield, 1977, pp. 36–71.

Petrunik, M. 'The Rise and Fall of "Labelling Theory": The Construction and Destruction of a Sociological Strawman' *Canadian Journal of Sociology* 5(3), 1980, pp. 213–30.

Pfohl, S.J. 'Labeling Criminals' in H.L. Ross (ed.) *Law and Deviance* 1981, pp. 65–97.

_____ *Images of Deviance and Social Control: A Sociological History* New York: McGraw Hill, 1985.

Philips, D. '"A Just Measure of Crime, Authority, Hunters and Blue Locusts": The "Revisionist" Social History of Crime and the Law in Britain, 1780–1850' in Cohen and Scull (eds), 1985, pp. 50–74.

Phillips, D.A. and L.B. Defleur 'Gender Ascription and the Stereotyping of Deviants' *Criminology* 20(3 and 4), 1982, pp. 431–48.

Pierson, C. 'New Theories of State and Civil Society: Recent Developments in Post-Marxist Analysis of the State' *Sociology* 18(4), 1984, pp. 562–71.

Piliavin, I. and S. Briar 'Police Encounters with Juveniles' *American Journal of Sociology* 69, 1964, pp. 206–14.

Pinker, R. *Social Theory and Social Policy* London: Heinemann, 1971.

_____ 'Social Policy and Social Justice' *Journal of Social Policy* 3(1), 1974, pp. 1–19.

_____ *The Idea of Social Welfare* London: Heinemann, 1979.

Pitts, J.R. 'Social Control' *International Encyclopaedia of Social Sciences*, Vol. 14 New York, Macmillan and Free Press, 1968, pp. 381–402.

Piven, F.F. 'Deviant Behavior and the Remaking of the World' *Social Problems* 28(5), 1981, pp. 489–508.

Piven, F.F. and R.A. Cloward *Regulating the Poor: the Functions of Public Welfare* London: Tavistock, 1972.

Platt, A.M. *The Child Savers: The Invention of Delinquency* Chicago: University of Chicago Press, 1969.

_____ 'The Triumph of Benevolence: The Origins of the Juvenile Justice System in the United States' in Quinney (ed.), 1974, pp. 356–89.

Plaza, M. 'Our Damages and Their Compensation: Rape: The Will Not to Know of Michel Foucault' *Feminist Issues* 1(3), 1981, pp. 25–6.

Plummer, K. 'Misunderstanding Labelling Perspectives' in Downes and Rock (eds), 1979, pp. 85–121.

Pollitt, C. 'The State and Health Care' in McClennan et al. (eds), 1984, pp. 119–49.

Posner, J. 'The Stigma of Excellence: On Being Just Right' *Sociological Inquiry* 46(2), 1976, pp. 141–4.

Posner, T. 'Magical Elements in Orthodox Medicine' in Dingwall et al. (eds), 1977, pp. 142–58.

Poulantzas, N. *Political Power and Social Classes* London: New Left Books, 1973.

Poulantzas, N. 'The Capitalist state: A Reply to Miliband and Laclau' *New Left Review* 95, 1976, pp. 63–83.

_____ *State, Power, Socialism* London: New Left Books, 1978.

Powles, J. 'On the Limitations of Modern Medicine' *Social Science and Medicine* 1, 1973, pp. 1–30.

Quinney, R. 'Is Criminal Behaviour Deviant Behaviour?' *British Journal of Criminology* 5(2), 1965, pp. 132–42.

_____ *The Social Reality of Crime* Boston: Little, Brown and Co., 1970.
_____ (ed.) *Criminal Justice in America* Boston: Little Brown and Co., 1974.
_____ *Class, State and Crime* New York: David McKay Co., 1977.

Rafter, N.H. 'Chastizing the Unchaste: Social Control Functions of a Women's Reformatory, 1894–1931' in Cohen and Scull (eds), 1985, pp. 288–311.
Rafter, N.H. and E.M. Natalizia 'Marxist Feminism: Implications for Criminal Justice' *Crime and Delinquency* 27(1), 1981, pp. 81–98.
Rafter, N.H. and E. Stanko (eds) *Judge, Lawyer, Victim, Thief: Women, Gender Roles and Criminal Justice* Boston: Northeastern University Press, 1982.
Rains, P. 'Imputations of Deviance: A Retrospective Essay on the Labeling Perspective' *Social Problems* 23(1), 1975, pp. 1–11.
Ratner, R.S. and J.L. McMullan 'Social Control and the Rise of the "Exceptional State" in Britain, the United States, and Canada' *Crime and Social Justice* 19, 1983, pp. 31–43.
Reamer, F.G. 'The Free-Will Determinism Debate and Social Work' *Social Service Review* 57(4), 1983, pp. 626–44.
Reidy, A. 'Marxist Functionalism in Medicine: A Critique of the Work of Vicente Navarro on Health and Medicine' *Social Science and Medicine* 19(9), 1984, pp. 897–910.
Reiger, K. *The Disenchantment of the Home: Modernizing the Australian Family 1880–1940* Melbourne: Oxford University Press, 1985.
Renaud, M. 'On the Structural Constraints to State Intervention in Health' *International Journal of Health Services* 5(4), 1975, pp. 559–71.
Renner, K. *The Institutions of Private Law and Their Social Functions* London: Routledge and Kegan Paul, 1949.
Rein, M. *Social Policy: Issues of Choice and Change* New York: Random House, 1970.
_____ 'Private Provision of Welfare' in R.F. Henderson (ed.) *The Welfare Stakes: Strategies for Australian Social Policy* Melbourne: University of Melbourne Institute of Applied Economic and Social Research, 1981, pp. 9–37.
Rein, M. and L. Rainwater 'Patterns of Welfare Use' *Social Service Review* 52(4), 1978, pp. 512–34.
Rheinstein, M. (ed.) *Max Weber on Law in Economy and Society* New York: Simon and Schuster, 1954.
Riback, L. 'Juvenile Delinquency Laws: Juvenile Women and the Double Standard of Morality' *University of California Los Angeles Law Review* 19, 1971, pp. 313–42.
Rich, A. *On Lies, Secrets and Silence* New York: Norton, 1979.
_____ 'Compulsory Heterosexuality and Lesbian Existence' *Signs* 5(4), 1980, pp. 631–60.
Richards, P. 'State Formation and Class Struggle 1832–48' in Corrigan (ed.), 1980, pp. 49–78.
Roberts, H. (ed.) *Women, Health and Reproduction* London: Routledge and Kegan Paul, 1981.
_____ *The Patient Patients* London: Pandora, 1985.
Robinson, P. 'The First Forty Years' in McInolty and Radi (eds), 1979, pp. 1–16.
Robson, W.A *Welfare State and Welfare Strategy: Illusion and Reality* London: Allen and Unwin, 1976.
Roby, P.A. 'Politics and Criminal Law: Revision of the New York State Penal Law on Prostitution' *Social Problems* 17, 1969, pp. 83–109.
Rochefort, D.A. 'Progressive and Social Control Perspectives on Social Welfare' *Social Service Review* 55(4), 1981, pp. 568–92.
Rock, P. 'Phenomenalism and Essentialism in the Sociology of Deviance' *Sociology* 7(1), 1973a, pp. 17–29.
_____ *Deviant Behaviour* London: Hutchinson, 1973b.
_____ 'Another Common-Sense Conception of Deviancy' *Sociology* 13(1), 1979, pp. 75–88.
_____ 'Law, Order and Power in Late Seventeenth—and Early Eighteenth-Century England' in Cohen and Scull (eds), 1985, pp. 191–221.

Rodberg, L. and G. Stevenson 'The Health Care Industry in Advanced Capitalism' *Review of Radical Political Economics* 9(1), 1977, pp. 104–15.

Roe, J. 'The End is Where We Start From: Women and Welfare Since 1901' in Baldock and Cass (eds), 1983, pp. 1–19.

______ (ed.) *Social Policy in Australia: Some Perspectives 1901–75* Stanmore, N.S.W.: Cassell, 1976.

Rogers, K.O. '"For Her Protection": Conditions of Incarceration for Female Juvenile Offenders in the State of Connecticut' *Law and Society Review* 7(2), 1972, pp. 223–46.

Rogers, S.C. 'Woman's Place: A Critical Review of Anthropological Theory' *Comparative Studies in Society and History* 20(1), 1978, pp. 123–62.

Ronalds, C. et. al. 'Policing Aborigines' in Findlay et al. (eds), 1983, pp. 168–83.

Room, G. *The Sociology of Welfare: Social Policy, Stratification and the Political Order* Oxford: Basil Blackwell and Martin Robertson, 1979.

Rosaldo, M.Z. 'The Use and Abuse of Anthropology: Reflections on Feminism and Cross-Cultural Understanding' *Signs* 5(3), 1980, pp. 389–417.

Rose, H. 'Rereading Titmuss: The Sexual Division of Labour' *Journal of Social Policy* 10(4), 1981, pp. 477–502.

Roshier, B. 'The Function of Crime Waves' *Sociological Review* 25(2), 1977, pp. 309–23.

Ross, E.A. *Social Control: A Survey of the Foundations of Order* New York: Macmillan, 1901.

Ross, H.L. (ed.) *Law and Deviance* Beverly Hills: Sage Publications, 1981.

Rossi, P.H., E. Waite, G.E. Bose and R.E. Berk 'The Seriousness of Crimes: Normative Structure and Individual Differences' *American Sociological Review* 39(2), 1974, pp. 224–37.

Rothman, D. *The Discovery of the Asylum: Social Order and Disorder in the New Republic* Boston: Little, Brown and Co., 1971.

Rubin, G. 'The Traffic in Women: Notes on the "Political Economy" of Sex' in Reiter (ed.), 1975, pp. 157–210.

Rubingon, E. and M.S. Weinberg (eds) *Deviance: The Interactionist Perspective* New York: Macmillan, 1968.

Rushing, W.A. 'The Supply of Physicians and Expenditures for Health Services with Implications for the Coming Physician Surplus' *Journal of Health and Social Behavior* 26(4), 1985, pp. 297–311.

Sallman, P. and J. Willis *Criminal Justice in Australia* Melbourne: Oxford University Press, 1984.

Salmon, J.W. 'Organizing Medical Care for Profit' in McKinlay (ed.), 1984, pp. 143–86.

Salt, A. *The Outcast Women: The Parramatta Female Factory 1821–1848* Sydney: Hale and Iremonger, 1984.

Sargent, L. (ed.) *Women and Revolution: A Discussion of the Unhappy Marriage of Marxism and Feminism* Boston: South End Press, 1981.

Scheff, T. *Being Mentally Ill* London: Weidenfeld and Nicholson, 1966.

Schervish, P.G. 'The Labeling Perspective: Its Bias and Potential in the Study of Political Deviance' *American Sociologist* 8(2), 1973, pp. 47–57.

Schlossman, S. and Wallach, S. 'The Crime of Precocious Sexuality: Female Juvenile Delinquency in the Progressive Era' *Harvard Educational Review* 48(1), 1978, pp. 65–94.

Schram, S.F. and J.P. Turbett 'The Welfare Explosion: Mass Society Versus Social Control' *Social Service Review* 57(4), 1983, pp. 614–25.

Schur, E.M. *Labeling Deviant Behavior* Harper, 1971.

______ *The Politics of Deviance* Englewood Cliffs, N.J.: Prentice Hall, 1980.

______ *Labeling Women Deviant* New York: Random House, 1984.

Schwartz, R.D. and J.C. Miller 'Legal Education and Societal Complexity' *American Journal of Sociology* 70(2), 1964, pp. 159–69.

Scott, H. *Working Your Way to the Bottom: The Feminization of Poverty* London: Pandora, 1984.

Scotton, R.B. 'Public Expenditures and Social Policy' in Scotton and Ferber (eds), 1978, pp. 1–37.
______ 'The Fraser Government and Social Expenditure' in Scotton and Ferber (eds), 1980, pp. 1–27.
Scotton, R.B. and H. Ferber (eds) *Public Expenditures and Social Policy in Australia: Vol. I: The Whitlam Years* Melbourne: Longman Cheshire, 1978.
______ *Public Expenditures and Social Policy in Australia: Vol. II: The First Fraser Years* Melbourne: Longman Cheshire, 1980.
Scull, A.T. *Decarceration: Community Treatment and the Deviant—A Radical View* Englewood Cliffs. N.J.: Prentice Hall, 1977.
______ *Museums of Madness: The Social Organization of Insanity in Nineteenth Century England* Harmondsworth: Penguin, 1979.
______ 'A New Trade in Lunacy: The Recommodification of the Mental Patient' *American Behavioral Scientist* 24(6), 1981a, pp. 741–54.
______ 'Deinstitutionalization and the Rights of the Deviant' *Journal of Social Issues* 37(3), 1981b, pp. 6–20.
______ 'Community Corrections: Panacea, Progress, or Pretense?' in Garland and Young (eds), 1983, pp. 146–65.
______ *Decarceration*: Community Treatment and the Deviant—A Radical View (2nd Edn.) Cambridge: Polity Press, 1984.
______ 'Humanitarianism or Control? Some Observations on the Historiography of Anglo-American Psychiatry' in Cohen and Scull (eds), 1985, pp. 118–40.
Scully, D. *Men Who Control Women's Health: The Miseducation of Obstetricians and Gynecologists* Boston: Houghton Mifflin, 1980.
Scully, D. and P. Bart 'A Funny Thing Happened on the Way to the Orifice: Women in Gynecology Textbooks' *American Journal of Sociology* 78(4), 1973, pp. 1045–51.
Scutt, J.A. 'Crime and Equality of the Sexes' *Crime, Punishment and Corrections* 5(1), 1976, pp. 57–69.
______ 'Towards the Liberation of the Female Lawbreaker' *International Journal of Criminology and Penology* 6, 1978, pp. 5–18.
______ 'The Myth of the "Chivalry Factor" in Female Crime' *Australian Journal of Social Issues* 14(1), 1979a, pp. 3–20.
______ 'Sexism and Psychology: An Analysis of the "Scientific" Basis of the Corroboration Rule in Rape' *Hecate* V(1), 1979b, pp. 35–49.
______ 'Admissibility of Sexual History Evidence and Allegations in Rape Case' *Australian Law Journal* 53, 1979c, pp. 818–31.
______ 'Spouse Assault: Closing the Door on Criminal Acts' *Australian Law Journal* 54, 1980, pp. 720–31.
______ 'Sexism in Criminal Law' in Mukherjee and Scutt (eds), 1981, pp. 1–21.
______ *Even in the Best of Homes: Violence in the Family* Ringwood: Penguin, 1983.
______ 'In Pursuit of Equality: Women and Legal Thought 1788–1984' in J. Goodnow and C. Pateman (eds) *Women, Social Science and Public Policy* Sydney: Allen and Unwin, 1985, pp. 116–38.
Sedgwick, P. *Psychopolitics* London: Pluto Press, 1982.
Shank, G. 'Review of M. Ignatieff: A Just Measure of Pain' *Crime and Social Justice* 11, 1979, pp. 62–6.
Shaver, S. 'Sex and Money in the Welfare State' in Baldock and Cass (eds), 1983, pp. 146–63.
Shaw, M. 'The Theory of the State and and Politics: A Central Paradox of Marxism' *Economy and Society* 3(4), 1974, pp. 429–50.
Sheridan, A. *Michel Foucault: The Will to Truth* London: Tavistock, 1980.
Sherman, J.A. and E.T. Beck (eds) *The Prism of Sex* Wisconsin: University of Wisconsin Press, 1979.
Shulman, A.K. 'Sex and Power: Sexual Bases of Radical Feminism' *Signs* 5(4), 1980, pp. 590–604.
Siltanen, J. and M. Stanworth'The Politics of Private Woman and Public Man' *Theory and Society* 13(1), 1974, pp. 91–118.

Simmons, J.L. *Deviants* Berkeley: Glendessary Press, 1969.
Simpkin, M. *Trpped Within Welfare: Surviving Social Work* (2nd Ed.) London: Macmillan, 1983.
Sinfield, A. 'Analyses of the Social Division of Welfare' *Journal of Social Policy* 7(2), 1978, pp. 129–56.
Skolnick, J.H. *Justice Without Trial* New York: John Wiley, 1967.
Skopcol, T. 'Political Response to Capitalist Crisis: Neo-Marxist Theories of the State and the Case of the New Deal' *Politics and Society* 10(2), 1980, pp. 155–201.
Smart, B. *Foucault, Marxism and Critique* London: Routledge and Kegan Paul, 1983.
Smart, C. *Women, Crime and Criminology* London: Routledge and Kegan Paul, 1976.
——— 'Regulating Families or Legitimating Patriarchy? Family Law in Britain' *International Journal of Sociology of Law* 10, 1982, pp. 129–47.
——— *The Ties That Bind* London: Routledge and Kegan Paul, 1984.
——— 'Feminism and Law: Some Problems of Analysis and Strategy' *International Journal of the Sociology of Law* 14(2), 1986, pp. 109–23.
Smart, C. and B. Smart (eds) *Women, Sexuality and Social Control* London: Routledge and Kegan Paul, 1978.
Smelser, N.J. *Social Change in the Industrial Revolution* Chicago: University of Chicago Press, 1959.
——— 'Toward a Theory of Modernization' in A. Etzioni and E. Etzioni (eds) *Social Change: Sources, Patterns and Consequences* New York: Basic Books, 1964, pp. 258–74.
Smith, D.E. 'Women's Perspective as a Radical Critique of Sociology' *Sociological Inquiry* 44(1), 1974, pp. 7–13.
——— 'A Sociology of Women' in Sherman and Beck (eds), 1979, pp. 138–57.
Smith, R. and M. Wearing 'Public Opinion and the Australian Welfare State 1940–1985' paper presented at S.A.A.N.Z. Conference, University of New England, 1986.
Smith-Rosenberg, C. 'The Hysterical Woman: Sex Roles and Role Conflict in 19th Century America' *Social Research* 39(4), 1972, pp. 652–78.
Smith-Rosenberg, C. and C. Rosenberg 'The Female Animal: Medical and Biological Views of Woman and Her Role in Nineteenth-Century America' *Journal of American History* 60(2), 1973, pp. 332–56.
Social Indicators No. 4 Canberra: Australian Bureau of Statistics, 1984.
Solo, R.A. 'The Economist and the Economic Roles of the Political Authority in Advanced Industrial Societies' in Lindberg et al. (eds), 1975, pp. 99–114.
Spector, M. 'Beyond Crime: Seven Methods to Control Troublesome Rascals' in H.L. Ross (ed.) *Law and Deviance* Beverly Hills: Sage Publications, 1981, pp. 127–57.
Speiglman, R. 'Review of A. Scull: Decarceration' *Crime and Social Justice* 11, 1979, pp. 67–70.
Spender, D. *Man-Made Language* London: Routledge and Kegan Paul, 1980.
Spitzer, S. 'Toward a Marxian Theory of Deviance' *Social Problems* 22(5), 1975a, pp. 638–51.
——— 'Punishment and Social Organization: A Study of Durkheim's Theory of Penal Evolution' *Law and Society Review* 9(4), 1975b, pp. 613–35.
——— 'The Rationalization of Crime Control in Capitalist Society' *Contemporary Crises* 3(2), 1979, pp. 187–206.
——— '"Left-Wing" Criminology—An Infantile Disorder' in J.A. Inciardi (ed.) Radical *Criminology* Beverly Hills: Sage Publications, 1980, pp. 169–90.
——— 'The Political Economy of Policing' in Greenberg (ed.), 1981, pp. 314–40.
——— 'The Dialectics of Formal and Informal Control' in Abel (ed.), 1982, pp. 167–205.
Spitzer, S. and A.T. Scull 'Social Control in Historical Perspective: From Private to Public Responses to Crime' in D.F. Greenberg (ed.) *Corrections and Punishment* Beverly Hills: Sage Publications, 1977a, pp. 265–86.
——— 'Privatization and Capitalist Development: The Case of the Private Police' *Social Problems* 25(1), 1977b, pp. 18–29.
Stacey, M. 'The Sociology of Health and Illness: Its Present State, Future Prospects and Potential for Health Research' *Sociology* 12(2), 1978, pp. 281–307.

Stacey, M., M. Reid, C. Heath and R. Dingwall (eds) *Health and the Division of Labour* London: Croom Helm, 1977.
Stang Dahl, T. 'Women's Law: Method, Problems, Values' *Contemporary Crises* 10(4), 1987, pp. 361–71.
Stanko, E.A. *Intimate Intrusions* London: Routledge and Kegan Paul, 1985.
Stanley, L. and S. Wise *Breaking Out* London: Routledge and Kegan Paul, 1983.
Stark, E. 'Doctors Inspite of Themselves: The Limits of Radical Health Criticism' *International Journal of Health Services* 12(3), 1982, pp. 419–57.
Stark, E. and A. Flitcraft 'Social Knowledge, Social Policy, and the Abuse of Women: The Case Against Patriarchal Benevolence' in D. Finkelhor et al. (eds) *The Dark Side of Families* Beverly Hills: Sage Publications, 1983, pp. 330–48.
Starr, P. *The Social Transformation of American Medicine* New York: Basic Books, 1982.
Stedman Jones, G. *Outcast London* Harmondsworth: Penguin, 1976.
______ 'Class Expression Versus Social Control? A Critique of Recent Trends in the Social History of "Leisure"' *History Workshop* 4, 1977, pp. 162–70.
Steffensmeier, D.J. 'Assessing the Impact of the Women's Movement on Sex-Based Differences in the Handling of Adult Criminal Defendants' *Crime and Delinquency* 26(3), 1980a, pp. 344–57.
______ 'Sex Differences in Patterns of Adult Crime, 1965–77: A Review and Assessment' *Social Forces* 58(4), 1980b, pp. 1080–1108.
Steffensmeier, D.J. and R.H. Steffensmeier 'Trends in Female Delinquency' *Criminology* 18(1), 1980, pp. 62–85.
Stevenson, J. 'Social Control and the Prevention of Riots in England 1789–1829' in Donajgrodzki (ed.), 1977, pp. 27–50.
Stevenson, N. 'Criminal Cases in the N.S.W. District Court: A Pilot Study' in Basten et al. (eds), 1982, pp. 106–45.
Stevenson, O. 'Social Services as Controllers' in J.F.S. King (ed.), 1976, pp. 1–19.
Stimson, G.V. 'Recent Developments in Professional Control: The Impaired Physician in the U.S.A.' *Sociology of Health and Illness* 7(2), 1985, pp. 141–66.
Stimson, G. and B. Webb *Going to See the Doctor* London: Routledge and Kegan Paul, 1975.
Stoll, C.S. 'Images of Man and Social Control' *Social Forces* 47(2), 1968, pp. 119–27.
Straus, R. 'The Nature and Status of Medical Sociology' *American Sociological Review* 21(2), 1957, pp. 200–4.
Strong, P.M. 'Sociological Imperialism and the Profession of Medicine: A Critical Examination of the Thesis of Medical Imperialism' *Social Science and Medicine* 13A, 1979a, pp. 199–215.
______ *The Ceremonial Order of the Clinic* London: Routledge and Kegan Paul, 1979b.
Suchar, C.S. *Social Deviance* New York: Holt, Rinehart and Winston, 1978.
Sudnow, D. 'Normal Crimes: Sociological Features of the Penal Code in a Public Defender Office' *Social Problems* 12, 1965, pp. 255–76.
Sugarman, D. (ed.) *Legality, Ideology and the State* London: Academic Press, 1983.
Summers, A. *Damned Whores and God's Police: The Colonization of Women in Australia* Ringwood: Penguin, 1975.
Sumner, C. 'Marxism and Deviancy Theory' in P. Wiles (ed.) *The Sociology of Crime and Delinquency in Britain, Vol. 2* Oxford: Martin Robertson, 1976, pp. 159–74.
______ 'Law, Legitimation and the Advanced Capitalist State: The Jurisprudence and Social Theory of Jurgen Habermas' in Sugarman (ed.), 1983, pp. 119–58.
Sutton, J.A. 'Sex Discrimination Among Social Workers' *Social Work* 27(3), 1982, pp. 211–17.
Swanton, B. (ed.) *Aborigines and Criminal Justice* Canberra: Australian Institute of Criminology, 1984.
Sweeney, T. 'Child Welfare and Child Care Policies' in Graycar (ed.), 1983, pp. 35–54.
______ 'The Meaning of Change in Child Welfare' in A. Jamrozik (ed.), 1986, pp. 85–107.
Sydney Labour History Group *What Rough Beast? The State and Social Order in*

Australian History Sydney: Allen and Unwin, 1982.
Szasz, T.S. *The Myth of Mental Illness* London: Secker and Warburg, 1962.

Taber, M., H.C. Quay, H. Mark and V. Nealey 'Disease Ideology and Mental Health Research' *Social Problems* 16(3), 1969, pp. 349–57.
Taylor, I. *Law and Order: Argument for Socialism* London: Macmillan, 1981.
Taylor, I., P. Walton and J. Young *The New Criminology: For a Social Theory of Deviance* London: Routledge and Kegan Paul, 1973.
——— 'Radical Deviancy Theory and Marxism: A Reply to Paul O. Hirst's Marx and Engels on Law, Crime and Morality' in Taylor, Walton and Young (eds), 1975, pp. 233–5.
——— (eds) *Critical Criminology* London: Routledge and Kegan Paul, 1975.
Taylor, R. *Medicine Out of Control: The Anatomy of a Malignant Technology* Melbourne: Sun Books, 1979.
Taylor-Gooby, P. 'Privatisation, Power and the Welfare State' *Sociology* 20(2), 1986, pp. 228–46.
Taylor-Gooby, P. and J. Dale *Social Theory and Social Welfare* London: Edward Arnold, 1981.
Temin, C.E. 'Discriminatory Sentencing of Women Offenders: An Argument for ERA in a Nutshell' *American Criminal Law Review* 11(2), 1973, pp. 355–72.
Terris, M. 'The Three World Systems of Medical Care: Trends and Prospects' *American Journal of Public Health* 68(11), 1978, pp. 1125–31.
Therborn, G. 'What Does the Ruling Class Do When it Rules?' in A. Giddens and D. Held (eds) *Classes, Power, and Conflict: Classical and Contemporary Debates* London: Macmillan, 1982, pp. 224–56.
——— 'The Rule of Capital and the Rise of Democracy' in D. Held et al. (eds), 1983, pp. 261–89.
Thio, A. 'Class Bias in the Sociology of Deviance' *American Sociologist* 8(1), 1973, pp. 1–12.
Thornton, M. 'Feminist Jurisprudence: Illusion or Reality?' *Australian Journal of Law and Society* 3, 1986, pp. 5–29.
Tigar, M.E. and M.R. Levy *Law and the Rise of Capitalism* New York: Monthly Review Press, 1977.
Titmuss, R.M. *Essays on the Welfare State* London: Allen and Unwin, 1958.
——— *Social Policy: An Introduction* London: Allen and Unwin, 1974.
——— *Commitment to Welfare* (2nd Edn.) London: Allen and Unwin, 1976.
Tomasic, R. (ed.) *Understanding Lawyers: Perspectives on the Legal Profession in Australia* Sydney: Allen and Unwin, 1978.
Tomasic, R. and C. Bullard *Lawyers and Their Work* Sydney: The Law Foundation of N.S.W., 1978.
Tong, R. *Women, Sex and the Law* Totawa, N.J.: Rowman and Allan Held, 1984.
Townsend, P. 'Inequality and the Health Service' *The Lancet* 7868, 1974, pp. 1179–89.
Travis, G. 'Police Discretion in Law Enforcement' in Findlay et al. (eds), 1983, pp. 200–19.
Trice, H.M. and P.M. Roman 'Delabeling, Relabeling and Alcoholics Anonymous' *Social Problems* 17(4), 1970, pp. 538–46.
Tudor Hart, J. 'The Inverse Care Law' *The Lancet* 7696, 1971, pp. 98–112.
Tudor, W., J.F. Tudor and W.R. Gove 'The Effect of Sex Role Differences on the Social Control of Mental Illness' *Journal of Health and Social Behavior* 18(2), 1977, pp. 98–112.
Tulloch, P. 'Normative Theory and Social Policy' *Australian and New Zealand Journal of Sociology* 14(1), 1978, pp. 65–75.
——— *Poor Policies: Australian Income Security 1972–77* London: Croom Helm, 1979.
——— 'The Welfare State and Social Policy' in Head (ed.), 1983.
Turk, A.T. 'Law Conflict and Order: From Theorizing Toward Theories' *Canadian Review of Sociology and Anthropology* 13(3), 1976, pp. 282–94.
Turk, A.T. and R.E. M. Grimes 'Legal and Social Scientific Views of Law and Deviance'

in H.L. Ross (ed.) *Law and Deviance* Beverly Hills: Sage Publications, 1981, pp. 251–75.

Turner, C. 'Welfare and Women: Changing Conceptions of Welfare and Problems of Women's Identity in Australia' in Grieve and Grimshaw (eds), 1981, pp. 168–77.

Twaddle, A.C. 'Illness and Deviance' *Social Science and Medicine* 7(10), 1973, pp. 751–62.

Van Dusen, K.T. 'Net Widening and Relabeling : Some Consequences of Deinstitutionalization' *American Behavioral Scientist* 25(6), 1981, pp. 801–10.

van Krieken, R. 'The Capitalist State and the Organisation of Welfare: An Introduction; *Australian and New Zealand Journal of Sociology* 16(3), 1980, pp. 23–35.

_____ 'Social Control and Child Welfare: Beyond Social Control' *Theory and Society* 15(3), 1986, pp. 401–29.

Verbrugge, L.M. 'How Physicians Treat Mentally Distressed Men and Women' *Social Science and Medicine* 18(1), 1984, pp. 1–9.

_____ 'Gender and Health: An Update on Hypotheses and Evidence' *Journal of Health and Social Behavior* 26(3), 1985, pp. 156–82.

Verbrugge, L.M. and R.P. Steiner 'Physician Treatment of Men and Women Patients: Sex Bias or Appropriate Care?' *Medical Care* XIX(6), 1981, pp. 609–32.

Verbrugge, M.H. 'Historical Complaints and Political Disorders: A Review of Ehrenreich and English's Study of Medical Ideas About Women' *International Journal of Health Services* 5(2), 1975, pp. 323–33.

_____ 'Women and Medicine in Nineteenth-Century America' *Signs* 1(4), 1976, pp. 957–72.

Versluysen, M.C. 'Midwives, Medical Men and "Poor Women Labouring of Child": Lying-In Hospitals in Eighteenth-Century London' in Roberts (ed.), 1981, pp. 18–49.

Visher, C.A. 'Gender, Police Arrest Decisions, and Notions of Chivarly' *Criminology* 21(1), 1983, pp. 5–28.

Waddell, C. and P. Floate 'Research Note: Gender and the Utilisation of Health Care Services in Perth, Australia!' *Sociology of Health and Illness* 8(2), 1986, pp. 170–77.

Waddington, I. 'The Role of the Hospital in the Development of Modern Medicine: A Sociological Analysis' *Sociology* 7(2), 1973, pp. 211–24.

_____ 'General Practitioners and Consultants in Early Nineteenth Century England: The Sociology of Intra-Professional Conflict' in Woodward and Richards (eds), 1977, pp. 161–88.

Waitzkin, H. *The Second Sickness: Contradictions of American Health Care* New York: Free Press, 1983.

Waitzkin, H.B. and B. Waterman *The Exploitation of Illness in Capitalist Society* Indianapolis: Bobbs Merrill, 1974.

Walker, A. 'Social Policy, Social Administration and the Social Construction of Welfare' *Sociology* 15(2), 1981, pp. 225–50.

Wallen, J., H. Waitzkin and J.D. Stoeckle 'Physician Stereotypes About Female Health and Illness: A Study of Patient's Sex and the Informative Process During Medical Interviews' *Women and Health* 4(2), 1979, pp. 135–46.

Ward, R.H. 'The Labeling Theory: A Critical Analysis' *Criminology* 9(2 and 3), 1971, pp. 268–90.

Warren, C.A.B. 'New Forms of Social Control: The Myth of Deinstitutionalization' *American Behavioral Scientist* 24(6), 1981, pp. 724–40.

Warren, C.A.B. and J.M. Johnson 'A Critique of Labeling Theory from a Phenomenological Perspective' in R.A. Scott and J.D. Douglas (eds) *Theoretical Perspectives in Deviance* New York: Basic Books, 1972, pp. 69–92.

Watkins, C.K. *Social Control* London: Longman, 1975.

Watts, R. 'Social Amnesia and Welfare History' *Arena* 47–8, 1977, pp. 133–45.

_____ 'The Origins of the Australian Welfare State' in Kennedy (ed.), 1982, pp. 225–55.

Wearing, B.M. 'Gender and Power in Social Work' *Australian Social Work* 38(1), 1985, pp. 11–18.

Weatherburn, D.J. 'Sentencing for What?' in Findlay et al. (eds), 1983, pp. 124–38.

Weatherburn, H. 'The Female Factory' in Mclnolty and Radi (eds), 1979, pp. 18–30.

Weber, M. in G. Roth and C. Wittich (eds) *Max Weber: Economy and Society* Berkeley: University of California Press, 1978.

Weeks, J. *Sex, Politics and Society: The Regulation of Sexuality Since 1800* London: Longman, 1981.

Weis, K. and S.S. Boges 'Victimology and Rape: The Case of the Legitimate Victim' *Issues in Criminology* 8(2), 1973, pp. 71–115.

Weisz, G. 'The Politics of Medical Professionalization in France 1845–48' *Journal of Social History* 12(1), 1978, pp. 3–30.

West, P., R. Illsley and H. Kelman 'Public Preferences for the Care of Dependency Groups' *Social Science and Medicine* 18(4), 1984, pp. 287–95.

Wheelwright, E.L. and K. Buckley (eds) *Essays in the Political Economy of Australian Capitalism Vol. I* Sydney: Australia and New Zealand Book Co., 1975.

White, K.L. 'Ill-Health and Its Amelioration: Individual and Collective Choices' in R.J. Carlson and R. Cunningham (eds) *Future Directions in Health Care: A New Public Policy* Cambridge, Mass.: Ballinger Publishing Co., 1978, pp. 3–19.

Wickham, G. 'Power and Power Analysis: Beyond Foucault?' *Economy and Society* 12(4), 1983, pp. 468–98.

Wiener, M.J. 'Review of Donajgrodzki, 1977' *Journal of Social History* 12(1), 1978, pp. 314–21.

Wilensky, H.L. *The Welfare State and Equality* Berkeley: University of California Press, 1975.

Wilensky, H.L. and C.N. Lebeaux *Industrial Society and Social Welfare* New York: Free Press, 1965.

Wiles, P. 'Introduction' in P. Wiles (ed.) *The Sociology of Crime and Delinquency in Britain: Vol. 2: The New Criminologies* Oxford: Martin Robertson, 1976, pp. 1–35.

Willis, E. *Medical Dominance* Sydney: Allen and Unwin, 1983.

Willis, S. *Purified at Parramatta: The Industrial School for Girls* 1979, pp. 77–82.

Wilson, E. *Women and the Welfare State* London: Tavistock, 1977.

Wilson, P.R. and J. Braithwaite (eds) *Two Faces of Deviance* St. Lucia: University of Queensland Press, 1978.

Wilson, T.P. 'Concepts of Interaction and Forms of Sociological Explanation' *American Sociological Review* 35(4), 1970, pp. 697–710.

Windschuttle, E. 'Feeding the Poor and Sapping Their Strength: The Public Role of Ruling-Class Women in Eastern Australia 1788–1850' in E. Windschuttle (ed.) *Women, Class and History: Feminist Perspectives on Australia 1788–1978* Sydney: Fontana, 1980, pp. 53–80.

______ 'Women, Crime and Punishment' in Mukherjee and Scutt (eds), 1981, pp. 31–50.

______ 'Women and the Origins of Colonial Philanthropy' in Kennedy (ed.), 1982, pp. 10–31.

Winkler, J.T. 'The Corporatist Economy: Theory and Administration' in R. Scase (ed.) *Industrial Society: Class Cleavage and Control* London: Allen and Unwin, 1977. pp. 43–58.

Woodward, J. and D. Richards (eds) *Health Care and Popular Medicine in Nineteenth Century England* London: Croom Helm, 1977.

______ 'Towards a Social History of Medicine' in Woodward and Richards (eds), 1977, pp. 15–55.

Wright, C. and R.E. Hilbert 'Value Implications of the Functional Theory of Deviance' *Social Problems* 28(2), 1980, pp. 205–19.

Wrong, D.H. 'The Oversocialized Conception of Man in Modern Sociology' *American Sociological Review* 26(1), 1961, pp. 183–93.

Young, A. 'Rethinking Ideology' *International Journal of Health Services* 13(2), 1983, pp. 203–19.
Young, I. 'Beyond the Unhappy Marriage: A Critique of the Dual Systems Theory' in Sargent (ed.), 1981, pp. 43–69.
Young, J. 'Mass Media, Drugs and Deviance' in P. Rock and M. McIntosh (eds) *Deviance and Social Control* London: Tavistock, 1974, pp. 229–59.
_____ 'Working Class Criminology' in Taylor, Walton and Young (eds), 1975, pp. 63–94.
_____ 'Left Idealism, Reformism and Beyond: From New Criminology to Marxism' in B. Fine et al. (eds), 1979, pp. 11–28.
_____ 'Thinking Seriously About Crime: Some Models of Criminology' in Fitzgerald et al. (eds), 1981, pp. 248–309.
Young, K. and O. Harris 'The Subordination of Women in Cross-Cultural Perspective' in *Papers on Patriarchy* Brighton: Women's Publishing Collective, 1978, pp. 38–52.

Zaretsky, E. *Capitalism, the Family, and Personal Life* London: Pluto Press, 1976.
_____ 'The Place of the Family in the Origins of the Welfare State' in B. Thorne and M. Yalom (eds) *Rethinking the Family: Some Feminist Questions* New York: Longman, 1982, pp. 188–224.
Zeldow, P.B. 'Sex Differences in Psychiatric Evaluation and Treatment' *Archives of General Psychiatry* 35, 1978, pp. 89–92.
Zola, I.K. 'Medicine as an Institution of Social Control' *Sociological Review* 20(4), 1972, pp. 487–504.
_____ 'In the Name of Health and Illness: On Some Socio-Political Consequences of Medical Influence' *Social Science and Medicine* 9(2), 1975, pp. 83–7.

Index

Name Index